Ethnographic Presents

STUDIES IN MELANESIAN ANTHROPOLOGY

General Editors

Donald F. Tuzin
Gilbert H. Herdt
Rena Lederman

Ethnographic Presents

Pioneering Anthropologists
in the Papua New Guinea Highlands

EDITED BY

Terence E. Hays

UNIVERSITY OF CALIFORNIA
Berkeley   Los Angeles   Oxford

University of California Press
Berkeley and Los Angeles, California
University of California Press
Oxford, England
Copyright ©1992 by
The Regents of the University of California

Library of Congress Cataloging-in-Publication Data

Ethnographic presents : pioneering anthropologists in the Papua New
   Guinea Highlands / edited by Terence E. Hays.
      p.   cm. — (Studies in Melanesian anthropology ; 12)
   Includes bibliographical references (p.   ) and index.
   ISBN 0-520-07745-8 (cloth : alk. paper)
      1. Ethnology—Papua New Guinea—History.   2. Ethnologists—Papua
   New Guinea.   I. Hays, Terence E.   II. Series.
   GN17.3.P36E84   1992
   305.8'009953—dc20   91-47735
                                                                 CIP

Printed in the United States of America

1   2   3   4   5   6   7   8   9

For the pioneer ethnographers will not read these words,
but who did much to shape them
Ronald M. Berndt
Beatrice Blackwood
Ralph N. H. Bulmer
Reo Fortune
Richard F. Salisbury
Paul Wirz
and to the people of Papua New Guinea,
our hosts, teachers, and friends

CONTENTS

ILLUSTRATIONS

EDITOR'S PREFACE

Until the middle of this century, the Western world knew little about the peoples of the Central Highlands of what is now Papua New Guinea, and vice versa. Only in 1930 was the curtain abruptly lifted on those valleys and mountain ridges, with their tens of thousands of inhabitants whose mineral resources, service as laborers, fealty as colonial subjects, and souls became objects of intense interest on the part of gold prospectors, Australian administrative officers, and missionaries. For the most part, these early interlopers were mere sojourners, and all were too preoccupied with their immediate objectives to learn or report much about the lives of people whose very existence had only recently been suspected.

Within a few years, another kind of outsider arrived, one whose goal was neither to employ nor govern nor convert the people, but only to understand them by living among them. In 1935 and 1936, two professional anthropologists settled in to begin the long process of ethnographic fieldwork: Reo Fortune, near Kainantu in the Eastern Highlands, and Beatrice Blackwood, on the Upper Watut River on the southeastern fringes of the region. But difficult field conditions, including chronic intervillage warfare that had not yet been suppressed through administrative "pacification" efforts, severely limited both the duration and scope of Fortune's and Blackwood's research, and they were forced to leave the field without completing their work. Soon the disruptions of the Second World War added to the complications, and it was not until the beginning of the 1950s that ethnographers became a significant presence in the Highlands.

Between 1950 and 1955 a veritable "wave" of anthropologists conducted sustained, intensive fieldwork there: Catherine H. and Ronald M. Berndt, Reo Fortune (again, revisiting his former field area), and James

B. and Virginia D. Watson, all in the Kainantu region; Kenneth E. Read and Richard F. Salisbury around Goroka, also in the Eastern Highlands; Marie Reay in the Wahgi Valley of the Western Highlands; Ralph N. H. Bulmer, Mervyn J. Meggitt, and Paul Wirz among various Enga groups far to the west; and Robert M. Glasse and D'Arcy Ryan in the Southern Highlands. It is these "pioneers"—what might be called the first generation of Highlands ethnographers—whose experiences are the subject of this book.

The research carried out by these ethnographers was "pioneering" not only in a temporal sense but also in that it was foundational to our current understandings of the astounding cultural diversity and richness of Highlands peoples. Moreover, their work has transformed much of the conceptual and theoretical armature of anthropology itself, as their descriptions and analyses of "big man" styles of political leadership, ceremonial exchange systems, challenges to "African models" of kinship and descent, and "sexual antagonism" have become compelling reference points in our attempts to understand societies and cultures everywhere. These intellectual legacies are insightfully and critically surveyed in this volume by Andrew J. Strathern, one of the "second wave" of Highlands ethnographers (with Paula Brown, L. L. Langness, and others) who began their work in the late 1950s and early 1960s.

While the "pioneers" produced, and continue to augment, a rich ethnographic record, what has been largely missing until now are personal, experiential accounts of their early fieldwork. Anthropological publishing conventions in the 1950s and 1960s left little room for such discussions; indeed, Kenneth E. Read became a pioneer in a second way by breaking with tradition in his sensitive memoir, *The High Valley* (1965; see also Read 1986). But we live now in a different era, one in which the historical and interpersonal context of ethnographic fieldwork is viewed increasingly as an integral part of the record. In my introductory chapter, I outline the general history of the European presence in the Papua New Guinea Highlands up to the 1950s and try to place the focal ethnographers within the institutional context that provided the impetus for them to go to the Highlands in the first place. But this kind of contextualization can be lifeless if we are left short of an appreciation of what they found when they got there.

Nine of the thirteen ethnographers whose experiences are the main subject of this book had conducted fieldwork elsewhere before arriving in the Highlands, but for all of them it was a new field given the paucity of information then available about the people with whom they would live. As for the latter, most of them had had minimal, if any, prior direct contact with representatives of the Western world, and certainly not with Westerners who wanted to live in houses built of native materials, eat the food from local gardens, learn their languages, and come to know them *as people*. With so much novelty to contend with from both sides, one has to wonder, what were these encounters like?

In 1985, while I was a Visiting Fellow in the Department of Anthropology of the Research School of Pacific Studies at the Australian National University, Marie Reay presented me with an opportunity to find answers to that question. For years, she related, she had discussed with Catherine and Ronald Berndt the idea of assembling a collection of original essays by those who, like the three of them, had been among the "pioneering" ethnographers of the Central Highlands. The essays would be memoiristic, focusing on the personal aspects of fieldwork in the early 1950s. Now she wondered if I might be interested in editing and introducing such a compilation. It was an offer I could not refuse. As a "third generation" Highlands ethnographer (beginning my fieldwork in 1971), I had tried to build on the work of the "pioneers" and had even been trained by some of them. Here was a chance to learn from them again.

At that time conditions were auspicious for such an endeavor. The then-emerging concern with "reflexivity" in ethnography guaranteed an appreciative audience for such a collection of essays, and all but two of the "pioneers" (Reo Fortune and Paul Wirz) were still active teachers and scholars, hence potentially available to contribute to the volume. Fortuitously, Ann McLean, niece and literary executrix of Reo Fortune, was then resident in Canberra while writing a postgraduate thesis based on Fortune's notes and papers. Her interest in the project and eventual contribution filled a lacuna that had seemed unavoidable.

Within the general framework of *how* and *why* they conducted their early Highlands fieldwork, but with the freedom to develop their essays as they chose, potential contributors were asked to reflect on a range of interrelated topics:

Before the Highlands: training and theoretical orientation prior to the experience; previous fieldwork; why the Highlands and a particular region were chosen; expectations and preparation.

Arrival: first impressions of the region and the people; the colonial encounter; selecting and establishing a field base; hosts' reactions and expectations; hosts' understandings of the fieldworker's objectives.

Fieldwork: logistics of living in the field; relationships with administrators and/or missionaries; the role of the anthropologists in the community; what the community gained from the ethnographer's presence; methods employed.

Analysis: how the anthropological climate of the times shaped or influenced analyses; how the Highlands experience may have changed the author's theoretical orientation.

After the Highlands: how return visits or later work has been influenced by the first encounter; how the early work relates to issues subsequently prominent in Highlands ethnography or anthropology in general.

Reassuringly, all of the invitees responded with enthusiasm although, in the end, not all were able to participate. A variety of circumstances and the press of other obligations lengthened the writing and editing process and, in a few cases, precluded contributions. The unexpected deaths of Ralph Bulmer and Richard Salisbury robbed us of the stories they might have told, but we are fortunate that Ronald Berndt was able to complete his essay prior to his passing. They are all remembered, as are their precursors, in the dedication of this volume.

In addition to thanking once again the contributors for their patience as well as for their essays, I want to express my gratitude to Patricia Hurley Hays, Gilbert Herdt, Fitz Poole, Donald Tuzin, the anonymous reviewers of the manuscript, and the editors at the University of California Press for their support and constructive criticism; the Australian-American Education Foundation and the Australian National University for their assistance in the early stages of the project; and the dean of the Faculty of Arts and Sciences and the Faculty Research Fund of Rhode Island College for later financial support. I am extremely grateful to Carolyn B. Kroian Costa for executing the maps, and to the Institute for Intercultural Studies for permission to republish the photograph of Reo Fortune.

Tok Pisin, or what some contributors refer to as Pidgin English, is a lingua franca throughout the Papua New Guinea Highlands. Words or phrases in Tok Pisin are always italicized and parenthetically identified as Tok Pisin or T.P. and provided with glosses or translations the first time they appear in each chapter. Glosses of words or phrases in local languages are also provided in parentheses following their first occurrences, with the language name (e.g., Kamano or Kuma) implied by the context.

THE CONTRIBUTORS

Catherine H. Berndt, a Senior Honorary Research Fellow in Anthropology at the University of Western Australia, was born in Auckland. Following her undergraduate education in New Zealand, she went to the University of Sydney (Dip. Anthrop.; M.A., First Class Honours), where she met Ronald. They married in 1941, and for the next decade spent virtually all their time in the Australian Aboriginal field. At the London School of Economics, she completed her doctoral thesis, "Myth in Action," in 1955, based on two periods of fieldwork focusing on women and on oral literature in the Eastern Highlands of Papua New Guinea. From 1956 she helped to develop teaching and research in anthropology at the University of Western Australia and concentrated on Australian Aboriginal research and writing.

Ronald M. Berndt, born in Adelaide, studied anthropology at the University of Sydney (Dip. Anthrop.; M.A., First Class Honours), where he met Catherine. Together from 1941 they carried out intensive field research among Australian Aborigines. His Papua New Guinea research covered two periods in 1951–53. At the London School of Economics, his Ph.D. thesis was on social control in the Eastern Highlands; a shorter version was later published (1962) as *Excess and Restraint.* In 1956 he was engaged to establish teaching and research in anthropology at the University of Western Australia and was appointed Foundation Professor in 1963. He continued to publish on Highlands material, although Australian Aboriginal research recaptured his attention. He formally retired as Emeritus Professor in 1981 but continued as an Honorary Research Fellow in Anthropology until his death in 1990.

Robert M. Glasse was born in New York City, where he graduated from City College of New York in 1951 with a B.S. in Social Sciences with Honors. After serving in the U.S. Army in Alabama and Japan, he enrolled in the Ph.D. program at the Australian National University, whence he conducted fieldwork among the Huli in 1955–56 and received his doctorate in 1957. A return trip to Tari in 1959–60 was followed by fieldwork among the Fore of the Eastern Highlands and in East Pakistan. In 1965 he assumed a faculty position in the Department of Anthropology at Queens College, City University of New York, where he is now Professor Emeritus following early retirement due to illness.

Terence E. Hays was born in Iowa and received his doctorate at the University of Washington in 1974. His major fieldwork has consisted of three periods, beginning in 1971 and most recently in 1985, with the Southern Tairora of the Eastern Highlands of Papua New Guinea. Apart from his continuing work on ethnography and ethnobiology, he is currently engaged in the ethnology of New Guinea and comparative studies of Highlands oral literature, gender ideology, and men's cults. He is Professor of Anthropology at Rhode Island College, where he joined the faculty in 1973.

Ann McLean is a native of New Zealand and a graduate of Victoria University of Wellington, the same university where her father's older brother, Reo Fortune, obtained his M.A. After her subsequent training as an archivist, a number of foreign service assignments with her family stirred leanings toward anthropology and brought her briefly into contact for the first and penultimate time with Fortune, then in his seventies. Following his death, she became his literary executrix. She took a postgraduate degree in anthropology at the Australian National University and is currently editing some of Fortune's unpublished manuscripts while also working with a New Zealand company that promotes the worldwide use of clean fuels technology.

Marie Reay is an Honorary Visiting Fellow (retired from a position as Senior Fellow) in the Department of Anthropology of the Research School of Pacific Studies, the Australian National University. Her major fieldwork has been with the Kuma of Papua New Guinea's Western Highlands, first in 1953–55 and with numerous further visits from 1963 to 1990. She has also done fieldwork among Aboriginal communities in eastern Australia, the Orokaiva of Papua New Guinea, and the Aborigines of Borroloola in the Northern Territory of Australia.

D'Arcy Ryan took his Ph.D. at the University of Sydney in 1962, following which he taught anthropology for a year at the Australian School of Pacific Administration, helping to train young patrol officers for service in Papua New Guinea. Thence he assumed a lectureship with the newly established Department of Anthropology at the University of Western Australia, from which he recently retired. His major interests include lunch and dinner parties, travel, theory of religion, India, art and cross-cultural aesthetics, creating an attractive and comfortable environment, and supervising his gardener.

Andrew Strathern was educated in classics and social anthropology at the University of Cambridge, where he was awarded the Ph.D. in 1966. After holding professorships at the University of Papua New Guinea and University College, London, he served as Director of the Institute of Papua New Guinea Studies, and since 1986 he has been the Andrew Mellon Professor of Anthropology at the University of Pittsburgh. Since the early 1960s he has conducted extensive fieldwork among the Melpa and Wiru, and most recently the Duna, people of the Western and Southern Highlands of Papua New Guinea.

James B. Watson is Professor Emeritus of Anthropology at the University of Washington, where he has been a member of the faculty since 1955. Throughout field research in four different cultural and geographic settings—Hopi (Arizona), Cayuá (Mato Grosso do Sul, Brazil), San Luis Valley (Colorado), and Kainantu (Eastern Highlands, Papua New Guinea)—his consistent focus has been the interaction of neighboring peoples and its cultural reflexes, as distinct from the study of individual peoples and cultures as isolates. From an initial use of the culture contact or acculturation framework, this inquiry has evolved to the comparative study of the regional settings and intersocietal systems within which the members of communities small and large are virtually everywhere encompassed and thereby both driven and constrained.

ONE

A Historical Background to Anthropology in the Papua New Guinea Highlands

Terence E. Hays

In 1971, newly arrived in Port Moresby to begin fieldwork in what was then the Eastern Highlands District of the Territory of Papua and New Guinea,[1] my wife, Patricia Hurley Hays, and I checked in with the Department of District Administration. After introductory small talk, we described to the administrator what we hoped to accomplish and showed him on a map the field site we had chosen. He said that he had no personal familiarity with the region indicated, as was usually the case in such interviews. Expressing surprise that we seemed already to have a general idea of what we were likely to find there, he said, "I've never understood how you anthropologists can choose villages for your research from halfway around the world."

The process didn't seem so mysterious to us, although, as is obvious from the essays in this volume, the choice of a specific field site for ethnographic research is always the result of a combination of professional priorities, personal tastes, and chance. I had been captivated by the Highlands literature, both popular and professional, and had chosen the University of Washington for my doctoral training because of the presence there of three Highlands specialists: L. L. Langness, Kenneth E. Read, and James B. Watson. All three had done their work in the Eastern Highlands and, with Watson as my supervisor, I soon became convinced that the Kainantu region served my needs concerning my intended research focus (folk biology in a subsistence-based economy) and that Watson's expertise and his continuing contacts there would aid in the logistics of fieldwork. As for the precise field location, several alternatives seemed equally suitable, but conversations with David Cole and Kerry Pataki-Schweizer, who had personally walked over most of the region, led my wife and me to choose a settlement they independently praised for its

1

friendly people and gorgeous physical setting. Those factors were important to us as novices who anxiously wanted our field experience to be
pleasant as well as productive.

Our case was probably typical of fieldworkers who went to the Papua
New Guinea Highlands in the 1960s as well as the 1970s, but what of those
who had trained us and guided us in our choices? Almost no intensive
ethnographic fieldwork was conducted in the Highlands by professional
anthropologists until the early 1950s, when the contributors to this vol-
ume were participants in an unprecedented boom, with a dozen ethnog-
raphers entering the Highlands from 1950 to 1955: Kenneth E. Read and
Paul Wirz in 1950; Catherine H. and Ronald M. Berndt in 1951; Richard
F. Salisbury in 1952; Marie Reay and James B. Watson in 1953; D'Arcy
Ryan and Virginia D. Watson in 1954; and Ralph N. H. Bulmer, Robert
M. Glasse, and Mervyn J. Meggitt in 1955. This was also the period when
Louis J. Luzbetak began his service as a missionary anthropologist in the
Wahgi Valley, as Heinrich Aufenanger, John Nilles, and others continued
their long-term work in this dual capacity.

Beginning fieldworkers today usually have a general appreciation of
the vast intellectual legacy of these "pioneers" (see Andrew Strathern's
discussion in the concluding essay in this volume). But they often lack a
clear sense of what field research in the Highlands was like before the
natural, social, and cultural landscapes were transformed by cash cropping, trade stores, and local government councils, and before the pain-
staking hand recording of texts and notes gave way to the tape recorders
and portable microcomputers increasingly regarded nowadays as indis-
pensable aids. Beyond providing much-needed historical perspective on
how fieldwork was conducted in the earlier days, the essays in this volume
address *why* questions as well. Both anthropologists and Papua New
Guineans can benefit from a fuller and more accurate sense—from the
viewpoints of those who were actually there—of what ethnographers
were trying to accomplish in the Highlands during the colonial period.
How and why did they choose the Highlands? On what informational
base did they make their choices? What did they expect to find there, and
how were their expectations met? What were they trying to achieve,
individually and collectively? And how did these factors inform the intellectual and social legacy of this burst of activity?

OPENING UP THE MIDDLE KINGDOM

In 1847, J. Beete Jukes, naturalist aboard H.M.S. *Fly,* wrote (Vol. I,
p. 291): "The very mention of being taken into the interior of New Guinea
sounds like being allowed to visit some of the enchanted regions of the

Arabian Nights, so dim an atmosphere of obscurity rests at present on the wonders it probably conceals." An aura of mystery still surrounded the Highlands a century later, when Paul Hasluck (quoted in Downs 1980: 174) assumed his duties as administrator in the territory in 1951: "It was as though [the] north of the great island was a coastal China, and from this the land rose in a Himalaya ruggedness of mountains that tumbled away in the south to a lowlands India . . . and nobody knew that a Tibet lay in between, in the heart of New Guinea."

Like other people, professional anthropologists were attracted by the mystique of the Highlands as they turned their focused attention to this "Middle Kingdom," as Australian Patrol Officer James L. Taylor had called the region (Downs 1980:175). Until his and others' exploratory patrols in the 1930s, little was known of this vast area and its peoples. Arriving within two decades of official discoveries of the densely populated high valleys, the "first generation" of ethnographers had an unparalleled opportunity. Perhaps nowhere else in the world could fieldworkers follow so closely in the tracks of first contact patrols, and while the Highlands were by no means pristine by that time, nowhere else was it possible to experience more immediately the "ethnographic present" of which most anthropologists write: "Here was the chance to study the social, economic and political life of people relatively 'untouched' by the influences which made analyses of Australian Aborigines or the [Nuer], for instance, seem, by comparison, more like reconstructions of the past than accounts based on first-hand observation" (Feil 1987:1).

In fact, the Central Highlands—that portion of the central cordillera bounded by the Strickland River in the west and Kassam Pass in the east (see maps 1 and 2)—was not, strictly speaking, a terra incognita even in the 1930s, when exploration and administration intensified. To be sure, it had not been the scene of major scientific expeditions such as those that had crisscrossed the central ranges of neighboring Netherlands New Guinea (now Irian Jaya) from 1904 to 1922, with resulting voluminous, detailed publications (mostly in Dutch) describing their peoples as well as natural environments (see van Baal et al., 1984). The sponsoring of such large-scale ventures was not the style of the British or Australian administrations of the eastern half of the island, though the Germans, whose domain included most of the Highlands until 1914, had begun to make similar inroads from the northeast coast: H. Zöller had seen and named the Bismarck and Kratke ranges from the Finisterre Mountains in 1888; botanist Carl Lauterbach had climbed the foothills of the Yuat headwaters in 1896, from which he saw and named Mount Hagen; and most of the major peaks of the Hagen and Wahgi Valley regions were probably seen by Walter Behrmann in 1912–13. These early scientific explorers, how-

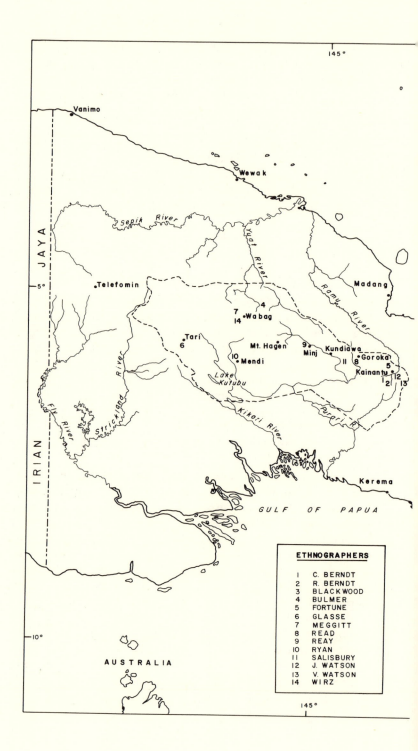

ETHNOGRAPHERS

1	C. BERNDT
2	R. BERNDT
3	BLACKWOOD
4	BULMER
5	FORTUNE
6	GLASSE
7	MEGGITT
8	READ
9	REAY
10	RYAN
11	SALISBURY
12	J. WATSON
13	V. WATSON
14	WIRZ

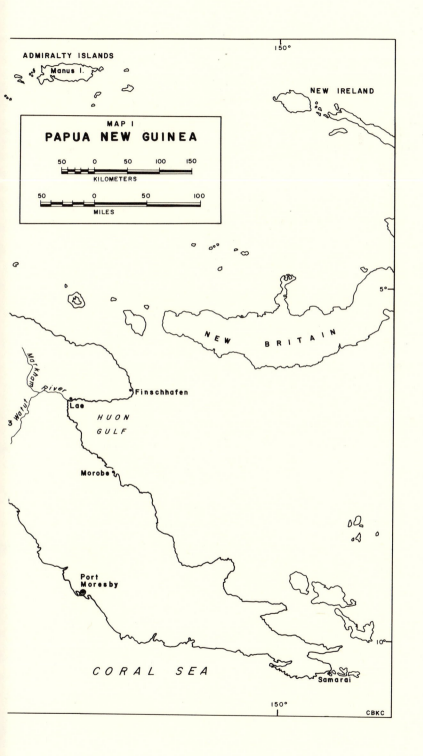

ADMIRALTY ISLANDS

Manus I.

NEW IRELAND

MAP I
PAPUA NEW GUINEA

50   0   50   100   150
KILOMETERS

50   0   50   100
MILES

5°

NEW   BRITAIN

Markham River

Watut

3

°Finschhafen

Lae

HUON
GULF

Morobe

Port
Moresby

10°

CORAL SEA

Samarai

150°

150°

CBKC

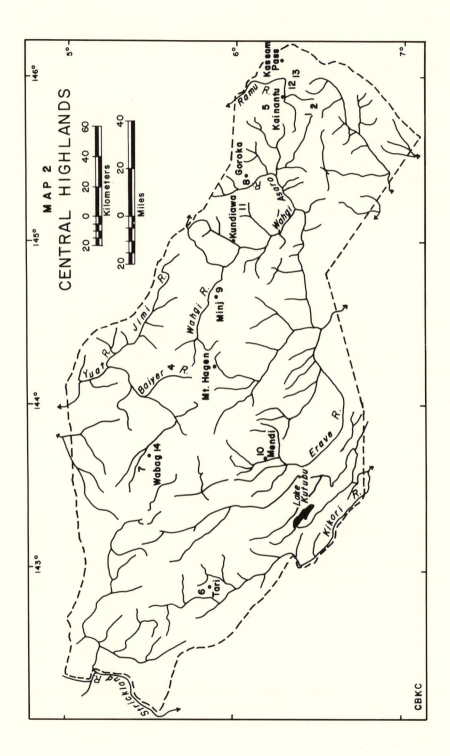

MAP 2

CENTRAL HIGHLANDS

Kilometers
20   0   20   40   60

Miles
20   0   20   40

CBKC

ever, only skirted or glimpsed the Highlands from a distance, and little information about its inhabitants was included in their published accounts.[2]

Indeed, prior to World War I the only substantial penetration was in the Territory of Papua, beginning with Donald Mackay's exploration of the Southern Highlands fringe in 1907–08 (see Schieffelin and Crittenden 1991). Seeking exploitable coal deposits, Mackay found Mount Murray (naming it in the process) and traveled through Pawaia, Podopa (Foraba), and Sau (Samberigi) populations. Shortly thereafter, in 1910, the administrator, Miles Staniforth Smith, ascended the Kikori River and explored the Mount Murray–Samberigi Valley region, to be followed by Resident Magistrate Wilfred Beaver (searching for the long-overdue Smith), who sojourned with the Sau and made initial contacts with the Foi people of the Mubi River. Various observations on these "Mountain Papuans" (Weiner ed. 1988) were included in published accounts of the journeys, but little information could be obtained systematically by parties preoccupied with physically making their way through this uncharted limestone country.

Following the great European war, administrative exploration of the Southern Highlands resumed with more patrols to the Samberigi and Kerabi valleys throughout the 1920s.[3] The potential existed for ethnographic research in the appointment of Walter M. Strong as government anthropologist for the Territory of Papua (1920–28), with F. E. Williams as his assistant (1922–28) and successor (1928–43). However, Strong never ventured into the Highlands (as here delimited), and Williams did not do so until the late 1930s.

Similarly, in the Mandated Territory of New Guinea an opportunity arose to initiate systematic ethnographic work with the appointment of E. W. P. Chinnery as government anthropologist (1924–32). From the start, Chinnery, who had studied under A. F. C. Haddon at Cambridge (but never completed his degree), was eager to begin the compilation and publication of information otherwise buried in patrol reports, and immediately he began giving "instruction in ethnographical methods" to the territory's district officers (Stocking 1982:4), providing them with handbooks based on *Notes and Queries* and questions formulated by J. G. Frazer (Commonwealth of Australia 1926:7). In a letter to Haddon in 1926 he indicated delight that research students from Cambridge would be sent to New Guinea, where they could build on his own work of "opening up new country, making an ethnographic survey of its inhabitants and generally preparing the way for intensive workers" (quoted in Stocking 1982:6). He appears not to have been thinking of the Highlands, however, declaring that "intensive work in new districts [was] of course impossible," owing to the "constant risk and worry" faced among newly contacted peoples (Stocking 1982:6). Over the next several years, Gregory Bateson, Reo Fortune, Margaret Mead, and Hortense Powdermaker would benefit from Chinnery's support as "gatekeeper" for field research in the Mandated Territory, but they confined their work to coastal and lowland regions or adjacent islands, as did Chinnery himself until the 1930s.

If ethnographic fieldwork did not begin in the Highlands as early as it might have done, there nevertheless were numerous Europeans entering the eastern portion throughout the 1920s. Northern fringe populations around Aiome were visited and photographed by a 1921 geological expedition up the Ramu (Stanley 1923), and government botanist W. D. F. Lane-Poole climbed Mount Otto in 1923. The major incursions, however, were made by missionaries, gold prospectors, and administrative pacification patrols (see Radford 1987 for a detailed account).

The German Neuendettelsau Lutherans were the most aggressive mission body during this period, continually expanding their domain from later 1919, when Stephan Lehner left the mission station at Kaiapit in the Upper Markham Valley and made the first European contact with the Binumarien, east of present-day Kainantu. He was followed by Leonhard Flierl and Georg Pilhofer, who thoroughly explored the Arona and Kainantu valleys and continued westward into the territory of the Kamano (Kafe) in the Dunantina Valley. By 1929, Yabem native evangelists from the Finschhafen coast were established in mission stations and villages throughout the Binumarien, Agarabi, Gadsup, Northern Tairora, and Kamano language groups.

In contrast to the missionaries, government patrol officers were slow to enter the Eastern Highlands and made only sporadic visits, which were almost exclusively focused on trying to stop the chronic intervillage fighting in the area. The first such patrols were not conducted until 1924–25, responding to reports of fighting in the Kainantu region. Such efforts at pacification multiplied toward the end of the 1920s as chronic warfare posed threats to the very survival of smaller groups such as the Binumarien and increasingly came to impede missionary and prospecting activity, both of which were accelerating as the decade was coming to a close. Some gold seekers, such as Helmuth Baum, may have penetrated the Eastern Highlands as early as 1918–19, but the area became thick with prospectors a decade later. At about the same time (1929–30) the "Akmana expeditions" were testing the creeks of the Jimi, Baiyer, and Maramuni rivers and making first contacts with Enga populations far to the west (Shepherd 1971), and the Arona and Kainantu valleys became major foci and staging areas for prospectors. From 1928 to 1931, Edward (Ned) Rowlands explored nearly every creek in the area and extended his search to the Fore populations around present-day Okapa.

Despite all of this activity, mainly concentrated in a relatively small part of the Highlands, the European presence was still scattered at the end of the 1920s, and "the paths of missionaries, miners and administration officials rarely crossed. Each group had different objectives and to some degree distrusted the others; they rarely sought each other out so that their encounters usually took place by chance" (Radford 1987:78). Moreover, neither the German missionaries nor the prospectors hoping to find big strikes comparable to those of the Morobe goldfields farther to the southeast were keen to draw the attention of the outside world. Apart from reports of the early Southern Highlands exploration in Papua, no accounts or descriptions of Highlanders were published until 1934.

The isolation of the Highlands from public awareness began to break down in 1930 (J. Watson 1964:1), with Rowlands's discovery of payable gold at Ornapinka and the arrival of more prospectors and missionaries. In early 1930, Edward Ubank and Alex Peadon continued to work claims near Rowlands at Ornapinka, and Michael Leahy and Michael Dwyer made their "epic journey" (Willis 1969). Setting out from the Lutheran mission station at Lihona, they entered the Highlands at the Dunantina Valley, in Kamano territory. From there they explored down the banks of the Asaro River, around Mount Michael, and down to the Asaro/Wahgi junction, eventually rafting down the Tua and Pio rivers in the Karimui area to the Purari and thence to the Papuan coast. At about the same time the Lutherans began to extend their mission field, also using Lihona as a base. Wilhelm Bergmann and W. Flierl made forays into the Bena Bena Valley in 1930 and again in 1931–32 finding, as had the prospectors, huge populations to which, for a brief time, they had exclusive proselytizing access.

Discouraged by their luck in the heart of the Eastern Highlands, Leahy and Dwyer turned their attention in 1931 to the southeastern fringe, making reconnaissance flights and exploring on foot the Watut headwaters and other mountain haunts of the Anga ("Kukukuku") peoples. Other prospectors had encountered the Anga in the Edie Creek region, but now parties were penetrating deep into their territory, and not without conflict. From Papua, Jack Hides made exploratory patrols into the Upper Purari region in 1931 and, like Leahy, was attacked (Hides 1935). For the next two years encounters between Europeans and these fringe Highlanders continued to be violent. Attracted by reports of gold in the Langimar, Tiveri, and Tauri headwaters, prospectors poured into the area, and some, such as Helmuth Baum, Emile Clarius, and William Naylor, would not emerge alive. Repeated clashes finally forced the hand of the administration, which sent Patrol Officer J. K. McCarthy to establish a post at Menyamya in early 1933, only to abandon it by November of that year because of continual attacks on prospectors who were, in any case, finding no payable gold (Sinclair 1978:205–210).

In ironic contrast, less than 100 kilometers to the north prospector Alex Peadon was settling into the Kainantu Valley in 1932 with his wife, cattle, and horses. In July of that year District Officer Eric Feldt built an airfield at Lapumpa, and a few months later James L. Taylor established the Upper Ramu Police Post (Kainantu) as the first in the Highlands. By November of that year, at least eighteen prospectors were settled near the post (by now a veritable European community), and expansion was beginning as Leahy, returned for another look and backed by the resources of the New Guinea Gold Company (NGG), set up a new base camp in the Bena Bena Valley.

In 1933, prospectors such as James Nason-Jones and Jack O'Neill continued to explore the Kainantu Valley and its southern, more rugged, hinterland as Leahy set his sights on the west. With NGG chief surveyor Charles W. Marshall, Leahy pushed into the western edge of the Goroka region, from which they saw the long, wide Wahgi Valley stretching into the distance—the main source of the numerous bodies Leahy had earlier seen floating down the Wahgi and Asaro rivers. On the previous Christmas Day the first landing had been made at the new Bena Bena airfield, and now the NGG and Leahy used it to launch reconnaissance flights over the Wahgi Valley. With their route planned and full support from the administration, Leahy set out in March with his brother Dan, surveyor Kenneth Spinks, and Assistant District Officer James L. Taylor, on what would be the largest patrol yet conducted in the Highlands—a six-month venture, complete with ad hoc landing strips in the Wahgi Valley and near Mount Hagen to resupply and stage more reconnaissance flights.

Taylor estimated that during this patrol "200,000 previously unknown people" had been discovered as the occupants of this "Middle Kingdom" (Downs 1980:175). According to Downs (1980:175–176):

> Up to that time, the Administration at Rabaul considered the Tolai of the Gazelle Peninsula, then numbering roughly 38,000, to be New Guinea's largest concentration of related people. In fact, the 1933 expedition . . . had come in contact for the first time with elements of population groups that probably exceeded 500,000. . . . [Thus in] the space of one month, in 1933, the Government of the then Mandated Territory of New Guinea had its administrative responsibility for people doubled. This was the real significance for all future administrations of what had been discovered.

Of course the expedition was significant in other respects as well: what could be considered the first anthropological reports on (Papua New Guinea) Highlanders was one product. Leahy's makeshift airfields had made it possible for E. W P. Chinnery (by then Director of District Services and Native Administration, but still devoted to anthropology) to visit Highlands sites during the expedition and report his own and Taylor's observations on the Kainantu, Bena Bena, Chimbu, Hagen, and Jimi River peoples to a worldwide anthropological audience (Chinnery 1934*a*, 1934*b*). In addition, while the huge, dense populations of the Western Highlands did not in themselves interest Leahy as much as did the gold (which he did find), his curiosity was sufficient to yield a rich harvest of recorded observations, photographs, and films of the Bena Bena, Chimbu, Wahgi, Hagen, Nebilyer, Kaugel, Wabag, Baiyer, and northern fringe peoples, which he eagerly shared with the world (Leahy 1935*a*, 1935*b*, 1936; Leahy and Crain 1937).

The Leahy-Taylor expedition was not the only group of Europeans in the Central Highlands at this time, for while they were finding the Highlanders useful as little more than sources of food and labor, missionaries continued in their concern for the peoples' souls. In 1933, Father Alfons Schäfer established the Society of the Divine Word (SVD) Catholic mission at Bundi (where he was joined in 1934 by Father Heinrich Aufenanger), and in October of that year, as Leahy and Taylor abandoned their temporary post at Mount Hagen, Schäfer and two colleagues were just beginning their exploration of the Chimbu and Wahgi valleys (Ulbrich 1960). Within a few months, SVD mission stations were established at Mingende (by Schäfer) and Wilya, among the Mogei people of Mount Hagen (by Father William Ross and Brother Eugene Frank). According to Mary Mennis (1982), the latter station was hurriedly put in place because the Catholics were worried about imminent encroachments by the Lutherans. Ross, Aufenanger, and Schäfer had encountered Bergmann and other Lutherans when exploring the Mingende region, and Ross had asked his bishop for permission to "beat" them to the Hagen area.

The Lutherans were indeed expanding into the central valleys as Seventh-Day Adventist missions started to compete directly in the Kainantu region. By September, 1934, Wilhelm Bergmann had settled into Kundiawa with his compatriots E. P. Helbig and Martin Zimmermann; Herbert Hannemann, and others were ensconced at Kerowagi; and Georg Vicedom and G. Harrolt, despite Ross's efforts, were beginning their long stay at Ogelbeng, near Mount Hagen. Tension was noticeably starting to build as Highlanders, having just seen their first Europeans and airplanes, were now being courted by even greater wonders that carried the price tag of undivided allegiance and faith. The rivalry among missions was increasingly seen by the administration as yet another stimulus to intervillage hostilities, which had not ceased despite the obviously revolutionary changes that were afoot (see Radford 1987:150–152).

Among these changes was one that would transform Highlands economic, political, and social organization forever. It warrants at least brief mention here as one of the reasons why the "pioneering generation" of ethnographers was faced with societies that were far from pristine, although only one of them, Richard Salisbury (1962), would make that fact a major focus of his work.

As Ian Hughes (1978:311) has characterized it, "It was in the eastern highlands in 1932 that a dramatic change occurred in the economics of Australian exploration in New Guinea, for it was then that the importance of adopting the currency of the land was realized." That "currency," in both the Mandated Territory and Papua, was shell: white egg-cowries, pearlshells, baler shells, dog whelks, or green snail shells, depending on the region. It was James L. Taylor who first realized the value of these commodities, which were infinitely available on the coast but precious in the high mountain valleys. At first, a day's labor could be purchased for less than a halfpenny's worth of cowries in the Kainantu region, and it was in this way that the airfields, police posts, and mission stations were built, miners' sluice boxes were manned, and food was purchased throughout the 1930s. The demand for shells for use in local bridewealth and compensation payments seemed limitless, and the Leahy brothers, like the government officers, tapped sources as far away as Manus and Torres Strait to meet it. Missions set up their own supply networks, with school children collecting shells on the beaches and the ever-proliferating airfields used to fly them by the ton into the Highlands. As the supply increased, inflation occurred, creating even more demand, in a spiral that lasted well into the 1950s. With incalculable millions of shells distributed by the end of the 1930s, local marriage arrangements, ascendancy to political leadership, and traditional ceremonial exchange and trade networks would never be the same again. Thus Hughes's (1978:316) cautionary note:

> Wealth increases of this magnitude and a consequent restructuring of exchange relationships during the 1930s and 1940s must be borne in mind when considering the "ethnographic present" encountered by the first anthropological field workers in the highlands two decades later. Not only had great changes been initiated, but they had had nearly a generation to spread and develop and become part of a pattern generally perceived as "traditional". The post-contact situation had become the norm.

Amid all of this change, one aspect of traditional Highlands life—tribal fighting—remained relatively constant, and for a few years, at least in the Mandated Territory, it looked as if the whole European colonial effort would fall apart (as, indeed, the outside world would appear to do not long thereafter).

The Leahy-Taylor expedition had not been without clashes as Highlanders learned that the men initially perceived as ghosts were in fact mortal and that their shells and other goods might be taken by force. In June, 1933, while that expedition was still in the field, Ian Mack became the first patrol officer to die in the course of duty in the Highlands, killed by Agarabi tribesmen at Aiamontina (Radford 1977*b*). Then, in February, 1934, prospector Bernard McGrath was killed by Kamano, who also attacked the subsequent investigative patrol and wounded the district officer as well as others in the party. The administration's response was prompt: "An advanced post was immediately established at Finentegu [sic] near the villages concerned, and close attention was given to the suppression of inter-tribal fighting in the area" (Commonwealth of Australia 1935:28). By the end of the year, peace had been restored, but government influence was not yet so effective "among the Kukukuku jungle-dwellers of the Watut watershed" (p. 29).

The peace was short-lived, however: "The people of Finintegu were peaceful while an officer was located there, but in the beginning of 1935, when the officer was withdrawn for more urgent duty in the Chimbu area, some of the more troublesome tribes began fighting, and the staff at Ramu [Kainantu] had to extend their patrols to Finintegu until the position improved" (Commonwealth of Australia 1936:23). The "more urgent duty" referred to was related to two more killings of Europeans. The Christmas season of 1934–35 was a sad one for the Catholic mission as Father Karl Morschheuser was killed near Kuglkane in December, as was Brother Eugene Frank near Gogolme in January. Again the administrative response was to establish new police posts, this time in the Kundiawa region in March, 1935.

This extension of tenuous "control" followed by only a month the arrival of Reo Fortune in the Finintegu area in February, 1935. As Ann McLean shows in Chapter 2, ethnographic fieldwork under these circumstances was nearly impossible, even for a veteran. Fortune was the very first professional anthropologist to undertake intensive field research in the (Papua New Guinea) Highlands, but he was far from being a novice. After earning his diploma in anthropology under Haddon at Cambridge, six months' work on Dobu in 1927 had already resulted in an ethnographic classic (Fortune 1932), and this was followed almost immediately by other projects, but not in Papua. During his work in the D'Entrecasteaux Islands he had repeatedly clashed with J. H. P. Murray, then administrator of the Territory of Papua, over what Fortune perceived as government interference with native customs. In the view of Deidre Griffiths (1977:174), "Perhaps understandably, when next Reo Fortune returned to the field he chose the Mandated Territory; and there he received every assistance from Chinnery and the Administration."

Such assistance contributed to Fortune's successful fieldwork (with his wife, Margaret Mead) on Manus in 1928–29 and on the Sepik in 1932–33 (with a venture among the Omaha Indians of the United States sandwiched in between). But neither Chinnery nor the administration could ameliorate the horrendous conditions Fortune faced between Kamano battle lines, and, in this instance, government "interference with native customs" may have saved his life, as he was forced to leave the field in August, 1935.

Whatever may have been the tragic consequences of this experience for Fortune, and perhaps for anthropology, his expulsion was part of a general administrative "closing" of the Highlands. From Kainantu to Mount Hagen, the region was declared an "uncontrolled area," and no new nonadministrative personnel were allowed to enter. The Leahy brothers were permitted to remain at their gold claims, and missionaries already in place could stay; also, at least for a time, native evangelists were free to continue expanding their activities. Thus, by mid 1936, ten mission posts were still staffed by Europeans and another seventy-four were in operation with native mission teachers only (Commonwealth of Australia 1937:25). But the situation had definitely changed. According to Ian Downs (1980:176), the Leahys' and missionaries' activities were severely restricted "within a defined radius of their stations," and concerns about the possible introduction of alien infectious diseases resulted in the repatriation of hundreds of indigenous mission helpers to the coast— concerns that may have been warranted given a pan-Highlands influenza epidemic in 1936 that took uncounted lives and doubtless added to the confusion and uncertainty as to the future of the Highlands and its people, who were by now fully caught up in processes of change that could not be stopped by administrative edict.

The rush to the Highlands in the early 1930s had itself been uncontrolled, and undoubtedly the administration's "closing" of what had been wide-open gates helped bring about a more stable set of conditions. In Downs's (1980:176) view, the restrictions "allowed intensive patrolling and pacification to take place," and by the end of the 1930s, "nearly half a million people between Kainantu and Wabag [had been] brought under a 'Pax Australiana.'" Where only a year previously Reo Fortune had been driven from his fieldwork among the Kamano (Kafe), in August, 1936, the Lutheran-missionized Kafe took part in a public burning of weapons in what Robin Radford (1977a) has called a "peace movement." And peaceful the region must have seemed, with permanent patrol posts established at Kainantu, Bena Bena, Chimbu (Kundiawa), and Mount Hagen, and 480 kilometers of bridle paths stretching from Gadsup territory in the east to the Chimbu Valley by October, 1937. Also by the late 1930s actual "development" was occurring, beginning with the establishment of the Aiyura Agricultural Experimental Station near Kainantu in 1936, with cinchona, tea, and coffee plantings and its own airstrip by 1937.

Even conditions among the notorious Anga of the Upper Watut River were sufficiently stable for permission to be granted to Beatrice Blackwood to become, in August, 1936, the second professional anthropologist to work in the Highlands (or, at least, on their southeastern fringe). Sent by the Pitt Rivers Museum to collect artifacts and make a thorough study of "a functioning Neolithic technology," her first choice had been the Mount Hagen area, but it was still closed when she began her work (Hallpike 1978:8).

Despite these conditions of relative peace, there were close parallels between Blackwood's and Reo Fortune's circumstances. Like Fortune, Blackwood was a seasoned fieldworker and had already produced her own classic monograph, on Buka (1935). Also, she was constrained by the government's concerns with her safety, being allowed to visit only the "safe" villages near Otibanda Police Post, where somewhat artificial settlements had recently been encouraged by the administration. An epidemic in the region shortly after her arrival was only a harbinger of the conditions she would have to face, and from her surviving fieldnotes C. R. Hallpike (1978:9) has reconstructed a picture reminiscent of McLean's account (this volume) of Fortune's sojourn among the Kamano:

> The linguistic difficulties, the absence of useful informants, the tiny settlements with their constantly changing membership, the rigours of the terrain, the dour and suspicious nature of the Kukukuku, constantly afraid of attack from lurking enemies and, in the last months, the frequent necessity to stay in roughly built government "rest houses", prevented from working by the pouring rain, combined to produce a notably depressing experience, and it is a tribute to her resilience that she managed to survive in the field for as long as she did without a period of rest, and remarkable that she succeeded in being well accepted by such a difficult people.

Again like Fortune, Blackwood had to contend with illness herself and finally had to leave the area after less than nine months' work when an assault by the Anga on a local Chinese storekeeper raised the administration's anxiety levels too high to allow her to continue (Hallpike 1978:9). So, viewing her "Kukukuku" fieldwork as incomplete, she made the most of what remained of her leave with brief periods of collecting and research among the Arawe of New Britain and the Bosmun of the Upper Ramu River before returning to England.

In the Mandated Territory, the intensive patrolling of the late 1930s included an expedition on a scale even larger than that of Leahy and Taylor in 1933. Again the leader was James L. Taylor who, with John

Black, was out for over a year, from March, 1938, to June, 1939, opening up the territory from Wabag to Telefomin (which by then had become much better known from the prospecting activities of J. Ward Williams in 1935–37, including airplane reconnaissance and landings at Telefomin). The "Hagen-Sepik Patrol" extended knowledge of the Hageners, Huli, and Enga, and yielded the first accounts (Taylor 1940*a*, 1940*b*) of the Duna people of the far western highlands.

This was also the period of great patrols in the Territory of Papua, with Jack Hides adding tens of thousands of people to its known population on his 1935 journey from the Mount Bosavi area in the far west through the valleys of the Huli, Mendi, Kewa, and Sau peoples (Hides 1936; Schieffelin and Crittenden 1991). Parts of this route were covered again, but much new territory was added, in major patrols of 1936 and 1937, with Ivan Champion and C. J. Adamson adding considerably to our early knowledge of the Huli and Mendi; southern fringe Enga populations; the Kakoli, Imbonggu, Kewa, and Wiru of the Mount Giluwe and Mount Ialibu regions and the Poru Plateau; the Fasu and Foi of Lake Kutubu; and finally, the Podopa, Daribi, and Pawaia of the eastern end of their travels. These patrols were also crucial in laying the groundwork for the establishment of a major police post at Lake Kutubu, which was accomplished following a seaplane landing on the lake in October, 1937. "Development" was still far off in the future for the Southern Highlands, but the stage was now set for intensive ethnographic research, and F. E. Williams, still government anthropologist of Papua, seized the opportunity.

Unlike Chinnery, his counterpart in the Mandated Territory, F. E. Williams was able to engage in several substantial periods of fieldwork, for example, fourteen months with the Orokaiva, and more than twenty-one months (albeit over a fourteen-year period) at Orokolo. Doubtless these circumstances helped make it possible for him to produce detailed monographs to an extent Chinnery (or most anthropologists, for that matter) was never able to do, including *Orokaiva Society* (1930), for which he received his M.A. from Adelaide; *Papuans of the Trans-Fly* (1936), his B.Sc. thesis (!) at Oxford; and his D.Sc. thesis (Oxon), *Drama of Orokolo* (1940). His work in eight "major fields" and at least twelve "minor ones" (Griffiths 1977:21, n. 5) established for him a solid reputation in anthropology, but it may have evoked little enthusiasm from his superior, J. H. P. Murray, for whom, in the view of Griffiths (1977:175), "there was a constant battle with anthropologists like Fortune who did not think he should be interfering with Papuan life. Whenever he had the opportunity he wrote or spoke to their discredit." Murray did not, at least in print, express the same antagonism toward Williams and, as Elkin (1943:99) has noted, Williams "was given a free hand, and the Government published his reports, whether they were regarded officially as acceptable and useful or not."

Despite Murray's general attitude toward anthropologists and severe limits on resources in the Papuan administration, Williams throve in his post and never wanted for support from the anthropological establishment, with introductions to his books written by R. R. Marett, A. F. C. Haddon, and C. G. Seligman. Contrasts with Chinnery—who seems always to have been overburdened with administrative tasks and never achieved either advanced degrees or his own ethnological goals—could not have been starker, and they apparently extended to the two men's roles as "gatekeepers" of anthropological research in New Guinea. Whereas Chinnery devoted much of his scarce time to recruiting and helping other fieldworkers, Williams seems to have been determined to keep in his sole possession the only key to the Southern Highlands "gate." On this topic, Griffiths's reading of Williams's papers and correspondence (1977:33–34) is worth quoting at length:

> Hearing that an Oxford Exploration Club party wished to be the first to enter the uncontrolled area of the recently discovered Southern Highlands, around Lake Kutubu, Williams wrote [in 1936] to the Administration forestalling the group's request for permission. . . . He was successful, although it was also unlikely that such a party would have been granted access to an uncontrolled area in any case; and it was "arranged that I [Williams] should be the first anthropologist to work in the . . . area". . . . And again, when an anthropologist named Bonington requested permission to work in the same general region, Williams suggested [in 1935] to the Government Secretary that he might find the [coastal] Aroma district "a very profitable one to work in" instead. . . . Referring to Bonington's desire to work on "ground which has been untouched", Williams commented: "I presume he refers to the gentle touch of the anthropologist only, not to that of the European in general". . . . It seems probable, however, that in requesting access to the Highlands, Bonington was asking permission to work in an area that Europeans had not yet greatly influenced; it seems equally likely that Williams, as a fellow anthropologist, would have gathered this impression. Instead he made a point of sending the other anthropologist elsewhere, informing the administration as he did so that "I should myself like to be the first anthropologist to go to see the new people discovered by Mr Hides".

And so he was.

Apart from a brief visit to Mount Hagen (Williams 1937), Williams conducted fieldwork in the Southern Highlands from November, 1938, to May, 1939, spending most of his time with the Mubi River Foi, using the new police post at Lake Kutubu as his base. Early in 1939 he visited the neighboring Mendi speakers of the Augu, Wage, and Nembi valleys for a total of about two months. There the absence of any lingua franca prevented him from following his usual practice of working through interpreters, and he began to learn the local language (Griffiths 1977:40). In his subsequent report on these "Grasslanders" (Williams 1940*b*), extensive word lists were given a place of prominence and went considerably beyond the "native vocabularies" often included in *Annual Reports*. These brief periods of fieldwork would be the only ones conducted by professional anthropologists in the region for over a decade, until D'Arcy Ryan arrived among the Mendi and Robert M. Glasse, the Huli (see their contributions to this volume). It is likely that Williams would have pursued his Highlands investigations further, but he lost his life in World War II, during which virtually all field research in New Guinea was put on hold in any case.

In the view of Downs (1980:176),

> The Japanese war was an interlude rather than an event in the history of the New Guinea highlands. The Japanese did not attempt to cross the Bismarcks and the people remained in relative isolation, occasionally entertained by visiting aircraft and VIPS. The highlands served as a rest area, mainly for American and Australian airmen. ANGAU [the Australian New Guinea Administrative Unit] had simply carried on when civil administration ceased. Medical services were greatly extended under army administration.

It is difficult, however, to dismiss the war so casually in terms of its impact on Highlanders; consider, for example, the history of the "Bena Force" (Dexter 1961). The Bena Bena and Goroka regions were regarded as strategically critical; by the end of 1942, the Japanese were entrenched in Madang, the Huon Peninsula, and the Finistrerre Mountains, needing only to move up the Ramu and Markham valleys into the Eastern Highlands to mount an effective campaign against Port Moresby and the southern coast. Accordingly, the Sixth Australian Division was sent to Bena Bena in January, 1943, to hold the entire area extending to the Ramu Valley. The operation was closed down in November, 1943, but during its main period of occupation of the Goroka Valley this "rest area" was host to sixty-five officers, over thirteen hundred Australian and American soldiers, and more than two hundred members of the Royal Papuan Constabulary. In addition, up to three to four thousand Chimbu were relocated to Bena Bena and Goroka as a labor force to help construct living quarters and airstrips. By the time of its removal, the force had constructed a permanent airfield at Goroka, established a hospital at Mount Hagen and increased medical services at the Kundiawa Lutheran mission, patrolled and mapped extensively from one end of the Highlands to the other, and flooded the region with Western goods and influences on a scale far greater than that of the European incursions of the 1930s. As for the visiting aircraft that "occasionally entertained" the Highlanders, in May and June of 1943 the entertainment included bombings and strafing of Asaroka, Goroka, Bena Bena, Chimbu, Kainantu, and Aiyura, with uncounted casualties among the indigenous population.

These wartime events, together with the previously mentioned shell inflation of the 1930s, must be taken into account when a long-overdue history of this early period is written. The received view, expressed, for example, by Peter Lawrence and Mervyn Meggitt (1965:20) is that

> the contact situation in the Highlands . . . was less disruptive than on the Seaboard. The people were able to reach a *modus vivendi* with the Europeans, who treated them with some respect, and left their social and religious systems largely intact. They still found their traditional way of life satisfying.

While the records of early colonialism in other regions of the world, and perhaps in New Guinea, may be filled with more violence and exploitation of native populations, we are now learning of some of the seamier aspects of the "first contact" period in the Highlands (see, e.g., Connolly and Anderson 1987), and, as Andrew Strathern discusses in his concluding essay in this volume, the "first generation" of Highlands ethnographers were, after all, working in *and were part of* a colonial context.

However benign may have been the treatment of Highlanders by early prospectors, patrol officers, missionaries, and military personnel—and most of it probably was—it is perhaps more the mystique of the Highlands than an appreciation of this historical context that has led to the impression, again to quote Lawrence and Meggitt (1965:20), that

> the problems facing the anthropologist in the Highlands were relatively straightforward. He rarely had to deal with antagonism to white men, which was normally expressed elsewhere through the medium of cargo cult. Such cargo cults or other 'revolutionary' movements as he met were usually only marginal and of short duration.

To be sure, the essays in this volume evince few indications of antagonism directed at the "pioneer" ethnographers, but some of the latter in fact found themselves in the middle of ongoing or recently abandoned "cargo cults."

It is still too early to answer fully Mervyn Meggitt's questions (1973:2) regarding the relative paucity of reports in the literature of "cargo" and millenarian cults in the Papua New Guinea Highlands compared to coastal and seaboard Melanesia: were such movements indeed rare, or had they dissipated too quickly and early for fieldworkers to study or be aware of them, or were they simply placed low on the list of ethnographers' priorities? Meggitt's recent documentation of "Ain's cult," which swept through Enga populations, as well as their Ipili neighbors (Meggitt 1973; see also Gibbs 1977), and Andrew Strathern's (1971*b*) account of a widespread cult in the Hagen area, indicate that the wartime period witnessed "adjustment movements" (R. Berndt 1954:274), involving vast numbers of Highlanders. The immediate postwar years, too, were ones of significant cult activity among the Kuma, Siane, Kamano, and Usurufa (Reay 1959; Salisbury 1958*b*; R. Berndt 1952–53), which continued in the Fore area during the period of the Berndts' fieldwork (R. Berndt 1954 and this volume).

These movements of the 1940s and 1950s, as well as the cults and "revivals" of the 1960s—including at least the ones described for the Baiyer Valley (Osborne 1970); Hagen (A. Strathern 1979–80); the Southern Highlands (Robin 1982; Clark 1988); the Asaro Valley (Steinbauer 1979:64–65); and Kamano (Steinbauer 1979:65–66)—still await full analysis, but the long-established "contrasts" between Highlanders and coastal and seaboard Melanesians in this regard are doubtless in need of revision. Of course, such an analysis will have to be sensitive not only to diversity among the cults themselves, but also among their antecedent events or conditions, which include enormous infusions of Western goods as well as traditional shell valuables, both human and porcine disease epidemics, the introduction of Christianity, and the devastation—even if limited—of the Second World War itself.

But if the war brought traumatic upheavals to at least some Highlands populations, it was also a stimulus to the extension of services to them. In the immediate postwar period, missions once again expanded their activities, moving into such areas as the Baiyer Valley in 1949, and by that year functioning native hospitals (products of collaborative efforts by missions and the military administration) were in place at Kainantu, Goroka, Kundiawa, Kup, Mount Hagen, and Wabag (Kettle 1979). Also by that time, the agricultural station at Aiyura had been reestablished and the townsite of Goroka had been purchased by the administration from the Gahuku people. If the Highlands were not yet completely prepared for intensive "development," the way had been paved for systematic anthropological research on a large scale.

HIGHLANDS ANTHROPOLOGY AFTER THE WAR(S)

The "first generation" of professional ethnographers began arriving in the Highlands in 1950, with Paul Wirz in the Wabag region and K. E. Read in the Goroka Valley. Beliefs that the Highlands were uninhabited or only sparsely populated had long been laid to rest by the patrols and prospecting activities of the 1930s. But with no organized institutional interest in the area, early efforts at fieldwork, such as those by Fortune and Blackwood, had been sporadic and, in the event, doomed to early curtailment by limited logistic support and continual problems related to chronic fighting among the local populations.

By 1950, the disruptions of World War II had ended and those related to tribal wars had been drastically reduced. While all of the Highlands, in the newly formed Territory of Papua and New Guinea, "came under the *Restricted Areas Ordinance* 1950, . . . pacification in the main valleys between Kainantu and Mt Hagen was regarded as complete" (Downs 1980:176). Thus, even allowing for administrative overgeneralization, fieldworkers such as Bulmer, Read, Salisbury, and the Watsons would find a radically different situation in the Central Highlands than had Fortune and Blackwood only fifteen years previously. On the other hand, the Berndts and Reay, as their contributions to this volume graphically indicate, began their work in areas "still to be brought under control" (Downs 1980:176). According to Nelson (1971), between July, 1951, and June, 1955, all of the Eastern Highlands (including much of the adjacent Anga territory) and the North Wahgi were de-restricted; the rest of the Wahgi and Hagen regions were so reclassified between July, 1955, and June, 1960, as were the Mendi and Huli areas, allowing Glasse and Ryan to begin their research at the beginning of this period; and the remaining parts of the Southern Highlands were finally de-restricted between 1960 and 1965, along with the Enga region, where Wirz and Meggitt had been able to work only within delimited zones or by accompanying official parties of patrol officers and armed police (Wirz 1952*b*; Meggitt 1956, 1957).

Administrative classifications applied to very large areas, and conditions were by no means uniform within them, with regard to fighting or anything else; forces of change had widely varying impact on village populations both between and within districts. For example, from 1950 to 1955, the Highlands Labour Scheme continually shifted its recruiting areas, drawing initially on the male populations of the Eastern Highlands District, then the Mount Hagen area, then the Wabag region, and finally the Southern Highlands. Mission expansion also continued, with virgin territories opened up in ever-widening circles from the main administrative posts; in 1950 and 1951 alone, new mission stations representing diverse creeds and denominations were begun at Menyamya, Kompiam (Enga), Kutubu, Mendi, and Telefomin. Nonmission European settlement was variably intensive and initially confined largely to the Eastern Highlands, where about a dozen Europeans resided at Goroka as early as June, 1951, and as many again were scattered on dispersed coffee plantations in the district to the east between 1952 and 1954. The lure of gold had mainly given way to other ventures, in coffee or cattle or employment within the administrative and economic infrastructures needed to support all of this activity. In the early 1950s Goroka became a major administrative center, the distribution point for shells (which were still pouring into the Western and Southern Highlands by the ton), and a favorite stop for journalists and filmmakers, who began to "tour" the Highlands with increasing frequency.

According to Downs (1980:176), in the reconstruction period immediately following the Second World War "highland development was put aside because there had been little war damage and no disruption in the lives of the people. There was a temptation to leave the people in a primitive illiterate and unclothed state and to postpone the 'culture clash' that would follow further development." Obviously, events soon overtook such a program of "benign neglect," and change, if not "development," dominated the early 1950s. While it bears repeating that the intensity and speed of change varied considerably within the Highlands, general processes were at work on a region-wide basis: missions, afforestation programs, labor recruiting, cash-crop introductions, and the building of roads—constructed so rapidly that by November, 1953, one could drive from Lae on the eastern coast to Mount Hagen—were transforming the physical, social, and cultural landscapes at the same time that many of them were still being charted.

The mystique of "the land that time forgot" (Leahy and Crain 1937) continues to the present day to attract the attention of the outside world, though by 1950 one had to go far off the beaten path to find Highlanders who had not been affected by the events and forces of change reviewed above. And yet, despite the hundreds of Europeans who had by then flown or walked into those high valleys, the Highlands were still poorly known, even where contact had been the earliest. By 1950 administration officers, prospectors, and travelers had published as many as fifty articles and books about the peoples considered in this volume (Hays 1976: 12–35), and many of these reports, which often were illustrated with photographs, are now invaluable documentary sources. But the vast majority of these accounts were the result of superficial observations by parties passing through the territory or otherwise preoccupied, and lacked the necessary contextual information within which an anthropologist could make sense of the customs reported.

Long-term European residents in the Highlands, namely, missionaries, had produced a richer, but diverse, fund of knowledge, and Garry Trompf (1984) is certainly correct in emphasizing how much they have contributed to Highlands anthropology—not only through the hospitality and logistic assistance provided to fieldworkers (as the authors in this volume attest), but through their own, often insightful, descriptions and analyses. When Louis J. Luzbetak settled into the Banz and Nondugl areas in 1952, contemporaneously with the "pioneers" who are the focus of this collection, he was following a long tradition of missionary anthropology by members of the Society of the Divine Word, and his subsequent publications (1954, 1956a, 1956b, 1958a, 1958b) would add importantly to our understanding of the societies and cultures of the Wahgi Valley. By 1950, both he and his professional counterparts were in a position to benefit from the already-published work of his predecessors, most notable of whom were Aufenanger, Nilles, Ross, Schäfer, and Vicedom (see Hays 1976 for references).

Father Heinrich Aufenanger entered the Highlands mission field at Bundi (with the Gende people) in 1934, transferred to Nondugl in 1948, and served for many years among lowland and coastal people as well as making short visits to the Chimbu, Duna, Gahuku, Kalam, and Wabag Enga. By the time of his death in the late 1970s, he had received a Ph.D. in anthropology at the University of Vienna (1955) and published fifty-two articles and three books on Highlands peoples alone. Apart from extensive vocabularies and grammars of Gende and Nondugl and an influential early monograph (Aufenanger and Höltker 1940), most of Aufenanger's publications, six of which appeared before 1950, were what might be called "customs reports," providing little or no analysis, but ahead of their time in reproducing masses of material recorded and translated verbatim from informants.

Father John Nilles also began his work in the 1930s and started publishing reports of Kuman Chimbu customs almost immediately, with six of his eight pre-1950 articles appearing in anthropological journals. While most of his early publications dealt with material culture and settlement patterns, his account (1940) of a Waugla male initiation ceremony observed in 1937 is a classic source for students of Highlands ritual and male cults, and a synthetic ethnography of the Kuman (1950), based on over a decade's residence, won him a Diploma in Anthropology at the University of Sydney.

Among the largely unsung Highlands missionaries (but see Mennis 1982) was Father William A. Ross, who had tried to "beat the Lutherans" to Mount Hagen. His prewar publications nearly all appeared in mission magazines and dealt only superficially with village life among the Mogei, but his early collection of "notes" published in *Anthropos* (1936) was an invaluable alternative perspective to juxtapose with the highly influential works of his contemporary, Vicedom (see below). While Ross's work was not part of an academic training program, a visiting military officer pumped him for information during a three-week wartime stay at Mount Hagen and produced a doctoral thesis that was published as the first monograph in English on a Central Highlands people (Gitlow 1947*a*, 1947*b*).

Father Alfons Schäfer was one of the true pioneer missionaries in the Highlands, establishing the Bundi station in 1933 and subsequently spending two decades with the Chimbu in the lower Wahgi Valley. Throughout the 1930s and the war years he published "customs reports" for his mission's magazine, but also in anthropological journals, including an extensive description (1938) of initiation ceremonies which ranks with Nilles's (1940) paper for historical value.

Perhaps the most influential of the prewar missionary-anthropologists was the Lutheran, Rev. Georg F. Vicedom. Although not trained academically as an ethnographer, his early (1938) detailed account of the Hagen *moka* ceremonial exchange system was an invaluable early source of information on one of the most complex Highlands societies. His collaboration with Herbert Tischner (1943–48) in a comprehensive ethnography of the Mbowamb totaled over a thousand pages and became, deservedly, a classic in Highlands anthropology.

By 1950, then, casual visitors and missionaries had produced a sizeable body of published information about Highlands peoples, but its scope and depth were very uneven. A prospective fieldworker interested in Bundi, Chimbu, or Mount Hagen—assuming facility in reading German—had available a substantial base on which to build, but none of the "pioneering generation" went to those areas. For other regions, one could get a general sense of the surfaces of traditional life, but little more, and sufficient diversity was apparent to caution against easy extrapolation from one area to another.

Nor, with the exception of F. E. Williams, had the prewar anthropologists gone far beyond "customs reports." Chinnery certainly had not had the opportunity to do more than make brief, though useful, observations. Blackwood's objectives had been fairly narrowly conceived, and given her field circumstances it is not surprising that resulting publications (1939*a*, 1939*b*, 1940, 1950) were largely contextless data reports. After the brilliance of Fortune's works on Dobu and the Arapesh, much might have been hoped for from his Kamano research but, again, conditions of fieldwork precluded in-depth, rounded studies; preoccupied in the field with the fighting around Finintegu, so too were his only early papers (1947*a*, 1947*b*) deriving from that research. Frustrated, one can only wonder what the impact might have been of his unpublished papers on patrilineal ideology versus actual group composition and "sexual antagonism," only recently discovered in his estate (see McLean, this volume).

As with Fortune, one might have expected more from Williams's Highlands research, considering the depth and sophistication of his earlier analyses of Papuan societies. Of course, a three-day visit at Mount

Hagen could not yield more than superficial descriptions (1937), but little more than that (apart from linguistic materials) came of his work (1940*b*) with the Mendi "grasslanders." Somewhat more of a rounded portrait was produced (1940–41, 1941) on the Foi of Lake Kutubu, with topical coverage comparable to that of standard ethnographic monographs of the period. However, the work has a survey quality, and may have reflected Williams's reputed disenchantment with "functionalism." In 1937 he had expressed the view to J. H. P. Murray (quoted in Griffiths 1977: 163) that culture was "only in part a system. It always remains to some extent a hotch-potch and a sorry tangle." According to Elkin (1943:95), Williams's years of Papuan research "had convinced him that the cultures which he knew were far from being fully organized systems, and that they were evolved to some extent by a process of accretion."

Later fieldworkers in both Mendi and Kutubu (e.g., Lederman 1986; Weiner 1988) would argue for more coherence than Williams seems to have found there, just as the intensive fieldwork done by the Berndts and others among Kamano and Fischer's (1965) with the Yagwoia would flesh out in detail the early sketches of Fortune and Blackwood (as would also be the case with groups described by the missionary-anthropologists). In any case, in 1950 it appeared that a good deal remained to be done in the Highlands, and research programs soon arose to address the perceived needs.

Prior to World War II, the Anthropology Department at the University of Sydney had been "the almost exclusive center in Australia for anthropological studies focussed on" the New Guinea region; this did not, however, ensure that it would become "automatically the staging center for students interested in New Guinea," as Keesing (1952:109) asserted. Since the late 1920s, government personnel had been trained in Sydney, but in 1930, then-Head A. R. Radcliffe-Brown clashed with J. H. P. Murray, as had Fortune, and the training stopped. After Radcliffe-Brown's resignation in 1931, an interim period ended with the appointment of A. P. Elkin as head in 1934. He smoothed out the difficulties with Murray, and in 1935 the training of Papuan officers and New Guinea cadets resumed (Wise 1985). According to Tigger Wise (1985:155) Elkin wanted to expand his influence over affairs in Papua and the Mandated Territory, and in 1943 he gave the region top priority in his "ambitious postwar reconstruction program."

But not all would go smoothly; with the end of the war, as with many other matters in Australia, attention shifted to Canberra where, in 1945, the new Military School for Civil Affairs in Duntroon took over the training of officers for New Guinea, and in the following year it became the Australian School of Pacific Administration (ASOPA). Sydney an-

thropologists would give courses there, but Elkin was correct in perceiving formidable competition, both at ASOPA and the Research School of
Pacific Studies at the Australian National University (ANU), set to open
in Canberra in 1951. In Wise's (1985) view, these developments led Elkin
to refocus his attention on Australian Aborigines, but he clearly was not
done with New Guinea.

As if in preparation for a major research assault on the region, in 1948
Elkin had supported a field survey of the Highlands by his department's
linguist, A. Capell. The resulting report (Capell 1948–49) included lex-
ical and grammatical sketches and provided tentative groupings of languages from Gadsup in the east to the central Enga and the Southern
Highlands. Then Elkin himself, in 1950, made a five-week tour of the
Territory of Papua and New Guinea for the South Pacific Commission.
In the published results (Elkin 1953a), he not only reviewed what was then
known anthropologically of the whole region of Melanesia, but articulated a detailed plan for future work, with special attention given to the
Papua New Guinea Highlands.

Elkin's main source of disquiet over the state of social anthropology in
Melanesia as of 1950 was expressed in his conclusion (1953a:xii) that

> our knowledge . . . in most of the total region lacks depth. . . . We can
> describe social structure, economic activities, magical forms and some
> myths. . . . But we have not learnt the system of values and of attitudes, nor
> the philosophy and religion of the peoples studied. Investigators do not
> seem to have been admitted into, or to have grasped, the meaning of life
> as held by Papuans and Melanesians.

This kind of "depth," of course, could not be achieved during the brief
visits of explorers, travelers, or administrators. Missionaries, however,
were singled out as a category of outsiders who, through long-term
residence and facility in local languages, had the opportunity for such
achievements, and Elkin (1953a:7) praised the work of Nilles and Schäfer
as outstanding models of what could be accomplished. By and large, the
anthropologists who had worked in New Guinea had not, in Elkin's view,
spent enough time in the field (usually six to twelve months) and had not
conducted "that longer and deeper research which leads to understanding. It means the devotion of five or six years to a project" (1953a:xiii).

Of course, he did not intend that a fieldworker would be in the field
for so long at one time; rather, he proposed (1953a:141–147) a schedule
for "new districts," such that the researcher would spend two years in a
first session of work, then a third year (including a survey of the total
"culture area") after a one-year break, and later return for a review,
covering a total span of five to six years. Aware that the number of
fieldworkers would always be limited, Elkin felt (1953a:137) that such

resource-intensive baseline studies had to be balanced with attention to "urgent problems of great consequence, concerned with the development of peoples and with social and cultural changes, for the direction and effects of which we must bear the responsibility" (1953a:137).

Rejecting as an unaffordable luxury the "individualistic selection of fields" that had been the rule in the past (1953a:137), for both kinds of projects Elkin targeted specific areas where work should be done, and one of these was the Kainantu region:

> Obviously there is great and pressing opportunity for research in this area, amongst almost unknown peoples. . . . There is a note of urgency to be struck here, for changes in the native economy may well be fairly rapid in the nearer parts.
> . . . Here then, is an opportunity and need to study a people settling down under a contact situation (1953a:76).

While Elkin (1953a:77) thought that either the Gadsup or Tairora "would seem to be the best to work in the first instance," another decade would pass before ethnographic research among the Gadsup (by Brian DuToit) would take place and James B. Watson would become, with Virginia D. Watson, the first ethnographer of the Tairora (see his contribution to this volume). Elkin would, however, play a large part in the Berndts' decision to work in the Kainantu region.

By 1951, Catherine and Ronald Berndt had already spent a decade in fieldwork among Australian Aborigines and, according to their accounts in this volume, they believed that field experience in a second area was desirable for an anthropologist; moreover, Catherine Berndt saw an opportunity to contribute to the filling of a near void, as the lives of women—one of her continuing interests—had received little attention previously in New Guinea ethnography. Advice from Chinnery and K. E. Read (see below) complemented the encouragement they received from Elkin and the linguist A. Capell, and they chose the diverse ethnolinguistic groups to the southwest of Kainantu as their "second area." Their doctoral theses (C. Berndt 1955; R. Berndt 1955a)—submitted to the University of London, with Sydney as yet unable to offer the Ph.D. in anthropology—and numerous Highlands publications would address both of Elkin's main concerns: intensive, in-depth studies of "new districts" and the study of social change and reactions to the contact situation (see, e.g., C. Berndt 1953; R. Berndt 1952–53, 1954).

Until it could establish its own Ph.D. program in anthropology, the University of Sydney was severely limited in the degree of support available for potential Highlands ethnographers, and especially so compared with the resources being assembled in Canberra (see below). But Elkin was resourceful and pursued his plan for the Highlands not only by recruiting anthropologists who formally took their degrees elsewhere, but also by turning to ethnographically oriented missionaries. Not only were such men perhaps temperamentally congenial to Elkin the Anglican pastor (Wise 1985), but he viewed them as unusually well-situated for anthropological research, given their long-term residence in an area and facility in the local language; moreover, they were perforce involved deeply in social change and its attendant problems, always one of his major interests. The only complaint he voiced (1953a:7) about the work they had published on the Highlands was that they seemed to view anthropology as little more than the recording of customs. This he could do something about, through training and guidance, as in the case of Father John Nilles in the Chimbu region. Prior to the war, Nilles had published a number of "customs reports" (see Hays 1976:96), but under Elkin's tutelage he produced a general ethnographic description of the Kuman, which won him a Diploma in Anthropology at Sydney and was published (Nilles 1950) in Elkin's journal, *Oceania*. With no other ethnographer on hand to send to the Chimbu, Elkin (1953a:80) asked Nilles to continue his studies, especially regarding the effects of contact, and Nilles soon produced just such a report (1953).

Elkin was not concerned only with social change, however, and it was in the "new districts" that he wanted to implement his plan of long-term baseline studies. One of the areas he targeted was in the Southern Highlands, among the Mendi people of the Nembi and Wage valleys. "Discovered" by the Papuan prewar patrols and described to some extent by F. E. Williams (see above), these large populations seemed to Elkin (1953a:83) to

> have been enjoying, right up to this moment [1950], a self-contained and self-directed life, with only such outside contacts as brought them what they desired. Such a phenomenon is fascinating, and should be studied for the purpose of throwing light on man and his communal relationships.

As D'Arcy Ryan tells us in his contribution to this volume, Elkin did send an ethnographer to Mendi at about the same time as the Berndts were in the field, but the project was aborted. Ryan, previously an undergraduate at Sydney, had gone on to Oxford and received a bachelor of letters in anthropology, returning to Sydney in 1952. By 1954, Elkin had research grants available and at last the possibility of Ph.D. students of his own; perhaps by then feeling the pressure of competition from the new program at the Australian National University, he sent Ryan off to the Mendi in May of that year. Ryan had done no fieldwork previously and began with "no clear programme," according to his own report (chap. 7), but he soon produced important pioneering papers (e.g., 1955, 1959) on Mendi social organization and a doctoral thesis (1962) that was one of the first systematic analyses of Highlands ceremonial exchange systems.

In July, 1950, on his study trip for the South Pacific Commission, Elkin had observed in operation at Wabag in the far western highlands another exchange system, of which he subsequently published (1953b) an account. Intrigued by what he saw there, he (1953a:84) ranked Wabag "as a first priority for research amongst what is, almost everywhere in the sub-district, an untouched culture and people. . . . This is an ideal area for the five year intensive type of project."

As with the Berndts, Elkin found in Mervyn J. Meggitt a seasoned fieldworker keen to do ethnographic research in a new area. Meggitt had previously completed two extended periods of work with the Walbiri of Central Australia, where he realized the "advantages accruing from a second visit to the same people" (Meggitt 1979:108); thus he was pre-pared to spend more than one period of field research on his next project, and this was exactly what Elkin seemed to have in mind for the Wabag study. (In the event, Meggitt's revisits to the Mae Enga and their neigh-bors would continue over more than thirty years, beginning in 1955.) As a Research Fellow in the department at Sydney, Meggitt was tapped by Elkin to be the social anthropologist/advisor to the Nuffield Expedition—a physical anthropological survey of the Western and Southern High-lands, organized by Elkin, and an extraordinary opportunity for an ethnographer to gain a regional perspective at first hand. Meggitt was Elkin's second Ph.D. student to work in the Highlands, but the first to complete a thesis at Sydney (1959). That thesis, on the Mae Enga lineage system, was published in 1965, by which time it was possible to incorporate the results of the work of the rest of the "pioneers" on a comparative basis, building on a foundation hardly conceivable at the end of the war and creditable, in large part, to the determination and efforts of A. P. Elkin.

But he was not the only person with a plan for Highlands anthropology in the 1950s; the other major force during the period was S. F. Nadel, who was building a program in Canberra that would compete directly with Elkin at Sydney in more respects than the training of administrative officers.

According to a departmental history (Australian National University 1977), the formation of the Research School of Pacific Studies and the Department of Anthropology at the new ANU began in 1948, under the advisement of Raymond Firth. In that year, Peter Lawrence was awarded the first Research Scholarship in Anthropology, but in the absence of a working department, Lawrence went to Cambridge for his formal de-gree. In 1949, W. E. H. Stanner was appointed reader in comparative

social institutions, and in the following year Cyril Belshaw and Kenneth
E. Read were awarded the first research fellowships. By 1951 the program needed only a director, and S. F. Nadel arrived in Canberra in
February of 1951 to become the Foundation Professor of Anthropology,
with K. O. L. Burridge and Peter Worsley as the first resident research
scholars (Ph.D. students).

Nadel began planning a research program immediately, and within a
few weeks of his arrival had recommended research projects on "the
societies of the New Guinea Highlands, social change (especially the
problem of cargo cults) in Melanesia, village communities in Indonesia
and India, and the process of assimilation among recent European im-
migrants to Australia" (Freeman 1956:7). Nadel's report (1951:1) is clear
about his priorities:

> The first research project is concerned with the analysis of the social or-
> ganisation and, generally speaking, the types of society occurring in the
> Highlands of New Guinea. . . . From the point of view of modern social
> anthropology this part of New Guinea is virgin ground; furthermore, it
> offers the attractive possibility of a geographically sharply defined and
> almost closed area, within which we can hope to obtain, in the course of time,
> an exhaustive "social typology".

Nadel's plans included the establishment of a field station in the Highlands to serve as a center for research and training, and collaboration with
other institutions—not, it may be noted, with the University of Sydney,
but the University of California at Los Angeles, whose anthropologists
"are interested in research in the same area and are very keen on joining
in my scheme (with funds of their own), thus increasing the number of
field workers available for this study" (Nadel 1951:1).

While neither the Highlands field station nor the collaboration with
UCLA would eventuate before Nadel's death in 1956, such intentions are
characteristic of the organized manner in which he began his project. Like
Elkin, he "declined to allow an inevitably small number of research
workers to spend themselves on piecemeal studies throughout Melanesia:
research was to have a strategic aim, not become a scatter of raids and
forays" (Stanner 1962:v). He would, in the few years left to him, send five
of the "pioneer" ethnographers to the Gahuku, Siane, Kuma, Kyaka
Enga, and Huli, but these studies were to be "no more than a beginning,
for he had hoped that such field work organized by his own and other
Departments of Anthropology would go on until there was a collection
of materials sufficient for a comparative study of all the main societies of
the New Guinea Highlands" (Freeman 1956:8).

It is not clear from available sources why the Sydney department was
not more explicitly or formally drawn into collaboration with the ANU

Highlands program. Relations between Elkin and Nadel may have been strained by competition for students and resources, but apparently this did not preclude collegial efforts such as a series of seminars at Sydney given by Nadel at Elkin's invitation (M. Meggitt, pers. com., 1989). In any case, in effect if not by design, Nadel and Elkin "carved up New Guinea research between them" (Wise 1985:209), and the first of the 1950s Highlands ethnographers was sent to the field by the ANU program, if not by Nadel himself.

In his survey of Highlands areas warranting particular attention, Elkin (1953*a*:77) noted that Pastor E. P. Helbig had been stationed at Asaloka (Asaroka) in the Goroka Valley since 1932, among the "Gafuguk" and "Gama," and he saw there an "opportunity for studying peoples, still living almost, and in many cases completely, in their traditional manner; but beginning to change." Kenneth E. Read was precisely the sort of person Elkin would have likely sent there had he been able to do so. Read had already conducted wartime research in the Markham Valley, which had led to several early publications (1946*a*, 1947, 1950), a master's thesis (1946*b*) at the University of Sydney, and, since a Ph.D was not yet offered there, his final degree at the University of London (1948). Following his Ph.D., Read was appointed lecturer in anthropology at ASOPA in Canberra, and in 1950 he found further support there in the new ANU department as a research fellow; soon he was off to the field for a two-year stay, as Elkin would have preferred.

As Elkin had noted, by 1950 the Goroka Valley was "beginning to change," and with a field site near the township, Read found the Gahuku poised precariously between the past and the future. In his recent memoirs (1986:129), Read recalls that

> intimations of change . . . in 1950 . . . were really no more than a surface vibration, an intermittent but premonitory flurry of wind across the deep waters of a lake. . . . Underneath the surface disturbance, everything continued to be as it had always been, that is for as long as any memory or experience could muster.

Such recollections, while consistent with Elkin's assessment that changes there were just beginning, may also have been colored to some extent by the mystique of the Highlands; elsewhere (1986:124–125) Read acknowledges that "the final initiation of males into the *nama* cult, was . . . on the brink of extinction in 1950," "the domestic separation of men and women was also breaking down," and there were, by then, "indications of a different economic future for men who sought it." This complex, dynamic situation allowed Read to speak to diverse interests and demonstrate with fresh data that the Highlands was, indeed, a new area with rich potential for any research program. For the ASOPA journal, *South*

Pacific, he sent papers from the field on development prospects for the Gahuku (1951*b*), missions and social change (1952*a*), and—in an area that was increasingly attracting European farmers and planters—issues related to land (1952*b*), all of which doubtless pleased Elkin, who felt strongly that anthropologists had moral obligations to guide administrators and other change agents toward humane approaches based on understanding of and respect for local beliefs and traditions. At the same time, both Elkin and Nadel would surely have been satisfied with Read's rich analyses of Gahuku religion and moral systems (1952*c*, 1955), marriage (1954*b*), and political leadership (1959), and his early delineation of regional patterns in the Central Highlands (1954*a*) was an auspicious beginning for the comparative studies to which Nadel was dedicated.

Perhaps to get another perspective on such institutions in a context of rapid change, Nadel sent his first Ph.D. student, Richard F. Salisbury, to the Siane neighbors of the Gahuku, specifically to study "social structure and religion" (Stanner 1962:v). In Canberra, Salisbury had the benefit of learning about field conditions directly from Read, and he was also "stimulated to collect economic statistics by Dr Cyril Belshaw," also a research fellow in the department at that time (Salisbury 1962:xiii). As matters would develop, this latter influence would turn out to be a crucial one.

Siane territory had been traversed in 1933 by Michael Leahy in his prospecting exploration, and by the time Salisbury arrived in November, 1952, stone tools and the precontact economy were living memories, but little more. Nevertheless, Salisbury recorded those memories and dutifully collected statistical information on economic change and its social ramifications. After a year in the field, he returned to Canberra and prepared a general monograph on the Siane, but left without submitting it as a thesis. Subsequently, at Harvard and then at Berkeley, contacts with Parsonian sociologists convinced him of the special value of his economic data (Salisbury 1962:xiii). With this new stimulus, a dissertation topic emerged and Salisbury wrote what would be a landmark study of economics and technological change, first as a doctoral thesis (1958*a*) and then as a book (1962). While Nadel did not live to see the work completed, W. E. H. Stanner (Salisbury's new supervisor) welcomed the shift in focus and later (1962:v) speculated that Nadel "would have thought the metamorphosis a good example of how to take up the challenge of unfolding facts."

It must be emphasized that Nadel's program for the Highlands was not rigidly conceived; as an experienced fieldworker himself (in Africa), Nadel knew that exigencies of the field situation would play a major role in final selections of sites and topical foci. However, he seems to have been determined not to let serendipity alone rule the field enterprise. According to Stanner (1962:v), Nadel's "ruling passion was a rigorous conception of research," and he "impressed on all his students that facts have to be collected for theroretical significance, not empirical interest, and that it is a moral as well as an intellectual duty to give inquiry as sharp a *Problemstellung* as knowledge and theory allow."

It was this insistence on "theory" as a guiding force behind fieldwork that resulted in the clash reported by Nadel's next Ph.D. student, Marie Reay, in her contribution to this volume. Reay had had considerable previous field experience, with Australian Aborigines and among the Orokaiva of Papua, and had been trained at Sydney under Elkin and Ian Hogbin. With a major interest in social change and the dynamic nature of social relations, an assignment to study "social structure" in British social anthropology terms may have seemed to her an inadequate way to capture the dynamics of Minj society in 1953 through 1955. In the event, she returned to Canberra with rich data on power and authority as they actually existed "on the ground," but which fit awkwardly, according to her account (chap. 5), Nadel's and Stanner's "preconceived notion of New Guinea society derived from Malinowski's account of the Trobriands." Reay would not be the last of the pioneer ethnographers to have difficulty with the "African models" that would be repudiated openly a few years later (see Andrew Strathern's discussion in this volume), but her thesis (1957), later published (1959) as the first English-language general monograph on a Highlands society, reflected the tension increasingly being felt between social anthropological models and the "facts" as they were unfolding in the Highlands.

Nadel's final two Highlands students would not return from the field until he had died, but the orientation of the ANU program had not changed by 1955, when both Ralph N. H. Bulmer and Robert M. Glasse became research scholars there. Indeed, in 1952, the department had been redesignated the Department of Anthropology and Sociology to reflect more accurately the predilections of Nadel and the other staff, all of whom had taken their Ph.D.s at the London School of Economics. In a concerted effort to map the social structure of the large and dense populations of the Western Highlands, Bulmer was sent to the Kyaka Enga of the Baiyer Valley in January, and Glasse followed soon after, with Nadel preferring that he work among the Sau Enga but leaving his final choice (Tari, as matters turned out) to him.

Bulmer's first field report (1955) suggests that he adhered to Nadel's choice of focus—social structure and political leadership—as did his thesis and first major Kyaka publication (Bulmer 1960*a*, 1960*b*), both of which were written under the supervision of John Barnes who, in 1958, declared the continuing interests of the department to center on twelve specified topics, all of which dealt with social organization, politics, eco-

nomics, and exchange (Australian National University 1977:4). It may be
that the Kyaka Enga, like the Mae Enga as Meggitt (1959) would portray
them at about the same time, provided a congenial case for the application
of "African models." And yet Glasse, in his contribution to this volume,
indicates that Bulmer was "struggling with nonagnates" when he visited
him in the field in March, 1955; for Glasse, such a struggle would become
his overriding concern among the Huli.

Unlike Bulmer, who had conducted fieldwork among the Sami Lapps
in 1950–51 prior to receiving his undergraduate degree in anthropology
at Cambridge in 1953, Robert M. Glasse entered Nadel's program with
little formal training in the discipline and no previous fieldwork experience. Arriving in Tari in April, 1955, he found it a restricted area and
was physically confined to the station environs, but this was not his only
constraint. As he tells us (chap. 8), Glasse continually had difficulties with
the segmentary unilineal models provided him in Canberra, concluding
by late 1955 that "Huli reality" could be captured only in a "cognatic"
model. Returning to Canberra in mid 1956, he came under the supervision of J. D. Freeman in an atmosphere that he judged was increasingly
conducive to departures from "African models," especially in Sydney,
where he exchanged ideas and frustrations with Ian Hogbin, M. J. Meggitt, and D'Arcy Ryan. After a subsequent field trip in 1959–60, Glasse
felt he had the quantitative data necessary to portray Huli society with all
its "anomalies," which he did in a thesis (1962), written in Sydney but
supervised from Canberra by Barnes, who would later that same year give
public voice (Barnes 1962) to the concerns that had been plaguing many.

From 1950 to 1955, Elkin at Sydney and Nadel at Canberra had sent
nine ethnographers to the Highlands, all of whom conducted intensive
fieldwork where none had been done before. But they were not the only
anthropologists turning their attention to this "virgin" (if not quite pristine) territory. Vying with K. E. Read for temporal priority was Paul Wirz,
who spent most of 1950 in the Kundiawa and Mount Hagen regions. Wirz
had already distinguished himself with extensive fieldwork and publications on the Marind-anim, Lake Sentani, and Swart Valley Highlands
peoples of Dutch New Guinea, and the Gogodala of Papua. As an inde-
fatigable fieldworker, his purpose in going to the Highlands appears to
have been the collection and documentation of artifacts for museums in
Europe, and most of his resulting publications (1952a, 1952c, 1952d) were
of a "salvage" nature, describing the material culture that was rapidly
disappearing, particularly in the Chimbu area. Taking more time—and
faced with much less obvious change—he was able to pursue general
ethnographic research in the Wabag area, but even there his interest

seems to have been greatest in material culture (1952*b*) and the ceremonies he was able to observe but did not explore in any depth (1952*e*).

This was not the case with the other non-Australian-sponsored pioneers, James B. and Virginia D. Watson, who spent eighteen months in 1953 through 1955 with the Agarabi and Tairora of the Kainantu region. V. D. Watson was a Ph.D. student at the University of Chicago, and her eventual thesis (1965) would comprise the first in-depth study of Highlands women and female roles in the midst of social and cultural change. It was this context of rapid but uneven change that attracted J. B. Watson to the Kainantu area. Having done his doctoral fieldwork on culture change in Brazil, he was intrigued by the contrasting potential of acculturation studies in the New Guinea Highlands, where one could see the change processes at work "at the beginning." For him, the Agarabi and Tairora promised almost a laboratory situation, allowing comparative studies of villages matched for intensity of contact but differing in culture, and vice versa. However, the very units of comparison soon became problematic. In the "crowded fields" around Kainantu, complex relationships between and among villages—both historical and ongoing—made *systems*, rather than "societies" or "cultures" the inevitable objects of analysis. Watson's essay here exemplifies well the profound impact Highlands "cases" continue to have as we advance beyond earlier naive hopes for neat social typologies and straightforward "before and after" studies of change.

The Watsons' work may be regarded as a second "opening" of the Highlands so far as fieldwork there is concerned. Neither Elkin nor Nadel, whatever may have been their own competitive situations, acted in any way to limit the Highlands to Australian-based researchers. But it was not until after the "pioneering" generation that the floodgates opened, and soon—especially in the early 1960s—new waves of ethnographers and new programs engulfed the area with fieldworkers. The University of Sydney and the Australian National University would continue to send students and staff to the Highlands, but the 1960s saw increasing numbers of British and American researchers and such team efforts as J. B. Watson's Micro-Evolution Project from the University of Washington, and Andrew P. Vayda's Human Ecology of the New Guinea Rain Forest group from Columbia University.

All of these investigators would have advantages unavailable to their predecessors: they could build upon not only a much broader and deeper information base but also on sophisticated analyses of a wide range of Highlands societies and cultures, exhibiting both the depth sought by Elkin and the comparative potential that so interested Nadel. Moreover, models had been tested and proven in need of revision, a state of affairs that made for a dynamic period of new agendas and problems, as Andrew Strathern discusses in his concluding piece to this collection.

Yet some aspects of fieldwork seem forever to remain the same, and I have been personally struck, in the papers collected here, by the many resonances with my own field experience as the 1970s began a third decade of Highlands anthropology. In my own part of the Eastern Highlands—the extreme southeastern corner—missions were, in 1971, a recently established force for change, as were the infrequent census patrols, and with the nearest trade store a day's walk away, my wife and I were almost the only sources of Western goods, for which a keen appetite had arisen. Fieldwork then, as always, was an exciting and bewildering experience and always full of surprises no matter how well prepared one might be. Still, while all of the chapters in this volume describe situations and societies that are in many respects comparable, amid the commonalities the uniqueness of peoples and fieldworkers emerges with the clarity of a mountain stream.

NOTES

1. The southern portion of the eastern half of the island of New Guinea was officially known as British New Guinea from 1884 to 1906, when it became the Territory of Papua until the Second World War; the northern portion was German New Guinea until 1914, then the Mandated Territory of New Guinea until 1942. Following a period of military administration during World War II, both were united as the Territory of Papua and New Guinea until independence was granted to Papua New Guinea in 1975.

2. No comprehensive history of European activities in the Papua New Guinea Highlands has yet been written, but the following general sources were useful in preparing this sketch: Souter 1963; J. B. Watson 1964; Steinbauer 1969; Bergmann 1971; Hasluck 1976; Sinclair 1978, 1981; Hope 1979; Kettle 1979; Munster 1979; Downs 1980, 1986; Mennis 1982; Connolly and Anderson 1987; Nilles 1987; Radford 1987; and Schieffelin and Crittenden 1991. For early published accounts of Highlands exploration see Hays 1976.

3. In this decade, too, Ivan Champion and Charles Karius made their historic crossing from the mouth of the Fly River to that of the Sepik. Their reports (e.g., Champion 1932) contain extensive important information on the Mountain Ok and other peoples encountered, but work in that region is outside the scope of this volume.

TWO

In the Footprints of Reo Fortune

Ann McLean

I have set my feet to follow a broken path,
From the sun in the groves below I have turned my face,
There will be no children's voices around my hearth
And the wind itself shall have more an abiding place.

But ever I follow on till the darkness falls
The ineluctable spirit of things unknown,
And I do not greatly care if none recalls
Whither it led; I shall sleep in the end alone.
—REO FORTUNE

Written nine years before his research among the Kamano in the Eastern Highlands of New Guinea, these words may well have been descriptive of his state of mind, as indeed they foreshadowed his subsequent career, as Fortune prepared for arrival in January, 1935, at Komonka. In its very title, "The Stoic," the rather indifferent poem of his youth indicates acceptance of a solitariness that places a major obstacle in the path of the latter-day researcher who would presume to speak for him; Fortune was always an intensely private person and has left very little of a personal nature on record.

In the thirty-two document boxes that escaped the flames of the numerous bonfires he lit in celebration of his indifference to academic immortality (Eileen Fortune, personal papers) there are nonetheless some clues upon which to construct inferences as to his motives for choosing to work in the New Guinea Highlands.[1] There are no surviving diaries and few field notebooks or letters, and most of the material is ruthlessly purged of subjective comment. However, a significant survivor is the draft of a book, at present in preparation for posthumous publication. It was written mostly in 1936, and originally titled *Men of Purari*; a later editing is headed *Amongst the Kamano*. There are numerous other draft articles on language, law, social change, and motivation, also never published, and fragments of lectures. As far as is possible this material will be allowed to speak for itself, but the reader will have to permit imagination to supply much of the weariness, worry, sickness, danger, and yet exhilaration of the experience of fieldwork in those remote times and places.

The difficulties and dangers Fortune encountered in his various New Guinea fieldwork locations seem to have increased in direct proportion to their height above sea level. The first was safe enough, on the island of Dobu in the D'Entrecasteaux group, where he spent six months in 1928. This research was later presented as his best-known publication, *Sorcerers of Dobu* (1932), a book that was very well received and is still an anthropological classic. It demonstrated what was perhaps Fortune's greatest asset—derived in part from his family background and partly from growing up in a bicultural country (see below) in which there was relative equality and remarkably little overt racial tension—that of accepting otherness with neither judgment nor condescension.

The second expedition was somewhat more hazardous, but the considerable successes of their respective first fieldwork studies lent Fortune and his co-worker and first wife, Margaret Mead, confidence to face the challenges of Manus Island. This was followed by their first encounter with non-Austronesian-speaking Melanesians on the expedition during which they studied three Sepik cultures. Mead's account of the trip, in the event very arduous, appears in her autobiography, *Blackberry Winter* (1972). Fortune published none.

The editor of *Oceania* in June, 1933, records: "Dr Fortune and his wife Dr Margaret Mead and Mr G Bateson have come down from the Sepik River, New Guinea, for a well-earned change." Behind this trite little piece of gossip lay twenty months of anguish for Fortune, spent in collaborative research on the Arapesh, Biwat, and Chambri.[2] It was on the last leg of this field trip that the couple met up with Gregory Bateson, who was studying the Iatmul at the time. After a period of close collaboration among the trio, the expedition ended for Fortune in physical and emotional privation and illness, malarial and marital collapse. At its conclusion Fortune and Mead traveled to Sydney, whence Mead returned to New York and Fortune to London.

Fortune's publications resulting from the trip were few (1939, 1942, 1943). It has been generally supposed that his relative reticence was due to personal distress. This is no doubt partially true, but it also suited Fortune to have it so interpreted, for the wider truth is that he was intensely disappointed in the collaboration on a professional as well as a personal level. He resisted descent to a full-scale *bataille de lettres* out of an ingrained inability to gainsay a lady—the same fundamental courtesy, considerably criticized, that caused him to acquiesce in what he felt to be an abuse of his Dobu material by Ruth Benedict (1935). Realistically, too, he may have realized that in the prevailing climate of Mead hagiolatry, professional considerations might have fallen casualty to accusations of sour grapes. Not that he was not tempted; in a draft book review he wrote: "Our own opinion is that Dr Mead is not articulate about her bias as an observer in this book [Mead 1935], and that she weights it, in her own terms, heavily with unacknowledged emotions." He did not proceed with the draft.

At the time of Fortune's descent from the Sepik, the coastal towns were agog with the first reports of large populations of horticulturalists in the wide, fertile valleys of the Highlands, hitherto unmapped but recently explored from Mount Chapman to Mount Hagen by the two Leahy brothers and K. L. Spinks. This knowledge, now a commonplace, caused great excitement at the time, as the earlier Karius-Champion traverse of the island from the Fly to the Sepik had completely missed these populations, and it was still popularly supposed that the central ranges climbed to inhospitable and uninhabited peaks.

The unexpected Leahy-Spinks find must have seemed tailor-made for Fortune; he needed professional occupation, and the excitement of opening an unexplored field must have stirred in him despite his dashed hopes and health. Moreover, he had not lost confidence in his professional judgment and would have exulted in the opportunity presented by an area near enough to offer the possibility of testing and developing the insights gained from Sepik studies, yet perhaps sufficiently distant to avoid casting aspersions on his erstwhile fellow worker.

Fortune's annotations to his copies of Chinnery's (1934a, 1934b) and Spinks's (1934) reports bear testimony to the quickening of his pulse as he noted mention of groups of accomplished horticulturalists, mild temperatures in the high valleys, and, most emphatically underlined, the implied absence of the anopheles mosquito at these higher altitudes (Chinnery 1934a: 408–410).

He must also have heard rumors of the difficulties and disasters suffered by prospectors in their progress into the Highlands. Gold-prospecting expeditions into the auriferous regions radiating out and up from Lae and Morobe had bred misunderstanding and mistrust, and a number of violent deaths on both sides had soured relations between the races. Fortune was later to find that official accounts of Papuan casualties did not always tally with the local people's reckoning, and that the sense of grievance against whites was accordingly greater than might have been anticipated. It is doubtful whether this would anyway have deterred him. Accustomed under normal circumstances to rude good health and a superior level of physical fitness, Fortune faced the prospect with a kind of reckless confidence.

Exploration was rapidly followed by the construction of landing strips near the headwaters of the Ramu at what was to become a permanent post at Kainantu (August, 1932), at Bena Bena (March, 1933), and at Wahgi and Hagen (April, 1933). Chinnery considered when he visited the Ramu-Purari area early in 1933 that "notwithstanding constant inter-tribal hostilities, steady progress was being made in bringing the people under control" (1934*a*:406).

In a perverse way, the knowledge that this area was in the throes of an imposed pacification may have strengthened Fortune's resolve to study there before the process was too far advanced. Reared in New Zealand at a time when Maori demography seemed to justify the view that the role of colonial governments vis-à-vis the indigenes was to "smooth the pillow of the dying race," he may well have subscribed to the prevalent view in anthropological circles that it was "sadly ludicrous, not to say tragic . . . [that] . . . Just now, when the methods and aims of scientific field ethnology have taken shape, when men fully trained for the work have begun to travel into savage countries and study their inhabitants—these die away under our very eyes. . . . The need for energetic work is urgent, and the time is short" (Malinowski 1922:xv). A similar viewpoint was still being expressed thirty years later by E. E. Evans-Pritchard (1951:9): "Another and very cogent reason for studying primitive societies at the present time is that they are rapidly being transformed and must be studied soon or never." Moreover, Fortune had worked in postcontact Dobu: "Dobuan population has now, after forty years of white influence, missionary, trading, and government, dwindled to where twelve persons replace twenty-five. (This is for Dobu Island; in Tewara the case is worse)" (Fortune 1932:30; original parentheses).

Fortune was atheist, the son of a renegade Church of England priest and former missionary; his sensitization to the effects of missionization on indigenous belief systems may also have contributed to his desire to study an almost pristine "primitive" society. An account of some other Papuan groups (Neuhauss 1911) had already been published by Lutheran missionary ethnologists, but Fortune did not even read the volume until after his return, at which time he declared himself "unconvinced" by aspects of these existing studies of Papuan groups in northeastern New Guinea. He seems, therefore, to have gone into the Highlands with no preconceptions and only the geographical information necessary to survival.

Though he was confidently, not to say possessively, claimed by Malinowski as disciple and evangelist for the functional school (Fortune 1932:xx), there is no documentary evidence that he had any prior plan as to what theoretical or practical bent his research would follow. In the light of his Sepik fieldwork, the value of which he felt to have been vitiated by theoretical bias, he may well have sought consciously to keep an open mind.[3]

There were no linguistic aids to the language in the area he would study; indeed, the language groups had not even been identified or named. It is a commentary upon Fortune's brilliance as a linguist that in a brief time, and amid the dangers and distractions of his first Kamano field trip, he became sufficiently familiar with the language to write a preliminary grammar and, apparently, to operate in Kamano. At the time, local people had had very little exposure even to Pidgin English, which Fortune used as a lingua franca for interviews upon his subsequent visit in 1951–52.

However it may be, during 1934 Fortune negotiated from London against considerable official opposition for permission to use his grant from the Columbia Council for Research into the Social Sciences to undertake fieldwork in the Eastern Highlands. The grant was to expire in July, 1936, and Fortune planned to spend a year in the field and to use the rest of his time writing up his work.

After his experiences in the Torricelli Mountains, where, as recounted by Mead (1972), their Arapesh expedition had literally bogged down under the burden of their hundredweights of supplies, Fortune probably sought to travel light into the Eastern Highlands, confining his belongings to his backpack. He was, of course, unencumbered by electronic or electrical equipment. It is not clear whether he even carried a camera on this field trip; at any rate, no progeny of his faithful Leica, which had produced a remarkably good visual record of the Dobu, Manus, Arapesh, Biwat, and Chambri, seem to have been born of this 1935 expedition.[4]

In the pack were included his sleeping bag, later to be a factor in his departure; his personal toilet gear, including a generous supply of razor blades (even the discards had been found in the Sepik to have the virtue of great acceptability as trade goods); and his clothing. Financial expediency as well as his experiences hiking in New Zealand would have tutored him in selection of spartan, functional apparel.

Of all his fieldwork, this was physically much the toughest. In his other study locations contact was relatively advanced, planning of supplies more ambitious, and transport easier. Among the nonessentials Fortune judged desirable, high priority was probably accorded to trade goods: an undated packing list specifies buttons, beads, seeds, salt, and cowrie shells. Since his notes mention dressing wounds, it is likely that a well-stocked medicine kit accompanied him. Professional paraphernalia was evidently severely limited; notes to check references suggest that Fortune had few books with him. His working tools included notably only powdered ink, penholders and nibs, pencils, notebooks, and a supply of flimsy bond paper. Fortune was frugal to the point of parsimony in his personal patterns of consumption; his only concession to extravagance was his pipe.

Heavier items, such as furniture of any kind—even pillow or mattress—were excluded by cost and by difficulty of transport. Even had finance been unlimited, the availability of carriers in this then-turbulent area of the Highlands was uncertain, and after the experience of being stranded for want of porters in Arapesh country, Fortune would have wished to limit his dependency upon the labor of others. And so he walked in alone.

Selection of a base posed no problem, inasmuch as the decision was largely taken out of Fortune's hands:

> The Government Secretary of New Guinea, then at Rabaul, initially declined to permit me to enter the central highlands, then closed to further penetration, by Order in Council, owing to three violent deaths of prior entrants, and a hanging of one. On Chinnery's representation on my behalf the Secretary then said that if I armed, equipped and maintained a bodyguard of twelve riflemen, as some of the prospectors for gold did, I would be permitted to enter. . . . Upon further talk with Chinnery [on the point of expense] the Government Secretary permitted me to enter the central highlands on condition that I slept at a police post, and not in a native village. . . . Accordingly I chose Komonka . . . and was in neighbouring villages daily.

Komonka has vanished from later maps but was notorious at the time as the site upon which the gold prospector Bernard McGrath had been killed in an affray with the local people not long before. Komonka was one of three staging posts intended for use as sleeping quarters between government headquarters at Kainantu, where Mark Pitt was assistant district officer, and Mount Hagen, where James Taylor held that position. The other two staging posts were at Chimbu and Goroka, disposed so that each was about a day's march from the next. Thus, in theory, messages could be relayed between Kainantu in the east and Mount Hagen at the western extremity of the chain in a matter of four or five hard days' march. The intention was that each post be held permanently by three or four native policemen—in the case of Komonka, by a sergeant and two privates of the Native Constabulary. It seems that staffing levels were not always observed: Fortune was alone in the post when some refugees asked for accommodation at the inception of one outbreak of disturbances during his sojourn. Moreover, at least one of the native police officers was removed for alleged procuring and extortion during the period.

Fortune arrived on 20 February 1935, almost certainly by plane from Lae or Salamaua, ascending over the Markham and Ramu valleys to alight at the Kainantu airstrip. He would then have shouldered his pack, walked for a day westward across the Ramu-Purari Divide, and descended along the headwaters of the Kamamentina River, an upper tributary of the Purari, to Komonka.

His first impressions were recorded in a letter to Ruth Benedict,[5] in which he scrawled a scant fifty words to the page in such evident haste and excitement that one can almost hear the accelerated heartbeat and sense the surge of adrenalin:

> The culture is very like Arapesh—only ultra-Arapesh in many respects—I think I know it all by heart before I do it in detail—like another language of the same grammar.
>
> It differs in that about 7/10 of their dead, men, women & children beyond weaning stage, die with arrows sticking into them.—the pace is terrific—It goes on still. They killed 2 under the eyes of the Govt. station the other day—They fight 100 yards from a Govt officer & police & rifles, knowing they may be shot up for it . . . —They have Govt puzzled. They're so stoical and used to it they eat their own dead, of their own village, own group killed in warfare—in sorrow—some they bury—not cannibalism of eating the enemy rejoicing and dancing—that never—unheard of—but to cut down mourning their own & get on with revenge immediately. . . .
>
> With repeated warnings I'm taking some care not to get killed—they are however certainly fair devils run riot on the masculine & patrilineal virtues carried as near social perdition as it is possible to carry them—with sanity delegated to women & despised accordingly.
>
> With best wishes . . .

The fighting to which Fortune refers, styled in his drafts "the first war of Komonka," broke out in March, 1935, a month after he arrived. From that time the situation in the area was at best one of armed truce. In a piece of typical understatement Fortune writes, "Conditions of work were not very good at the time, as white and native relations were regarded with some mistrust by both sides." It was not until 1936, back in the almost tedious tranquility of Paraparaumu, New Zealand, where he wrote the first draft of his unpublished book, that Fortune was able to render a calmer and more measured account of his impressions.

He provisionally dubbed the people he was studying "Purari," after the river at whose headwaters they resided. They occupied at that time, he calculated, some four hundred square miles of the Eastern Highlands, lying between 145° 35' and 145° 50' East longitude, and 6° to 6° 20' South latitude. He reckoned that ten to fifteen square miles of this area consisted in fertile river-valley land, and the remainder was hill country, with all of the area relatively timber-poor: "It is a fine country, warm by day and cold by night, of long reaching river valleys and rolling hills, with the flats covered in tall nine or ten feet high grasses."

In 1935 there were thirty-six settlements in the area, vagrant village populations of which only one had not been evicted from its lands by war within living memory. Most had suffered several routs and regroupings. Typically the village comprised three or four patrilineal lines. Fortune reckoned that the population of the area was from twelve to fifteen thousand, though he was uncertain exactly where the linguistic boundaries were and had too little time to determine this.

Fortune commented at some length on the appearance, sound physique, and health of the local people, and on the manufacture of their garments. He managed to assemble and take out a collection of some seventy-five artifacts, including a fairly complete selection of apparel for both sexes, which he donated to the Otago Museum in Dunedin on his return to New Zealand in 1936. In the light of his previous New Guinea research it did not strike him as strange that the male should be the dandy of Highlands society and the female the drab and the drudge, though the recollection of the strangeness of this phenomenon to Europeans at first encounter led him to detailed explanation in his book draft of the finer points of coiffure and costume that distinguished the sexes.

Fortune was somewhat nonplused by some of the customs and behaviors confronting him. One such concerned the niceties of greeting. The precontact courtesy between persons in certain familiar relationships was by reference to and handling of the genitals. Essentially a prudish person, he records with obvious relief that he was only once put to this test. In presenting an account of the greeting, he hedges with various formulations to convey the meaning of the utterance accompanying the gesture— "thy virility greeting"—"thy male member greeting"—before finally settling for "thy penis greeting," and a clinical account of its usage and abusage.

Sometimes a cri de coeur escapes into his book draft, to be firmly suppressed later by the editorial pencil. For example, he describes with barely disguised distress the miserable dress and demeanor of recently widowed women and the severing of their finger joints in token of mourning, then notes in the margin the instruction to himself to "edit out all this less-than-gallant stuff." Likewise in his description of initiation rites, which involved a good deal of gore in Kamano as elsewhere in the region—noses, tongues, and urethras were cut and thrust with razor-sharp twisted sword grass, and stomachs evacuated with vomiting canes— he suppresses the word "sadistic" that springs unbidden into his notes and retreats into the safety of unemotive professional prose.

It is remarkable in view of the terror and revulsion the reader of Fortune's notes occasionally glimpses that at no point, even in his notebooks, does Fortune convey any hint of personal dislike or judgment of the local people as individuals. To the contrary, Fortune writes of his Kamano *friends*, and never ceased for the rest of his life to puzzle over how to render an account of their culture which made it intelligible in its own terms. He would probably have concurred with the prospector Jack O'Neill (Sinclair, ed. 1979:77): "They were just men; most very likeable, a few nasty bastards, just like our own kind. A few were very real friends."

What the Kamano thought about Fortune is of course not recorded, and there is no indication of how he explained his presence to them. He merely states: "The people of this stone age society have found a great deal of surprise in our uses of metals, political institutions and government, and in our aviation and our industrial science." To gain some more vivid idea of the encounter, the reader must conjure to mind sequences such as those captured on film only two years earlier by Michael Leahy, and recently rescued and restored to enrich the ethnographic film record as "First Contact" (Connolly and Anderson 1983). By the time Fortune arrived, many people in the area would have encountered Europeans at least by hearsay within the preceding two years, but the contacts of some in the area had been singularly inauspicious.

A minor influx of white people—administrators, missionaries, and prospectors—had swarmed into the newly explored Highlands. Unfortunately, among the earliest was a prospector who cut a swath of rapine and murder from the Dunantina River westward through the Wahgi Valley to Mount Hagen, arming some groups against their enemies and participating in tribal fights. The effects of his career in this already volatile political situation are incalculable; suffice it to say that some of the locals were ready to shoot at white people almost upon sight, possibly honoring the local law of revenge by taking one of the white man's clan for one of their own dead. A series of killings of whites and subsequent punitive raids had ensued, souring relations and leading to the closing of the Highlands by Order in Council while the administration attempted to gain control.

Having argued his way through the red tape, Fortune, like the Leahy brothers and other members of their party, was approached with circumspection and was taken by some local people for a ghost. Kamano ghosts were believed to impede their avenging were they not exorcised. Since Fortune was residing at a police post, one purpose of which was precisely impediment of these customs, the misconception may have been hard to dispel. These factors may explain why on more than one occasion Fortune found himself at the point of dispatch, with a brace of arrows at full drawn strings pricking his back.

Luckily, the first time this occurred he stood his ground and faced down his aggressors, which proved to be the laudable local solution to such a situation, and for some ill-understood reason the war leader chose to let him go. However, Fortune had already seen that the simple weapons of the Kamano could transfix an opponent from a distance of about eighty yards, so it is not surprising that he chose, when war broke out, to comply with a magisterial order to return to the coast and buy a rifle. His book draft, scrupulously academic, is devoid of any reference to such personal experience. Only in his later lectures, and even then in somewhat mordant jest, was he able to refer to the events that left him, his brother recalls, with some seventeen facial tics at the time of his return:

> The war leader and his men were away beating off the attackers. They returned, and two young men who were beside me telling me that the souls of the dead had gone to the sky, at a sign from their leader moved behind me and drew their arrows full on their bows. At the same moment I looked up at their war leader, who was ahead of me and against the sun, just then risen, and who had drawn an arrow directed at me full on his bow. This was merely a security precaution which they used against all unlikely persons who wished to talk with them, as I discovered later by seeing them use it amongst themselves. . . . Mark Pitt, who had quelled the attack made by Faganofi on Fukaminofi at the beginning of the month, advised me to go to the coast to buy a rifle. He reasoned that if I remained unarmed and were killed by the natives the government would be expected to mount a retaliatory expedition for me, as it had done for McGrath and also for a German missionary. But there was now no money in the treasury for such an expedition. If I were armed I would be safe, unless I killed a native, in which case the cost of hanging me was within the Treasury's meagre means.[6]

Despite the terror of the moment, Fortune did not take such incidents personally, nor, it seems, were they so intended. On the whole he got on well with the people and found them willing informants. At this early period of contact the Kamano do not appear to have regarded him as a potential source of cargo, nor to have attempted any form of extortion consonant with the fact that his life was indisputably in their rather nervous hands. In fact he recounts, in illustration of their lack of venality, that after the first outbreak of intervillage hostilities during his stay, the patrol officer arrived from Kainantu with a posse of native constables to quell the action. He obliged the aggressors to pay a pig in compensation to the offended village. The aggressors also paid him a pig, which he treated as an invitation to exchange, and he gave them an axe in return. This totally unexpected gesture occasioned the first and only time Fortune ever saw Kamano men break down and weep.

His position vis-à-vis the Kamano was, however, unquestionably compromised by his residence at the police post, which rendered full participant observation impossible. Local people also seem to have had some expectation consonant with his residence at the post that he would protect them. He recounts that one night two men stole up to the post under cover of darkness and asked for accommodation. Apparently no native constable was present, for it fell to Fortune to disarm them. He arranged for them to bed down for the night but told them they must leave in the morning. They had been visiting a neighboring village where they had kin. However, they had stolen away during the night, sensing unease in the village. Unknown to them, or to Fortune, a man's death had occurred there. Natural deaths of men were at the time attributed to enemy sorcery and concealed while a secret retaliatory raid was being mounted. As outsiders, the visitors would have been, on the one hand, the most likely suspects of sorcery responsible for the death and, on the other, likely targets for its avenging. The next day, two men were shot in an early morning raid, only a hundred yards from the police post.

The following thirty-six hours were a war of nerves, as two villages took arms together against a third, the sorcery suspect, and fighting continued all around the police post. The victims of aggression, very much the underdogs, were surrounded, and all cover was burned. They applied at the post for aid. Fortune had to tell them that his orders forbade it. Eventally some allies came up, and they fought their way out, totally routed, in the early hours of the morning. Then "the victors made a demonstration against the post, but we managed to avert bloodshed by bluff and fair words." In fact, the Native Constabulary had no instructions to cover such eventualities either, and it seems that Fortune was using the editorial "we," as the sergeant was apparently not present, having declared the post untenable.

The incident highlighted the fact that Fortune was indubitably professionally hampered by not being party to the deliberations by night in the men's house, where all males over the age of about four years slept. However, in view of the wars that erupted, residence in a village would have compromised him politically vis-à-vis all other villages. He found that he had blundered unwittingly into a hot spot, as it was the village in which he had spent most of his time during his phase of orientation which was divined as the sorcery suspect. This village was nearest the post. Had he been resident in the village, which he described as "an easy mark," it is likely that he would have been at considerably increased personal risk as a preferred *akonage*, vengeance victim. "I knew," he wrote later, "that Kamano warfare was not murder," but held under arrow drop and surrounded by pitched battle in the dead of two consecutive nights, "[I] shared something of the social psychology of the white frontier about it."

There is a well-substantiated rumor that after this incident Fortune took to heart the advice of the patrol officer that it was desirable to appear dangerous, and that he shot a Kamano in the leg. I have been unable exactly to date the incident, but it is said to have been in response to a telegram from Mead advising him that she proposed to file for divorce. The divorce was granted on 26 July 1935, which places the shooting between his return from the coast with a rifle about 3 April, and that date, during the period of the two wars of Komonka.

Certainly shooting in the leg is a subject that recurs in his papers, as a well-established Kamano custom to register displeasure: as a sanction for adultery against either the man or the woman, but more usually the latter; for laziness over gardening; for stinginess in marriage payments; for polluting the food by cooking while ritually impure; or simply because one felt like it. The only record in Fortune's papers which may refer to the affair is his expression in a letter to his second wife, Eileen, when he was en route back to the Highlands in 1951, of some unexplained misgivings about his personal safety: "I asked Chinnery what he thought about it. He said he thinks the people forget old incidents here and there. He may be right." Whatever the facts of the case, it appears that compensation was paid in accordance with Kamano custom, but at the colonial going rate—sixpence.[7]

In sum, the Kamano must have found Fortune an enigma in an anyway incomprehensible situation—he was white, but was not looking for gold; he did not seem, like the missionaries, to care to tell them about his all-powerful Ancestor, but was on the contrary extremely interested in theirs; he was careless in the disposal of the skins of his *kaukau* (Tok Pisin, sweet potato) and ignored their warnings of the danger in this; he was not shocked by their apparel and even exchanged valuables for some, but did not wear it, and kept his own body concealed. Nor did he behave like a *kiap* (T.P., administrative officer). He possessed the weapon of the white man but used it in a context that was more Kamano than European, and he paid compensation accordingly. He did not instruct them not to use their own arms but, judging from his repeated questions, did not seem to understand why this was necessary; to the contrary, on occasion he showed absurd concern when they acted against the authors of their misfortunes—women and children, who might either pollute or betray them, bear arms against them, or bear children to their enemies. Altogether, the Kamano probably made much the same assessment of Fortune as did most of his later associates—that he was manifestly mad, but relatively harmless.

Indeed his activities were innocuous enough, though the native constables voiced their disapproval of his fraternization with the locals. In the month that passed after his arrival and before the outbreak of hostilities, Fortune seems to have occupied himself with linguistic study. There is little documentation about how he handled the humdrum business of housekeeping and laundry—whether, as on his later trip, he had a garden (though apparently no village "sister" to work it) or a *manki* (T.P., local child) to help—other than a passing reference to a cook and native servant at the post, presumably for the native constables.

On the evidence, Fortune's working day in the village began early, shortly after dawn. He describes people emerging from their places of sleep. Men would exit noiselessly from the cult house, *wonafa* (vomiting canes) on their backs and bows and arrows in hand, constantly alert to the possibility of early morning ambush, to leave the palisaded village and attend secretively to their toilet at the stream. Sentries would change at the entrance to the village. Slowly, along with the thin smoke of the fires in individual cook-houses where women were preparing the *kaukau* that would last the family until the communal meal in the late afternoon, would rise the babble of conversation. Fortune would note this phonetically, observing accompanying action and jotting odd words of translation and explanation as he went along.

He apparently followed the daily round in this manner, notebook and pencil at hand, symbols scrawled hastily on each alternate line, tidiness manifestly sacrificed to the need to observe intently in the attempt to assign meaning to the sounds he was transcribing. He appears sometimes to have eaten the early evening meal in the village, for he describes in some detail its preparation, content, and distribution. Fortune would then retire to the post to spend what little natural light was left sorting out his day's texts, striving not merely to translate the words but to tease out their significance in indigenous terms.

It was fortunate that one of the events Fortune observed early in his sojourn was the marriage of a girl from the valley village only a hundred yards or so from the camp, to a youth in a hilltop village half an hour's walk to the north. The ceremony conveyed to Fortune an appreciation of many of the dominant themes of the culture he was studying. More than that, it served as instruction in intervillage etiquette, without which he might not have survived his survey of the thirty-six villages in the environs. He observed the importance of exercising care about the company one kept, since the friend of an enemy was automatically an enemy also, liable for all the consequences that enmity carried. Fortune learned, too, the potential dangers of marginal members of society traveling alone, and of the desirability of escort by people with kin at both one's point of departure and one's point of arrival.

In some respects Fortune's position in the social constellations in which he revolved was akin to that of recent initiates, and he tended to fall into the line of march toward the back with them. They were excellent informants, recently admitted to the mysteries of the cult and immensely mindful, with the fresh recollections of the ordeals they had recently endured in the getting of wisdom, of the comportment appropriate to an adult male of their society. Yet their recollections of childhood were also still vivid, and through them Fortune gained some appreciation not only of how men should behave, but also of how women and children fared in this ultra-patrilineal society.

He observed the phlegmatic good humor of the women, their affectionate pleasure in the little children in their care, and the stoicism with
which they undertook their numerous and onerous tasks. It astonished
him that, consigned to the margins of society after marriage and often
suspected, reviled, and abused, the women nonetheless usually developed
a solidarity and affection for the husbands they had often not chosen and
beside whom they sometimes were called upon to stand even against their
own kin, and that on the whole they complied. A son of the soil himself,
Fortune was interested in their garden produce and took some time and
care to collect specimens to be identified by experts (Dickie and Malcolm
1940). He may have hoped that this shared interest would gain him an
entree into the confidence and worldview of the Kamano women, who
were here, as elsewhere in the Highlands, the principal producers of
staple foods.

If so, his hopes were disappointed, for most of his time was necessarily
spent with the men, who would not readily tolerate strangers near their
womenfolk. If, on the one hand, men reserved and exercised the right
to abuse their own wives verbally, physically, and metaphysically, on the
other hand they were at pains to shield them from perceived external
threat. In this part of the Highlands in 1935 the men even collected the
firewood from the forest margins, held to be too distant and dangerous
for the women to perform this duty. Men were also the builders and
carvers, the warriors, breakers of ground and fence builders, and usually
the cooks of the communal evening meal. Not surprisingly, it is of some
of these activities that Fortune's descriptions are richest.

He regretted the limitations on social contact with women, for he
suspected the existence of a women's cult associated with menstrual and
childbearing seclusion and would have liked to investigate it. However,
his questions about it to the men were invariably met with derision. He
would have been unable to question or observe the women in any systematic manner even if fighting had not broken out and become perforce
his major preoccupation, in the interests of personal survival as much as
those of ethnology.

Warfare held Fortune in horrified fascination, though naturally it
circumscribed his movements and disrupted the orderly process of observation, notation, translation, and interpretation. It was, however, the
occasion of one of only two visits from a patrol officer during the five
months he was in the field. Though he did not wish to be too closely
associated with the administration in the view of the Kamano, the visit
afforded Fortune with a splendid opportunity to witness interaction
between administrators and newly contacted Papuans. The second visit
followed the outbreak of the "first war of Komonka." By the time the
patrol officer arrived on this occasion, Fortune had spent thirty-six hours

concealed in the *pitpit* (T.P., cane grass) with a party of the routed warriors, attempting rather unsuccessfully to take notes in the pitch dark. He spent the next night, he records, drinking gin with the *kiap*. It may well have saved him some embarrassment that at the time he had very little idea about the roots of the trouble. While valuing good relations with the administration, Fortune had very strong feelings about the ethical responsibilities of the ethnographer. In a draft monograph dating from about 1931, a cross-cultural comparison of Dobu and Manus dedicated to Mead and never published, he writes in the foreword:

> It is the somewhat delicate position of the anthropologist that his conclusions regarding native society may differ so radically from the established practice of his hosts and befrienders of Mission and Government in dealing with that society that he knows beforehand that they will be received with a conservatism that may amount to rejection. This would be bad enough in itself if it were all—but it is by no means all. For the anthropologist makes public information of facts which native reticence would else have kept private and unknown to Mission and Administration; especially as in New Guinea the native is well aware that white knowledge is invariably the precursor of white interference.

Fortune distinguished, however, between policy and personnel; he records with sympathy that the patrol officer was sleepless with fatigue and misery the evening of his arrival, knowing that he had to perform the punitive execution of a member of the aggressors' village at dawn. The horror and pity of this spectacle were accentuated by a converted coastal native constable returning from the task of the firing squad intoning the *Te Deum Laudamus* in impeccable Latin. This same individual was subsequently relieved of his duties for taking into protective custody at the post a number of comely young local women—to liberate them, he explained, from the bonds of heathen matrimony.

The sequel to the execution was no less solemnly farcical. The patrol officer summoned all the men of the village that had opened the fighting and harangued them on the civic responsibilities inherent in their recently acquired privileged status as subjects of the king. He instructed them that "their lives were not their own in disposition, but the King's." Having delivered himself of this homily, the *kiap* turned about, went to the village that had been victim of the aggression, and delivered to its men the same speech.[8]

If Fortune was unimpressed by this performance, he nonetheless liked and admired personally the actor, a medical student whose financial resources had failed him during the Depression before he had been able to complete his studies, and whom Fortune saw as a pawn in a process that was largely inevitable and uncontrollable.

Fortune also developed a long-standing regard for the assistant district officer at Mount Hagen, James Taylor, who married a Papuan woman and had an abiding love for people and place. Indeed Fortune himself entertained the fantasy of "going native" and living out his span running a trade store in the Highlands. There are draft letters to Taylor alluding to this notion. Fortune also mentioned the idea in correspondence with R. F. Salisbury, to whom I am indebted for this information (pers. com., 1986).

Mission influence was unfelt in the Kamamentina Valley in 1935, though a Lutheran mission had opened at Kainantu not long before. Fortune was thus eyewitness to unadulterated indigenous rites of marriage and to the numerous rites that took place in the context of fighting. He saw the various funerary rites appropriate to different circumstances—to men killed in battle, to men and women who died naturally, and to a woman who was killed accidentally in fighting by allies of her husband's village. He observed forms of exorcism, or their absence, as appropriate to the mode of death, and noted means of divination, both practical and theoretical, all of which were to become central to his later studies.

Fortune had too little time before "the constable at the post reported our life insecure, and our permission to reside longer was withdrawn" to piece together completely the practical politics behind these religious rites. He was, however, lucky to have gleaned sufficient information on which to resume inquiry upon his return. By that time, 1951–52, missionization had bitten deeply into indigenous practices if not beliefs, and some of his informants were startled and embarrassed to be confronted with a white person who knew some of what they believed to be the closely kept secrets *long guttaim bipo* (T.P., "from the good old days"). Fortune regarded the missionaries as personally admirable but misguided; it is probable that this assessment was mutual, and relations cordial but not close.

There is no surviving written account of Fortune's withdrawal from the Kamano area. It occurred with indecent haste, after less than six months of the twelve he planned, during a prolonged and bitter series of raids and routs. His permission to work was withdrawn partly because the post at Komonka, encircled by warring communities, was indefensible, and partly, he later learned, because James Taylor at Mount Hagen found out that he had only a sleeping bag by way of bedclothes: "his worry about my sleeping bag was that I could not get out of it in a hurry—typical of 1935 sentiment in this particular area." Fortune, then aged thirty-two, carried away with his scanty personal possessions a prodigious quantity of disorderly notes and a considerably strengthened conviction of the basic correctness of his earlier insights into Papuan cultures. But his physical and mental health were considerably weakened. His brother doubts that he ever fully regained either after the ravages wrought by the Sepik and the Highlands experiences.

He left the Kamano also facing a period of decline in physical and mental health, though not as a result of his passage through their lives. His own influence was probably neutral in the cavalcade of utterly incomprehensible white people they encountered in the early period of contact. They may have gained from it only the passive knowledge that there was a category of white man who was interested and willing to participate in most aspects of their lives, different in some way from those who assumed the authority, and who possessed and used the firepower to dictate to them what they should think and how they should live.

Fortune was, after all, himself unwilling to take dictation from anyone else as to what he should think or how he should live. This unpreparedness to bend before the wind posed something of a problem to him in the matter of how—or whether—he should present his findings. His difficulty in drawing a line between academic difference and *ad hominem* attack, which his admirers would label courtesy and his detractors cowardice, resulted in his publishing very little for the rest of his career. He was not, however, inactive, as the volume of unpublished drafts he left illustrates; he was simply unconvinced that the anthropological public would accept what he had to say. Rather than cast himself as Cassandra, fated to speak what he saw as the truth only to be disbelieved in the light of Mead's opposing views of Papuan cultures, he sat stoically silent, certain that ethnographic accuracy would ultimately out and that he need neither betray his professional convictions nor denigrate the work of others who had more taste or talent for academic salesmanship.

But Mead's was not the only specter with which Fortune wrestled. As stated before, Fortune was claimed by the functionalists on the basis of his most substantial published work, *Sorcerers of Dobu* (1932). He never cared to correct this impression during his lifetime, except in a few acid asides, but it was perceptively refuted by one of his most admired students, Peter Lawrence, in Fortune's obituary (Lawrence 1980). Lawrence refers semihumorously to the problems faced by the doctoral students whom Fortune supervised as they faced "trial-by-thesis," in which theoretical orthodoxy was felt to be required—theoretical orthodoxy that Fortune neither possessed nor valued, and from which he no doubt encouraged apostasy, especially in his most promising students.

However, he certainly borrowed the fieldwork method of participant observation that was the hallmark of the functional school, and enriched it with his own capacity, praised by Malinowski in his introduction to *Sorcerers of Dobu*, for perceiving the significance of minutiae—the facility that Geertz (1973) would later characterize as essential to "thick description." He observed, for example, two women pass unharmed between enemy lines in a fight. From this simple fact he was led to inquire into their mission, which in turn led to investigation of their kin connections. The next step was to find out more about the norms of brother-in-law relations in time of war, which invited comparison with other kinship relations in similar circumstances. Eventually, by focusing on one apparently insignificant event he pieced together a complete picture not only of the norms of kinship behavior, but also the possibilities for their abrogation (Fortune 1947a). It was entirely characteristic of Fortune's relentless honesty that when he found on return that an informant had misled him on the facts of one set of relations, he published a correction (Fortune 1960a), even though the mistake did not invalidate the theoretical principles he had distilled from the incident. He would not, in spite of the unlikelihood of contestation of his original findings, allow theory to command the interpretation he put upon the facts.

It was thus, perhaps, his excellence at the method of participant observation which led him into strife with the theoretical stance that became associated with structural-functionalism: that, to paraphrase the psalmist, to everything there is a reason, and a paradigm for every purpose under heaven. In the field it was manifest to Fortune that this was not necessarily so, especially in the Highlands. As indicated in his letter to Benedict, it seemed to him that, so far from forming an integrated, much less a harmonious whole, Kamano society was staggering along on the brink of self-destruction.

On the basis of the complete genealogies he was able to elicit, Fortune's incredulous predictions that, at the termination of a genealogy, fifty percent of the population would be seen to have died violently, proved correct. It also astonished Fortune, the son of a priest turned farmer, that women, the breeding stock of the society, were held in such low regard by the Kamano, whose physical and social survival had a great deal to do with numbers, and who trusted unreservedly only homegrown members of their group. These two factors alone would have been sufficient basis for him to question the reigning paradigm of the day.

This rejection left something of a vacuum in his analysis. He flirted in a marginal note with the observation that the high violent mortality rate kept population proportionate with the productive capacity of the land, which in this part of the Highlands is at the lower end of the gradient. It is tempting to interpret this as prefiguring cultural ecology; perhaps having rejected on the evidence of his own observation the notion that the institutions of a society form a complexly interrelated interdependent whole, he may have looked to some other wider principle according to which social institutions were providentially ordered. In his marginal jottings, Fortune questioned himself, "How did war solve their problem: 1. helped meat supply 2. made medicine unnecessary for ⅓ of them." But there is no evidence that he pursued any such line of thought; he concluded "scarcity a pipe dream." Though he was intensely interested in religious and symbolic systems, he was not disposed to indulge in their mystification as some form of ecological providence, in his own or any other culture. Thus, although he was aware of the effect of war in maintaining congruence between population and resources, he was unprepared to assert that it was causal in any overt or covert sense. He indeed declared himself contra Wedgwood (1930) on the subject of the social utility of war: "It is doubtful whether reprisals and feuding have any use in the advancement of the arts and sciences in general, or even in the art of political organisation in particular" (Fortune 1947a:255).

Langham (1981) places Fortune in the intellectual line of descent from W. H. R. Rivers and the Cambridge school of kinship studies. Fortune himself declared that he would most have liked to study under Rivers, and among the few material possessions in which he took pleasure was the Rivers Medal he was awarded. He retained a lively theoretical interest in kinship, as evidenced by his paper on the subject (Fortune 1933) and by subsequent correspondence with David Maybury-Lewis, Rodney Needham, and Claude Lévi-Strauss on apparently anomalous systems. But though he was fascinated by the mathematical beauty and symmetry of kinship systems on the level of theory, he was never in the slightest doubt that they do not always work on the ground.[9] His work anticipated the questions later raised by Barnes (1962) as to the applicability of African models. Fortune saw at first hand the fighting that was one of the major mechanisms for redistributing and reclassifying individuals, and even whole descent groups. Having witnessed three or four routs take place around him, it was no surprise to him either that there should be such strong expressions of the agnatic idiom or, paradoxically, that they should not be reflected in social realities. Fortune undoubtedly continued to believe and expect that kinship would be a very important organizing principle among the Kamano, but as with his stance on structural-functionalism, he found the theory inadequate to accommodate the facts and withdrew allegiance to it.

Of Dobu he wrote: "It has become one of the best known facts in anthropology that the use of terms in reckoning relationship normally mirrors social custom. This fact is very aptly demonstrated in Dobu" (1932:36). But in subsequent theoretical discussion he would "not wish to urge that this is true for other parts of the world, but only that such a degree of integrated development has occurred in Dobu" (1932:40). Fortune was, before "models" became a buzzword, quite clear about their utility and limitations: "We might pursue theories in the subject of sociology, but we have a business of recording plain observations of native customs to perform, and theory may wait."

To some extent Fortune's analysis resembles neo-Marxist technique, not in conscious intention nor in terminology, but in the sorts of questions he set himself to answer. As a child of structural-functionalism he was concerned to describe an exorcism or a divination and to place it correctly in the social scheme, but what really interested him was not how an action was done but why it was done: given that divination manifestly was not directed by natural forces, what motives dictated its findings? How were supernatural sanctions underpinned by economic considerations? Whose interests were served by the subjugation of women? What prompted parents to perpetuate to their children stories about ghosts which they themselves knew to be untrue?

Fortune would no more have subscribed to a doctrine of determinism in the last instance by the mode of production than he would accept other determinisms—by kinship, by structure and function, by ecology, or by temperament or sex. His drafts and notes suggest that he believed in very few universal immutable social laws. As a consequence he was unable to espouse any universal principle of analysis or any grand theory.

Fortune's experience in and prior to the Highlands did, however, leave him with a preoccupation that was the unifying theme of his work for the rest of his life—that of human motivation. His initial impetus may have been his personal hurt at Mead's accusation that he was the sort of person who causes wars:

> There should be a general explanation of what the matter has been to make wars here or there. However, I am not sure yet what it is—are you? I was hurt by your saying it was persons of my temperament—the Arapesh & Gregory and your "maternal" in contrast. (Fortune to Mead, 1949, quoted in Howard 1984:269)

In the Eastern Highlands, not surprisingly, his concern with motivation found expression in the need to find some satisfactory explanation for the bitter and apparently pointless fighting he witnessed. This quest assumed for Fortune something of the dimension of a personal search for an explanation of evil. His mental meanderings led him past consideration of Lucien Lévy-Bruhl's theories of prelogical thought, but only to find that the Kamano were a negative illustration. He dismissed equally explanations in terms of culture and personality: "A member of a culture has at least 2 or 3 'personalities'—to take a person in his hell-raising personality & say he has psychologised his culture into a hell of a culture misses the universality underlined by the social processes that appear as the result of analytical abstraction of the anthropological method."

Nor did he find the study of child-rearing patterns a useful analytical tool. For Fortune, explanations of a society in terms of socialization practices or culture and personality simply begged the implied question as to why certain patterns of behavior or child-rearing practices evolve. "Chicken and egg," he wrote in the margin, as he scored through a draft paragraph musing on the possibilities of Oedipal influences upon the sexual antagonism he observed among the Kamano.

If Fortune was apparently able easily to dismiss whole bodies of theory as either self-evident or obviously flawed, he dwelled obsessively on other theoretical concerns that would appear of little interest to many. A case in point was Christian Keysser's theory of motivation for war among the Kai (Neuhauss 1911). Keysser suggested that the Kai were naturally peace-loving—he gave as a singularly unfortunate comparison the citizenry of metropolitan Germany—and would not have exacted vengeance for their dead had they not feared retribution by the ghost of the departed. Frazer in turn read this account and used it to support a theory about the role of the belief in immortality in motivating primitive peoples to fight (1913).

Fortune was certain from his researches among the Kamano that Keysser had grasped the wrong end of the stick, and he was at great pains in a short and obscure article (Fortune 1954), and in many lectures, to demonstrate that Keysser could not actually have witnessed the alleged events upon which his explanation stood. Why was he so determined to illustrate the error of a long-gone obscure missionary whose work was available only in German, and of an armchair ethnologist, much of whose work had long since been consigned to the category of the fascinating and well-told "Just So" story? Fortune's aversion to missionary activity may have been a factor. Perhaps more importantly, he used the case as a parable that exemplified the potential for magnification of error in work undertaken with the kind of theoretical bias and flawed scholarship that he felt ruined his collaborative Sepik research. Fortune felt strongly enough on the point to have styled Frazer's derivative theory "a most outrageous fake." This illustrates the fact that Fortune saw ethnology in quite strongly moral terms; this attitude immunized him from untested acceptance of any flavor-of-the-month hypothesis, and rendered his theoretical position, as Lawrence was to comment, "almost impossible to pin down" (1980:3).

It was fitting that Fortune, with his capacity to accept the peoples he was studying as intellectually responsible individuals, should have derived from a Highlands woman, the wife of James Taylor, the most illuminating comment on the subject of the relationship among sorcery, ghost fear, and the motivation to fight. People must be aware, argued Fortune, that the divination of guilt for deaths was politically motivated. How then did they sustain their belief in sorcery, to the point of being prepared to kill and to die for it? Mrs. Taylor simply asked him how Europeans form their ideas of causality. Fortune conceded that most people took the information on hearsay. "Well," she replied, "so do we. That is why we fight to avenge ghost or sorcery deaths."

The comment crystallized Fortune's personal view of what the task of anthropology should be. This might be summed up simply in all its grandiose idealism as the development of understanding of other peoples in terms of indigenous meanings. Doodling in the margin of an article about proposed linguistic translating machines, Fortune observed, "that's what we are from one point of view." For Fortune, this task of cultural translation was too vast to be accomplished within the confines of any single analytical technique or theory. Aware of the cultural and intellectual conditioning he himself carried with him, he always took into account an informant's likely biases and limitations. It was typical of Fortune that if he was reporting hearsay rather than eyewitness observation he invariably declared it, and his book draft confines itself largely to the latter. He does not attempt analysis of the psychology or the symbolism inherent in the social facts he observed. It was not that he was unaware of or uninterested in this dimension—quite to the contrary—but he seems to have regarded such analysis almost as a private indulgence. Since it was necessarily speculative and culture-bound, it was unproductive to his project of presenting an account in what would later be labeled "emic" terms.

The research underpinning the book draft Fortune wrote in 1936 was, however, incomplete. He hoped to return when the Highlands were under control to further his inquiries, but it was to be fifteen years before the opportunity presented itself. During that time, Fortune took a number of positions for short durations, hoping to be available for return when it became possible. At the expiry of his grant, he took a position at Lingnan University, sailing in January, 1937, to be joined in July by his bride, Eileen. He undertook some research during the vacation among the Yao and Miao. Invasion, evacuation, and war ensued. There followed brief periods working in Toledo, Ohio, and at the University of Toronto, service with the Canadian Auxiliary Force, and a short period as government anthropologist in the Shan states. Shortage of shipping and of funds, especially of overseas funds, together with the turbulence of the times, contrived to keep Fortune physically separated from his draft and his papers until 1948, when he, his field notes of thirteen years, his draft of twelve years, and his wife of eleven years of marriage were finally reunited in Cambridge.

Research funds in postwar, rationed Britain were scarce. Fortune turned down an offer from the Rhodes-Livingstone Institute to work in

South Africa and took on a heavy lecturing load at Cambridge until a grant from the Leverhulme Research Institute made possible his return to Kamano country. It was his aim, he told friends and colleagues variously, to study social change, work on a dictionary, pay compensation to the man he had shot in 1935, and find out why the war leader who had held him under arrow drop in 1935 had let him go unharmed. In addition to his unanswered questions from 1935, he no doubt hoped to see the ceremonies that had not occurred during his earlier visit. He set out from Rotterdam via Suez to Melbourne in July, 1951. As no shipping to New Guinea was available for some weeks, he finished his preparatory purchasing and, biting rather deeply into his funds, bought an air ticket to Port Moresby.

Transport from the coast was, as before, by air to Kainantu; this time Fortune was somewhat more lavishly equipped, and in addition to his scanty essential personal possessions—only two pairs of trousers, one of which was so decrepit as to require cutting down to shorts after three or four months—he carried a camera bought on the way at Port Said, film, saucepans, some food, salt—forty pounds, half the total weight of his consignment—matches, writing paper and pens, a medicine chest—this time including penicillin and sulpha drugs as well as antimalarial medication—a garden fork, and seeds for himself as well as for gifts. On this trip Fortune carried no firearm, though he was not entirely confident of his personal safety. He advised his wife against purchase of a piece of land adjacent to their Cambridge cottage in case she should find herself widowed and need the money:

> I think the job's secure enough, but one never knows—I'm going back into what was murderous country fifteen years ago. . . . It should be secure as a house, but we should probably be careful of money anyway as one never knows for certain.

Fortune was still unable to afford to transport a bed, mattress, pillow, table or chair, or kerosene lamp. As before, he brought a few shells. Surprised to find that money had not displaced them, he wrote back to England to attempt to obtain some more for his friend James Taylor, still at Mount Hagen.

As in 1935, access to his fieldwork site was a day's walk, but now instead of lying concealed in the valleys, safe from enemy surveillance, the tracks ran in plain view along the ridges. Progress was no longer signaled by yodeling warning of a stranger's approach from one village to another. The villages themselves had moved—though this was not new—but instead of commanding strategic crests as in 1935, they had relocated in the valleys, closer to the rivers and more fertile flats. The palisades, sentries, and the *djoraka noni*, the cult houses that had formerly commanded the central plaza, where men now said they had slept formerly as a matter of military contingency, had vanished. Gone too were the trophy posts festooned with arrows recovered from enemy corpses.

The gardens beside which he walked had changed a little—they were larger and better fenced—and there were some steel tools to be seen. Some introduced vegetables were cultivated, but the predominant crops were still sweet potatoes and local greens such as spinach, *pitpit* (T.P., an edible garden plant), and the goa bean, which was cultivated to produce either a root or pod crop. Pigs were more securely housed, separately from living quarters.

The well-insulated little round houses whose construction Fortune describes in his 1936 draft had largely given way to the imported coastal rectangular style with flimsier woven panels for walls, though corrugated iron for roofing was "still well beyond the natives' means." It was in one such, in the village at Finintegu, that he resided during his return trip. This impressed upon Fortune one aspect of the change he had come to study; he wrote home, "I have not much room to myself to think—a crowd of natives around—they gape still and have not enough to do . . . but I do want to perfect the lingo, so I put up with it." And indeed his linguistic notes reflect this cavalcade: "Will the white man go to the river now, or will he sleep?" "Will he not fall in the hole while walking along writing?" "Is that the way the white man chews tobacco?"

As time progressed it became obvious that the problem was less one of unbridled Kamano curiosity than of their lack of occupation, for the irritant continued long after Fortune's novelty value wore off. The pre-contact manner of reckoning time by seasons or by the intervals between fights or deaths was less apparent; locals now "counted days by sleeps, as in Cambridge," he wrote. This was not Fortune's only source of irritation. At age forty-eight, his formerly excellent physique was letting him down, and he suffered constant niggling back pain from the absence of chair or bed. Annoyed, he finally gave in and had a chair flown in from Lae. This simply served to increase the size and concentration of the audience. A private and modest person, he found this invasion of his personal space hard to bear. He felt obliged, he complained, to wear underpants under his pajamas, and the best part of his day was his swim in the river when, apparently, mission-instilled prudery protected his privacy from Kamano surveillance for as long as he could bear the arctic water temperatures.

Most villages now built and maintained Christian churches and schools. Many Kamano were baptized, which was not, Fortune found, synonymous with conversion. The niceties of greeting had undergone missionization, though; the appropriate courtesy was now "thy breaches-of-taboo greeting." Kamano dress and grooming had also altered: the bark-cloth men's kilts were giving way to the cotton *laplap* (T.P., cloth used as a wraparound garment), which were obligatory for baptism, and bark-cloth capes were now rarely found. The flamboyant plaited hairstyle of initiates was less in evidence, and the *wonafa*, which men used to carry openly and store in their sleeping houses, had vanished altogether. A few old men confessed that they still possessed and occasionally secretly used one.

The transformation in the appearance of the women was even more dramatic. In 1935 they had worn grass skirts, and their heads and shoulders were draped with the ubiquitous *bilum* (T.P., net bag) of their own manufacture, which served as a garment as well as a receptacle for produce and babies. Frequently women's garments had been disheveled, and perhaps the joint of a finger had been recently severed and their heads shaved and covered with ash or clay in token of mourning. These extreme manifestations of grief were no more to be seen, and the long cotton dress, also obligatory for baptism, was becoming commoner, despite the fact that it inhibited performance of garden and domestic work and the suckling of babies. Craft work, which in 1935 had focused largely on cult and military artifacts, had also declined, excepting the multifunctional *bilum*.

While neither Fortune nor his informants were disposed to deny the benefits of peace—which was what the Kamano avowed they fought for in precontact times—Fortune was, on the whole, depressed by the changed scene. It was the rainy season, of which the only blessing was that the vegetable seeds he planted throve modestly. He was initially skeptical as to whether he would be able to find the answers to the questions left unanswered in 1935. Having reentered the area full of hope and optimism, he was dismayed to find himself delighted to escape from it on patrol with the local patrol officer, to sleep in a real bed, to have a lamp by which to read, and, above all, to have the hubbub of village life recede to a distance that left him some personal space in which to operate.

As he settled down, Fortune was relieved to find that despite the dramatic apparent change in Kamano society he was still able, with patient and tactful selection of informants, to elicit answers to some of his unsolved puzzles. On the evidence of his interview notes, he spent much of his time in 1935 with adolescents. On return, he sought out the older and more mature Kamano. In some instances these were, of course, the same people whom he had earlier come to regard as friends and repositories of cultural knowledge.

His research design for this return trip was, as the reasons he gave for going suggest, contingent on his earlier work—he wished to fill gaps in his earlier understanding and to study change. It is not surprising that the list of questions he prepared for interviews updates the map rather than changes the course he charted in 1935. Most questions concern religion and war, with motivation always an underlying unifying thread. Even questions relating to mundane matters, such as the treatment of wounds, require discussion of magical beliefs and the implied question as to what in the Kamano view made things happen. It seems that it was still difficult to obtain information from women, for even those questions about women are cast in such a way that it is evident that they were posed to men: What do the women do with the placenta after a birth? Do the older women break the hymen of a girl at puberty? Why do the older women still teach the children that ghosts will eat their vital organs?

Thus one cannot state on the documentary evidence that Fortune's work changed direction on return. Kamano society, however, had. Fortune was one of the few people to undergo the archetypal Rip Van Winkle experience of living in, then leaving, a stone age society, only to return and find it flung future-shocked into the 1950s in the interval of fifteen years. It was a journey that ethnology had made in much the same space of time; after the Second World War there was no corner of the world that was not, at least in some indirect way, drawn into the global nexus of metropolitan political and economic systems. The much-criticized tendency of anthropologists of structural-functional persuasion to study small-scale societies as if they were isolates was now clearly untenable.

For Fortune, to see the connectedness of small, remote social configurations with larger ones had never posed a problem. When he first arrived in Kainantu in 1935, comparing and contextualizing, he scribbled notes placing Kamano within a nexus of cultural traits shared by peoples from Malays to Australian Aboriginals. However, he evidently felt no temptation to elaborate on the observation or to construct any theory of regional heliocentrism. As he settled in, he depicted the landscape, then set aside the broad brush to work on the miniature at which he excelled. In his use of language and choice of subjects, however, the wider frame is always in evidence: he wrote of Kamano "sovereign states" and of the operation of "international law," of the Kamano version of the Geneva Convention, and of "officers of the commune." Nor is this in any way to be interpreted as condescension or bathos. Fortune's outlook across the anthropological spectrum could be described as formalist; he debated with himself in his notes, "how can a difference in kind, if it exists, be distinguished from a difference in complexity?" The question was always on his mind; if he used the language of concepts and institutions in his own society it was because "savage" man and society were to him no less rational or comprehensible than his own.

Fortune's 1935 field trip had commenced in February and been interrupted in August. His return, from August, 1951, to March, 1952, completed an annual cycle of study, but left him in a dilemma as to what to do with the material he had gathered. Clearly, in the light of the changes that had occurred, he felt that what he had written in 1936 was no longer relevant. That work was not complete, and now the possibility of completing the book he would have written in 1936 was gone. After the second field trip he began to update the draft, but apparently abandoned the scheme. Changing tack and writing about social change as a topic seems to have held little interest for him, perhaps because of his profound disrespect for hidebound theory and his skepticism as to whether any universal truths might be distilled from the particular. It was easy but boring to catalogue the observable physical changes, yet as of then too early for an objective assessment of profounder cultural change. By this time, too, Fortune had acquired such a contempt for what he saw as the power games and politics of academia that he may simply have declined to contaminate himself by association with it. His attitude was exemplified in a draft article commenced with the "aim . . . to have it published in the *American Anthropologist*, even if, in some respect, this may, perhaps, be like an aim of writing the truth and having it buried in a Sunday newspaper of glottochronology, dogma, opinion, attitude and self righteousness." And elsewhere he observed, "The truth in anthropology does not travel first class." The rest was almost total silence.[10]

Moreover, little that was coming out of the post–Second World War wave of anthropological investigation in the New Guinea Highlands was novel to Fortune. His unpublished work had already touched many of the bases of anthropological interest that sprang from the pens of the numerous other pioneers who were part of that wave, some of whom were his students and perhaps to him his surrogate fieldworkers.

He had already observed in his unpublished papers the misfit between patrilineal ideology and the actual composition of local groups, and perhaps after fieldwork among the Biwat (Mundugumor), on whose kinship organization he wrote a long but unpublished draft, he may have expected this to be so. But so far from seeing this as problematic, he saw the strength of the articulation of the patrilineal idiom as actually arising from the weakness of its realization, as in his own society a convert might be the most vigorous proponent of an ideology. In his view, endemic war was catalytic. His observation and documentation of the effects of fighting on clan and place names, inheritance, damages claims, fictional kinship, rout, and refuge, indicated to him that patrilineality carried a different connotation, and that what one should investigate was not the genealogical connectedness of group members but the whole range of criteria for recruitment and residence.

Similarly, the sexual antagonism, which was often seen as being such a riddle in a people-poor area, as the Eastern Highlands was, seemed logical to Fortune. He early identified male fears as being at its root, and war again as being a touchstone. First, there was constant fear of unexpected violent death, which might in emic terms be either physically or

supernaturally caused. Since belief systems left little alternative explanation of differential life expectancy and luck, and supernatural aggression was believed to require the cooperation of an insider to secure
exuviae, in-married women were the logical suspects. Second, girls appeared to grow spontaneously to maturity, leaving their male age-mates
small and undeveloped, thus fueling male fear that women were possessed of some supernaturally endowed vital force. Clearly, men would
feel compelled to seek means to compensate and to "grow" adult men out
of adolescent boys. The sanctions against dwarfs, and against initiators
whose efforts failed to procure the desired growth despite copious and
spectacular shedding of "maternal" blood, again seemed logical to Fortune. Third, women were in social fact the vital providers of both people
and produce, and those same women were outsiders. If pregnancy failed
to occur, miscarriage ensued, or crops failed, there lurked the sneaking
fear that women were in some mysterious way manipulating fertility, as
they were believed to have done in mythical times. Worse yet, they were
suspected of using their powers to the detriment of their husbands'
groups, possibly to benefit their own kin groups, with whom their loyalties
were assumed still to reside. There could be little more logical than that
men would elaborate fantasies of superiority, and invest them with the
supernatural sanction and physical expression that their greater strength
made possible.

But Fortune was also aware that women had secrets, too: "there is a
little spiritualistic seance religion run by women." He recorded the angry
outburst against the uselessness of women by a man who implied that
women turned the teaching about female pollution against men, and that
women manipulated male fears to escape the drudgery of women's lot of
gardening and cooking to spend time off in seclusion on the pretext of
being, as Kamano men conceptualized it, in bad odor. This practice left
the menfolk furious but impotent to do anything against it. Fortune
regarded the severe postpartum and menstrual taboos, and the physical
and supernatural sanction invoked for adultery, as proceeding quite
logically from these male fears. He believed that it was not in the least
coincidental that pollution beliefs alienated the small boy from his
mother, an outsider, but consolidated his ties with his sister, a lineage
mate. Again, in Fortune's view, the contradiction contained the seeds of
its own creation as well as those of its destruction.

Fortune's work identifies in Kamano culture a series of contradictions:
the concept, familiar from his own, of fighting to end war; of honoring
the village officials who prompted it, but who were thence agents of social
undoing; of desiring natural increase but abusing the women through
whom it must be brought about; of elevating the social status of the
daughter, who would bear children to rivals, but denigrating the wife,

who would bear lineage members; of procuring vomit and bleeding to secure growth; of placing in competition for the mother's attentions the father with the son who would be his heir and ally. All of these internal tensions Fortune saw as being expressed in external warfare. He regarded fighting as the venting abroad of those practices which would be intolerably disintegrative at home.

It is a very great pity that Fortune did not proceed with publishing his book. But on the evidence of his corrections and annotations to the draft, he was severely self-critical and would not go to press with less than what he perceived as the whole truth. For he did conceive the task of anthropology in just such moral terms, and regarded error, omission, or misinterpretation—his own or anyone else's—as nothing less than moral turpitude. His own reservations about presenting work that he regarded as incomplete may well have been shared by publishers in the era of postwar strictures. Gaps in the research remained, though, even after the second field trip: Fortune was never to see an initiation, for example, and was unable to pursue his interest in women's traditional religion. But even as it stands, his work would have outlined some of the background ethnographic history against which later ethnographers could more readily have set their research in context. It should even yet provide a valuable historical source.

The draft contains a standard descriptive introductory chapter, a full and perceptive account of social organization, a chapter on warfare (which indeed is an inseparable theme throughout), and a chapter on rituals of the life cycle. It may well have been the want of eyewitness to some of these which caused Fortune to stop in his tracks, write a short and impatient chapter on material culture—barely more than captions to photographs of the artifacts he collected in 1935 (a gesture to his association with Franz Boas at Columbia, perhaps)—and then to lay the work aside.

Fortune continued to work on the Kamano, though, and his later lectures and articles, published (1947a, 1947b, 1954, 1960a, 1960b) and unpublished, contain bodies of detailed information on the language, lore and law, history, and, above all, motivation. In the light of subsequent accounts, Fortune's confidence in his interpretation, expressed in his letter to Benedict after arriving in the field, was justified: "I'm pretty sure it's all right—even in general perspective."

In 1941, writing to her mother from Toledo, Ohio, where Fortune was working hard on research and writing before going to teach at the University of Toronto, his wife wrote:

> I feel about Reo that it is a bit like being married to a National Museum; you can't assert your private thoughts too much, he being rather something

in the way of a people's asset. Not that I think his last stuff will be very widely acclaimed for a while; it is too daring and too erudite for that. But I imagine it will be in the long run.

Perhaps more than fifty years after his first Highlands research the run has been long enough.

NOTES

1. The Fortune Archive, comprising both Reo and Eileen Fortune's personal papers, was donated in 1980 after his death to the Alexander Turnbull Library, National Library of New Zealand, Wellington. My thanks are due to the Librarian, Mr. J. Traue, and to the Manuscripts Librarian, Ms. D. Meads, and her staff for facilitating special access to the archive, which is not yet arranged or catalogued, and hence not normally available for research. As it is therefore not possible to give library references, I shall simply use quotation marks or indentation, without reiterating where this is the case that the material is drawn from Reo Fortune's unpublished papers.

2. Mead refers to the two latter as Mundugumor, possibly a corruption of the name of the nearby village Mundukoma, and Tchambuli, respectively.

3. It is, however, notable that his writing about the Kamano is to a degree a one-sided polemic with Mead, Benedict, Malinowski, and a number of others.

4. The Leica has come to rest among the ethnographic artifacts at Auckland University, New Zealand. Some photographs from the subsequent trip, 1951–52, but of a latter-day, inferior machine, are to be found in the Fortune Archive in the Alexander Turnbull Library in Wellington.

5. The missive was faithfully preserved, as Fortune requested, "for its freshness of aspect." It was unearthed from the American Museum of Natural History in New York by Rhoda Metraux and was sent along with some Sepik fieldnotes to join the rest of the archive in New Zealand.

6. The reference to official intolerance of Europeans committing violence against the local people was not altogether frivolous; Ludwig Schmidt, the offending prospector referred to above, had in 1934 been arrested and was subsequently hanged for crimes against Papuans.

7. I am indebted for some of this information to personal communications from Professor Anthony Forge and the late Professor Peter Lawrence.

8. The fighting did not cease in indigenous terms, but predictably went underground in the form of sorcery accusation and countersorcery, felt to be an inferior weapon. Fighting resumed and the scores were leveled in about 1942 during the period when administration was withdrawn while Australians were demonstrating their devotion to the precept that their lives were not their own but the King's in disposition.

9. In retirement, Fortune's fascination with mathematics was expressed in his taking an advanced university course in Euclidean mathematics, and in the legacy of scores of sheets of calculations, sometimes on the back of or even over his ethnographic notes.

10. In his later professional years (he retired in 1971), Fortune became an increasingly cantankerous and difficult colleague, and his lone crusade against what he saw as corruption in academia bordered on paranoia. Numbers of his friends would have agreed, however, that he was at least partially justified. In retirement he was a benign, whimsical character, and a devoted nurse to his terminally ill wife, who predeceased him by two years.

THREE

Into the Unknown!

Ronald M. Berndt

Our first encounter with Papua New Guineans began late in 1951 and continued through two intensive periods of field research, terminating in the first quarter of 1953. In one sense it was like a serious diversion that removed us temporarily from another field in which we were heavily committed. Since our marriage in 1941, Catherine and I had been carrying out anthropological research in various parts of Aboriginal Australia, with hardly a break away from the field. We had become emotionally involved with the people and the problems that faced them in the light of prevailing policies and practices regarding Aborigines. Work in that direction was often rather frustrating. Over and above such issues, we were absorbed in the intricacies of traditional Aboriginal cultures, some of which in those days remained in many respects relatively intact. Of course the writing was on the wall for them, as it had been for others, and alien influences were harbingers of massive changes.

The reasons for our digression to a new field were mixed. Funds supporting anthropological research were not easy to obtain. Catherine applied to the International Federation of University Women and was fortunate in being awarded an Ohio State Fellowship. However, this stipulated that research should be carried out in a country other than her own. Having been born and brought up in New Zealand, she hoped that the grant could perhaps be transferred to Aboriginal Australia without doing violence to its terms of offer. As she had been resident in Australia for just on ten years and was married to an Australian, that view was not accepted. On the advice of Professor Elkin and others, we decided on New Guinea; Dr. Capell had been urging us to go there and perhaps to study what was happening in areas where Christian missionary zeal was bringing about the destruction of traditional ceremonial materials. I was able to obtain a matching grant from the Research Committee of the University of Sydney. More generally, our rationalization for being diverted in this way rested on what we considered to be an important academic principle: that a professional anthropologist should have field experience in a region other than his or her chosen area of specialization—if for no other reason than, one hoped, to bring a more objective approach to it.

In passing I should mention that it was this proposed move that later triggered a further decision—to go to the London School of Economics rather than to the newly established Department of Anthropology at the Australian National University. Although Professor Nadel had offered us each a fellowship if we would join him at the ANU, what we regarded as the abrasive and arrogant manner of Nadel at the August, 1952, meeting of the Australian and New Zealand Association for the Advancement of Science gave force to that decision. (I had presented a summary of my paper "A Cargo Movement . . ." [R. Berndt 1952–53].) Sydney University at that time did not offer a Ph.D. in anthropology, which several overseas visitors (including Margaret Mead) assured us was a professional necessity.

So far I have been speaking mostly in terms of "we," but as Catherine is a contributor to this volume, I should conceptually separate her from my own experiences and attitudes. To do this is a difficult task. While our foci of concentration differ, they inevitably overlap. Perhaps a major contrast between us is that she normally works almost entirely with women and I work entirely with men. This division of labor has been a long-standing one, throughout all our Aboriginal research. In the Eastern Highlands in which we were to work, it was even more apparent: it would not have been possible for me to cross the male-female "barriers" without drastic disruption to my research. Those points aside, we have both had more or less the same kind of anthropological training and shared common experiences. For instance, neither of us has been in the field without the other; we have always been a husband-wife team. Thus, in regard to our respective individual differences of approach, they are not necessarily apparent to me. One thing is clear. There are tremendous advantages in working together as such a team, and these outweigh any contrasting variations there may be on the basis of gender. In simple terms, then, we were in a position, as we have been in Aboriginal Australia, to concentrate on exploring male-female relations in trying to achieve an overall view of the society—and not to see women solely through the eyes of men, or vice versa. We attach considerable importance to that perspective.

It was, therefore, with a feeling of adventure that we began to prepare for our Highlands research, although we had not yet decided which part of that region would be most appropriate. Reading *The Land That Time*

Forgot (Leahy and Crain 1937), *Through Wildest Papua* (Hides 1935), and *Vier Jahre unter Kannibalen* (Detzner 1920) had paved the way for me by creating romanticized images that served as a backdrop to more serious reading. Phyllis Kaberry's Abelam articles in *Oceania* (1941–42), G. F. Vicedom and H. Tischner's *Die Mbowamb* (1943–48), and H. Aufenanger and G. Höltker's *Die Gende* (1940) provided a wealth of general and specific information. Camilla Wedgwood had kindly given Catherine a bibliography of the Highlands. It was, however, A. Capell, following his linguistic research in the Highlands (see Capell 1948–49), who encouraged us to choose the Eastern Highlands as being among the areas least known anthropologically. Dr. Capell wrote to the Reverend A. C. Frerichs, who was in charge of the Lutheran mission at Lae; he, in turn, contacted Mr. and Mrs. Tews, then in charge at Raipinka mission station, near Kainantu, who welcomed our working in that area. We had already been in contact with E. W. P. Chinnery (whom we knew quite well from our research in the Northern Territory of Australia) and K. E. ("Mick") Read. Mick Read was particularly helpful in giving us advice on fieldwork conditions in that region. In fact, it was his published papers in *Oceania* and *South Pacific* (see bibliography) that stimulated me more than any other writing on the Highlands at that time. These were the first systematic research results available; and although Goroka and the Gahuku-Gama were socioculturally different from the environment and people of what became "our" area, there were many relevant linkages.

The Highlands were being penetrated by prospectors and missionaries in the 1930s, but from early in 1935 entry was restricted up to the time of the Japanese invasion that was felt more in the extreme eastern sector than in other inland parts. Gradually, administration posts were established, and after the war the official intention was to bring all of the Highlands under Australian government control. This was, however, a piecemeal affair. The whole region was heavily populated, with a multitude of small villages and hamlets, only a few of which had been visited by sporadic patrols that rarely spent more than an hour or so, sometimes a night or perhaps two, in any one place outside the main centers. Kainantu district was gradually being brought under control from 1930 to 1931, but that process was delayed by the war, and it was not until 1947 that the first patrol (by R. I. Skinner) visited Kogu district, among others. At that time interdistrict fighting was the norm. Through interpreters, the local people were told to cease fighting and to break down the palisades or fortifications that surrounded each village or hamlet, but changes in that direction did not take place immediately. Nor did destruction of the palisades necessarily herald the cessation of interdistrict conflict; in many respects it was exacerbated. To ensure that a modicum of order was maintained, a "native police" post was first established at

Kemiyu in 1949 and then at Moiife (both places being fairly close to Kogu). By the time we reached our first fieldwork base in Kogu, the whole area as far south as Moke was deemed to have been brought under control. All the country beyond, to the southeast, south, and southwest, was still "uncontrolled." The formally "controlled" area, except in the immediate vicinity of Kainantu and Raipinka, was pervaded by an atmosphere of uneasy "peace." Many villages had not then been visited by Europeans. That, roughly, was the situation that faced us when we arrived at Kainantu. But that was yet to come.

Our permit to enter the Territory of New Guinea had come without difficulty. On the late afternoon before we were due to leave Sydney by Qantas, Catherine sprained her ankle severely in alighting from a bus in town on our way home from the University. Although in considerable pain, she was able to have it tightly bandaged at a nearby chemist. Inconvenient as this was, she could manage to walk for short distances, and so we left for Port Moresby as scheduled.

Professor Raymond Firth and a couple of his colleagues from the Australian National University were staying at the same hotel as ourselves, and that gave us an opportunity to discuss with him our proposed fieldwork. On the following day we visited the administrator, but spent most of the time at the Office of District Services going through copies of patrol reports relevant to the Kainantu district. Next morning we were on our way to Lae. Paul Hasluck (whom we knew), then minister for territories, was on board making an official visit, and he was met in appropriate style at Lae airport. Frerichs, who had come down to see his wife off by plane, took us back to the Lutheran mission settlement. We spent six busy days preparing our stores and attending to other matters, in between visiting various places in and around Lae and discussing our plans with government officials. Instead of going directly to Kainantu we went on to Goroka to see the district officer. However, he was ill, so we caught the returning plane to Kainantu and were in time to have lunch with the local district officer. We borrowed some of his patrol reports, mustered up some carriers, and, with Catherine riding a horse (one of the very few in the area) and myself walking, we set off in a long line with some of our boxes to Raipinka. Heavy rain on the way had dampened everything, including ourselves. On arrival at the mission station we spent the rest of the day and all of the next drying out our stores and clothing.

We stayed for twelve days at Raipinka. We saw this as providing us with an opportunity for orientation, and as a practical introduction to our proposed area of research. There is no need to detail our activities in this respect, except to say that by the fourth day we were each recording interlinear texts in Kamano. Although most of the material I wrote down at that time concerned myths and stories, in general they gave me an excellent introduction that presaged well what was to be expected farther south. Linguistically and socioculturally, the Kamano belonged to one sector of the overall interactory sphere that included three other basic sectors on which we were eventually to concentrate. During this preparatory period Reo Fortune, who was revisiting Finintegu, came over to see us. Messengers had been sent south to inform people that we would like to come and visit them. Eventually we heard sounds of distant chanting, coming closer, and a large group of men armed with bows and arrows arrived to carry our possessions and ourselves away. The local people and the missionaries viewed these events with some trepidation. The stage was set.

THE FIRST PERIOD

The Journey South

Our progress south consisted of scenes reminiscent in some ways of those from *King Solomon's Mines*. The terrain was rough and at times very steep; the track, often edged with jungle, was slippery and narrow. A long line of carriers (more than we wanted), with our boxes lashed to poles, stretched out farther than I could see. At the head was Catherine, mounted on her horse and surrounded by plumed and decorated men with their bows and arrows, singing as they walked and danced along. At the end of the procession came myself with the main interpreters and more warriors. We had started at 6:30 A.M., and we arrived at Sonofe village at noon. At each village crowds of men, women, and children came from the surrounding areas to see us. Clusters of dignitaries met and addressed us volubly as we paused. On our arrival at Yababi, dozens of people rushed noisily to embrace us, flinging themselves upon us, caressing and feeling our bodies. Catherine was the first European woman who had come so far south, and many had never seen one before, and never in such close proximity. For that matter, no European man had come that way without being accompanied by "native police" or an evangelist. It was a novel event for them as it was for us!

We were urged to recruit more carriers at Yababi, because thirteen of our men insisted they were afraid to go further. We therefore obtained the services of eighteen others and by 7 A.M the next day were on our way to Irafu, slowly climbing a long steep hill. We were accompanied by mobs of excited men and women, probably hundreds of people, grabbing and pulling us back, making sucking and hissing sounds, shouting and calling out greetings, "I eat you!" (which was apposite in the light of what we got to know about these people a little later). But the greetings seemed genuine enough; they were obviously overjoyed to see us and, of course, the spectacle we presented. From the bush on either side of the track sacred flutes were being played, echoing and resounding across the countryside, inviting others to join in the throng. Passing over some more hills, I reached Moiife; by this time Catherine was already at Kogu. At Moiife I was met by the local *luluai* (Tok Pisin, village official appointed by the administration), *tultul* (T.P., assistant to the *luluai*), "native police boys," the "doctor boy," and others who embraced and welcomed me. Then up and down some more hills, and Mairapa (in Kogu) lay before us, its central clearing packed with dancing and singing men and women.

I should have said, it lay before me unexpectedly since we had not known exactly where they were taking us. A comparatively large house (of about 20 by 15 feet) had been constructed of local timber, with walls of woven banana leaves, thatched with *kunai* (T.P., sword grass), and floored with plaited bamboo, all securely tied with lengths of jungle creeper and bush twine; a screen partly marked off a small sleeping and storage compartment within it. Attached to it was a small "washroom" with an open window; nearby was a small semi-open cook-house, and at the opposite side a deep-pit latrine with a conical roof and a bamboo screen; around this amenity had been arranged a small garden edged with crotons and flowering plants. Within the house itself, bunches of bananas had been hung. It was a princely welcome.

By this time vegetables were piling up in front of the house, as well as fowls and a pig for the feast. Ovens were being prepared. First, however, there were the carriers to be paid, and other men to be recruited to return to Raipinka in order to bring down the remainder of our boxes. Apart from those men we had paid off at Yababi (thirteen), there were twenty-one others, the additional men from Yababi (eighteen), and twenty-seven others to bring down the second batch of stores. Two youths were installed (or, rather, installed themselves) in our cook-house, where there was just enough room for an open fire on the ground. And there were gratuity gifts to twelve other men, not to mention those who had built our house and supplied food for the initial feast.

The next five days were devoted to "settling in." Additions were made to the house: for instance, a verandah, bamboo walls to reinforce the banana-leaf ones, more roof thatching since the rain was heavy, a woven bamboo platform bed, and a bench around the main room for our goods and for people who wanted to sit there instead of on the ground. We also had two houses built for our interpreters and their families, as well as a large round traditional style "men's house" in which I could work. Catherine was to use our "domestic quarters," which were more in line with local women's interests. We were interrupted by the visit of the only other European in the region, Ron Fiegert, a Lutheran missionary in charge of an outstation at Taramu (Tarabu) which was established late in 1950 at the edge of the "uncontrolled" country. During this period and afterward, we were constantly visited by parties of men and women from the surrounding area and even from more distant places, bringing garden produce in exchange for some gift, especially salt and newspaper (in which to roll the local tobacco, as an alternative to a bamboo pipe). There were always large heaps of vegetables outside our cook-house, which supplied not only ourselves but most of the people of Mairapa. Regularly there were *singsings* (T.P., festivals) of mixed village membership, each group vying with the others in the construction of emblems and in patterns of dancing.

I have devoted some little space to this introduction to our fieldwork, perhaps more than I should have since some references have been made to it elsewhere (R. Berndt 1952–53:150–151; 1962:vii–viii). However, I make no apology for dwelling on it. First impressions are significant—whether or not they may have to be modified later, with greater awareness of the situation. Exotic as the context was in our eyes, its meaning was clear enough. The area had been subject to a sequence of what turned out to be abortive "cargo-cult" movements, resulting from unsettlement deriving from the entry of Europeans into the Highlands: on each occasion, expectations were raised, only to be deflated. Our own coming was viewed as a possible fulfillment of these expectations: superficially, we manifested all the signs that portended that in this case things would be different. No doubt the exuberant welcome we received was only partially in relation to our being a novelty. More particularly, it was in celebration of (what appeared to them to be) our vast range of goods.

This attitude rested on a deep-seated belief about the nature of Europeans. They were regarded as spirits of locally dead persons or, in some versions, as their intermediaries. This was substantiated by the basic mythology. The major creative beings and establishers of traditional custom, Yugumishanta and Morufonu (or other names), a wife-husband pair, emerged from the ground at Rivetiga, near Oka, in Fore country and traveled northward until they eventually reached the Markham Fall, where they entered Anabaga, the Land of the Living Dead. Europeans also first came into the Highlands from the east, presumably, so it was held in local belief, from Anabaga.

The first point, however, is that when spirits of locally dead persons went to Anabaga, they eventually returned to their home territories *as* Europeans, having the same physical appearance and characteristics that were sufficiently identifiable to establish him or her as a previously known dead person, resuscitated as a European. As it was said, "My brother dies, the face belonging to him comes up [as a European]. We know it is the same person, but you [European] do not understand!"

The second point concerns the material possessions of Europeans. It was the old story that what they had really belonged to the local people. But the explanation went further than this. Because Europeans did not realize the incontrovertible fact that they *were* returned relatives of the local people, the local people were ashamed—ashamed that they were not recognized by their own close kin. The correlation between this view and our own spectacular journey to Kogu was clear to them: it was in a sense an expiation on our part, absolving them from feelings of shame. We had produced the long-desired goods, and tensions inherent in the earlier situations, when we were not there, found some release in celebration. During our two periods in this region we were regarded as spirits of the dead. This had both advantages and disadvantages. One advantage was that it served as an explanation of what we were attempting to do—our wish to know everything we could about their life. In other words, our anthropological research substantiated their belief that we *were* spirits, refreshing our memories about what we already knew! And what we already knew was enshrined in what we recorded in our notebooks.

Being close as we supposedly were to the people themselves, as spirits of the dead we were now alive again and potentially willing and able to take over some of our social and interpersonal obligations. But as such, we were to some extent unpredictable. We did not specifically conform to their expectations. Inevitably and unavoidably we were agents of change. We were the same but different. One major and indeed shocking difference in their eyes was that Catherine and I shared and slept in the same house. Traditional custom decreed that the men of each village or hamlet slept and spent most of their time in and around the men's house, while their wives lived in small separate houses where the men visited them from time to time. This disparity between ourselves and them was muted somewhat since I spent a large part of my time in the men's working house they had built for this purpose, and Catherine spent most of the day with women.

Imperatives Influencing the Course of Research

It was obvious that at least one local language had to be learned. Hardly anyone had more than a few words of Pidgin, and to rely on interpreters (as we did initially) was obviously unsatisfactory. The two who were available demonstrated quite early in the attempt that they were not in a position to undertake serious translations. Moreover, it was not practicable to concentrate solely on the Kogu people, when our and their interaction with members of other nearby districts was vitally significant. For example, the list of names of persons I met or talked to, or worked with consistently, or heard about in the recording of cases, numbered approximately seven hundred drawn from over forty districts (without my distinguishing here villages and hamlets; see R. Berndt 1962:449–

455). According to our perspective at that time, five primary languages were spoken in this region: Usurufa, which was the smallest, covering six districts; Kamano, sixty-seven districts; three divisions of Yate—Kemiyu-Yate, thirty-three districts, Ke'yagana-Yate, forty-one districts, and Friganu-Yate, at least twelve districts; Fore, approximately thirty-six to forty-five districts; and Koga, about fourteen. Since Usurufa was a minority language, I concentrated on Ke'yagana-Yate; Catherine on Usurufa and Kamano. Little consistent work was carried out with Koga speakers, and I used Yate in speaking with the Fore (although I recorded Fore texts).

My interests in Aboriginal Australia had been, and are, mostly focused on religion and social organization, but not to the exclusion of other aspects. In traditional terms, I saw religion, particularly, as constituting the mainspring of social living and providing those features and values that hold a society together, that supply meaning to life and death. At the same time, in most of the areas of Aboriginal Australia in which I had carried out research, external pressures were intrusive. In some cases, the intrusion was so extensive that resulting changes were irreversible and sufficiently assertive to push aside traditional elements, replacing them with non-Aboriginal ones. In choosing such an area as the Eastern Highlands, my expectation was that it should be possible to explore the processes of externally sponsored change almost from their beginnings; to discover the relative strengths and weaknesses of some institutions as contrasted with others; and, hopefully, to make some suggestions that might direct those changes, in order to modify the trauma of radical disruption that was so apparent in parts of Aboriginal Australia. I argued that in the Eastern Highlands context, where many of the people were experiencing substantial alien impact for the first time, it should be possible to influence the course of change through local awareness of the problems and through administrative goodwill. The euphoria occasioned in those years immediately following the cessation of World War II hostilities, and the reopening of the Highlands, gave hope that such aspirations were, indeed, realistic and possible.

The major issue that faced me in this respect was to know what the local situation was like, how that society (or societies) functioned, and what the aspirations and expectations of the people were. To obtain answers to that complex package involved detailed anthropological research. In approaching this I recognized, of course, that Papua New Guinean societies and cultures were different, and markedly so, from the Australian Aboriginal ones I knew. Looking back, I admit that my Aboriginal experience provided me with few guides to enable me to cope with and interpret the situations we eventually came to know about in our "new" area. Where the Aboriginal experience did help considerably was in the way I approached my raw field data and the procedures I used to obtain them. As far as techniques were concerned, I had still cameras but no tape or other mechanical recorder, pencils but no ballpoint pens. Apart from questions of observation and personal participation, my primary approach was to record everything, wherever possible in the local language, in phonetic script and with interlinear translations. Every text recorded in writing not only helped me with learning the language, but provided opportunities to expand discussion as well as leads into cognate topics.

Apart from myths, on which I did not concentrate except for those of a religious and especially of a ritually linked kind, all of these texts were person-oriented, concerning events that had taken place in the immediate past and those that occurred or were occurring in the present. Even where I witnessed a particular action-sequence, I also got people who were involved in it to tell me about it, to elaborate on specific issues that were raised, and to comment on and discuss ramifications. I was concerned with what was really happening around us, not so much with what had previously taken place, except insofar as it had a bearing on the contemporary situation.

Wherever possible, my approach was nondirective, although it had to be directive in at least two areas of inquiry: in order to provide information on (1) village and hamlet names in particular districts, the patrilineages ("ropes" or "lines") said to be represented in these, issues of segmentation and what constituted a "clan," and so on; and (2) the organization of kin, and other relationships, and associated rights and responsibilities. This information served as a guide in exploring the large number of genealogies I recorded. However, I did not commence my work, as I would have done in Aboriginal Australia, by recording genealogical material. I delayed that task in the Eastern Highlands until I had more control over the language and a greater understanding of interpersonal relations (that is, until I was halfway through the first period), because I was seeking personal details over and above simply genealogical ones. For instance, by that time interdistrict fighting and sorcery had made a deep impression on me and I wanted to know about the actual and alleged causes of death of many of the persons whose names appeared in the genealogies. (An example of this sort of information is outlined briefly in three tables in R. Berndt [1958:17–18].) The procedure I adopted generally in obtaining data demanded maximum collaboration on the part of the local people, who were remarkably frank in all respects. In fact, they were at pains to spell out in considerable detail every aspect of their living, a task that they saw, so I was told, as a process that aided my remembering what indeed I had been a party to prior to my transformation as a European!

Understanding Context

While I was nondirective in my approach when obtaining information, inevitably some features interested me more than others. I did persist, sporadically, in my attempt to come to grips with the religious orientation and have discussed this briefly in R. Berndt (1962:39–84; 1965:78–104). An understanding of the religion rested in the myths relating to Yugumishanta and Morufonu. These contained much information relating to basic assumptions as well as to the conduct of social living. While this stipulated what these mythic beings did "at the beginning," it did not provide specifically a guide for action—except in the ritual sphere. For instance, it spelled out in detail how the pig festivals, the *avagli* (sweat house), and the initiation rites were to be organized and performed, but left matters of interpretation to participants. The myths associated with those two major characters did underline what were, or should be, the "natural" preoccupations of men and women—fertility, their own and that of their pigs and gardens; the importance of strength and fighting prowess in men and, in a complementary way, in women, too; and they emphasized the inherent physiological contrast between men and women which had social-personal implications, not least in the ritual spheres, and they asserted that this meant conflict between them.

The pig festivals were on a much smaller scale than have been reported for other parts of the Highlands, partly because of a disease that had seriously affected the number of pigs available. They involved the spilling of pig blood on the ground as a libation to Yugumishanta in order to ensure fertility of pigs as well as the fertility of gardens. It was an inter-district affair and both men and women participated. It was also an occasion when the sacred flutes were played. Of equivalent importance insofar as garden fertility was concerned was cannibalism, on the one hand, and, on the other, the large repertoire of secondary myths (see C. Berndt, chap. 4). Personally, looking back on all my published discussions of Eastern Highland religion, it would seem I have adopted a more formal approach than I intended. Be this as it may, the secondary myths offer the only viable clues to what the rules are likely to be—although within them there are many obvious contradictions. What is revealed in them is an emphasis on action rather than on belief, and, as regards action, much is left to the person as to how he or she should interpret any injunction that may be articulated. We also accumulated a large corpus of material on spirits of the dead which, if analyzed, could appreciably amplify our understanding of Eastern Highland religion. This, in turn, was related to cannibalism and, where there were corpses to spare and in certain circumstances, to the desiccation of heads and sometimes of whole bodies.

The focus in the *avagli* sweat house rites was on fighting, on enhancing a young man's strength and efficiency in the use of the bow, as well as his attractiveness to members of the opposite sex. Initiation sequences followed that theme, but went much further: cane swallowing (to induce vomiting) and penis and nose bleeding were all intended to achieve inner cleanliness and strength through physical suffering. Cane swallowing, particularly, was concerned with preventing or counteracting contamination, especially that derived from women and sorcery. In every village and hamlet women had their seclusion hut, closed to men, analogous to the men's house (which women were not permitted to enter), and except for cane swallowing, penis bleeding, and possession of sacred flutes, women's religious rites were much the same as those of the men. The religious spheres of men and women were seen as being not only partly separate but in a sense diametrically opposed. Women were potentially dangerous to men, especially in regard to menstrual and afterbirth blood, and men had to take ritual precautions to safeguard themselves, but so did other women.

In short, the attitude of people toward their religion was essentially a practical one and one motivated, moreover, in terms of self-interest. I think it is possible to go further than this and speak of a purposeful dramatization of social events. The quiet life was not for them. They lived on the edge of excitement, and excitement was not far away from tension and fear. Interdistrict fighting was or had been the order of the day. Although patrols had instructed people that village stockades must be broken down, many had not been. Men invariably carried their bows and arrows, especially when they moved outside the precincts of their own house places (villages). Women owed allegiance primarily to members of their own lineage and some immediate relatives, not necessarily to their husbands and *their* lineage members; affines were traditionally potential enemies; and when women were attending to the gardens, men would stand guard with bows at the ready to protect their womenfolk *and* themselves. Expectation of physical violence was always present, as was the threat of sorcery. Even when fighting was strictly forbidden by the Australian administration and the positions of villages and their populations had been frozen (see, e.g., R. Berndt 1962: 250–254, 266–268), the tension was still there.

My notebooks for the 1951–52 period have within them dozens of actual cases of warfare with the names of persons involved in such encounters, as well as their district and village affiliations. These ranged from small forays to full-scale affairs, and the reasons for them varied from a vague but infectious and escalating suspicion and fear of others based partly on rumors, to reprisals for real or imagined offenses, sorcery accusations, and so on. The main intensive areas of aggressive interaction involved districts that were spatially close to each other. Enmity between them was sustained over a period of time, although alliances between different villages varied and were dependent on bribery or arrangements that involved the payment of compensation. I have discussed these patterns comparatively for the Highlands in general (1964:183–203). The point I made there for "our" area was that the further apart any two districts were, both spatially and affinally, the less likelihood there was of warfare between them. Warfare concerned people one knew and was related to; there were only a few categories of kin whom one could ordinarily trust—but even then, a conflict of loyalties could intervene. Against that frame, or rather contained within it, was what perhaps could be called a syndrome.

For instance, any particular case of fighting would almost certainly involve at least two or three, if not more, of the following features: sexual aggression and/or abduction of a woman; destruction of property and/or burning of houses; forcing defeated inhabitants to seek refuge elsewhere; violent behavior toward those who had not escaped; duplicity and theft; and cannibalism. In principle, warfare between any two districts consisted of a series of "backings" and "counter-backings." The defeated, as I have said, sought refuge elsewhere and bided their time until their fighting force had recovered and they were strong enough to return to their home settlement and assert their independence, but that in itself provoked reprisals. Coupled with sorcery, there were no effective controls for achieving and maintaining any sort of a lasting peace. That was the dilemma that faced them; but as far as I could judge, it was not one that worried them overmuch. Warfare was for men a serious game, and arrow making an enjoyable and absorbing task. With the advent of and intervention by the Australian administration, as I have mentioned, people were "frozen," including refugees, and were unable to recover lost territory. This in itself provoked other responses, accentuating the occurrence of sorcery but also placing more emphasis on individual acts of aggression. Administrative control of the area in which we were working was very uneven, as we shall see more clearly when I discuss our second period.

It is not my intention to dwell on the incidence of cannibalism (see R. Berndt 1962:269–290). From all reports, considerable violence took place, not always during the killing of a victim but often when the corpse was cut up and the flesh apportioned after being cooked. While I have a drawing that depicts how a body should be dismembered, my evidence suggests that this formal procedure was rarely carried out. The same is the case when I formally recorded who (males or females) may or may not eat whom (defined in male or female kin terms). In practice, it seems, the niceties in this respect were not adhered to. The gap between what should happen and what in fact did happen was marked in this area of activity, as it was in other aspects of social living. Mortuary feasts that involved eating the flesh of a dead person took place in the gardens and contributed to their fertility. Eating such flesh was said to transfer the strength of the deceased to the eater, and was also a mark of respect for him or her. Again, in practice there was little evidence to support such views. I was intrigued to read in a recent paper by Gillian Gillison (1983), based on fieldwork in 1973–75, that among the Gimi, in the Lufa area of Mount Michael, cannibalism was exclusively associated with women. While the Gimi were outside our own interactory research zone, they are sufficiently close to Friganu and Taramu that I would query such an assertion.

It was the steady accumulation of material of this kind, on more or less endemic fighting and conflict, on violence and sexual excess that included frequent cases of adultery, abduction, and seduction, that made me ask questions about the nature of social order. What were the checks and balances? What were the rules? On the basis of the evidence I had, it was not an easy matter to construct a meaningful frame to explore these vitally important issues. It was for that reason that I focused later on the theme of "excess and restraint," discarding the concept of anomie. In spite of difficulties, I preferred to think in terms of patterned conflict and explore the limits to which certain persons would go to achieve their own ends, and what reactions this form of behavior engendered among people who were involved. Within that pattern, however, there were overriding, culturally congenial imperatives supported by basic assumptions: the battle went to the strong. And a really strong man, in spite of what deeds he perpetrated, could get away with almost anything—until another, more powerful, person appeared on the scene.

That state of affairs was exemplified in the informal courts that emerged with the appointment by the Australian administration of local dignitaries—the *luluai, tultul*, and "mouth-boy" (a spokesman or interpreter). These courts, although unauthorized by the administration, were presided over by such men. I have dealt at some length with many of the cases that took place during our first and second periods in the field (see R. Berndt 1962:318–380). The majority concerned marital upsets and sexual offenses on the part of men and women. In fact, the blocking of many avenues through which aggressive and violent behavior could customarily be manifested highlighted sexual misdemeanors that would ordinarily have been settled by fighting. The dignitaries, sometimes the strong men, assumed a new guise in the context of administering their own rule of law in a manner to which they were accustomed. This often involved punishing "transgressors" publicly in a violent physical way for the vicarious excitement and satisfaction of onlookers. Such public enactments without violence (except where simulated) had a precedent in many of the farces that accompanied *singsing*s.

Leaving the Area

A few weeks before we left Mairapa, conflict was brewing between Kogu and Asafina, which was as close to Kogu as Moiife was. In contrast to Kogu (Usurufa-speaking), Asafina was Fore. Dissension had allegedly been rife between members of these two districts long before our arrival, but it was exacerbated when we settled in Kogu. Asafina people considered that the Kogu people had stolen a march on them, having got us to live in one of their villages. Although I visited Asafina on several occasions, the people of Kogu warned me against them. There were some skirmishes, but not much harm was done. Unsettlement was intensified one morning (February 26, 1952) when we saw smoke and flames rising from Tofenaga. It was reported that a Kainantu "police boy" had set fire to them because the local people refused to be recruited for roadwork. On the same morning, the *luluai* of Agura came to me to complain that the *luluai* of Numparu had told him that a Kamano "police boy" had put all the Agura people "in *kalabus*" (not, in this case, in jail, but he had commandeered their services) for road making. They were accused of having "spent too much time on *singsings*." A further delegation reached me the next day, requesting me to take some action in the matter.

A few weeks before this incident, according to reports, the Lutheran missionary from Raipinka, accompanied by another from Goroka as well as by Reo Fortune, had gone down to Wamio, near Ki'o in Kamano territory (northwest of Kogu). The intention was to perform a *waswas* (T.P., baptism), to incorporate the villagers within their church. Some of the local people, I was told, had invited them to come. During the course of the proceedings the sacred flutes were brought out, displayed, and played before the uninitiated, women, and children. Native evangelists (*bapatara*) exhorted the people to give up their old ways and called the flutes "the mother of Satan." The repercussions of this event were felt throughout the southern villages with considerable shock. However, this was by no means an unusual event. Lutherans and "Seven-Day" Adventists were competing with each other for nominal control over the northern villages. Kemiyu, a little west of Kogu, was a "Seven-Day" stronghold with a resident *bapatara*. Not to be outdone in this respect, a Lutheran adherent built a *lotu* (T.P., church building) at Mairapa and arranged for an "open door" ceremony of inauguration (see R. Berndt 1965:101–102). Catherine and I were present. Almost all the ritual and proceedings that were carried out in this context were in the traditional manner, even in regard to the singing and the farces that were performed. It was certainly a very different situation from the one reported to me as having taken place at Wamio.

All of these events were signs of radical changes—not so much in the case of the burning of the houses, but because the person who had done this was not within the traditional local interactory zone of conflict. Not only were new ideas coming into the region that were in direct contrast to traditional ones, but representatives of new power points (the "state" and the "church") had assumed the strength to impose their own particular regimes. While, as I have said, people accepted the manifest strength of others even to the extent of permitting it to override their own interests, they had the expectation that it would not last. The general view was that all that was happening was ephemeral; administration patrols were irregular and hardly left a mark on the area they traversed. *Bapatara* settled down with their own small coteries, with only an occasional evangelical "outbreak." European missionaries were more persistent but, there again, they were only at Raipinka and one was at Taramu. "Police boys," however, were a different kettle of fish—there were a couple at Moiife and at Moke.

A few days before we left Kogu, reports reached me that an Aitape (north coastal) "police boy" had come to Grufe and set fire to some of its houses, for reasons that were unknown. He had also sent three adherents to several other villages (Tevio, Tiroka, Yumana, Agura, Numparu, and Yagamaifa), where more houses were burned. Many of the people who were absent at the time, visiting Mairapa for our large farewell *singsing*, were most distressed: they lost most of the possessions that had been stored in their houses. They asked me to help. I immediately sent word saying "Stop!" and wrote to the Kainantu district officer asking that such activity should cease, the "police boy" be removed from the area, and an explanation be given.

I mention these events because they underlined for me at that time, as now, the uncertain nature of administration control and the lack of any real understanding or appreciation of the problems facing the local people. In this context, the only person to whom they could appeal was myself, although they did not realize that my influence as an anthropologist was strictly limited. (I should perhaps mention that Catherine and I devoted a large part of each Sunday to informal discussions with groups of people. It was something they themselves had suggested, saying, "We are telling you about ourselves; could you tell us about yourselves?" We welcomed this reversal of roles.)

Finally, "payday" came and we distributed money and gifts. Speeches were made and embraces exchanged. The people appeared to be overjoyed at what they received. It was a boisterous evening with feasting, singing, and dancing. Next morning, ash-covered men assembled in the porch of our house and wailed, mourning our impending departure. At last we left, closing our houses to await our return. The Taramu missionary had sent a horse for Catherine, but her foot had long since healed. We set off, with Catherine at the head of a long line of carriers, making our way through Kemiyu and southwest to Inivi, Tatagufa, and Amufi, where the narrow track became almost impassable and heavy rain had

made the steep hills slippery. Passing through dense jungle, we reached
the river near Henagaru only to find the jungle-fiber "bridge" broken
down. Eventually, making our way across, we reached Taramu and had
our first glimpse of Mount Michael in the distance. We had intended to
visit Ke'afu and Kasa (both Yate-speaking) in the uncontrolled country,
as well as Moke (Fore-speaking) nearby, but the roads were far too bad.
We were especially interested to see Moke since we intended to work there
on our return to the Eastern Highlands.

We spent a few days at Taramu working with local people, and on
March 22, 1952, we commenced our return trip to Raipinka. Passing
through Henagaru, Wezu'epa, Ke'yagana, Amufi, Tatagufa, and Inivi,
we came through the Tatanitaka jungle to Uwa'mi, reaching Kemiyu.
Next day we continued through Tofenaga, Kimi'agumu, Numparu, and
Ki'o into Hafaru: the roads in this part of the country were the roughest
and steepest we had yet experienced. Leaving Hafaru on the following
day, we reached Grufe, where the "No. 2 *Kiap*" (second-in-charge at the
Kainantu district office) met us to discuss the recent burning of village
houses (see above). He assured us that orders had been given that this
would not happen again, and that the "police boy" responsible would be
transferred. Next day we went on to Sonofe, through Yababi, where we
spent the night, reaching Raipinka the following day. Exhausting as the
trip was, it was especially rewarding since we were able to visit dozens of
small villages and hamlets. It meant, moreover, that we had encircled the
whole of the area that concerned us and met many of the people who had
come to see us at Kogu, or had heard about us.

Raipinka gave us an opportunity to "rest" for a couple of days and at
Kainantu to go through the district office records, especially the Register
of Courts from 1948. We visited the Aiyura Agricultural Experimental
Station, the hospital, and so on. On April 5 we went on by plane to Goroka,
where we stayed in Mick Read's house in his absence and talked with some
of the local people. We had decided to visit the rest of the Highlands, or
at least some of the main settlements. So we continued on to Kerowagi,
Mingende, Kundiawa, Ogelbeng, Mount Hagen, and Wabag, taking a
plane in some cases, walking in others. Our rationale for this excursion
was that it could conceivably help in placing our own research area in
perspective. When we eventually returned to Lae and Port Moresby, we
took the opportunity of discussing our work with all interested parties—
with missionaries, administrative officers, and representatives of the Education Department. We also went through patrol reports and visited
schools—for instance, at Sogeri.

THE SECOND PERIOD

The six-month interval between leaving the Highlands and returning
provided us with an opportunity not only to review and assess our re-

search data and discuss these with other persons at the Sydney Department, but to consider our relationship with the people themselves. In this last respect, our feelings toward them were ambivalent. We certainly did not find their emphasis on violence congenial. While Max Gluckman's dictum that "conflict is the essence of social living" had its appeal, as fitting rather comfortably into the sociocultural orientation of the Eastern Highlanders, it seemed to me a little forced. It begged the question regarding the limits of conflict, how far it could go before drastically undermining social order—whatever that meant! It also had a lot to do with the kinds of conflict that were involved. It was in this state of mind that I contemplated the nature of basic assumptions, the obvious gap between ideal and actual behavior, and how the controls that did exist and were more or less recognized as serving that purpose actually worked. I realized that a good argument could be made for social order being identifiable within patterned forms of conflict, however extreme these might be. Increasingly, however, I was considering the place of individual persons vis-à-vis their responsibilities to others, and their expectations of what constituted "the good life."

On the one hand, we liked the people as *persons*, perhaps mainly because of their flamboyance, frankness, and largely extrovert approach to social living. On the other hand, and speaking generally, they were excitable, emotional, and unpredictable, quick to take offense and act aggressively at the turn of a hand. Even in aggression they were sentimental, although that did not seem to affect the outcome. It was mainly for that reason that I took with me on our second trip to the Eastern Highlands W. E. H. Stanner's small pistol that had been stored, among other weapons, at the Sydney Department.

On leaving Sydney for this second period (Mick Read was on the plane, too, bound for Goroka) we went to Lae, via Port Moresby, made arrangements for our stores, and reached Raipinka on November 8, 1952. Having sent messages down to Kogu alerting the people to our impending arrival, we assembled our carriers and set off, sleeping the first night at Yababi and reaching Kogu on the following afternoon. There was a marked contrast between our first and second trips south. We had a much better knowledge of the local languages. People greeted us all along the way, but we were no longer such a novelty; mainly we discussed what had taken place in our absence. There were no uncontrolled crowds of people. On our arrival at Kogu, our welcome was calm; they had known, they told us, that we would return and were ready to resume what they must have looked upon as "our, and their, custom." We were slotted into our niche only too well! Although we utilized our first house and slept there for two nights, they had built a more commodious place for us nearby.

We had originally intended to spend only a short time in Kogu, and were eager to go farther south. Their expectation, however, in spite of being told to the contrary, was that we should settle permanently in Kogu. We were a source of desired goods and, although I hesitate to say so, I was regarded as a "power figure" who could be called upon to react in the appropriate way as occasion demanded. Even though I was unpredictable from their viewpoint, I was much less so than other Europeans: they *knew* us and how we would respond to certain situations, and they knew no other Europeans in that way. Moreover, we were a living reminder that a "cargo cult" movement could effectively be transformed into reality. We settled down to our routine, realizing sadly that they would eventually be disillusioned.

The Same Themes, but More So!

Once I began working, I tried to modify my nondirective approach. I suggested various themes that might conceivably lead away from physical aggression. I thought of two relatively "safe" topics—economics on the one hand, marriage and family on the other. I also revived my exploration of religion. I should have known better. Economics opened the door to acrimonious discussions relating to distribution of pig meat during festivals, "payment" of betrothal gifts, compensation for injury, and so on. A focus on the gardens and the production of vegetables and other foods led in the same direction. Men's hands were soft, women's were rough; men handled the bows and, although they were responsible for fencing and other heavy work, it was mainly women who produced the food. Gardens were related positively to cannibalism and to fighting, although fighting also, negatively, involved their destruction, and people (men and women) quarreled over the boundaries of their gardens. Moreover, gardens were ideal places for sexual assignations. The question of marriage, too, immediately triggered off a multitude of cases relating to adultery, abduction, fighting, death and/or punishment, not to mention sorcery.

I was back to square one, compiling accounts of near-past and contemporary cases within the sphere of conflict. An interesting thing about all these was that men recounting the details of a particular event were helped, excitedly, by others who made their contributions on an eyewitness or participant basis. Or, if it were an incident or series of incidents that I knew about personally, all the various aspects would be gone over thoroughly. The more extenuating circumstances that were involved, and the more participants, the greater the degree of interest expressed. For instance, one case might focus on marriage, but include seduction, bribery, and killing, followed by reprisals and temporary resolution through compensation. Or, in a case of sorcery resulting in death, the theft of a pig had led to fighting and a mortuary feast involved eating the corpse, with further sorcery reprisals following. There were dozens of variations on such themes, spelled out in considerable detail with the names of the kinds of arrows used by particular persons and the songs that were sung during an attack or when a death occurred, or during *singsings*, in memory of such an event.

Generally speaking, tensions were rising in the area we knew. Many activities that clustered around interdistrict fighting were temporarily suspended, officially. That is, the administration had called for the cessation of hostilities, but what was involved was not spelled out to the local people. They interpreted the situation to mean that, while interdistrict fighting was frowned on, a number of other aspects associated with it could not reasonably be terminated at short notice. People continued to act as they had before. There was, for instance, no direct ban on personal physical aggression. In any case, the behavior of some of the "native police boys" made it clear that there was not. This state of affairs accentuated an unevenness and uncertainty throughout the area that contributed to, rather than militated against, conflict.

An indication of the unsettlement that penetrated into the "uncontrolled" area to the south was manifested in attempted or actual suicide. While its occurrence for various reasons (see R. Berndt 1962:179–207) was not uncommon traditionally if the evidence available is any guide, during our second period I recorded many more cases than I expected. In the northern part of the region, especially among the Kamano, ideally (as *one* ideal response) a wife should commit suicide on the death of her husband. Yet there were many other situations in which a man or woman might be provoked to carry out such an act of self-destruction for a real or imagined wrong, in order to "punish" the person responsible for causing it. We can perhaps read into such cases, or tentatively infer from them, that the channels available to an aggrieved person had narrowed, making it more difficult for him or her to respond in a more direct way. However, the informal courts were becoming more active and during our second period were held more frequently. The reasons for convening such courts were widening, and the courts were replacing, at least to some extent, personal and social reprisal.

This was not necessarily a matter of local dignitaries imposing their "rule of law." In a sense, it was through public demand. More aggrieved persons brought their problems to the courts. It was not that they especially expected a resolution. The matter of impartial judgment was virtually absent. People hoped that those who had done them harm would be punished, but they often misjudged the climate of opinion and what the attitude of their "judges" would be. The courts punished those persons supposedly responsible for causing the trouble. As in other circumstances, judgment only rarely went against the strong, and in that respect women were fair game—although, from looking at the cases, it might seem that they were often responsible for exacerbating the situation. The number of sexual offenses coming before the courts increased for the simple reason (or so it appeared) that they provided the most interesting and exciting public displays in regard to the punishment involved. Many of the cases, too, were of a trivial nature. In one example, an old friend of mine, T——, had gone to Moiife to collect pig meat and bananas from the husband of his recently dead sister. On his way back to Kogu he was watched by some women engaged in enforced roadmaking. They asked him where the pig meat had come from and with whom he intended sharing it. He resented this, and consequently approached the local *luluai* to hold a court so that the women could be punished. But nothing was done about it. Another case involved the recovery of marriage payments because a man's betrothed wife had left him for someone else, but comments on this emphasized that P——, the deserted husband-to-be, was jealous of other people "making court": if they did so, why shouldn't he? Court case after court case continued almost interminably. On occasion, my working house was used for this purpose. To get away from these for a while, I struggled to explore various aspects of the Yugumishanta and Morufonu mythology, especially the relationships between myth and ritual.

Interruptions became obtrusive. A young patrol officer visited us from Taramu, where a patrol post was being established: he asked to see our permits! I almost asked to see *his* credentials. A district officer from Goroka visited Kemiyu in the belief that it was located in the Bena Bena Subdistrict. His intention was to take a census, and he asked to see the "village book." A *luluai* was supposed to keep a record of the names of persons resident in his district. Needless to say, all the *luluai* I knew were nonliterate and no such books existed (not compiled by them). Then the newly appointed district officer at Kainantu sent instructions to the southern villages that all "police boys" and *luluai* should come up immediately to see him; a few weeks afterward this particular district officer visited us at Kogu.

More unsettling for the local people were the repercussions arising from a series of small-scale "cargo cult" movements that had reappeared in our absence. It is likely that our temporary withdrawal from Kogu stimulated some strong men, especially those in the Fore-speaking villages, to try their luck in magically materializing goods that they desperately wanted. On our return, things quietened down in that direction. But dissension, as I have said, appeared in other ways. In late November, a disturbance broke out over the "shoot nose" (that is, ritual nose bleeding) of a young boy, E——. Pigs had been promised for the occasion but were not forthcoming. The matter was resolved after my intervention, at the request of the boy's father. On December 2, general fighting broke out early in the morning. On inquiry, the reason was soon given. H—— had commenced planting (or rather his wives had, under his direction) in a section of garden land belonging to K—— and his brother (see R. Berndt 1962:296–297). The upshot of this argument found kin taking sides, with men rushing to the men's house to get their bows and arrows and shields. The uproar attracted people from some nearby villages. Eventually, the *luluai* of Kogu brought it under control.

Each day brought new excitements. When we returned to Kogu, we thought we had made it clear that we intended to go on to Moke after Christmas. As I have already mentioned, the people were loath to believe this. On the night of December 20 we were awakened by cries that *sangguma* (T.P., assault sorcery) men were lurking in the surrounding bush. Local men rushed to and fro with drawn bows. It turned out to be a false alarm. It was explained to us that, if such intruders had been there, they would have been Fore sorcerers out to kill us! From that time, armed men watched over us at night, guarding us (they said). Five nights afterward, howls and cries were again heard coming from the bush, with answering calls from the huts. N—— announced that he had caught a *sangguma* man who had slipped from his grasp and run away. The whole of Kogu turned out to scour the immediate vicinity, lighting huge fires in the nearby jungle. Again, we were warned. A few days afterward, when our stores were packed, a group of fully initiated men staged an *avagli* (sweat house) ritual in the enclosed area of our porch, hoping to prevent our departure. After a great deal of persuasion that took up most of the day, I was able to convince them that we really intended to leave. On January 8, 1953, we recompensed the people for helping us.

Farther South

With a long line of carriers we set off for Moke. Many of the Kogu people accompanied us to Kemiyu. Although some of them were disappointed with what they had been given because they wanted *everything* we had (we could magically replace it in no time!), most volubly expressed their satisfaction. Nevertheless, it was not difficult to see that they did not want our goods, and presumably ourselves, to go to an area they feared and considered to be a stronghold of sorcery. After leaving Kemiyu, we were in Fore country. Passing through Ifusa, Tonerikogu, Hetasena, and No. 2 Moke, we reached what we originally believed to be No. 1 Moke. However, this turned out to be the village area of Pintagori in the district of Busarasa; it had wrongly been named Moke by an administration patrol. Interdistrict fighting and the prevalence of sorcery had forced most of the residents of Pintagori to leave it in 1952 for hamlet and lineage strongholds, and some of the people had only recently returned. We were welcomed by the "police boy," several *luluai* and *tultul* from surrounding districts, and the resident "doctor boy." We were taken to the administration "rest house" that had recently been built, and told to use it as our own house. We had three houses built for our three Kogu companions and their wives (who for most of our period here lived in fear of sorcery) and a men's house in which I could work. Two men working on these houses were shot at by arrows but were not seriously injured.

From the vantage point of Busarasa, we had a clear view of Wanevinti mountain (hill) to the south. On the second day, while scanning the villages around Wanevinti with a pair of binoculars, in one village I saw a leisurely game of "kickball" being played; another village, Kawaina, not too far away, was being sacked, the palisades broken down and houses aflame, with opposing warriors shooting their arrows. It was a salutary experience. Reports were also coming in of fighting at Ya'agusa, near Kawaina. Next day a number of refugees came to Pintagori from Wanitavi, near Wanevinti; they said they had been driven from their villages by Kamira men who came from south of the mountain, below Ke'akasa and Amora.

In these circumstances, it was difficult to persuade people to sit down consistently over a period for discussions. Men and women came into Pintagori from distant villages to see us, but made excuses that they were unable to stay because fighting was going on. Especially, I hoped to work with Ora men, but only some came over at my invitation, as they were at enmity with Moke and the latter with Busarasa. To achieve some kind of reconciliation between these opposing groups, it was suggested that a large *singsing* be held. Consequently, immense quantities of vegetable food were brought up and piled high before our house.

On the scheduled day, only groups from Busarasa villages appeared: there were no emblems and no *singsing*. However, people from Ora and Moke turned up later and accused Busarasa of not being properly prepared for dancing. Arguments raged over the distribution of pig meat, coupled with accusations of sorcery. Masses of people had now assembled and general fighting broke out between men armed with bows and arrows, knives, sticks, and so on, while some men jumped onto the *kunai* grass roofs of the women's houses. Several women and children sheltered in our house in fear, while other women joined in the affray. So serious did the melee become that I took the unprecedented course (as far as I was concerned) of threatening with my pistol. Repeated threats and exhortations eventually quietened them. An officious *bapatara* broke up a number of bows and arrows of the combatants, who were incensed and threatened reprisals. On the next day, although the weather was indifferent, with rain following heavy mist, the *singsing* was held. A contingent from Ora came first, followed by people from Miarasa, then Busarasa, with a mixed group from Moke, Emasa, and Mage; some people had even come down from Moiife. The occasion was marred, however, by arguments between men from Busarasa and Moke. The Moke *luluai* condemned Busarasa for holding a *singsing* when relations between them were strained. Busarasa, remembering the broken bows and arrows of the day before, damaged and removed fencing from the *bapatara*'s gardens and stole some sugarcane. Singing and dancing ground to a halt as people feared another outbreak of fighting. The Moiife people were a bit superior (although they had no reason to be) about the whole business, explaining to me that what we had experienced was quite typical of the Fore. Arising from this conflict, the Moke "police boy" convened a court at the "doctor boy's" house to persuade the Moke and Busarasa *luluai* to talk over the recent fighting. After mutual accusations, they agreed to meet for a peace ceremony on the following day. They promised to bring along their sorcery objects so that these could be destroyed, hold a feast, break sugarcane, and plant crotons in order that the peace should hold fast. Ovens were prepared, but nothing else happened. The matter remained unresolved.

I have gone into these points in summary form, since the continued threat of fighting interfered drastically with the more formal aspects of my recording, and there were other cases, besides those I have mentioned. In mid January the patrol officer from Taramu visited us, and at the end of the month so did the Kainantu district officer, who had come south to Moke through Tairora language territory.

Much of the area in which we were now working was officially "restricted," but we received oral permission from the Kainantu district officer to venture as far south as we thought could be done with safety. Since at that time I was concentrating on "mapping" (charting) and recording information about the smaller villages and hamlets and lineage lands, as well as garden ownership and usage, I took the opportunity of visiting all areas in the vicinity of Busarasa. Many hamlets still had their stockades intact; some had recently been mended. I followed this up a few days later by visiting Moke villages. I then went south through gardens (since tracks were almost nonexistent) to Kasagu, Oka, Rivetega (the emergence place of Yugumishanta and Morufonu), and on to Ya'agusa at the foot of Mount Wanevinti. In most of these places (outside Moke), the hamlets almost within the jungle itself were heavily protected with stockades, with small women's houses of four to five feet in diameter and about the same height. The men's house was domed or conical, usually built on an elevated position, with one aperture (or door), mostly too small for me to press through. The floors of those I did enter were strewn with debris, benches for sleeping on with their headrests, shields and bundles of arrows and bows, among other things. Small pig houses were within the stockades. In the gardens near each hamlet, women were working under the protection of armed men. Around the men's house, men were sitting making arrows. The hamlets were dirty and dank; everything was in shade, and wet, and the tracks between the hamlets (where there were tracks) consisted of mud and slush or running water. In most cases I was accompanied by the *luluai* of the respective districts. Except among ourselves, there was little talking or excitement. I recognized a number of men who had visited Busarasa, Moke, and Ora, but was told they were not talking because they were preoccupied with fighting. I did not attempt to go farther south or climb Wanevinti, as I would have liked to do. I was warned not to do so, that it was far too dangerous. In any case, the men accompanying me would not go farther.

During our last phase of research at Busarasa, N——, the *luluai* of Kogu, came to see me, to report that disaster had befallen our old home at Mairapa. It will be recalled that Asafina was at enmity with the Kogu people, and both had many scores to settle. Hostility had broken out from time to time during our first period at Kogu, mainly over Asafina claims to Mairapa land. Before we left Kogu for Busarasa, I wrote a letter, addressed to the Kainantu district officer, substantiating the claims of Kogu. According to the evidence presented to me, it had never been Asafina land, although Asafina had occupied it for a while on defeating the Kogu people. But that was a couple of years prior to our arrival at Kogu. I gave this letter to N—— in case of any trouble in that direction. During the Kainantu district officer's patrol of this area, and since the matter was raised by Asafina, N—— gave him my letter to read. As it was reported to me, after reading it, the district officer returned it to N—— and punched him. Having destroyed some of the Kogu houses and part of our own—which was, incidentally, defended by some of the Kogu men—the district officer told the Kogu people to go back to their own villages and forthwith allocated Mairapa to Asafina. I was told that the whole affair had been engineered by a "police boy" who had received as a bribe pig and cassowary meat, a fowl, and some vegetable food. I took the matter up with the administration, but as far as I know, there was no attempt on its part to remedy this act of injustice. It left an unpleasant flavor as far as we were concerned. It was humiliating for N—— and the local people. It no doubt confirmed the opinion of Kogu that, once we had left them, they had no "figurehead" to protect them.

Leaving Busarasa

Looking over my notebooks of the Busarasa period, I was interested to see that, in spite of the difficulties, I recorded so much data. Certainly the coverage was similar to that obtained at Kogu. The differences lay primarily in the direction of emphasis. Sorcery, fighting, and cannibalism, in that basic combination, served to supply the main topics of conversation. However, at Busarasa we also witnessed important initiation sequences that brought out for me a greater understanding of the part women played in these and, particularly, their attitudes toward their "co-wives"—the sacred flutes (see R. Berndt 1962:65–73). *Singsings*, on the whole, were less well attended, less frequent, and did not display the imagery of emblem design that was so apparent at Kogu. In the light of what I have said about the atmosphere of the region, this was not surprising.

In the Kogu area, full-scale fighting was less likely to take place because of the spread of external control. At Busarasa and in the surrounding districts restraints of this kind were minimal. Again, in the Kogu area, cannibalism was less frequently practiced, and then only surreptitiously; it was being pushed into the background, if not into the past. In the Busarasa area it was still a fairly common occurrence and by no means hidden. Among the number of cases I have for the Fore, I mention one that took place on February 4, 1953. A woman of Ke'akasa, who was married to P——, had reportedly been sorcerized by men from Karu who used *guzigli* sorcery (thought to produce the fatal nervous degenerative disease *kuru*). As a result she died. Her body was anointed with pig's blood and buried in the Koburayanti gardens. The corpse, however, was exhumed by her brother and three women, and the flesh removed and cooked in hollow lengths of bamboo mixed with native spinach. Since I had expressed interest in the case, some was sent up to me: however, I declined to accept it. The whole matter, along with other examples, occasioned no particular interest. It was simply regarded as normal behavior. An officious Ora "mouth-boy" wished to bring the matter to the attention of an informal court, but the court decided not to do anything about it since it was the custom of people at Ke'akasa.

The period at Busarasa provided me not so much with new material as ratification and elaboration of what I had already obtained. And that was valuable, particularly in the ritual sphere. For instance, I was able to record a large range of songs relevant to this, which I had not done at Kogu. These presented a wealth of symbolic allusions that opened up new ways of looking at the religious orientation. In a sense, the Fore people were closer to the "source" of the Yugumishanta and Morufonu mythic beings whose home, as I have said, was at Rivetiga, near Oka and reasonably close to Moke. For that reason alone, the time at Busarasa was well spent. Experiencing the atmosphere of the region, and living in a situation constantly under threat of fighting and/or sorcery, provided an extra dimension that played a part, and I believe a major part, in helping us to understand the people themselves and their culture. Living under the shadow of threat was quite wearing. I do not think we were unduly nervous—although the people around us were.

We left Busarasa at the end of February, having given gifts to all the people who had helped us. With a long line of carriers we walked west to Awanti (Kasa), through Ke'afu, then northward to Hogateru and into Taramu. It was a switchback track made worse by heavy rain, and we were more than pleased to reach Taramu. The missionary from Taramu came out to meet us during the last hour or so of the journey. Four days later, after obtaining local carriers, we left Taramu taking the northern track to Goroka. The same missionary accompanied us for a short distance. Then, passing through Lalabu we came to Kagu (not Kogu), where it commenced to rain heavily. Since our boxes were covered with *karuka* (T.P., pandanus) leaf mats, we continued along some very bad tracks running with water, and at times it was like climbing up a series of waterfalls. Eventually we reached a Lutheran mission rest house at Keipafina, and after the rain had eased we went on to Keipafina *kiap* house. This was in the heart of the Friganu-Yate dialect group territory. We had met many of the people at Kogu when they visited us for *singsing*s. Rain continued overnight, but next morning we went on to Friganu, Kitsibiru, Oroguti, and finally to Kami: the track had been steep and slippery, at last coming into the *kunai* grass country. At Kami, however, we paid off our carriers, who had no wish to go farther from their home villages, and enrolled another batch. As we were extremely tired, we rested on the following day, and the next morning left for Goroka. The track led us to the Asaro River and its several tributaries. So strong were the currents after heavy rain that Catherine had to be carried over, while I had to be held as I struggled across against the rapids. The Kami Hills marked the northern extremity of Friganu-Yate territory, and once we had passed through these we were in the hot *kunai* plain that stretched into Goroka. We arrived late in the afternoon, and our carriers had to be paid before sunset since a curfew existed at that time—"the natives" had to be out of town by then!

There is no point in expanding on our trip out of the area, except to say that on the following day we left Goroka by plane for Lae. As with the termination of our first period, we decided to visit some other places in order to broaden our knowledge of Papua New Guinea. So we went to Madang, Wewak, Manus, Kavieng, and Rabaul, returning to Lae to assemble our luggage, and back to Sydney, via Port Moresby.

EPILOGUE

This is a personally oriented contribution covering my/our experiences within a section of the Papua New Guinea Eastern Highlands which, at that time, had not been studied or even surveyed anthropologically. It has not been my intention to provide any sort of analysis of the material I obtained. To have attempted this without the support of detailed empirical data would have been like embarking on a conjuring trick without the appropriate props. Instead, I have preferred to focus on the atmosphere of the area, on my personal feelings, and to make some comments on likely implications for the people.

I for one (and I think it is true for both of us) went into the area with eyes open and a sense of adventure, tempered, I trust, with a social scientific approach. Our introduction to the people and their culture gave flame to our interest. It was, however (and not just in retrospect), as we soon learned, a deadly serious affair. When Reo Fortune told us at Raipinka that his real intention in returning to Finintegu was to find out why he had not suffered an arrow in his back during his first visit (see McLean, chap. 2), we thought that this was another of his idiosyncratic approaches to research. We did not appreciate his point until we had been working in the area for some little time. Not many anthropologists have had the opportunity of carrying out research in an indigenous situation that had experienced a minimum of external contact. Had there been less of that contact, it would not have been possible for us to have worked there. Our experience at Busarasa underlined the tenuous nature of so-called external control. Much of what we saw, heard, and wrote about we found personally uncongenial. It was not always possible to separate out the personal affection we felt for many of the people from other features that were more difficult to rationalize in our terms. What must be kept in mind is that we ourselves were actors on the cultural stage, along with the people themselves. Our presence in the area, and our interaction with these people, inevitably provoked changes in their own lives.

I have published only a fraction of the material I recorded in the field. What there is of it should be sufficient for interested readers to seek out and get a reasonable idea of the social anthropology of the region. I am reminded that when *Excess and Restraint* was published (1962) some reviewers of that book were shocked at the scenes (or cases) I presented and discussed. The feeling that came through was that I had overemphasized some of those features. Perhaps this attitude was understandable at that time. The carnage of World War II had made a deep impression on most of us. The "brave new world" that was to emerge from all of that ostensibly had no place for behavioral patterns of the kind we had witnessed and written about. *Excess and Restraint* was, in fact, the partly rewritten thesis I submitted to the London School of Economics for my Ph.D. degree in the English summer of 1955, when the data were fresh in my mind. As Eastern Highland society and culture had made such a deep impression on me, I chose it for that purpose rather than Australian Aboriginal material, perhaps because it offered such a contrast to the other.

We did not return to the area, as we had expected to do. Aboriginal

Australia reclaimed our attention and, moreover, we became enmeshed in the problems and issues associated with it. At one stage, we were invited to participate in the election surveys that preceded Papua New Guinea independence. However, we declined because we did not wish to become involved in what we regarded as a purely routine activity; we wanted to look again at the themes that had been so significant in the early 1950s, and at the changes that had been taking place in those respects, but we lacked funds to do so. Moreover, the Eastern Highlands received considerable attention in regard to *kuru*, which was popularly called a "laughing disease." Vincent Zigas and D. C. Gajdusek initiated an intensive "Kuru Research Project" in March, 1957, at Okapa (which I understand is located at our old village, Pintagori, in Busarasa). Because of that, I wrote my *Sociologus* paper on that topic (R. Berndt 1958). We had earlier tried to interest staff at the Sydney University School of Tropical Medicine in carrying out research along those lines, and other medical personnel, too, but without success.

We were convinced that what was unknown in 1951, anthropologically speaking, was *reasonably* well known by the time we left Busarasa in 1953. I am not saying that a great deal more material could not have been obtained, nor that particular topics could not have been focused on in more detail and, perhaps, with a greater degree of objectivity. Conditions, however, were radically changing; the Kuru Project was operating, with the presence of various kinds of scientists and short-term visitors. Moreover, the momentum of administrative control was being speeded up, and mission infiltration became much more encompassing than it had been. Access roads by then made traveling easy for jeeps and even for other traffic. On the main arteries, the area was no longer isolated. What we witnessed in 1951–53 was gradually being muted, even transformed. In this respect it is useful to compare R. Glasse and S. Lindenbaum's (1971) article (on the basis of fieldwork among the South Fore, 1961–63) with mine (R. Berndt 1971), both on political organization.

In conclusion, then, there are just a couple of points I would make. The first relates to issues of change. Without doubt, these changes have been far-reaching for the Eastern Highlanders. Nevertheless, a significant comment can be made here along the following lines: what we *were* (as being relevant to those people during 1951 through 1953) is not all that different from what we *are*. Although that statement may seem ambiguous, I am simply saying that the past is, in one way or another, always relevant to understanding the present. In this example it is particularly so. "Traditional" patterns of belief and assumptions, but not necessarily actions, can be remarkably resilient (see R. Berndt 1971:417–419). The second point is perhaps even more important for understanding the Eastern Highlanders and their culture. On the one hand there were social imperatives that obliged persons, out of self-interest if for nothing else, to stand together in the face of adversity—for instance, external aggression—or, alternatively, obliged them to contribute toward a ceremonial network (*singsings*) or the religious festivals for the benefits that would, or might, accrue to them. On the other hand, the culture and society of the Eastern Highlanders offered considerable scope for individual self-expression in a wide range of activities. The right to exercise personal initiative, and to bear the consequences if one could not get away with it, was perhaps the most marked attribute of their life (see C. and R. Berndt 1971:59–71). It certainly played into the hands of the new regime, through the people's pliant acceptance of innovation and of the changes that were thrust on them. Both these points, in my view, have had and will continue to have ramifying implications for their future.

FOUR

Journey along Mythic Paths

Catherine H. Berndt

Long before we first went to the Territory of New Guinea, one of my favorite books was F. E. Williams's *Drama of Orokolo* (1940a). Years later, after fieldwork in the Eastern Highlands, it still is. I am not sure why. Certainly it makes no pretentious claims to be theoretically "important." One reason was that I found his choice of topic congenial. Another was his attention to ethnographic detail; he was obviously interested in what he was exploring and documenting. Also, his interest clearly extended to the people involved, and to their personal perspectives and emotions. And he was especially concerned about the impact of the changes that were taking place among them in consequence of outside pressures—concerned about their responses to these, as well as about the wider implications. A further dimension that was significant in his dramatic portrayal, but rather elusive, was what is now sometimes called "gender relations."

All of these themes have been of major interest to me in the course of fieldwork in Aboriginal Australia from 1941 onward. My focus has always been on women's perspectives, although I have tried to see these in broader context. That kind of contextual approach has been a basic feature of anthropology, at least as an ideal. It is easier to enunciate in general terms than to embody in specific research designs, except within rather arbitrary limits. Where does a "relevant context" end? And what is "relevance" in any given project? Feasibility, or practical possibilities, obviously impose one sort of boundary, however the conceptual ideal may be defined. In some studies that concentrate on women, for instance, men appear on the periphery or as an almost separate population. In others that purport to be more general accounts, it is women who appear to be submerged, and the main emphasis is on men. Phyllis Kaberry, first in her

Australian Aboriginal fieldwork and later in New Guinea and Africa, argued that women should be seen in the overall setting of social relationships, attitudes, and activities, which inevitably include men. My own fieldwork has differed from hers in many respects (see, e.g., C. H. Berndt 1988), but in principle I share her views on this subject.

Except for informal discussions and conversations, I have consistently worked with women, not with men. I could do that more easily because my husband was working with men, and the people we were with recognized and approved of this division of labor. I struck problems in the Eastern Highlands in this regard, but they were partly resolved, after some initial difficulty.

THINKING ABOUT GOING THERE

R. M. Berndt's chapter outlines something of this, and how we became involved in New Guinea research.[1] Looking back at the two "reports of fieldwork" that I submitted to the International Federation of University Women (the second, in the middle of 1953), I see that the "aims of research" I noted were framed broadly enough and comprehensively enough to cover the main points of social living for women in almost any society. The categories I set out were as useful in the Territory of New Guinea as in Aboriginal Australia, although of course the content was very different; but then, it varied within Aboriginal Australia as well, according to region, and also according to the degree and nature of contact with the outside world.

Margaret Mead, in New Guinea, had used the label *"tamberan* cultures" for situations where men had their own clubhouses (*tambaran* in Tok Pisin) from which women were normally excluded on the basis of religious sanctions. There was enough similarity here to some aspects of traditional Australian Aboriginal culture to suggest one intriguing line of research, but, as in the *Drama of Orokolo* case, there was not enough information on women's points of view. Mead had worked more systematically with men than with women, partly because men were more proficient in Pidgin English as a lingua franca. Kaberry encountered the same obstacle in her New Guinea research, and she reported that she had to work with men until she knew enough of the local language to talk directly with women. Other women fieldworkers had spent varying periods in New Guinea or in outlying islands: Camilla Wedgwood, Beatrice Blackwood, and Hortense Powdermaker. But women did not emerge from their studies except in a minor way—much less forcefully than from the work of a male anthropologist, Malinowski.

So, I wanted to learn more about women's "world views"—but women in what area?

THE EASTERN HIGHLANDS, 1951–53

The region that later became our temporary home was one of ridges and valleys, with stretches of bush and of open *kunai* (T.P., sword grass), intersected by small rivers that ran turbulently during the rainy season from about November to March. The basis of the local economy was subsistence horticulture, with shifting cultivation. The staples were sweet potato and taro in the north, yams in the south. They were supplemented by other garden foods, including bananas, maize, and various legumes and cucurbits, also wild fruits, different kinds of fungus, and edible leaves. Small animals and reptiles were hunted during the dry season; pigs and fowls, and occasionally dogs, were domesticated and eaten, and trapped cassowaries were sometimes kept in small pens and fattened for eating. During the heavy rains, villages and hamlets more than 6,000 feet above sea level were enveloped for much of the day in mist and drifting cloud, and the nights were often cold. Nevertheless, the conventional dress while we were there was a skirt or fringe of bark strips in varying styles; women's skirts were bulkier than men's and they usually wore more than one at a time. Small bark-cloth capes were everyday wear in the south, but farther north they appeared mainly during ceremonies. Gardens of different shapes and sizes were scattered among the slopes, fenced to keep out pigs. Clusters of round houses with conical thatched roofs of *kunai* dotted the open plains and lay hidden in the bush or in clumps of coarse wild cane, but even in 1951 the introduced rectangular style was becoming popular, especially in the north.

The Eastern Highlands include a number of language groups, but I was concerned with only four—Kamano (Kafe), Usurufa, Yate, and Fore—and to a lesser extent the Agarabi (Agarve) around Kainantu.[2] In the Kainantu Subdistrict the Kamano numbered nearly twelve thousand; there were several thousand more in Bena, including the Kamamentina Valley. On their southern boundary was the small Usurufa (Uturupa, Uturapa) language unit of about nine hundred people, and farther south again the Fore (Porei), with a population estimate varying between about five and ten thousand according to the way this composite label was interpreted. On the west of all these were three linguistic divisions that together, in 1951–53, were often called Yate, with a total population of perhaps fifteen to twenty thousand.

The territory of each of the language units was made up of a number of "big names," which I translate as "districts." They varied in size, and in the extent of more or less fertile garden land they included. In all of them there were named sites, "small names," on which might be clusters of houses, gardens and garden-huts, or solitary pig-keeping huts. Villages or hamlets ("house places") were traditionally built on ridges or hilltops, where they were more easily defended, but by 1951 the northern Kamano, especially, were moving down to the valleys. Even the largest village usually had no more than thirty houses. At the time of our research some of the southern settlements, still fortified with wooden stockades, were no more than small hamlets.

R. M. Berndt's chapter has sketched the uneven time-space spread of administrative control up to 1951–53. Administrative and other European influences were being diffused southward from the main centers, extending the "controlled area" to include new districts. (It is to the far south that some of the major creation myths point in their statements about "origins.") In 1951–53, active warfare had ceased over much of the region. This was, in fact, the main official criterion for deciding whether an area should be classed as "controlled." In the south, however, in territory still officially "restricted" at the time of our study, interdistrict warfare and cannibalism were continuing and efforts were being made to bring that area under control.

Of the four language units, the sophisticates insofar as European contact was concerned were the Kamano and northern Yate—but less obviously so than their Agarabi neighbors. Next came the Usurufa and northern Fore and many of the Yate, and then the southern Fore and Yate in the "restricted" area. Individual exceptions aside, both administration and mission influences appeared to be strongest in the north. Among other signs, a crude kind of football or "kickball" game was popular among boys and men up to about middle age; *laplaps* (T.P., cloth used as wraparound garments) and shapeless calico frocks worn over bark skirts were much admired, although not universal, and altogether there were more introduced goods, in rather greater variety. For instance, we saw no stone axes in use among the Kamano and, conversely, very few steel axes among the Fore. Most Kamano had obeyed official and mission orders to cut their hair and stop greasing it with pig fat, and the fashion was spreading rapidly southward, but many Usurufa, Yate, and Fore, both children and adults, still wore their hair in thin braids firmly greased and flattened.

The most far-reaching change was one that none of them seemed to have grasped, at least in its implications for their future. Some, especially in the north, echoed the "native" evangelists and others who urged that traditional ways of living should be abandoned because the "time of Satan," or "*kanaka* [T.P., derogatory term for native people] time," was over and a new era had dawned. Even the most ardent supporters of Christianity, in its local forms, saw this emphatically as an era of material plenty, but to achieve the prosperity they wanted, they had to make use

of Europeans who held the keys to it, and that entailed temporary sub-
ordination. What they did not realize then was that this state of affairs was
likely to continue, and to bring in its train more drastic changes.

Nevertheless it was obvious, however much a number of them resented
it, that for the time being Europeans (especially, male Europeans) stood
at the summit of the local pyramid—whether people attributed that
dominance to magical techniques and special status as ghosts, or saw them
simply as paler but more fortunate, more knowledgeable, and therefore
more wealthy counterparts of themselves. There were some doubts about
the connection between the Australian administration and missions. It
was often claimed that the two worked hand in hand and had to be
accorded equal loyalty, but news that a missionary was approaching a
village seemed to spark off less confusion and apprehension than when
the expected visitor was an administration official with his "native police."
These last had much more authority and power in 1951–53. At the level
of practical affairs they had a fair amount of freedom of action. In
keeping with official policy, they came from other areas and rarely spoke
or understood any of the local languages; for communication they depended on their interpreters. Australian administrative officers, partly
because they were not stationed for long at any one base, were in much
the same position. They depended heavily on the police and their interpreters, and it was through these, and the few people speaking Pidgin
English, that virtually all their local contacts were made.

By 1950 there was an administrative outpost in the region under a
"native police" official, by 1951 a second, and by the middle of 1951 a
third, at Taramu, which by 1953 had an Australian in charge. From the
middle of 1952 more police were sent in as part of the drive to put
through roads and bring the southern districts under control. In exerting
pressure on the local people the native police could draw on a number
of sanctions, limited but apparently quite effective. The main ones, in
threat or actuality, were physical violence, detention in Kainantu jail or
its unofficial local counterparts, and reporting offenders to Australian
officials. They also presided over unofficial informal courts and decided
on punishment and compensation (see R. M. Berndt 1962:318–380).
Any district or village that held a pig feast when a native police official
was somewhere nearby was expected to make him and his satellites a
generous "present." A number of feasts were deliberately postponed in
the rainy season of 1952–53 because of increased police activity; people
claimed that they would not have enough pig meat left for themselves to
make the effort worthwhile.

Other agents of the outside world in this situation were medical aides,
or "doctor boys." Some young Kamano and Agarabi men were taking up
this occupation. It involved undergoing a period of elementary training

and then being supplied with instruments and drugs to treat all but the most serious cases of illness and injury. These men were responsible to the European medical officer at the main centers, Kainantu or Goroka. In 1951–53 there were perhaps three in the southern Kamano area, and one each in the Usurufa, southern Yate, and northern Fore, but they were not there continuously. From all accounts, most of them preferred to wait for patients to approach them for treatment. Then there were a few self-styled "native" evangelists without formal backing and with virtually no awareness of what their profession entailed, though their claims were accepted locally almost without question, as men aligned with the new order of things. With few exceptions, the authority and power of all the mission evangelists rested on the threat of supernatural intervention and supernatural punishment rather than of direct force.

Police, evangelists, and "doctor boys" wanted people to settle in large villages where they could be more easily supervised and controlled. It was harder to keep an eye on small hamlets and dispersed huts, they said, and people who lived in that way were like wild pigs and dogs, not human beings. (From a local standpoint this was an issue on which people were especially sensitive to criticism.) Traditionally, the isolated huts scattered outside the palisaded settlements were sheltering places where people would spend only a night or so now and then while attending to gardens or pigs, or hiding from pursuit in "war time," or segregated because of sickness suspected of being contagious. But the coming of European control and the breaking down of palisades brought a corresponding increase in decentralization. The suppression of warfare was partly responsible, although sorcery fears counterbalanced it to some extent. Another reason was a desire to escape from official supervision, and particularly police supervision, with all that this was believed to imply. The tension between village concentration and dispersed dwellings reflected a dual trend, one that had traditional as well as contemporary relevance.

This was a time of transition. Formal control by the Australian administration extended through much of the region, except for the southern Fore, but apart from obvious features like the ban on warfare and cannibalism there was much confusion among the local people about its immediate implications. Misunderstandings and ambiguities were rife, regarding not only "what should be changed" but also the relative authority of those who were trying to bring this change about. Claims that the administration and missions were in complete accord were offset at times by clashes and disagreements. There were differences of opinion, competing interests, and conflicting loyalties. Rites of various kinds were still being performed in many districts. Betrothals were being arranged in traditional ways. Ceremonies and trade exchanges were taking place.

The cessation of warfare was recent enough for people to behave as if they were uncertain how long the new peace would last. And cannibalism was continuing, in partial secrecy, in the south.

At the end of 1951, in Kainantu, we read through patrol reports at the administration base to supplement what we had learned from the head office at Port Moresby. Apart from sometimes contradictory notes made by traveling patrols, there was little information on the area south of the Kamano villages, but all the patrol notes agreed that in that large area, barely mapped, the language went under the general label of Porei (Fore). During our week at Raipinka Lutheran mission station we were considering possibilities and exploring, tentatively, the social and cultural scene among the Kamano around Raipinka.

It was clear that language would be a major difficulty. None of these languages had been recorded beyond some initial work in Kamano on the part of a former Raipinka missionary. There were Pidgin English speakers among the Agarabi and Kamano near Kainantu, as well as people speaking the Lutheran lingua franca, Kâte, but none of them knew "Fore." In the villages around Raipinka, I could find only one Kamano-speaking woman who knew more than a few words of Pidgin English; she had once lived for a short time, she said, with one of the native police. In any case, she did not want to leave the Kamano language area. "Fore" territory was said to be dangerous, and travelers there could expect sorcery attacks at least, if not open violence. In the end, and in desperation, I agreed to having a male interpreter, provided that his newly married young wife came with him. (A youngish man with no accompanying wife could have been suspected, however wrongly, of wanting to find local sweethearts, causing some unrest among jealous local men.) Kaso was a serious "schoolboy," an adherent of the Lutheran church but still a junior in that hierarchy, who came from one of the southern Kamano districts. He had a sense of humor, was quick and perceptive, and throughout our association was more helpful than I had ever imagined he would be. His young wife, Eto, who knew no Pidgin, was helpful too, but rather overawed by the course of events as our journey proceeded.

R. M. Berndt's chapter outlines our dramatic journey to our unknown destination. I shall not repeat or add to that, except insofar as a personal comment is necessary. He has noted that I was obliged to travel on horseback. I had been on a horse only once before, when as a teenager I was induced to mount a horse bareback on an uncle's farm, my cousins set it galloping, and I somersaulted over its head. The point is that I could not display an accomplished standard of horsemanship, and in mounting and dismounting to accept the greetings and welcoming speeches of people assembled at various places along the way, I provided an entertaining spectacle. It was a case of mutual strangeness, if not mutual culture shock, and I am sure that the horse had a lot to do with the excitement of that journey for everyone concerned.

At last, preceded by a group of chanting men twanging their bow-strings as they advanced and retreated in unison, I saw from the top of a low ridge a crowd of shouting adults and children. Light rain was falling. Some women were digging feverishly at one side of a wide clearing beside the roadway. Nearby, men were excitedly finishing a house of native materials, thatched with *kunai*. But most of the crowd simply stood waiting noisily alongside the borders and surged forward triumphantly to clutch at us. We were told that men and women from neighboring districts had combined with the Kogu people, whose choice of a site for us had won the day. The village, Maira, was not Fore, after all; that was only a general name from a northern perspective. It belonged to the small, hitherto unrecorded language unit called Usurufa (Uturupa). But it was strategically situated. The nearest Kamano villages were about four hours' walk to the north, the Kemiyu-Yate about twenty minutes' walk to the west, and the so-called Fore about an hour to the south—with a refugee Fore group from Asafina only ten minutes' walk down the ridge to the east. In the days that followed, fresh visitors kept arriving to greet us. Many brought vegetables to sell. Others came empty-handed to look, listen, and comment. A crowd of adults and children refused to let us out of their sight, even to the extent of opening little eyeholes in the leafy walls of our house so that they could watch us by night as well as by day. There seemed to be no doubt of their interest and also their friendliness.

Many of the Kogu people spoke and understood Yate, and my husband concentrated on that. Also, many of them spoke and understood Kamano; I had already started working on this. There were no reliable Usurufa interpreters, and as a Kamano speaker had come with us from Raipinka, it seemed best to go on with that as a bridge between Pidgin English and Usurufa. We learned later that Usurufa speakers rarely, if ever, composed songs in their own language. If they wanted their songs to be taken up and spread through the region during *singsing*s (T.P., festivals), they had to use one of the languages of the larger populations surrounding them. At that early stage, however, their plans for us did not extend to teaching us their languages. They wanted to be able to speak with us, but they did not see why this should be a problem.

Broadly, they argued along three lines. First, as returning ghosts we should have no trouble in recapturing our father tongue now that we were back among our kin. Second, Europeans were so powerful and so skilled in magic that these "easy" languages would be a simple matter. Third, whatever else we did, our main role was to supply them with goods. We were to employ gangs of men in manual labor—roadwork, house building, fencing, and felling trees. Europeans at Kainantu seemed to be interested in that kind of thing, they said, and we should be, too. There were plenty of people to use the houses and roads, and so such projects could continue indefinitely, but of course we would have to finance them. They hoped we would buy all the vegetables they brought us. To ensure that, they were ready to dispose of the surplus themselves, preferably by selling it to us again. In any case, we were to provide a continuous flow of gifts. Because we were Europeans, we could replace everything we gave them almost immediately and at no cost to ourselves. The wet season gardens all over the region were producing far more than their owners could use. Men, forbidden to make war, were restless, with time on their hands. We seemed to represent an instant answer. They wanted the novel things they had heard of or seen, but did not know how to get them. The region south of Kainantu was not officially open to labor recruiting while we were there, as the Goroka area was. Individual men from the northern villages had volunteered for it, but people in the south had limited access to such things.

They had high expectations, and the atmosphere of tense excitement that surrounded our arrival reflected their conviction that something new and different was happening. Inevitably, we disappointed them. We had nothing like the resources we would have needed to cope with even a fraction of what they wanted. Nor did we have the resources to move to a less complicated, less demanding area, as we were half-tempted to do when we began to realize what a difficult situation we had been caught up in.

"Getting there" is more than a matter of physical arrival at a place. In another dimension it is almost like the beginning of a journey, with a destination that is less specifically defined and the paths less clearly visible. Being in a strange environment with a minimum of cultural bridges and verbal clues to communication is always a frustrating experience; being physically present but otherwise remote, on the outer fringes of under-standing—an intolerable state of affairs for an anthropologist!

BEING THERE

After the singing and dancing and exuberant greetings we settled down for our first, rather unsettled, night's sleep. Next morning there was a great deal of commotion all around the village, especially around our house. We were told that the house was not safe: it was surrounded by too many tall trees that might fall on it during lightning storms. Before the trees could be cut down, as they should be, all our things would have to be moved out of the house for safety. So our boxes and other belong-ings were stacked about in the clearing, and I spent the day mostly sitting among them, surrounded all the time by people greeting me, and looking at what we had. They had not been able to assess that properly the day before, in the turmoil of our arrival. Now, some of them (I was told) renewed their assurance that they would soon be building the huge storehouse that we would surely need for all the goods we were going to get for them. I did my best to note down the names and other details (places, language affiliations, and so on) of the people who were speaking to me, along with what they were saying, but it was a very preliminary effort, and the noise and constant crowd movements would have made recording difficult even with mechanical aids. At last the crashing of tree trunks stopped, our boxes were moved back into the house, and some of the crowd began to melt away.

Next day another obstacle emerged, this time in regard to having women as teachers and guides. None of the women in the area spoke or understood Pidgin English. I was told indirectly that women were suspicious and afraid of Europeans. (So, to a lesser extent, were men who had not visited Kainantu or had direct contact with them.) That did not prevent women from embracing me enthusiastically, especially on first meeting. It was part of the local scheme of things. In peace ceremonies, for instance, a show of goodwill said nothing about the intentions of the participants, who might very well be planning further hostilities. (Some women told me later that they had discovered I had "soft hands, like a man's," whereas their palms were rough and scaly from continuous gardening.) Also, in those first exuberant meetings, several women were able to pull out single hairs from my head and wrap them carefully around their fingers; they were taking them home to show the people there who could not come to the spectacle themselves.

Watching from a little way off or being an anonymous figure in a crowd was safe enough. Being singled out individually for closer and more prolonged association was not: "We might die!" What was more, the men strongly opposed the idea that women could help me in learning the local languages, or in anything else except growing and selling vegetables. It was not so much that "women's place was in the gardens." One reason was that men wanted to keep these dangerous and potentially profitable contacts with the outside world in their own hands. To them, such contacts were men's business. They were encouraged in that view because I came with a male interpreter. Even when that hurdle was overcome, the problem of "danger" remained. Except for interpreters' wives, the first women who were willing to talk to me beyond an exchange of greetings were wary and nervous. They anxiously chewed special leaves to protect themselves, and a couple of them were trembling with fright. It seemed best to avoid for the time being any but more or less impersonal subjects. Genealogies, case histories, or even a preliminary attempt at a census, were suspect.

SORTING OUT PROCEDURES

To begin with, therefore, I decided to spend most of this formal recording time on "stories," *kinihera* (see below). I had already made a start on these at Raipinka. This was simply a matter of expediency. They were a convenient means of learning the language and at the same time making friends. It was only when I already had a fairly large number of them that their most interesting features began to emerge in perspective—perhaps because by that time they were no longer a central topic. In the course of discussions in which I emphasized my intention of working with women, not men, I recorded two short *kinihera* from men, and later several others from the Kamano interpreters, but the great majority were told to me by women.

In our Australian Aboriginal fieldwork, whenever we had our own camp I attended to cooking and food preparation without local help except for firewood and sometimes water. In the Eastern Highlands I evaded most of these domestic tasks. The two teenage boys (see R. M. Berndt's chapter), who spoke no Pidgin English but were sure they could cope if they were told what to do, were eagerly determined to handle all such affairs, and we were told it was our duty to employ them. I was pleased that they, not I, would be the ones to scramble up and down the slippery tracks to the stream to fill the long bamboo containers with water, to keep the open fire burning to cook our vegetables on the coals, and to deal with all the produce we could not avoid acquiring. We had a minimum of utensils to care for: enamel mugs and plates, billycans, and so on. (A well-equipped patrol visiting our place on one occasion gave the impression that we were "letting the side down.") "What happened in the cook-house" could be a story in itself, but without those two boys I would not have been able to do much systematic research.

The total population of the five Kogu villages was less than 220, but almost every day, morning and afternoon, people from neighboring districts would visit Maira. Some came laden with vegetables to sell to us, others merely to see what was going on. During ceremonies the crowd was much larger. It was evident that just through being there we were having an unsettling effect, not only on Maira but also on the whole area.

It was impossible to talk more than casually with the great majority of women I met. There were so many. I therefore relied heavily on several who spent most of their time with me. In Kogu during our first stay there were thirteen-plus. In our second fieldwork period there were fifteen to twenty at Kogu, and eight-plus at Busarasa-Moke. I kept the number fairly small in order to establish a continuing relationship and, I hoped, get to know them in more than a superficial way. There were others I talked with less often, in different circumstances, who sometimes joined this group. They provided further links with the transient informal contacts represented by most of the local and visiting women. During such periods of formal recording (in writing), unweaned children up to about three or four years old stayed with their mothers. Any women, from any district, who wished to do so were welcome to join us provided they kept quiet enough for me to hear what was being said. This was a necessary proviso. People who were used to shouting from one hilltop hamlet to another could sound very loud indeed in an enclosed space during animated conversations.

Women came and went, attending to their domestic affairs and discussing current events. I concentrated quite strenuously on learning enough Kamano and Usurufa to talk with them—very clumsily at first, inviting corrections—and to understand what they said to me and to one another. Vocabulary lists and formal recording of narrative material helped a great deal. But to sort out the specific meanings and the proper framing of some words, especially verb forms, I focused on these in short sessions of about an hour or so each day, looking at them in a variety of speech contexts and clarifying their use. Because Kamano was my main medium, I became much more familiar with this than with Usurufa. The two languages differed to some extent in structure as well as in vocabulary. I tried to overcome this by using Usurufa directly as much as possible, and later with increasing confidence. Apart from group sessions, I was able to practice while walking about the neighborhood with a few of the women, meeting a wide range of people during ceremonies and other gatherings in and around Maira, and watching from the outskirts the fights, informal court scenes, and other highlights of ordinary life in the area.

I worked in much the same way when we returned to Maira the following wet season. Again I had a male interpreter, because I thought I needed someone to keep check on interpretations as well as translations. He was also a southern Kamano man with Lutheran affiliations, quiet and interested in words and languages and in his own traditional background. His wife had no command of Pidgin English, but she spoke some of northern Fore as well as her own language, Kamano. For this second visit, the Kogu people and their Usurufa neighbors had built us a new and larger house and tried hard to prevent us, and above all our goods, from leaving the district. Nevertheless, this time we spent only six weeks with them.

Our second base was half a day's walk farther south, in Fore territory but still quite close to the Yate—in this case, Ke'yagana. It was at Pintagori in Busarasa, almost on the boundary with Moke.[3] The combined population of Busarasa and Moke was approximately four hundred, mainly in small dispersed hamlets. Other large districts adjoined, and a few yards away began the restricted area that stretched south to the Papuan border. The people here, as the Usurufa and northern Fore had warned us, were timid and wary. Many of them resented the new administrative road-making drive. They complained that it not only interfered with their gardening and pig festivals but had already led to a number of deaths from sorcery. Interdistrict hostility flared up from time to time in accusations and counteraccusations of sorcery, and in fights, and they gloomily prophesied further deaths.

Here, too, fear of the dangers stemming from contact with Europeans brought a few difficulties at first. Some of the men had met us or seen us already, when curiosity led them to Kogu during our first period there. Others had heard of us, and seemed friendly. Nevertheless, there was now a new language to learn; I had been able to do only preliminary work on it before. As usual, I began with formal recording (again, in writing; we still had no tape recorders at that time) in order to communicate directly with the local women. Usurufa was not spoken or understood here. Yate had a wider currency, but the Kamano range was narrow and had mission overtones. To begin with, I used as medium a mixture of Kamano and Yate, which both my interpreters knew. In the circumstances it was the only way of obtaining, fairly quickly, a working knowledge of Fore. Later, during a short stay at Taramu (Ke'yagana Yate), I concentrated mainly on individually composed songs dealing with events in everyday life.

Most of the material I recorded formally in Kogu and in Busarasa was in Kamano, Usurufa, or Fore and occasionally in Yate, with interlinear translations. Nearly all of it took place in a group environment. This meant that women were able to settle down more easily in the company of people they knew. Secrecy, or "hidden talking," had a negative connotation outside the spheres of religion and warfare. It was often associated with sorcery. Also, "private" quarrels rapidly became public property. So a group atmosphere probably had a less stifling effect on discussion than it would in a situation where privacy was highly valued. One person's account of an incident was open to on-the-spot checking by others who had witnessed it or participated in it. They might interrupt or argue out their differences, or put forward their own versions at other times when the first speaker was not present. There were plenty of opportunities for confidential accounts, as well as for informal sessions when I took rough notes or simply listened and wrote up the material later (or tried to find time to do that!). These groups provided some scope for observation, too, within a rather limited range. After their first hesitation, the women came to treat the working part of our house as their own during the time they spent in it. They cooked sweet potatoes and cobs of maize on the open fire, made new shredded bark skirts, or worked on netted twine bags. Children played and fought and were scolded and petted, and women gossiped and joked in the intervals of formal recording. This communal atmosphere also was appropriate to the telling of *kinihera*.

I supplemented formal recording with firsthand observation over a much wider field. This covered not only such spectacular occasions as ceremonies and rituals, informal court cases, and fights, but also numerous small-scale incidents involving, particularly, interpersonal behavior of various kinds. It was a slow but absorbing process.

LEARNING ABOUT MYTH, DRAMA, AND SONGS

The basic mythology mentioned in R. M. Berndt's chapter accounted for contrasts between northern and southern peoples, and between local people and Europeans. It also accounted for women's as well as men's religious ritual sequences. Women told me a great deal about these, including their blood-drawing rites, and I witnessed some of them. Another kind of ritual that the main creative characters introduced was the telling of stories, *kinihera* in Kamano. Ideally they should be told in a special house at the beginning of the rainy season, around an oven of edible leaves, to encourage the growth of garden crops. The link between storytelling and garden fertility was strongest when a person, on his or her own ground, was telling a story directly associated with that place. But at such gatherings anyone with a story to tell was at liberty to do so—men or women. That was one way in which stories spread.

Some stories contained songs that were said to be *kinihera* songs, not composed by human beings. Other songs were made by living human beings, on a tremendously wide range of topics. These were sung casually by people moving about the villages or in their gardens, but the most popular were taken up and sung by groups of men and women parading about the ceremonial ground on *singsing* occasions. Such occasions were also the scene of *krina* (in Kamano), dramatic enactments of various kinds (see C. H. Berndt 1959), which were sometimes based on *kinihera* themes and sometimes on actual or hearsay events among human beings.

My life at Maira and later at Pintagori became absorbed in all of these happenings and discussions. Their crosscutting themes and the range of variations and similarities were endlessly fascinating. In this chapter, I thought it best not to attempt any kind of complete coverage, but to look briefly at a few examples. In each case, I noted the name of the storyteller, the date of telling, and other relevant details.

Stories about relations between men and women in general, and specifically between, for example, husbands and wives or brothers and sisters, were numerous, as were co-wife stories. The example below is a little

different. It was an Anonana story (a Kogu district) combining punishment and erotic humor. The storyteller was Maiino, who said she had first
heard it as a small girl from her mother. The women sitting around the
fire as she told it listened attentively, clutching at one another with
screams of laughter as she described the victim's predicament.

> They made houses and lived there, got vegetables, and cooked them. This
> woman here cooked food and called to her husband, "Come and get sweet
> potato!" A despised [*kefo*] man came and got it, gave it to him, and he ate.
> Another woman cooked food and called to her husband, "Come and get
> sweet potato!" This despised man came and got it, gave it to him, and he
> ate. [The episode was repeated for four more women, three with sweet
> potato and one with sweet potato and *hefara* leaves.] That's how it was.
>
> The women complained, "We get and cook vegetables for our husbands
> and keep saying to them, 'Come and get it! Come inside the house and get
> it!' Why do you, this man, come and get it and take it to them? Are their
> legs broken, that you do this?" They asked their husbands, "Why do you
> all stay away? And as for this despised man, you've started something
> different here!"
>
> They went to the edge of the water, the good water at Meki, and there
> they stopped and lay down in a row. They had got that despised man and
> put him there, too. The women were all in their finery, lying there in a row;
> and he had intercourse with them all, one after another, down the row.
> When he came to the water's edge he stopped to rest, then started again,
> stopped to rest, then started again. His buttocks were broken ("loose") and
> his "eyes were round." He stopped altogether. The eldest "sister" of all the
> women plucked healing nettle leaves and gave him a massage, and warmed
> him by the fire; he was put into his house. The eldest "sister" went there,
> and warmed him by the fire, but he died.
>
> "We cooked food, ready, and called out to our husbands. You despised
> man, you're not to come and get it and take it to them. If they have ears,
> they can come inside and they will eat. You yourself brought this about!"
> they said. "You did this, and so you die."
>
> They took him from where their eldest "sister" had put him, they went,
> and they buried him. They said to her, "You put him there, you came and
> got nettles and gave him a massage, and you warmed him . . ." She remained
> for a time, then she died. Her brother[s] went and buried her, they all
> buried her.
>
> What the story did, may that remain. "In future, if a man's wife has
> cooked vegetables ready for him, he can freely come, get them, and eat!"
> [he] said. [He] cut *tazítazófa* crotons, planted them that way and this way,
> at Uvata Hill. Thus the story!

Although the story seems to imply that the eldest "sister" died because
she had helped the victim, the storyteller insisted that nobody took steps
to bring this about: "She was just sick, herself—she was a *kinihe* woman!"
For the storyteller and for the others who were listening, the nature of

the punishment followed logically from the man's own actions. A husband accepts food from his wife: this is one indication and one criterion of their marriage (see R. M. Berndt 1962:128–129). The despised man deputized for the women's husbands, putting himself in their place, and so they forced him to accept the sexual implication of the relationship as well. Here the wives did not bring the food to the men's house, as was often done in everyday life. Instead, they called the husbands to their own houses to eat the meals they had prepared. This anticipates the climax of the story: an invitation to a man, other than a close relative, to enter a woman's house could have only one connotation—and so could his acceptance. Conversely, rejection of a "lawful" offer of food would be taken as a slight, as a gesture of antagonism or at least of unfriendliness. The neglectful husbands were not punished, but simply admonished, yet the threat was there: "women can retaliate," and a man should not ignore his wife if he wants their relationship to endure.

Despised people, *kefo* people, were a target of jokes and abuse in everyday life. What has been called "banana peel" humor was well established locally. A misfortune or accident that made someone else look foolish would be talked about with enjoyment around the house-fires at night or dramatized in *krina*. Sayings and doings of children were repeated with laughter, too.

Everyday life appeared to provide much more scope for humor than the *kinihera*, but the *kinihera* did mirror, although imperfectly, the range of subject matter that people found amusing. The *kinihera* did not make much of the ridicule-shame combination that was used as a weapon in social control, especially in the informal courts, although the basis for it was there. But it was the dramatic ceremonial scenes, the *krina*, that provided the main vehicle for humor, in a social setting that was oriented toward entertainment. The moral lessons that were more or less implicit in these were, instead, spelled out in the *kinihera*. In this sense the two complemented each other. In the same way, the "contemporary" songs supplied a running commentary, sentimental and usually serious, on an assortment of crises, small and large.

SETTING A PRECEDENT

Aside from the immediate object of garden fertility, a major aim in the *kinihera* was said to be the instruction of children. In discussing the conventional telling of *kinihera* in a traditional setting, women (and men) were emphatic about this purpose—the passing on of information and, above all, of precepts and rules. It was not simply that *kinihera* were used in the teaching context of initiation, but rather that *kinihera* in general had this orientation. They were seen as a link between generations. In many instances the time of first hearing a story was reported as childhood, from about five to about nine or ten years old, although that was evidently not enough for recall, and certainly not for detailed recall, without later reinforcement and amplification. And the penalty, apparently the only one, associated with "letting the sun hear the *kinihera*" was the growth of body hair on children: the threat of too early physical, and perhaps emotional, maturity.

Nevertheless, the *kinihera* were obviously directed at adults as much as at children. In this they resembled the ordinary blood-letting and purifying rites, which were age-grading devices for the young but routine procedures for adults as well. Only the charcoal-initiation rite, confined to boys, was an exception. There were no stories designed specifically or solely for children. Nor were there children's versions of ordinary stories, modified in regard to language or plot. Like the *krina*, and in fact like social living in general, the same material served both. Children would play among themselves away from adults, but other than that there seemed to be no readily distinguishable children's subculture. Even the few songs said to be composed by children could not be identified as such on the basis of structure or content alone.

One assumption seemed to be that very small children were too young to understand what adults did not want them to understand. Another was that older children, who were excluded only from the secret rites of men and women respectively, would learn whatever they needed to know for later life without having material slanted expressly in their direction and labeled "for children." (In effect, "once they are old enough to understand, let them do so.")

Certainly more than a few *kinihera* included fairly unambiguous models for children to follow—or avoid: a little girl avenges her mother's death at the hands of an old man; a boy rescues his father who has been swallowed by a huge python; another boy tries in vain to warn his grandfather of a cassowary attack; because a small boy keeps pestering his mother, she goes off and leaves him; a greedy boy is drowned by his elder brother; a girl who killed and ate her elder sister's baby is herself killed; two brothers who stole taro are killed or commit suicide. As against this it could be argued that the *kinihera* offer just as many "undesirable" models, showing children who have behaved badly but received no punishment at all, and others who meet with misfortune and death despite their good behavior.

In any case, in line with the forward-looking local orientation where children were concerned, the implication was that it was more important for them to prepare for what lay ahead than to dwell on models that had only passing relevance. Childhood was seen as a transient phase. Once boys had left their mothers' houses to live with male kin they were expected to concentrate on preparation for adult living. Girls at puberty were young adults, marriageable if they were not already living with their husbands. Adorning small children with armbands and necklets of dried pig genitalia or pig skin was one of a number of ways, magical and otherwise, of urging on their growth (see R. M. Berndt 1962:90–91).

Although there was much in the *kinihera* that could be drawn upon by and for children, very few of the maxims were explicitly framed in terms of what children, as such, should do. One exception was the general directive, "Don't steal from gardens." Another declares that a small boy is not to "answer back" to a big man. In a Kogu story from Zava and Tono, a little bush spirit boy eats the babies he has been minding. The maxim urges, "If your elder sister gives you a child to mind, look after it properly while she works in the garden so she can get it again afterward." An example advising unmarried girls not to bear children obviously belongs in the broader sphere of "looking ahead to puberty and adulthood."

The fact that nearly all the maxims I recorded were addressed to adults was not because there were no children in the audience. It is true that for most of the time, during these formal storytelling sessions, four-year-olds were about the oldest who were allowed to stay. Others were discouraged from playing too close. But that alone would not have prevented the women from orienting the maxims toward children. The overall range of the *kinihera, krina,* and the dramatic scenes staged as part of the initiation of boys, all gave the impression of concentrating on behavior appropriate to adults. The maxims attached to many of the *kinihera* are a good indication of this.

Generally speaking, the good example was not singled out for special comment but simply implied, or mentioned quite casually. In that way the *kinihera* underlined the noncontroversial "realities" of local life. Some features were not taken up for negative comment. The maxims did not say, "People are not to cultivate gardens," "Widows are not to hang themselves," or "Men are not to work sorcery." (In one *kinihera* a group of men declared that *women* were not to do so, that sorcery was men's work.) For the story of a pregnant woman killed by sorcerers, the maxim is not "Do not work sorcery" but "If you are killed by sorcery lie down and die [and don't molest other people]."

The pattern of proper and praiseworthy behavior in the domestic sphere that was most often cited in other contexts was rarely crystallized into maxims. Whatever excitements and adventures punctuate the *kinihera,* and whatever else they do from time to time, there is a substratum of routine in which husbands and wives work in their gardens and share the produce, rear pigs, and bear and rear children. Outside the *kinihera,*

too, numerous statements remark on the virtues of conformity in that
direction. This is one of them:

> Marai had been talking about her own experiences, ending with her
> marriage to a widower—against the advice of his sister. He married her, she
> said, as a matter of convenience to himself, on the understanding that the
> arrangement would lapse if she proved unsatisfactory or if he found an-
> other wife he liked better. At the time she told about this she had been with
> him for about 6 or 7 years. Her final remarks, in a raised voice, were
> directed at the other women present, and they listened in silence, their eyes
> on the ground. "I've behaved properly with this man. I've borne children,
> made gardens, given food to everyone so that they ate. I've made ovens. I've
> borne children and reared pigs—and you all say I'm a promiscuous woman!
> Promiscuous women don't know how to look after gardens and pigs and
> children. And yet you all talked against me!"
>
> Marai had brought up the same features in another account where they
> were interpreted as dangerous, as well as commendable. A Kogu woman
> married in Ifusa [Fore] was said to have been killed by sorcerers from Amufi
> [Yate] just because she approximated the ideal. She made gardens, bore
> children, tended pigs, and was generous in distributing food: "And Amufi
> men, looking at her, said, 'Here is a good woman. We will kill her.' "

In other words, as several examples show, a woman who made herself
conspicuous even through good behavior might expect to be "rewarded"
by some sort of unpleasant attention. She could be a target for hostility,
much more so than if she conformed in a more modest and unassuming
way. For some women, local prestige counterbalanced this threat, especially since in the great majority of deaths attributed to warfare and
sorcery conspicuousness does not seem to have been very important:
district membership was apparently much more significant than personal
reputation. But in times of stress the threat was more immediate. Women
from the region south of Busarasa (Fore) early in 1953, when interdistrict
fighting was in progress, went so far as to avoid wearing any finery at
ceremonies on the grounds that these might attract the eyes of sorcerers,
who would surely kill them.

In other *kinihera* the good example, the positive precedent, is summed
up in a command that sets the human and natural world in the right
perspective: "Bird, you fly about. Human being, you stay on the ground!"
"Fungus [listing the varieties], in rain-time we people will come and get
you. You're food for us!" Or it is underlined by spelling out what *not* to
do and putting negative and positive commands together: "Man, don't
copulate with bananas but with women!" Or two precedent-statements
are made simultaneously from opposing standpoints, as in the story of a
man married to a shape-changing *wanume*-girl: the husband and his kin
insist that *wanume* are small animals, to be hunted, killed and eaten, while

the girl's kin say resentfully that human beings will never again be welcome among them. And so on. After a man has been attacked by a hostile
creature or a ghost, the maxims interpose a barrier between these events
and everyday human life. They reassure, or exhort, or affirm that this is
not to happen again: "Human being, you can go to the bush and come
back safely." "Wild pigs, you are not to destroy gardens. And men, you
can kill wild pigs!"

But the conventional form of the *kinihera*, their concern with "what *not*
to do," means that the messages they conveyed were less straightforward
than those in the basic mythology. Even a creation myth presented in this
framework is negatively oriented, followed by the maxim that women are
not to give birth to anything but human beings. Another maxim about
edible fungus puts it in this way: "Man, this kind of thing is food. Don't
say, 'Don't eat, it's not food.' It *is* food."

Whether or not a narrator supplied a maxim in these storytelling
sessions seemed to rest on personal choice. A maxim was an appendage
to a story, a drawing-out of implications, rather than an intrinsic part of
the action. This choice did not extend to the negative pronouncement
which conventionally concluded each *kinihera*, and the accompanying rite
of croton planting that sealed or closed off the events within it. On one
occasion a Yate man who spoke Pidgin English added his own translation
of the customary formula: "*Dispela samting pinis, em i no ken kamap moa!*"
("This is a thing of the past, it must not happen again!") The *kinihera*
characters behaved in one way, human beings are to behave in another:
the "bad example" is to be avoided, not imitated. Nevertheless, actual
behavior inevitably diverged in varying degrees from the ideal, and often
it coincided with the pattern described as wrong. In this sense the "bad
example" could be taken to indicate "what does happen, although it
shouldn't." It is doubtful how far this was acknowledged, but probably
only in isolated instances and not by people in general. Kaso articulated
it once. After listening to a woman telling the story of the wife-who-
danced-and-neglected-her-husband's-dinner, he commented laughingly: "That's what we do. When there is singing and dancing we can't keep
away. We go, even if we're cooking food, and when we come back the food
is spoiled!"

Some of the *kinihera* are straightforward, directly intelligible in their
comments on the local situation. Among them are symbolic statements
that were more or less common currency or could fairly readily be "translated." "Men are not to be *wayafa* birds," says one maxim, but, perhaps
because the creative being Morufonu once took that shape, men were
often referred to in this way in song. "A vulva is not a full moon," says
another, but in conversation and song the two continued to be identified.
Arrows and sugarcane were commonly spoken of as phallic symbols, and

crotons had many and varied associations. The story of the man-who-removed-his-skin-while-hunting-and-deceived-his-wife, and others like it, could be interpreted in the light of conventional hostility between men and women. In other cases the content of a myth, as a "set of signs," cannot so easily be related to everyday reality.

"Sealing off" the actions of their characters suggests the need for constant renewal of ritual pronouncements against them; this sustains the "pattern for misconduct," simultaneously reinforcing both types of precedent. Moreover, just because these negative pronouncements can be applied so vaguely and loosely, and because (as in everyday life) the bad example is so closely mixed with the good, there is room for differences in interpretation of the rules and precedents laid down in the *kinihera* as a whole. As a set of symbols, they do not "speak for themselves." Their meanings and their practical significance must be elucidated: they are not fixed, but open to change as circumstances alter around them.

At the time of this study, direct contact with the outside world was too recent for the effects to be noticeable in the *kinihera*, but they were certainly a ready-made vehicle for expressing and transmitting "alien" norms. This was illustrated in two stories dealing with the origin of cannibalism.

On December 17, 1951, early in our first period of fieldwork, Eto, a young Kamano woman, gave a short and rather cursory Grufe version:

> There was a cave beside a large stand of bamboo, and whenever a man died they used to put him in there. [But the bodies always disappeared.] So, one day they put a living man in there too—a despised man, a *kefo* man. Men hid, in ambush, outside the cave, ready with sticks and with bows and arrows. An old bush spirit man came and poked the living man—not "ripe" yet! Then he poked the corpse, but as he was about to eat it the men rushed in and killed him.

Eto's husband, Kaso, translated the story, adding the maxim, "In future we will bury them, men will dig holes in the ground (and bury the dead, not eat them)." This was consistent with Kaso's general approach. In other stories that ended with the killing and eating of a bush spirit or a man, Kaso in translating used to add his own comment in Pidgin English, which none of the local women understood: in effect, "Those who had not heard the Word ate both man and pig. Those who had heard the Word left the man and ate only the pig." This statement was confusing until I had learned enough Kamano to discuss it and identify it as Kaso's own contribution.

On December 30, 1952, when Kaso and Eto were no longer with us, Tava gave a Viteve version of the same story localized at Moruravezyaka. Tava said she had first heard it as an unmarried girl from her father, who

had heard it first from his mother. It was longer and more detailed than
Eto's:

> The old bush spirit had many sons. Whenever a corpse [a "ripe banana"]
> was put in the cave, he would prick it in the chest with a sharp stick to test
> its "ripeness," and when it was ready his sons would cut lengths of bamboo
> to cook the flesh in, dancing and singing, "Cut this bamboo, cut that
> bamboo!" ["*irontafei arontafei*"; *tafe* means "bamboo"]. Then they would eat,
> leaving only bones. [This happened every time.]
>
> Another man was killed [shot], and they put him there, and they kept
> watch. Next time, a living man went with the corpse.
>
> The old white-haired man came and his "line" of huge-headed sons
> came, and again they cut lengths of bamboo and put them down: "Let's cook
> it!" But the living man killed them all: he killed the old man and all his sons,
> and put all the boys together in a heap. "We come and give people to the
> ground and you eat them, finish them completely. 'What's happening?' we
> ask. You started this!" he said. He went away, slept, and [next day] came
> back and looked: bush beads protruded from the old man's anus, and he
> lay there in the shape of a pig. Instead of the heap of dead boys, there was
> a heap of dead pigs. He went to kill the old man's pigs, made an oven and
> cooked them, and cooked the old man [and his sons].
>
> Tava, who had been at Maira when Eto gave her version, included at this
> point the same comment: some people ate both man and pig; those who
> "had heard" ate only pig. But she added: "We men [people], we cut and eat
> men. If [someone] says, 'I'll give him to the ground, don't eat,' we bury him
> in the ground, [like] *tugefa* [garden magic, a word used also for prehistoric
> stones]. If [someone] says, 'It's all right, you can cut him and eat him,' we
> do that. The *kinihera* did it, and we eat."

This suggests that the *kinihera* can take a negative stand on features that
may not have been presented in that light in the past. But there seems to
have been a fair measure of choice, traditionally, in regard to the disposal
of nonenemy dead. Genealogies and case material suggest that, despite
disagreements in individual cases, eating and burial were equally favored
(see R. M. Berndt 1962:chap. 13). In other words, there was a traditional
precedent for opposing the eating of the dead, or at least supporting the
alternative procedure. Opinion was less flexible on another feature that
was outlawed by the Australian administration—interdistrict fighting,
which appears to have been universally approved in a much more positive
sense. In fact, up to the time we left the area the official ban on warfare
was not reflected in any *kinihera* maxims.

In northern Kamano districts, biblical stories, especially from the Old
Testament, had supplanted the *kinihera* as a collective rite, but not otherwise. *Kinihera* were still told informally there, and could very well have
begun to absorb something of the content of these new stories. Probably
the main reason the *kinihera* were not being used as a medium of change

was simply that evangelists and other agents of the new order either were unaware of their potential, or regarded them as too integral a part of the local culture to be usefully encouraged. They occasionally drew on *krina*, however, in performances deliberately arranged to show "what people should not do" (see C. H. Berndt 1959:180–181). Among their targets in these performances were fighting and sorcery; but because *krina* interpretation was flexible, too, the "bad examples" they dramatized were taken by some spectators to include ordinary gardening practices as well. Because of their potential, however, it seemed possible that both *krina* and *kinihera* could very well survive into the future and reappear in modified or diluted form—as compact statements ostensibly focusing on what should not be done, but at the same time, and at least as much, pointing to more positive precedents.

Going Away, Coming Back

When we went away at the end of our first research period, the Kogu people and their neighbors told us confidently that they expected to see us again before the next wet season. And of course we did go back (see R. M. Berndt's chapter). In the interval, I checked carefully through my notebooks, looking for anything that seemed to need clarifying or amplifying, compiling lists of questions and comments, and working at Kamano and Usurufa; my Fore notes were only preliminary then.

Back at Kainantu and Raipinka, we spent four days in and around that neighborhood. We discussed local conditions with the retiring assistant district commissioner and were able to bring up to date our notes from official records, especially patrol reports. There had been cargo cult "trouble" in "our" area while we were away, and some patrol activity in regard to it. Most of the Agarabi and northern Kamano men were still reluctant to go south into "dangerous" regions of sorcery and fighting. Word was sent south to Kogu, and before long a group of men came hurrying to Raipinka, singing with pleasure because their special source of trade goods had returned.

We noticed some changes almost straightaway. The assistant district commissioner at Kainantu during our first visit had been opposed to the construction of large interdistrict roads in the region. He contended that the southern people were not ready for such developments. His two successors, however, thought otherwise. There was a tremendous burst of activity in road and bridge making, except in the officially restricted region. "Native police" were going to and fro, as far south as Busarasa-Moke. On our first visit we had been accustomed to hearing the sacred flutes night after night and often during the day as well, sounding from our own or neighboring districts. This time the flutes were almost silent, heard only on rare occasions and then only in one or two districts. One reason, people said, was the presence of so many "native police," eager to share in any pigs killed at such times. Related to that was conscription for roadwork, and the breaking up of initiation and other rituals when the flutes were normally played. "Native evangelists," mainly from the coast, attached to the Lutheran and Seventh-Day Adventist missions, preached against these and proclaimed that sickness or disaster would overtake anyone who did not abandon the cult of the flutes. They were more active and more numerous in the north than in the southern districts, and our interpreters, being more junior and also more locally oriented, were less obviously single-minded.

As we came through the southern Kamano districts, the atmosphere of our journey was again one of busy excitement, but not nearly as tense as before—and without the almost-larger-than-life intrusion of a horse. This time, the crowds of welcoming women were less unrestrained in their embraces. For me, the most positive and pleasurable part of this reintroduction to the region was not so much that we already knew something about it, nor even that I recognized some of the people who had visited Kogu for ceremonies or for selling vegetables. It was that I could manage well enough with Kamano to understand roughly what they were saying, and to speak to them if in a simple and rather clumsy way. Nearing the top of a steep incline, for instance, I was able to tell them, "I'm pausing for breath!" (*"haha-huwei!"*), and to understand when the women nearest me told me kindly, "You pause for breath!" (*"haha-hanei!"*) and called out to tell others farther away who asked what was happening (*"haha-hiyei!"*). When I was immobilized by the pressure of the crowds on such a steep incline, I could say, in effect, "All right, if you want me to move up the hill, pull me and push me!" And, laughingly, they did.

On the second day's walk from Raipinka, as we approached our old "home" at Maira the crowds gathered to welcome us almost in silence. The women who had helped me most were waiting in the forefront. They stood back while one of them who had been almost the first to speak with me, and the most frightened, came forward with outstretched arms, gesturing toward her dirty bark skirt, her matted hair and torn net bag, with one of the English words she had learned from me in the course of translations during our first visit: "Widow!" (She was not a song composer, and she always had trouble in organizing her stories and narratives, so that other women sometimes got impatient with her. But she had an interest in words and verb forms and would listen eagerly to the course of discussion and translation. She was puzzled at first that one Kamano word, *agona*, could be translated into English as either "hill, mountain" or "nose," but she quickly pointed out that they had something in common. And she was patient and conscientious in going over series of verb categories, in Kamano as well as Usurufa.)

This time at Maira I was overwhelmed with women wanting to become regular "full-time" members of the group, as contrasted with those joining in casual discussions. I tried to limit the number to twenty, but even that was really too many. Some of them complained that they did not have enough opportunities to tell me all they wanted. A number of them had interesting items of news they had been keeping for my return. Others had *kinihera* which they said nobody had yet told me, or incidents from their own life histories, and so on. Most of the women were with me all day (except Sundays, when, as R. M. Berndt has noted in his chapter, anyone who wanted could ask us questions or talk about anything *they* wanted to talk about). They could bring their youngest children or grandchildren, and occasionally others as well. It was one situation in which writing had an advantage over a tape recorder! The background noise would have been formidable. As it was, I could at least single out or join in or observe especially interesting items of discussion or behavior: "red herrings," perhaps, but useful leads to be followed up later.

As usual, and later at Pintagori, these solid talk (plus observation) sessions were interrupted by such diversions as fights, informal courts, ceremonies (*singsings*), visits to the gardens, greeting visitors, and so on. The days and evenings became packed even more tightly as the time for our departure drew closer. There were long discussions, as women tried to persuade me that Maira was the place for us, not the southern "enemy" districts where there was no defense against the most lethal kinds of sorcery.

I had hoped that one Usurufa woman in particular would be willing to come with us. During our first period at Maira she looked in sometimes or even joined the main group for a while, and I met her occasionally at ceremonies or around the village. But she was always busy, a thin, quick-tempered, and lively person, an organizer: rearing and exchanging small pigs, arranging betrothals and bridewealth payments, and doing a host of other things. She was knowledgeable, too; in many respects other women deferred to her. ("We'll ask Zava, she knows.") She was highly articulate, a composer of individual songs, with a flair for words. As I found out when she told me two *kinihera* (saying these were the only ones she knew) and talked about a couple of incidents in her own life, she was a superb raconteur and knew exactly how to shape narrative material to achieve maximum effect. And she was fluent in Kamano, Yate, and northern Fore as well as in her own language, Usurufa (but not Pidgin English). She knew that I was trying to learn everything I could about the local situation and about people's own views of their lives in that situation—*and* that, according to some of the women, they were trying to help me to remember what I myself must have known in a former life there (see R. M. Berndt's chapter).

One day I asked her if she would spend some time in helping me. She looked at me sharply, considering. Eventually she agreed that she would come as often as she could. She spent more and more time with our group, commenting on what the other women said, and playing a major part when it came to religious rituals and *singsing*s and healing rituals, as well as talking about them. She knew, also, a wide range of *kinihera*, shrugging off with a laugh her first denial of this. However, although she had been to Busarasa and Moke, she would not come with us. It was sure death, she asserted, to spend any length of time there, even for not-quite-human beings like us. (She was in the group one afternoon when the sky darkened in a violent thunderstorm. As lightning flashed all around, and some high trees burst into flames, at each loud crash the women uttered shrill, almost formalized, cries. I admitted, eventually, that I was frightened, too. But she and the others would not accept that. They gathered closer to me, laughing incredulously: "No, no! You [you plural] make [are responsible for] this sort of thing!" There were plenty of other such examples, too. One related to the so-called cargo cult. It was a great surprise to us, when we returned to Maira, to find that quite a large number of husbands and wives had abandoned their strict rule of living in separate houses. All questions of "Why this sudden change?" brought the same answer: "You two shared the same living-house, and look at all the things you have! If we copy you, if we do as you do, we will have such things, too!")

On our last afternoon in Maira, when the people were at first angry about our imminent departure but then reluctantly accepted it, Zava helped one woman to tell a *kinihera*; then an older woman talked about an incident in an interdistrict fighting sequence and an unsuccessful marriage arrangement; another woman told about a childbirth dilemma in which a baby was born with no anus, and after a lot of discussion was finally killed—raising the general question of what to do in such cases. The afternoon concluded with nine songs composed by various people, including three about the men's sweat house, two that one of the women present had made when her brother died, one remembered by Zava from her childhood, one made by her husband when he was worrying about the safety of their small son during a fighting episode, and two provided by Zava from another composer. As Zava began to sing one of these, the second-to-last, the other women joined in. Soon tears began to run down their cheeks. I thought it was a mourning song; but they said, "We sing this song when we are sorry, or we sing it and it *makes* us sorry. Now we sing it and we cry because you are going away." The song is a simple one:

> uri-karahei,   eri-karahei
> ("that way, creaking")   ("this way, creaking")
> nehuno   Guza'i   zafa'o
> ("it speaks/does") (place)   ("oh, tree")
> "It sways creaking, that way, this way.
> Oh, tree at Guza'i!"

One tree was left standing on a ridge between Kogu and Kemiyu. All the others had been cut down, and it stood with branches creaking and turning, turning in the wind. "Why were they cut down?" I asked.

"Because Kemiyu were fighting us all the time, and they could hide [make an ambush] in that bush. So we cut them all down except that one tree. Now we are sorry about that tree, standing all alone!"

It was a tearful exit that afternoon and next morning, from Maira.

A LONG JOURNEY TO UNDERSTANDING

At the very beginning, when we were at Raipinka and I was making a start on Kamano vocabulary, my interpreter and his wife taught me how to say such things as, "You two come in the afternoon and tell me *kinihera*!" and "I would like you to tell me *kinihera*!" The first *kinihera* he told me, in Kamano, was about a quarrel between two "place-men," house dwellers or village dwellers, and a "wild man" (*afi-vahei*, analogous to a wild pig, *afi-afu*, which lives in the bush as constrasted with a domestic pig). The "wild man" had marked a bird, a jungle fowl, for himself, but the other two killed it to cook and eat it. He came in pursuit of them and broke down the stockades of their "house-place" one by one, but he was finally killed with a blunt arrow. After checking that he was really dead, all the men cut him up, cut up a pig, made an oven, and ate them. The *kinihera* ends with the statement that "This is not to happen again!" (There are other details that make it into a reasonably coherent story.)

I did not realize at the time that this was not such a simple story as it appeared to be. It has implications for bush versus settled living, a sensitive point in areas where administration officials openly drew this contrast in urging the development of large, settled villages. It points to rules regarding property and ownership claims. There is the theme of the blunt arrow—and so on. I recorded (in writing) as many stories as I could, noting each one down, then having it gone over again less slowly, and finally making an interlinear translation. I had done this consistently in Aboriginal Australia and was reasonably satisfied with the speed at which I could manage it.

In Kogu, once I had settled down with women around me, they went on telling me *kinihera*. These became interspersed with other accounts (see below), and interruptions of various kinds. Except for a few examples, I tried not to record more than once what they said was "the same" story. I learned that partly similar stories could be accepted without comment in the same area; that all *kinihera* were linked with specific places, and were responsible for the meanings attached to some, but not all place names; yet at the same time *kinihera* traveled along the paths that ran between different places and different districts, and across language boundaries. Some discussions focused on the matter of sameness and difference, along with routine considerations of meaning. By the end of the first period in Kogu, I had been told just under four hundred stories. At the end of the second research period I had well over five hundred. The problem in Busarasa was, the women there complained, "Those Usurufa women have told you all the stories!"

While we were away, in looking at the *kinihera* and their maxims I had begun to understand more about their living significance, and the way they intermeshed with "real-life" accounts and the material of observation. So, during that second period, at Maira and at Pintagori, I resolved to record all the *kinihera* I could, to try to make sure that none escaped me. And despite the continuous difficulties of fighting and sorcery scares and other upsets, women (and interpreters) helped me enthusiastically in this quest.

Many *kinihera* are long and very detailed. The most popular theme, of relations between an elder and a younger brother, comes into this category, and one point that emerged quite plainly was that no one *kinihera* could be taken as a "model" of that relationship. It was the totality of stories that counted, with each set of *kinihera* treating different facets of it. The same applied to the next most popular theme, relations between husband and wife (see, e.g., C. H. Berndt 1966). But in the dramatic scenes on ceremonial occasions only one or two aspects were selected, and the rest of any *kinihera* was taken for granted. That could be done more easily in the case of *kinihera*, but when the basis of a *krina* was an "everyday" incident, the actors could not be sure that everyone would understand what it was all about.

In going over the *kinihera* again, I did not attempt to look at them in relation to "the local culture" as a general construct or a summary of what that culture (those cultures) seemed to be like. Instead, I wanted to know what individual people said about the topics and problems and maxims that made up the *kinihera*. What about relations in everyday life between brothers? Between husband and wife? And so on. What about the issues of bridewealth, courtship, and conflicts of an often more deadly sort that came up in both spheres?

Women talked to me about situations that they regarded as interesting or important, and in which they or people they knew personally had been involved. Each case was then discussed in some detail. The setting was defined, roughly, as one in which they were helping someone from another social and cultural environment to learn about themselves and their lives: "This is how we live, these are the things we do." The reports covered a very wide range of topics. Inevitably, they varied in length and also in clarity. Some were straightforward descriptions of feasts or ovens, without other incident, mostly in the form of long lists of people who shared in the distribution or contributed to it. There were numerous reasons for such occasions: a birth, a death, a betrothal or marriage, the preparation of a garden or maturing of a crop, or a repayment to people who had helped in any of these—a continuous interweaving of obligations and credits, with feasts of different size and social coverage as sorting-out points at intervals in the process. More often, material of this kind was included in other contexts and not presented separately. There were also a few "construct" statements, generalized outlines on such topics as growing up, gardening, and various ceremonies and rites. I tried to keep these to a minimum, but they were useful for comparison with reports and firsthand observation of actual events.

Of course, every situation, and every person's account of a situation, is in a sense unique. Classifying the narratives into categories, as I did in my larger study of them, emphasizes their uniformities, the features they hold in common; for example, some of them give a lot of attention to dissension between husband and wife, or between brothers. The selection included here is arbitrary, but it does indicate the sort of material with which the narratives deal and, broadly, the way it is arranged and presented.

This is an excerpt from a longer narrative, so I have put it in a third-person framework. It came from Urera, of Agura, married to Rabu of Kogu:

Rabu had given her a bundle of indigenous "salt" to keep in her house. Now the men were having a sweat house, and he called for it. "You can have a little, because you're pregnant." But it was nearly all gone. ("I'd eaten it," said Urera, giggling.) When she did not bring the salt, he came with a stick to fight her. She was afraid, and at first would not emerge from her house. When she finally did so, he beat her with the stick, and rubbed the remains of the salt into the wounds. This was so painful that she struck him on the head with a stick, and he fell bleeding. She was afraid. Putting the stick on top of his body, she ran away to Numparu [Yate], adjoining her home district of Agura. . . . Then men went through the women's houses getting food and goods to take back to the sweat house, and they took Urera's pig. . . . Afterward her husband called out, sending a message to her: "You can come back now, we've killed and eaten your pig!" . . . He and a few other Kogu men went hunting for animals to give her brothers and father, and presently she went to the birth hut. She bore a girl. When word of this was brought to Rabu, he was angry. [He wanted a boy.] "You salt-stealer! If you had borne a boy, I would look at it. I won't look at a girl!" So Urera gave the baby to Pau [her first, deceased, husband's younger full brother in Moiife—she called him "brother"], and he gave her a pig. He reared the girl, she grew, and he arranged her marriage. . . . [The account is a detailed one, including a description of the marriage arrangements.]

A number of such examples show that a wife's rights in relation to her husband and his relatives depended very much on how far she had the support of her "brothers"—in other words, the able-bodied men of her own lineage and clan. They represented the only organized group on which she could rely. Cross-cousins and mothers' brothers might act individually on her behalf, but she could not expect any concerted help from them. Nor could she depend on nominal or relatively distant kin, because in a crisis her opponents might have stronger claims on them.

For instance, Urera was, she says, once confronted on the track near Moiife by her second [Moiife] husband whom she had left. He reminded her bitterly of this, saying he had always treated her well, and demanding the return of his [and her] small daughter. He struck her several times, threatening to shoot her. . . . When she cried out, her former co-wives came up, but would not help her. Then her second husband's younger clan brother, whom they both had reared as a son, came on the scene. She asked him for help, reminding him that she had "grown" him and helped to initiate him, but he simply wept for her and stayed neutral. Her second husband's father also attacked her with an axe. During all this, her nominal brother, whom her third husband had sent to escort her past this dangerous patch of road, had stood by. He would not intervene, because he called her second husband cross-cousin. Finally, however, he led her away.

Ideally, women should not fight men, but occasionally they did. In a number of cases women claimed to have fought back when their husbands, or others, attacked them.

Fenaki claimed that on one occasion she defended her adopted daughter, Igusa, against the girl's husband, Gova [of Wezu'epa]. When Gova returned with his younger lineage brother from a mixed sorcery-and-stealing raid on Tatagufa, he found that his wife did not have food cooked ready for him as he had instructed. He beat her. "Oh, mother!" she cried. "I got a stick" [said Fenaki] "and came running. 'Have you been hunting?' I asked him." [This is an allusion to *kinihera* husbands who come home from hunting empty-handed but expect to find cooked vegetables waiting for them.] "He went to shoot me, but I broke his arrow. Together, we fought him. . . . Then we went to his garden, cut bananas and sugarcane and other foods, and cooked and ate them ourselves. . . . He said, 'I can beat my wife—but now you come fighting me! I have never seen this before. It never happens in other places that a man's mother-in-law should fight him!' " He disowned his wife. " 'This is your concern,' he said to me [Fenaki]. 'You two can stay together.' And he told his wife, 'Your mother fought me!' " He didn't mean it, Fenaki added: he said it because he was angry. His wife was now living with him again.

A wife who defied her husband ran the risk of being punished, even if she had male relatives to call on, but this need not stop her. Some women refused to return to their husbands on the grounds that the men were physically unattractive or old. "Your hair is white, I want a young man," two are reported to have said.

In one case the result was an informal court, but the wife repeated her remarks and would not leave her younger lover. When she died soon afterward, her first husband expressed pleasure at the news, and it was rumored that he had caused this through sorcery. In the second case the wife took refuge with a series of men in another district, all clan brothers, who first defended her against her husband and then fought over her among themselves. Angry about this, she took a course of action sometimes followed in such circumstances. Gathering together a party of women and girls, all with grievances against their menfolk, she led them to a district then on unfriendly terms with the one they had left: "They will kill us or marry us, it is their affair." But in this instance they were seized from their new "husbands" and punished with some violence.

It was easier for a husband to reject his wife than vice versa, even though as a rule the bridewealth was not returnable.

Marai told about her first betrothal to a man in the Fore district of Ofafina. He had not seen her before. When the bridal party brought her to him, adorned in finery and laden with pig meat, he said rudely, "What is this faeces-thing? I don't want it!" He wouldn't accept her. She returned home in tears, helped by a nominal "brother" from that district.
    Her lip trembled when she came to this part of the story, and the women who were sitting listening around the fire expressed sympathy with her and disgust at him. No reason was given, although, she said, his relatives tried to persuade her to give him another chance.

In other cases more specific explanations were forthcoming for such a rejection, involving temporary or permanent dissolution of a marriage—either before or after it had been consummated. They included a wife's failure to consider her husband's wishes; her unattractive appearance (implied in Marai's case, although other men seem to have taken a different view); her loyalty to her own kin against his; adultery (on her part, not his); or, from the standpoint of her supporters, his unreasonable behavior, or "hot" temper. From the cases, it was not always clear where one marriage ended and another began. A man might live separately from his wife for a long time, or "lend" her to a brother, but still object if she tried to set up a new relationship on a long-term basis. Alternatively, even a husband who formally rejected his wife might give a public demonstration of grief and affection for her. As in other situations, one way of doing this was for him to turn his rage, or display of emotion, against his own belongings (a solution that has been reported for other parts of Papua New Guinea as well).

Ivuo told of one such case. The husband and wife concerned were both of Grufe:

> Gruso could not control his wife, Eso. She kept having sexual relations with other men, although he took her from one place to another hoping to keep her away from them. At last he gave up. "I'm upset about this. You are to go to another man, but when I come you can give me food." (This implies a sexual claim as well.) He took her to Newa (whom he called "brother") in the adjoining district of Hintegrufe. Then he came home weeping to Kaga in Grufe. He smashed up his sugar garden, his hollow-log oven, his wooden plates, and tore up his bark-strip skirt. "Eso made a good garden. Good food she cooked, and I ate. She was always cooking *faga* beans for me." He brought out his bamboo of pig fat and his bamboo of *faga* beans, and called his "brothers-in-law" to look at him. Mue and Hafaki (mother's sister's sons to Eso), Haravi (Hafaki's young son), and Fave (Eso's brother) came to him. "Now that she's gone, I'm going to break these up," he told them.
>
> "No," they urged, "just rub yourself with ashes, don't break your bamboos!"
>
> "No, I can do that, and then I'll go to Taramu!" They wept with him, "helping" him.
>
> Afterward, in return, he gave them beans, skirt fiber, and wooden plates. Another man also came to weep with him. This was Vasuhu, who called him by no kin term at all. "He came because he thought Gruso would give him something for helping him weep." The others noticed this and afterward gossiped about it, and they made a *krina* of it.

A man who was reluctant to treat his unfaithful wife too harshly, or kill her, had a socially acceptable alternative here. By a dramatic gesture of renunciation he could win the sympathy of her male kin, put an extra-district "brother" under an obligation to him, and still retain some claim on her while perhaps marrying again, as Gruso did. Nevertheless, most people seemed to prefer more direct measures, and many of the narratives dealt with such events in great detail.

The partly static tableaux that were a feature of ceremonial displays did not deal with conflicts. Nor did the emblems, impermanent beaten bark creations either worn as masks or carried as separate sheets on frameworks. Patterned with colored designs, they might be shaped as various birds and adorned with feathers or plants and flowers. These made different kinds of statements, more concerned with innovation and with individual imagination, although within a fairly conventionalized framework (see C. H. Berndt 1959). Women rarely made such emblems, though they knew that could happen in other areas, and a few women from such places actually carried emblems when they came to Maira with their singing groups to join in ceremonial occasions. In each of these gatherings, I tried to find out the meaning of all the emblems that appeared: the meaning to the persons who had made them—who were usually also the persons carrying them—and also how the spectators interpreted them. This was fairly straightforward for the conventionally named types of emblem, although these could have additional personal meanings. But in most cases, even though the spectators might hazard a guess or two, they nearly always ended up by saying, "You'll have to ask him! He's the one who really knows!"

At Maira and at Pintagori, then, in the intervals of watching and listening to *krina*, I spent a lot of time following up individual emblem bearers. Most of them pretended not to know about this, and tended to melt away into the crowd and even to hide. At first I thought they were reluctant to tell me, until I realized how interested and entertained so many of the others on the dancing ground appeared to be. When I finally caught up with the particular emblem carrier I was after, it was usually to find him giggling, sitting unobtrusively behind some of the others, and very willing to explain what he had had in mind when he made it. The pursuit through the crowd was rather like a *krina* episode, though more subdued. It was also, I was told, rather like a scene in some of the *kinihera*, where a coy and elusive man is chased or importuned by a determined woman: he has to submit in the end, but he puts up a show of resistance. (This was one of the contradictory themes, not only in myth but also in everyday living; cutting across it was the assertion that men were aggressive and brave, and war was their favorite occupation, an assertion supported by a number of women who used to say of any courageous woman, "She is like a man!")

Although the *krina* based on *kinihera* were popular, erotic scenes and mildly violent ones were more so. Some sequences parodied police activities, or informal court scenes. The *krina* during boys' initiation rites emphasized the aspect of "what not to do," the bad example, but not in the same hilariously entertaining way.

Individually composed songs covered the same spectrum as these other aspects of a ceremonial (*singsing*) performance. They ranged from rather slight (but mostly neat and appealing) individual statements about particular scenes and events, to more poignant expressions or accounts of personal tragedy. (A few short, simple examples appear in C. H. and R. M. Berndt 1971, and one in C. H. Berndt 1959.) They were like little vignettes, or glimpses into people's lives—not spelled out in the songs themselves, which merely alluded obliquely to them. Discussions of these were much longer than the actual songs themselves: who sang each song, who composed it, and when; who were the other people involved; if they were living, where were they now; if they were dead, how and where did it happen; and what did each word mean.

On the morning when we finally left Busarasa, I had managed to fit in a few more songs, but there were two women still waiting, each with a song for me. Everyone was beginning to move off: a hilly, rather rough walk lay ahead. I could not delay longer. But after all these years I still regret that, and wonder what the songs would have been—what I had missed. In regard to all the songs, I was particularly sorry not to have had a tape recorder, because it was obvious that the tunes, or melody, were an important part of their appeal to the people who chose what they would sing in district groups during ceremonies. Some of them were very "catchy" indeed.

By the time a popular song was far away from its place of origin, after traveling along various *singing* paths, its specific meanings could be lost. (We heard in Busarasa some of the same songs we had heard in Kogu several months before.) In the district where a song had been composed, where the places as well as the people's names were familiar to at least some singers, it was more likely to be remembered for a long time. Individual composers did not seem to mind the loss of their names in the process of transmission. They were proud if their songs were able to spread and be sung publicly. Similarly, *kinihera* that were not linked to specific places and circumstances, and being told as a ritual garden fertility activity, were said to be told only for "nothing," as entertainment. In such circumstances, anyone could tell them. In rather the same way, colored crotons and other plants were grown in gardens simply for decoration or personal adornment. In a setting where so much emphasis was placed on reciprocal obligations and payments, these exceptions point to another facet of local values, where people expected no recompense except acclaim and enjoyment.

Among the women who were with me more or less regularly in Busarasa were several good singers and song composers. Two came almost every day, with their husbands, from the Fore district of Ora. The younger one had been a central figure in a series of "ghost wind" (cargo cult) episodes. The other, Tina, white-haired but very energetic and quietly self-assured, had a large and varied repertoire, including her own compositions. The Ora people usually came a little later than the others, and left a little earlier. One afternoon, when Tina had been sitting chatting with the others and eating sweet potato for most of the day and had sung only one song, I was hoping to hear one more from her before she went. So I asked, "Tina, have you a song for me?" She said, "I'm just eating my sweet potato, then I'll sing." Looking at my disappointed face, she put the rest of her sweet potato into her mouth and came and sat close beside me, trying to swallow it and to smile at the same time, but smiling with her eyes. The following morning she sang a song that she said she had made the afternoon before, after I had asked her for one.

This is the song. The Fore words at the top of each line are written down as they were sung. Below them are what were said to be the Kamano equivalents. The approximate English translations are in the third line. (I don't discuss here the words or constructions or translations.)

maata'i

(masta)

kamanaka(wari)
kegu
("for talking")

negisaavisa
nagiyafinti
("on my foot/leg")

nasona
natagarifei
("it pains")

neyapisa
nazompinti
("on my hand")

yavava-muta
yavava-riga
(place name)

kanayingka-muti
kanayika-mutiga
(place name)

wewera
gora
("ground")

avayagupopo
afaza-geka
("near dawn")

yemipavinti
nehiyangkopi
("it makes")

misus-yaa

(misis)

avintogo-pinti
zokagu-pi
("net bag of hair")

tumpa-nauka-kavomayuwei
mo-navesiyaza-huwei
("I like to go, talk/do")

neyapisei
nazampinti
("on my hand")

nasovina
natagarifei
("it pains")

navainamayu
navesiyei
("I like")

tumpa-navumayuwei
mo-navesiya-huwei
("I like to go, talk/do")

It was a reproachful as well as a reassuring song. In essence: I should remember that she and her husband didn't live nearby. They liked talking to us, but they had to come rather a long way, and they were not young people. Their hands and feet easily got tired. The two place names refer to her own ground, in Ora. In the song she says "dawn," but means half-light, or twilight. "Net bag of hair," or "bundle of hair in a snood," is a conventional song expression for "nice hair," *azoka-gura*; an alternative song term is *intompa-gura*. The reproach shows up in the slightly formal use of the Pidgin English words *masta* for "a European man," *misis* for "a European woman." I was rather disconcerted by these, but I don't think she used them as Pidgin speakers farther north would have done. She did not know any other Pidgin words. In any case, the colonial authority connotations were much less obtrusive in this southern area. People who acknowledged the more effective weapons controlled by Europeans, and the power of the administration officials, the *kiaps*, supposed that if only they could find the right key to all this, they themselves would be in the same position of power. They had a strong sense of pride in themselves, and the older Fore women I knew, such as Tina, seemed almost to have a protective attitude toward me. During some of the fighting and skirmishing that punctuated our period there, they were quick to shout to me that I needn't worry: "We'll look after you!"

There are some students who decline to study songs (pop songs, folk songs, and the like) because they are not in a position to study or even merely to record the music. If I had taken that stand, I would have neglected a significant avenue to understanding—not only the songs as such, but the ramifying discussions about them, and the extra insights these provided into a complex situation with all its cross-cutting contrasts and contradictions. I was fortunate in the women I came to know, with their varying personalities that could have stimulated a study in themselves. I continued to be intrigued by their resilience and their blend of sentimentality and hard-headedness in the difficult and volatile and often violent circumstances of their lives. We saw and heard enough of these aspects to realize what they must have been like for everyone involved in them, men and women, and children. I was fortunate also in having interpreters who served as actively helpful bridges into this situation.

The people of this region were economically aggressive as well as being aggressive and often ruthless in fighting and warfare (although they had rules of neutrality and ideas about "enough is enough" which set limits in any specific warring encounters). They struck hard bargains with one another in their dealings in such commodities as pigs, and in bridewealth arrangements, for example. Their delight in songs and adornment and dramatic performances, their sense of humor, and sentimental personal attachments and emotional relationships provided another integral, but contrasting, part of their overall culture.

Dramatic *krina* scenes helped to reinforce and feed back into the *kinihera* as well as into everyday life. And the *kinihera* reinforced one another, because no one story stood alone. The complex of stories about bridewealth, courtship, marriage, and so on linked up with other story sequences about other aspects of social relations. And the stories, *krina*, and songs were all interlocked in a constellation of cues, which were amplified in certain circumstances. It was not simply a matter of each of these items being related to its sociocultural context, or seen in a complementary relationship, for example, between myth and ritual, or song words and music. What was involved here was a pattern of interconnecting linkages over a wider spectrum, each facet making its own kind of contribution to the whole—and each allowing a different kind of scope to individual people and groups of people.

The situation was especially interesting to me for several reasons. At the level of "raw material," for instance, there was the range and quantity of narrative and dramatic and song material, and its quality: the great variety of stories, the handling of words and images, the clever "packaging" of content in all of these fields. Beyond all that, there are the obvious possibilities for analysis and interpretation. Then, in regard to individual performance, there were the noticeable differences in skill and ability between persons. Some were clearly more competent in dealing with words and arrangement of verbal material. Others showed a special flair for acting and for organizing dramatic events. In some cases these were the same persons who demonstrated skills in several fields. Then again, there were men who concentrated on strategy and tactics in warfare, and on organizing such events as the informal courts.

All through the region there appeared to be a number of basic assumptions held more or less in common: shared views about, for example, the importance of warfare, the importance of gardening, the nature of social relations between people and between groups—and the importance of continuity in human affairs. At the same time, there was also an emphasis on change: on innovations, diversions, the need to incorporate new things and ideas. The basic mythology and basic religious rituals included some provision for this. But the *kinihera* and *krina* and individually composed songs did more than make allowances for it: they were ready-made vehicles for communicating changes as well as continuities. They also provided opportunities for individual self-expression, as an explicit, socially recognized, and socially encouraged facet of ordinary living. This deliberate, positive acceptance of the advantages of flexibility and innovation extended "across the board." Individual people went out of their way to acquire new seeds and new plants for their gardens. They looked for new items such as these that they could get through trade and exchange and could develop further for themselves. They thought that they could cope with these changes and these new items. They were adept at fitting new things into their own framework, modifying and adjusting that framework, up to a point, to accommodate them. Even when the changes began to accelerate beyond their earlier expectations, they still worked at it. They were used to the idea of changes and cultural differences—but against a background of similarities and continuities, and the *kinihera*, especially, illustrate this point. (More widely, such story similarities are evident throughout Papua New Guinea, as I noted in C. H. Berndt 1977, but the differences are crucial, too.)

One thing that we were increasingly conscious of, as our research proceeded, was the progression from almost total strangeness to a modicum of familiarity. This was a two-way process. For the local people as well as for us, it was a transition from largely uninformed observation alone, to more comprehensive possibilities of communication. Most noticeable of all was the development of a common verbal understanding (along with nonverbal language) that went part of the way to reducing the "cultural distance" that had been so conspicuous when we first met them. It was a slow business for them, as it was for us: building up and intermeshing so many varied "strings of meaning," making tentative patterns out of a multitude of experiences and interpretations.

In preparing this chapter, I was not sure how best to convey the nature of this journey, the accumulation of items that made it possible. They are not like a paper flower that opens into a complete blossom when soaked in water. I have noted some of the ingredients that went into my own overall perspective, but they are merely examples, not "typical," because the range in each case (e.g., of *kinihera*, *krina*, songs, and narratives as well as incidents of firsthand observation) is so wide. Our research was rather in the nature of an extended pilot survey, but because we were able to concentrate on specific aspects, it became more than that. The *kinihera* and *krina* and songs, in particular, drew my attention more consistently than before to the relations between verbal and dramatic material, and other aspects of living—the "sex and violence" issues in the so-called mass media, for instance, and problems of censorship and rules, and permissiveness. I have not commented on these issues here.

For the people of this region, caught up in such overwhelming changes, the full and detailed record of this "journey into myth" will, I hope, one day become part of their archives: an account of their own past from a constellation of local perspectives, even though it is mediated through someone who started off as an "outsider" but tried quite hard to be in one sense, if only temporarily, an "insider."

NOTES

1. This chapter should be read in conjunction with R. M. Berndt's chapter. Our procedure was that in order to minimize repetition he wrote his first, providing a general coverage along with his particular perspectives. In writing my chapter, I had to bring in something about the background of the area and how it became a "foreground" of our combined and separate interests—as the people there became a part of our lives and we became a part of theirs. I have not included

comments on several topics of shared interest that R. M. Berndt mentions, such as sorcery, cannibalism, informal courts, and cargo cults, or disruptive incidents such as the potential escalation of interdistrict trouble in Busarasa, or the house-burning "spree" engaged in by "native police" in villages north of Maira toward the end of our first period there. (Women from those villages who had come to Maira for a ceremonial farewell to us reacted with consternation and tears as runners came panting in with the news. Among other things, they had left some of their best skirts and an assortment of belongings inside their houses; and in any case there was a general anxiety about "What next?" "Where will they stop?" and "Are they coming this way?")

I have deliberately made no attempt to consider, even in outline, what has happened since 1953 in that region specifically or in Papua New Guinea as a whole. That could not be done in a few words. In the light of what I (we) have said about the rapid changes that were noticeable even between our two visits, perhaps it is unreasonable to be surprised by statements and interpretations relating to the northern Kamano, and even more so by some of the huge volume of material that has accumulated around the subject of *kuru*. A critical assessment of all this, even one confined to assertions about the "traditional past," would have to be a substantial study in itself.

When referring to people's personal names I have altered them, for privacy. Regarding place names, where R. M. Berndt has "Mairapa," with the customary Usurufa and Yate locative suffix, I have kept to the basic form, Maira. This is because, for convenience, I have used Kamano words for stories and so on; to be consistent in this in using a locative suffix, as was commonly done even in cases where direction or movement was implied, I would have felt obliged to use the Kamano form, Mairangka (cf. the name Raipinka or, to Kamano-speakers, Repingka).

2. The linguistic picture outlined here is based on our own field research. (I made some preliminary comments in C. H. Berndt 1954.) For a different perspective drawing upon later work, see Wurm 1960.

3. As R. M. Berndt points out in his chapter, the *kuru* investigation center was later established in this neighborhood, but during the initial search for a suitable site the locality was mistakenly identified as "Oka." When we were there, Oka was the name of a Fore district to the southeast of Moke, an important area in creation mythology.

FIVE

An Innocent in the Garden of Eden

Marie Reay

The interesting thing about living memories, the ones that we carry in our heads, is the way we modify them, changing them, improving upon them, censoring them. It's only later, when you're confronted with hard copy of old times (as in a photograph) that you realise the subtle amendments you've been unconsciously making.
—PHILIP ADAMS

My hard copy of old times was my 1953–55 field diary.[1] There I came across the names of Jo and Poli, two young men from Chimbu who wanted to work for me. The wages set by the administration were paltry, but working for Europeans was the only sure way of obtaining money. Many young men called at my base seeking work. They were often equipped with a magic *pas* (Tok Pisin, letter), a fragment of a torn-up letter or a scrap of paper decorated with squiggles in imitation of writing—the nonliterate person's response to demands for references. I rejected these applicants summarily, for I had no jobs for them. Jo and Poli, however, were adamant that they would work for me. Jo, the more aggressive of the two, insisted that I must cut their hair, since men in employment always had their hair cut. This was my opportunity to get rid of them. I kept Jo talking while I cut his hair and Poli gazed in fascinated horror. Then I handed Jo a mirror and let him see the *kalabus* (T.P., jail or prison) crop I had given him. He screamed and left hastily with Poli following.

I remembered the whole incident vividly. But the hard copy of old times startled me by recording that I had been bullied into letting Jo and Poli work for me for nearly a week before managing to get rid of them in that manner. My memory was untrustworthy when it could telescope events like that. What else will be telescoped or omitted or reinterpreted when I recall events of more than thirty years ago? Memory can project a slanted image when time chips away parts of its mirror finish.

Of all the colorful characters at Sydney University during World War II, Ian Hogbin and Camilla Wedgwood were the two in whose footsteps

I wished to follow. They made New Guinea come alive for me, but the prospect of going there seemed remote. In and out of tutorials, students discussed the growing literature on fieldwork method, but this concerned tribal societies and it was hard to see its relevance to my work among Aboriginal fringe-dwellers. Their situation was pitiful and I longed to work with a proud people—in Hogbin and Wedgwood's New Guinea, of course, rather than Elkin's Aboriginalia.

The opportunity came when, as lecturer in anthropology at ASOPA (the Australian School of Public Administration), I was able to go to the Northern District of Papua to study the changes that had taken place among the Orokaiva since the time of F. E. Williams. Port Moresby, then a ramshackle settlement, housed a colonial society of bizarre pretensions. The administration had selected for my base in Orokaiva country an extremely isolated resthouse. There was not a village in sight. My visits to the villages, always greeted with a fresh coconut to drink, were more like royal tours of inspection than the fieldwork of an anthropologist. But soon Mount Lamington, an allegedly extinct volcano, erupted and I was evacuated along with the other surviving Europeans.

I intended to complete my study of change among the Orokaiva and in 1953 was awarded a research scholarship in S. F. Nadel's department at the Australian National University (ANU) specifically to do this. I was familiar with some of Nadel's papers but had no acquaintance with his major works and no preconception of what he might be like. I found him domineering. "Anthropology" was British social anthropology. Practitioners who came to Australia were convinced of their superiority over Sydney's A. P. Elkin, the only other professor of anthropology in Australia, who, as churchman, man of practical affairs, and eclectic at that, was "theoretically unsound." Elkin did not share their preoccupation with Africa but, focusing on the Pacific, was ready to learn from new developments in American anthropology, which Nadel ignored. The British social anthropologists made arrogant attempts to wrest the journal *Oceania* from his control and run it from Canberra.

Nadel intended that his students would provide him with the data for classifying and explaining the varieties of social structure in the New Guinea Highlands. He asked me whether I would like to participate in this project but, mindful of unfinished business, I declined. Months passed and I could not get his permission to set off for the field. At last I told the god-professor I was willing to go to the Highlands and he instructed me to go to Minj immediately.[2] I was content with this change of plan. In my short time with the Orokaiva I had discovered the difficulty of interpreting differences between the findings of an earlier ethnographer and my own: they might be his errors or my errors or a genuine change with a course I might or might not eventually manage to trace. At least in the Highlands the changes brought about by colonialism were recent and should be readily identifiable, so the only changes I would have to worry about were the changes inherent in any ongoing society. At that time many anthropologists assumed that primitive societies were unchanged "from time immemorial," the only change they underwent being cyclical change that left the status quo ante intact. I myself believed that societies could not persist without continually experiencing change. I admired Radcliffe-Brown and indeed had listened reverently to him speaking in London as a very old man, but I could not accept his insistence that the basic element of society and social structure was the individual. It seemed obvious to me that the building blocks for social structure were social relationships, which were inherently dynamic.

There was a pecking order among the students at ANU: first, Nadel's "bright boys"; second, the other male students; and last, "us girls." The select band of Nadel's bright boys excelled in seminars. Nadel himself dominated these with lofty orations which purported to draw out the theoretical implications of the material presented in the papers. His flow of ideas was impressive. He then allowed one of his bright boys to chime in, and we heard an unwitting caricature of the master's own method, bold theories that were not simply abstract but impossible to relate back to social reality. Nadel was definite that we should go into the field with a "problem," that is, a theoretical problem to solve. I tried to devise such a problem but, testing each attempt against my knowledge of the Orokaiva, I found it just as inconsistent with human behavior as the theories of Nadel's bright boys and the wilder excesses of Nadel himself. I stormed into my supervisor's office. I had not been there before and I found it surprisingly bare but for a photograph of H. M. the Queen.

"Nadel insists," I cried, "that we go into the field with a theory. But what is a theory? What is a theory?" I demanded rhetorically.

He took the question seriously. "Leave it with me," he said. "I'll give you something tomorrow."

The next afternoon I received a typewritten half-page of his considered thoughts.

At that time I was a somewhat dilettante anthropologist. I was serious about anthropology during the time I devoted to it, but I spent more time on other things and had published more in literary magazines than in anthropological journals. In selecting books to take to the field I began with the poems of Jose Garcia Villa and an anthology of modern verse. I took half a dozen whodunits, which generated further reading when I found I could exchange them for paperbacks other Europeans in the valley had finished reading. I joined the Readers Union to receive regularly books I would otherwise not have read. My basic anthropological text and frequent source of disagreement was *Notes and Queries* (Royal Anthropological Institute 1951), and I took some African works to read for the first time. My African reading had been confined to clumsy studies of culture contact and dull stuff on separatist churches and other movements that suggested some kind of parallel to cargo cults. Now I armed myself with several books by Nadel, Meyer Fortes, and E. E. Evans-Pritchard. The most useful was Nadel's *Nupe Religion* (1954), which never ceased to remind me of things I had not yet investigated. When I read *The Nuer* (Evans-Pritchard 1940), I found it a highly idealized version of the Kuma segmentary system.

I had no acquaintance with field budgets and financial statements and simply bought what I thought was necessary, including a set of notebooks made to my own specifications. In the end, having arranged for McIlraths (Sydney) to send me a monthly supply of canned food, cigarettes, and one bottle of Rhum Negrita, I went to the field not with a theory as such but with a general intention of studying socialization and authority.

I voyaged to Papua New Guinea in the legendary M. V. *Bulolo*. A friendly planter from Karkar told me I should learn Pidgin and proceeded to teach me while the other women were knitting and gossiping and the other men were drinking below. A memorable stop was Samarai, where I walked around the island and took a stunning photograph of palms waving over a beach and the sea, the kind of picture that is now hackneyed chocolate box.

At Lae I saw a fellow student who, according to Nadel, would be handing over his field equipment to me. Richard Salisbury had been urging me to go to Chuave, adjacent to his Siane, and may even have been expecting Nadel to send me there. (Salisbury was one of Nadel's "bright boys.") I did not relish going to an area adjoining one with all the information still in the anthropologist's notebooks, so I told him firmly that I was going to Minj to study the Kuma people. (In fact I need not have worried. Salisbury produced a splendid ethnography of Siane, mysteriously never published, in record time.) Our respective itineraries had prevented us from meeting in the obvious place, Goroka. In Lae the question of my destination arose yet again. He told me triumphantly that he had left his equipment for me not at Goroka, as I had expected, but at Chuave. I presumed that I could get it sent from there to Minj. (At Goroka the *kiap*s [T.P., administration officers] promised to bring the equipment to Goroka and forward it to Minj the next time a patrol went to Chuave. After five months at Minj I had real tables and chairs instead of eating, typing, and sitting on McIlraths' invaluable wooden packing cases.)

My voyage ended at Madang, where I had to stay overnight before flying to Goroka. The hotel bedroom was stifling, so I left the high window wide open. I awoke to find a New Guinean in my room. My newly acquired Pidgin failed me, so I let out a blood-curdling scream and he climbed through the window again. I pretended not to recognize the intruder in a police lineup that morning since it seemed obvious that his punishment would be undeservedly harsh. To the little band of expatriates the presence of a native in a white woman's room was equivalent to rape.

A DC-3 transported me to a magical region of green mountains folded against each other as if in some divine plan: here and there, a spur bearing a line of native houses looking like stud batteries or strange sea forms from the air and, wherever there was human habitation, a riot of plumed bamboo. In Goroka I stayed at the *kunai*-thatched guest house run by Mrs. Pitts, a kind of colonial matriarch. There I learned that Minj airstrip was "out" and would probably remain so for the duration of the wet season. But the author Colin Simpson and a photographer accompanying him were headed for Nondugl in the north of the Wahgi Valley, so I shared a charter Dragon with them. We stayed in Sir Edward Hallstrom's house (very grand for the Highlands and uniquely constructed of permanent materials) before undertaking a three hours' walk across the valley to Minj.

Brian Corrigan, the assistant district officer (ADO) at Minj, was away at the time investigating murders at Telefomin, but after a few days a new ADO, Jack Emanuel, arrived. I had been staying with a hospitable couple, Patrol Officer Bob Daugherty and his wife, but was very conscious that I could not impose on them much longer. Still, I needed more time to select my field site. Jack Emanuel allocated me the house of the district medical officer, who was away on leave. He also allocated me a *manki masta* (T.P., general household servant), Wau, who had been trained by Jim Leahy, and he gently explained to me the rules of the colonial game. As a conscientious administrator he had definite views on everything concerning his subdistrict, including the place of the anthropologist within it. I was one of his subject people and if I did not obey his rules I would be expelled from the district and possibly the territory.

I was deeply shocked when I learned in 1971 that Jack Emanuel had been murdered by Tolai. I had grown to think of him as a kindly man and a generous host on my monthly visits to Minj. But with the "hard copy of old times" as a reminder, I can understand why someone might eventually stab him to death. He was the perfect public servant of his time. He venerated the law, the power and responsibility of government, and the British Empire. As officer in charge of the Minj Subdistrict he saw all its inhabitants, "European" and "Native," as his charges. With few staff at his side and few other Europeans in the valley, vis-à-vis many thousands of belligerent natives just recently pacified but still organized in their warlike groups, he dreaded any manifestation of "antiadministration sentiment."

He feared there would be a bloodbath for the Europeans, who were so hopelessly outnumbered, if antiadministration sentiment should go unchecked. "Maintaining white prestige" was most important, and he felt it his duty to inculcate respect for Europeans.[3]

It was forbidden for a European to "go native," to live with the local people as one of themselves. (There was no danger of my abandoning the shower bucket culture in favor of the natives' life-style, even if the natives had allowed me to do so.)

Well-trained servants were scarce in the Highlands and the most heinous offense a European could commit, short of "going native," was to steal someone else's *manki masta*. (Wau was exceptionally well-trained and was one of the best cooks in the Wahgi Valley; I had no intention of replacing him with someone else's servant. But I did unwittingly commit this offense when I hired him. Wau had simply been on leave when the district officer found him, though I did not know this until Leahy snubbed me on my return in 1963.)

I had to pay my employees standard pittances together with rations of food and clothing. I could pay cash for fowls and eggs, but a pig had to be purchased with a goldlip or bailer shell, and vegetables with measured spoonfuls of salt, beads, or face paint. To deviate from these standards, Jack told me, would upset the native economy.

One of the rules I had to obey on pain of expulsion was that I must inform the ADO whenever I was going any distance from my base, for the *kiap*s had to know the precise location of all Europeans in the subdistrict "in case of trouble." I was not permitted to enter any uncontrolled territory. (When I thought it necessary to visit the East Kambia, south of the Kubor Range, I tried in vain to persuade Jack Emanuel that it was safe. I had come to know some Kambia people; they had invited me to visit them and had begun, unasked, to build a house for me, but I did not get there. When I walked into the Jimi Valley I was not permitted to cross the river. I found a good vantage point for watching a tribal fight in progress in the uncontrolled territory on the other side.)

Of course, the ADO told me, there was no record of any cargo cults in the area, but I must realize that it was an offense to witness cargo cult rituals and if I should ever come across any I must not stay to observe them but must report them immediately. (Of course I did not report any of the manifestations of cargoism I found, but when I stumbled upon a Table ritual [Lawrence 1964:194] during a visit to another group I did not stay to investigate it. I did investigate a cargo cult of five years earlier when it came to my attention and, during a short absence of Emanuel from Minj, gained access to the record of this cult in one of those highly classified "Native Situation" patrol reports.) Plainly the ADO viewed cargo cults as subversive movements for the administration to deal with and therefore not suitable subjects for anthropological enquiry.

I must on no account interfere with his work. Disputes and court cases, for example, were his concern, not mine. Since I had every intention of making a close study of disputes, I interpreted this rule as a warning not to interfere in the judicial process. (Once, when a dispute with a particularly complex history was to be heard by the *kiaps'* court, I sent the ADO an account of the background, being careful not to make judgments or favor either party. If he found this helpful he did not admit it. Promptly by special messenger I received a curt note requesting me to stick to my own work and not interfere with his.)

Then there was the rule concerning *Mande Brum* (T.P., literally, "Monday sweep"). *Mande Brum* was Monday, devoted to roadwork officially classified as "voluntary" because unpaid, though known defaulters spent a few days in the lockup. The administration's argument was that the roads (not yet vehicular roads) were for the benefit of the local people. The Big Road linking all groups with the government station was sacred to peace and authority. All could walk along it without fear of molestation. Jack Emanuel impressed upon me the importance of respecting *Mande Brum*. I was not to interfere in any way with all the people's attendance at roadwork. (In fact I was not tempted to keep the people from their roadwork, for it gave me a weekly day of rest to devote to correspondence, going over my notes, reading, and the enjoyment of solitude.)

Visiting various groups in search of a field site, I found them unanimous in pressing me to stay with them and discouraging me from settling with their neighbors on either side, alleging that these were thieves and cheats and not to be trusted. I visited as many groups as possible, but three of them—Konumbuga, Tangilka, and Kugika—had begun to celebrate the great pig festival so I had to choose one of these. I selected the Kugika clan. They numbered 313 persons, so I had a good chance of knowing them all individually instead of as mere numbers. They were only three miles from Minj and directly across the Minj River from the airstrip, but my visits convinced me that they were a world away. Importantly, I found most of them instantly likable. I recognized the quality of *Luluai* (T.P., government-appointed village official) Wamdi's oratory. His older brother, *Tultul* (T.P., assistant to the *luluai*) Tai, was more reserved but exhibited as much authority as Wamdi did. The other two *tultuls*, Tagba and Tunga, seemed likable but undistinguished. Tunga seemed overshadowed by Ko-ba, his predecessor as *tultul*, who had been dismissed for taking part in interclan fighting and presented the appearance of a charming rogue. Tagba was upstaged by Mangindam, who had declined the appointment as *tultul* because he knew he was short-tempered and felt unsuited to the task.[4]

When I told Wamdi that I would like to settle with his group and wanted to live in the ceremonial village, then scarcely begun, rather than in an expatriate compound, there was much rejoicing and Mangindam gave me a generous house site "until you die." (The ADO's instruction to Wamdi that he must build me a house came when the *luluai* and his clansmen had already told me enthusiastically that they would do so.) I sketched in the dirt a floor plan of the house I wanted. It was a round house divided into an outer workroom and inner bedroom. Remembering my experience in Madang, I specified that the bedroom window must be very small indeed. The roof was conical and had no ceiling, which was a playground for rats in government resthouses. (An additional advantage was that a ceiling would certainly have caught fire when my pressure lamp flared.) The house was finished in record time and cost £50. I watched while Wamdi distributed my money to his workmen and was startled to see that he kept the bulk of it for himself. I asked several workmen about the distribution and they all said smilingly that it had been fair and just. Wamdi had done all the real work, negotiating with me, making all the decisions, and supervising the work as well as himself working hard on the actual construction. Further, he had brought me to Kondambi as earlier he had brought the first *kiap* (Jim Taylor) to Minj.

When I arrived to take up residence the true meaning of the enthusiasm all groups had shown for me to stay with them became clear. Mangindam's house site was on the Minj side of the ceremonial ground and my round house was nestled in a grove of strong bamboos. I had wanted to live on the eastern side, but the sheltering bamboos had reconciled me to the Kugikas' decision. Now I was horrified to find that all the bamboos on the Minj side had been cut to the ground. Anyone on the station who had a pair of binoculars could, if he wished, observe me going to my outside bathroom or farther down the slope to my toilet. I stared aghast, but Wamdi was proud of what he had done. "The airstrip is just opposite," he said. "Now you can see every aircraft that comes in and you will know when your cargo has arrived."

Fortunately the bamboo grew up again quickly, but until it did so I felt exposed whenever I went to my shower or walked farther down the slope.

In Australia the Aborigines had classified me as "Madha *dhuli*" (a sand goanna belonging to Mari/Madha section), thus placing me in various kin relationships to everyone in the community. Those at Borroloola had put me in Nangalama subsection. I understood that it could be awkward for the people of a face-to-face community to share much of their daily life

1. Reo Fortune with Ngasu,
Pere village, Manus, 1928
(Courtesy of the Institute for
Intercultural Studies, Inc.,
New York)

2. Ronald M. Berndt on the way to Kogu, 1951

3. Catherine H. Berndt among *singsing* onlookers at Mairapa (Kogu), 1951

4. Marie Reay with her Swiss Evangelical mother Ain (left) and her Catholic sister Non at an innovative Lutheran wedding, Minj, 1960s

5. James B. Watson and daughter, Anne, at Aiamontina, 1954

6. D'Arcy Ryan and Mendi men, 1956

7. Robert M. Glasse in Huli dress, 1955

with a stranger from another culture who was not so placed, and I was not surprised that Wamdi adopted me immediately as his daughter. This identified me with Penkup subclan and its dominant subdivision, Baimankanim. But Wamdi was proud of his clan as a whole. The Kugika had once been a very large group before their enemies had decimated and scattered them; but later, as a very small group, they had fought the Kondika again and put them to flight. I had already learned in Minj that the Kugi-Kondika enmity was notorious as the most bitter and long-lasting in the area and that the Kugika had a formidable reputation for fighting.

Kugika territory is dominated by a series of ridges jutting from the foothills of the Kubor Range into the Wahgi basin like the deformed fingers of a giant hand. Most of the "women's houses," where the pigs slept, were on the rims of deep wooded gullies where they could root all day. Group and individual "men's houses" were nestled in groves of bamboo and sugarcane. The wet season had begun and I went sliding down slippery clay paths to conduct my sociological census. At first a persistent horde of chattering children dogged my footsteps, but the muddy gullies deterred them and I was left with only Tunamp, a lad of eight years who insisted on carrying my notebook and accompanying me wherever it was permissible for a child to go.

It was evident very early that the men of the Kugika organized their lives in terms of group membership. They called upon groups, not individual men, to perform particular tasks, and the only absentees permitted were the infirm and those who were in jail or on a trading expedition. Wherever they went they walked in company with age-mates from their own groups. They called these groups "groups of men" (*yi ndugum*), distinguishing them only as "big" or "little" in relation to one another. Kugika, as a putative descent group with a rule of exogamy, was clearly a clan and its divisions were subclans. I decided to call the least inclusive corporate groups "lineages." They did not conform precisely with the definition in *Notes and Queries*, but obviously the members thought of themselves as the kind of group anthropologists called "lineages," and they assumed that their leaders and other elders knew the genealogical details. (Later, back in Canberra, senior anthropologists were adamant that it was not permissible to use the term "lineage" for any group within which the actual unilineal links could not be accurately traced. I was intimidated into inventing a neologism, "sub-subclan," for this controversial group. Mervyn Meggitt was not so intimated. Perhaps those scholars who accepted his use of the term "lineage" did not read his definition of the patrilineage [1965:285], which fits the Kuma sub-subclan very well.)

For the first month or so life at Kondambi was quiet. I was discovering
a lot and I was identifying a lot of things that I had to discover. I
recognized a number of maneuvers the Kugika made to find out whether
I would report their misdemeanors to the *kiap* and I passed these tests
easily. But then, reassured, they resumed ordinary behavior that the
chance of my betraying them to the *kiap* had interrupted. They resumed
the "pulling" (*tine*, literally "taking") of brides. One was a girl whose father
had arranged to give her to the Kugika and another, Nimbigl, was a girl
Yuaga had kidnapped to pay for three debts owing from her clan. I was
to see many girls taken forcibly as these were—straining away from their
captors, dragged screaming over the sharp stakes of pig fences, and
arriving bruised and bloody, tearful and shaken. At first I could not
conceal my abhorrence and urged the men to treat the girls more gently.

I was away when Nimbigl arrived at Kondambi. Yuaga's party paused
and a man of another subclan tore the goldlip crescent from Nimbigl's
neck, saying that this would satisfy that part of the debt that was owing
to him. Nimbigl took the opportunity to escape, but she was physically
unable to go far and she took refuge in my house. I arrived home later
to find my workroom a shambles: papers were scattered on the floor,
some had been trodden on, and a few things (including one of McIlraths'
precious packing cases) were broken. Yuaga's elder brother, *Tultul* Tagba,
gave me a fowl as compensation. But the matter did not end there. Wamdi
alarmed me by telling me that a *pas* had arrived from the *kiap* informing
me that I was to go back to Australia some months before I planned to
leave. This was transparently "hidden talk" (*tok bokis* in Pidgin, *yu ogil* to
the Kuma), and I assumed—incorrectly, as it happened—that Wamdi
himself wanted to get rid of me. I told him that what he had said was quite
untrue. He said then that he was concerned because many marriages were
to take place during and after the pig festival, and he knew I disapproved
of his "pulling" girls against their will. I told him that I wanted to learn
about all of the Kugikas' customs, even those I did not like much, and
would not be interfering with their "pulling" brides. Wamdi brought me
a piece of cooked pork that evening.

At this time I was pondering the impossibility of trying to learn the
language while simultaneously collecting ethnographic data. Wamdi had
deputed his two senior wives to teach me, but their interest (to get me to
know all recognized varieties of the vegetables they grew) was not mine.
Only one woman in this community spoke any Pidgin at all and her
version was so idiosyncratic that understanding the drift of what she said
was a feat of imagination. Many of the young men spoke Pidgin with
varying degrees of fluency. There were marked differences between
Coastal and Highlands Pidgin, and some items of the vocabulary of the

coast had not reached the Highlands, where words built on English often sufficed. The young men took it in turns to interpret for me. I could not employ one of them full-time as my interpreter, for they were all under the command of their elders and had plenty to do. I tried to find a young man from another clan who had a good command of Pidgin and could act as my linguistic informant. The best I could find was Kis, a surly young man from North Wahgi, whom I employed on the strength of his competence in Pidgin. He dictated to me some useful texts, which I copied down laboriously. But he was very slow and appeared to be unintelligent. (In retrospect I think he was undernourished.) He was also extremely prudish, refusing to interpret any reference to sexual matters or to tell me terms for sexual organs or activities. I found it awkward, too, working with an informant from North Wahgi, a different dialect area.

My best linguistic information, however, came from a study of the Banz (North Wahgi) dialect by Louis J. Luzbetak, who kindly made it available to me in manuscript. Luzbetak, who was stationed at the Roman Catholic mission at Banz, had tried to persuade me to go to the western boundary of the Wahgi people (in the area now known to be inhabited by Nek-Ni speakers) and study the transition to Melpa or Hagen culture. Until I arrived in the Wahgi Valley I had not known that another anthropologist was already resident there. I understood his concern that my work might duplicate his, but I thought that the differences between north and south would justify the two studies. I had no wish to embroil myself in a complicated border study. The Upper Jimi might have been acceptable to me as an alternative but, while Nadel might conceivably have agreed, I knew that Jack Emanuel would not. The East Kambia, with its mysterious small population just beyond those marvelous mountains, beckoned futilely, absolutely forbidden. I stayed with Nadel's choice.

Difficult as it was to explain to the Kugika precisely what I was up to, it was even more difficult to acquaint them with my name. With Catholic missionaries already in the area, I was prepared to answer to "Maria" but the occasion never arose. I was stereotyped as "Misis," the (Tok Pisin) term of address and reference for any white woman. When I told people that I wanted them to call me by my real name, Marie, they refrained from calling me anything at all until they reverted on our next encounter to "Misis." The term had already been used in this community in two contexts. When a female cargo cult leader had appointed various people to posts in her shadow administration five years earlier she had appointed Wamdi's No. 1 wife and two other women as Europeans, and for the duration of the cult they had been addressed and referred to as "Misis." Their role had been to "purchase" (by delayed credit) vegetables from the other women as the white women did with their beads and face paint. But the term had also been used as a name. Kanant, Tunamp's mother, had a little girl on whom her husband had bestowed the name "Misis." Whenever I appeared she literally thrust the child forward (once dumping her unceremoniously into my arms), insisting that she was my namesake (*jimbenan*). Misis was a charming child but I was irritated at being identified exclusively as a white woman and I avoided Kanant as much as possible. If I had realized, so early in my stay, the oppressive obligations an adult incurred toward his or her namesake, I would have been alarmed as well as appalled.

I felt strongly about the Kugikas' insistence on rejecting my name and calling me "Misis" because I believed that when anthropologists are getting to know the people in the field they should allow those people reciprocally to get to know them as individual persons. The Kugika were curious about my parents and my siblings and were deeply shocked when I told them that my mother had been cremated and (on my second visit) that my father had willed his body to a medical school for dissection. Otherwise they seemed to be content to know me as a purchaser of vegetables, a provider of jobs and whatever wealth they could wheedle out of me, and a first-aid clinic. Named as a market for local produce, I did not feel that this constellation of roles constituted an individual personality for them to get to know.

(Yet there was a term for "white woman," *ambang* [from *amp mbang*, "reddish woman"] which the Kugika used for me increasingly. While I was still "Kondambi misis" ["the European woman of Kondambi"] to outsiders, the Kugika referred to me as "*kil ambang*" ["our, exclusive, white woman"]. "Ambang" became my name and this was so ingrained that when Kombuk wished to give his baby daughter my "real name" [*kangem wei*] he had to ask me what it was.)

After a few months in the field, not recognizing my own impatience to learn everything at once, I wondered why my discreet inquiries about religious beliefs were yielding so little. By this time my notebooks should contain many pages of laboriously written exegesis, not simply odd remarks and intriguing hints. The older men were reluctant to tell me myths, saying that they would not be credible to a white man or white woman, and I could recognize that the few I collected were greatly abbreviated. When *Tultul* Tagba called to express his gratitude for his "miraculous cure" I steered the conversation around to asking him what happened to people after death. (Tagba had developed a raging boil on a private part of his anatomy. He had endured it as long as he could before limping shamefacedly to my morning first-aid clinic. I took him into my house to shield him from prying eyes and applied some drawing ointment while he held his genitals protectively. The ointment worked wonderfully and soon he was walking normally and was free of pain. He was pathetically grateful.) Surely he would tell me about the spirits. But, instead, Tagba looked at me with displeased surprise and asked me not to make fun of him.

"You should not ask me about things like that," he reproved me, "when you know so much more than I do."

I tried to explain that it was part of my work to find out what the people themselves knew about spirits, but he was adamant that I was making fun of him. I thought of the men who occasionally found some excuse to enter my workroom so that they could show their visitors the paper clips and stapler the spirits had given their white woman.

Jo and Poli worked (ostensibly) in my garden. Other anthropologists had told me that they had been able to save a lot of money by growing their own vegetables. I was no gardener, so I welcomed the Kugikas' insistence that I must have a garden *boi* (T.P., young man, employee). I sacked the first *boi* Wamdi found for me. It took him over a week to fence the tiny garden and then, instead of taking a traditional rest-day (*kor*) or an equivalent of the white man's weekend, he expected to go on drawing his pay for doing nothing further. When Tige repeated this pattern, taking three days to dig a single drain, I decided to hurry the garden along myself. Late one unusually quiet Sunday morning I started digging. There were several interruptions: I knocked off for lunch; a dispute broke out which I had to transfer to my notebook; and, grubby-fingered, I had to record a compensation payment. Nevertheless I had completed two drains by the end of the day. It would not be unreasonable to require Tige to do the same. His reaction to this suggestion was to look away from me with an expression that was close to a snarl. Offered the alternatives of working harder for pay and doing nothing for nothing, he went off huffily. His age-mates told me later that he had left because I was too hard and expected him to work like a prisoner. Other people, he told them, received payment from me for doing nothing but talk. I was scrupulous about reimbursing informants for the time they spent helping me with my work, as Nadel had instructed us; but they had no real conception of what my work was and scarcely any considered telling stories, dictating texts, answering questions, and giving explanations to be work.

My garden did not flourish. After six months I was still buying all my vegetables. By that time I realized what was happening. It was important to my hosts that I should employ a garden *boi*, providing pay for one more member of the clan. But a productive garden would deprive the women of their domestic market. Their sale of vegetables constituted the only steady income, albeit a paltry one, for their menfolk. But when the women took their vegetables to the government station they might meet lovers and kinsfolk and undermine their husbands' control over them. I did not employ another garden *boi*—preferring, I said, to buy the Kugikas' own vegetables. I purchased surprising quantities, for I had to provide for my *manki masta*'s swelling household and keep a good supply of bananas and cucumbers to refresh informants. One day none of the women brought food for me to buy, for they had all heard that a patrol officer's wife had run out of beads and was making all her purchases with money. Many of the husbands had gone along to witness the transactions in case the women tried to keep the shillings and sixpences from them.

Luluai Wamdi was a flamboyant character. The *kiap*s dismissed his glowing oratory as the effusions of a "windbag" and "blatherskite" and sneered at his attempts to please them as *gris* (T.P., currying favor). His habitually proud demeanor seemed to Jack Emanuel to border on insolence. Wamdi did not criticize "Masta Jack" but he spoke to me nostalgically of the former ADO, Brian Corrigan, whom he liked and admired, while he suffered repeated humiliations from the new *kiap*.

For example, one *Mande Brum* a visiting malariologist arrived to take blood samples, record spleens, and search houses for mosquitoes. The Kugika were just departing to do their roadwork, but he called them back and kept them at Kondambi for most of the morning. Wamdi assumed that the malariologist was a government man and that Masta Jack had given his work priority over the usual roadwork. But when this new white man was leaving, two policemen arrived to round up the Kugika. They went to Minj as directed but were told to come back on Thursday instead. On the Thursday, Wamdi sang out for everyone to go to Minj. Many stayed away, so he sent a young man back to sing out again. Because some of the Kugika did not go to Minj the ADO took away the *luluai*'s badge of office and put him in the lockup for the afternoon. He decreed that the Kugika must be punished. They were to do roadwork at the Wahgi River the following day and every day for the next fortnight. *Tultul* Tunga was among the people who did not go to Minj as ordered, but there was no talk of removing his badge of office.

A week later, when the Kugika were still required to go to the Wahgi, a policeman called out across the Minj River that the *kiap* wanted them to bring firewood to the station. About half the Kugika took firewood to Minj and the rest hid in their houses. The ADO said he would remove the badges of *Tultul* Tai and *Tultul* Tagba but not that of *Tultul* Tunga, since he had turned up with firewood.

The bed of the swiftly flowing Minj River was a jumble of rocks in the shallowest part, but when I had to visit the government station it was much shorter to wade across than to follow the road and use the bridge. When the river was up I gladly accepted the help of hands grasping mine. One day, as I was leaving the ADO's residence, the torrential roar of the river was plainly audible. Jack Emanuel, mindful of his responsibility for all expatriates in the subdistrict, insisted on accompanying me part of the way to see that I got across safely. A noncommissioned officer of police escorted us at his command. When we arrived at the bank of the rushing river the ADO ordered the policeman to carry "Misis" across. Obediently the man bent his knees to receive my weight on his shoulders. I was appalled. He was a very small man and I was a strapping young woman. I protested that I only needed someone to hold my hand. But the ADO was adamant. He was the law in his territory, the subdistrict, and I did not dare to argue with him about "white prestige." Eventually, to avoid antagonizing him, I gave in and straddled the policeman's shoulders. All the way across I kept planning how I would save him when his foot slipped and we collapsed into the roaring stream, for swimming was not a customary accomplishment of his people in Chimbu. But he negotiated the flooded river successfully. I thanked him profusely, but I was deeply ashamed.

Sergeant Major Siwi was still at Minj when I returned there in 1963. I saw him occasionally over the ensuing years but did not think particularly of the river crossing. In 1982 I discovered that he had been stationed near Mur during the Komugl Tai cargo cult and I resolved to ask him for his version of it. I thought I had found my opportunity when the police were counting the votes for the national election in the Minj courthouse and the only available and permissible seat was on the bench beside him. I greeted him cordially, but Siwi had been drinking to excess and his own greeting was over-warm. Straightaway he reminded me that he had once carried me across the river, and he kept repeating this, giving me nudges and lascivious looks. I would have to ask him about Komugl Tai some other time. I encountered him once more, but again he spoke of carrying me across the river and gave me more suggestive looks. He was now retired, but I thought he might misinterpret my calling at his home, in spite of our now advanced age, so I sent Ka Non to interview him. Ka, nervous at interviewing an old and distinguished character, fluffed it. He obtained some useful information but forgot to get Siwi remembering some of the most important items.

Anthropology and anthropologists are among the uncounted victims of colonialism. It had not occurred to me in 1954 that "carrying" a white woman across a stream was terminologically indistinguishable from the Pidgin for "carrying" leg (courting) with a local girl.

In any field situation people sort themselves into those who are immediately congenial and others whom one does not care for much. My personal liking for Wamdi and Ko-ba and Mangindam, my sympathy for Tagba and Tunga, and my desire to understand Tai had coalesced into one factor in my deciding to settle with the Kugika. I took an instant liking to Aragont, a young married man, and although I did not associate closely with him or his wife I worried when he became ill. Wamdi, too, was worried. The *kiap* had threatened him with jail if anyone sick should be hidden and die without being admitted to the hospital. Wamdi tried to get people to take their sick relatives to hospital as soon as they became ill, but the people took no notice of him. The hospital was built on the land of the Kondika, their old enemies, and Kondika medical orderlies were employed there so it was a dangerous place for the Kondikas' own enemies. Thus, by the time the *kiap* or the orderlies learned of an illness the patient was already dying, and the hospital gained a reputation as a place of death.

Tomorrow was *Mande Brum*, when all hands had to be present at roadwork, so the next day Wamdi would send for some youths to make a stretcher and carry Aragont to Minj. But, predictably, when Aragont's older brother, Azip, heard of this plan he refused to allow the sick man to be moved. The Health Department had supplied me with a plentiful stock of medicines so that I could treat various ills of the people among whom I worked. I held a first-aid clinic daily at 7 A.M. mainly patching up the wounds of men who cut themselves chopping firewood with steel axes but also treating yaws, boils, burns, colds, and stomach upsets. My skills at diagnosing serious illness were severely limited. (Once I treated what I thought was a tropical ulcer every day for a week before I learned that the patient had escaped from the leprosarium.) Aragont's illness was indeed serious. He had the symptoms of dysentery but others besides which I could not interpret. I wanted him to go to hospital, but Azip was adamant and insisted that I must treat his brother at home. I treated the dysentery symptoms and hoped that the others would cure themselves. They did not.

Aragont's condition fluctuated dramatically but through it all he still smiled a greeting and clasped my hand. But now a subclansman was urging Azip to reciprocate for a pig Palme had given him because he would be needing all of Palme's pigs for the mortuary feast if Aragont died. When it was obvious to me that Aragont was dying, a gash of sorrow that this most likable man was soon to be no more struggled with the hope that Wamdi and his clan would not be involved in trouble through failure to report an illness and the hope, too, that the *kiap* would not form the impression that I had encouraged the sick to stay at home and submit to my own unskilled treatment. A medicine man from North Wahgi came and produced a stone allegedly lodged in Aragont's forehead by someone unknown and far away.[5] These ministrations gave the patient and his brother some comfort, but Azip agreed at last to the youths' transporting Aragont to Minj and there he died.

I more than half expected to receive some of the blame for his death. This did not happen. Many people congratulated me on my understanding of the case and the effectiveness of my medicines. The sick man, they said, had shown signs of improvement while he was in my care and then died when he was out of touch with my medicines. Azip told me that if his brother had stayed and continued to be treated by me he would have lived. In fact Aragont's death was a mystery to me since he had seemed a little better before he left for Minj. "Perhaps," I wrote somewhat priggishly in my diary, "the *hausik* [T.P., hospital] is as bad as they say? I have not examined the patients' quarters in the *hausik* at Minj, but those at Goroka are decidedly [illegible], with neither comfort nor cleanliness to compensate for strange surroundings and perhaps hostile fellow occupants of the same ward. Aragont's body had not been washed during his stay at Minj and I am inclined to think that the lack of hygiene may be an index of a general standard of carelessness."

Azip told me sorrowfully that he was now completely alone. His parents and his wife had died and he had no children (meaning no male children, since I knew he had two daughters). Now that he had no brother living he intended to chop off one of his fingerjoints. I did not know whether to try to dissuade him from doing this or not. A severely depressed Konumbuga man had recently died after such an operation. But I felt that I had interfered enough in the sickness of poor Aragont— giving him sulfaguanadine for what turned out to be beriberi, nagging Azip to take him to the *haus sik* while the illness appeared to be curable, and conniving with Wamdi's sending him there when all the visit could accomplish was to protect the *luluai* from a spell in the lockup. So I asked Azip lamely whether he was going to chop off his fingerjoint today or wait till tomorrow when the burial was to take place. He was plainly disappointed by my response.

The death of Aragont disturbed me, for it made me question the value and the propriety of an anthropologist doling out tablets and applying dressings to sores and cuts and burns. Certainly my morning clinic helped me to identify and get to know a wide range of people and establish some kind of rapport with them. But not everyone fronted up for treatment, and I had no hope of eradicating the disgusting and appalling skin diseases, especially since all the close associates of a child with yaws vied with each other to pull off the scabs. The ordinary first aid—treating headaches and snuffles, abrasions, burns, and boils—was so effective that I gained an unwarranted reputation for miracle cures, which was easily extended to an expectation that I could prevent the seriously ill from dying. I was on good terms with the two orderlies at the nearest aid post and used to refer to them people who seemed to need an injection of penicillin. I also told them of the serious illnesses I encountered. They had come to visit Aragont and quietly advised me that he should go to the *haus sik*, but they lacked the authority to command Azip to take him there. Afterward I felt I should have used Nadel's "bullying technique, the method of the last resort," for I knew that I myself did have that authority as a white person and it might have saved Aragont's life. Still, at the time it did not seem to be my decision to make.

In the Wahgi Valley of the 1950s I was not a woman anthropologist but a white-woman anthropologist. Women were chattels. White women, however, had unlimited money and trade goods for purchasing food and artifacts; they employed servants; they selected their employees from a wide range of applicants, all eager to learn about the world of the white people; they directed the work; and they dismissed those who displeased them. Their employees were all men. The policy of "white prestige" required the *kanakas* (T.P., derogatory term for native people) to show respect and obedience not only to white men but to white women as well. White women were thus of higher status than local men, more powerful than males rather than honorary males.

My knowledge of other cultures made it unnecessary to pry into matters that might have been forbidden: when I wanted to learn about male initiation I related anecdotally to a few of the leaders what some distant people did to boys. They considered their own methods superior, described them enthusiastically, and invited me cordially to witness the rituals. (White men [*yimbang*] slept with native girls and clan secrets were not safe with them: these would soon be known to the girls' fathers and brothers as well as to all the women, but they knew that I slept with no one and could be trusted.) Still, *Tultul* Tai was not so eager for me to watch the prefabricating of the *Bolim* spirit house. But he wanted to borrow my brace and bit for the task, so I made the loan conditional on my being able to observe the work. Perhaps that was an insensitive thing to do; Tai had only wanted to continue the tradition of keeping the process secret to the few men who had a hereditary obligation to perform it. In the event, he agreed readily to the transaction and invited me to be present at the finding of the hidden materials.

When my twelve months were up there was still no way of predicting when the pigs would be killed in the final ceremonies. If all went well this could happen in about a month, but my experience so far suggested that all was unlikely to go well. In any of the three groups men might be jailed for fighting, there might be a death, or the ADO might impose more government work. The administration wanted an "Assistant Government

Anthropologist (Female)" and, in a surge of desire to continue doing fieldwork in New Guinea forever, I applied, but I was too busy with my present fieldwork to attend an interview in Port Moresby and resigned myself to returning to Canberra. Then Nambawan Konangil, undisputed leader of the Konumbuga and one of two "great men" in the area, died. This delayed the pig killing for two months, and Mangindam's search for the witches responsible for his relative's death might take longer.

The death of the great man occurred when Ralph and Eileen Bulmer were due to visit me on their way to Baiyer River. In anticipation of their visit I delighted the Kugika by asking them to build me a little guest house. "A storehouse?" (They had been nagging me to build one ever since I arrived.) *"Maa-baa!"* ("Definitely not!"), I exclaimed. I described minutely the tiny house I wanted them to build and they assured me that it would be finished by the time I returned from my stay in another part of the area. I came back pleased with the information I had obtained on extinct groups and intergroup relations, but displeased with the Kugikas' interpretation of a little sleeping house for a couple of guests. I stared aghast at the lofty, capacious structure: at last they had built the storehouse of their dreams.

I had seen very little of Luzbetak and knew that he thought I was trespassing on his territory. Ralph Bulmer's visit was my only extended encounter with an anthropologist while I was in the field. He helped me enormously by identifying birds and collecting more names of birds. It was helpful, too, to have grass-roots ethnographic talk, to hear his impressions of things he observed, and be forced to find answers to questions about matters I had scarcely begun to analyze. His wife amazed the Kugika by prancing far ahead of them over the hills on the way to Konmil for Konangil's funeral. Bulmer himself astounded them by his height (nearly 6'6"). Konts, their tallest man, sidled up to him and said wistfully, *"Ngagl kembis mei"* ("I am [only] a little boy").

Late in the *Konggol* (pig feast), when the ceremonial ground was lined with spectators from near and far, Wamdi insisted that since I was Kugika I must dance one day with the men and girls. It was a simple dance, pumping the body up and down by bending the knees to the beat of hand drums and energetic songs. Wamdi stipulated that I must wear my white shirt and white shorts, and he and his wives would decorate me. The women fastened several new sets of fluffy pubic strings around my waist. Wamdi himself added shells and furs and finally constructed a magnificent concoction of bird of paradise plumes on my head. I danced proudly. Afterward I received a message that a man from another clan had greatly admired my performance and wished to bathe me in pigs' grease. I declined. But the men of Koimamkup subclan, jealous of my having danced with the Penkup, insisted that I must dance with them, so I donned my white shirt and shorts another day, let them decorate me, and performed once more on the ceremonial ground with the other dancers.

Ian Hogbin once said that there was no difficulty in getting Melanesians to talk about sex; the difficulty was to stop them. I did not inquire about sex, but I learned a good deal from information volunteered to me and from discussions at which I was present. All I heard about homosexuality, however, was that it was an abhorrent and disgusting custom practiced by employees on the government station who came from the coast. I could not tell whether this was the Kumas' authentic attitude or, as I suspected, a parroting of Jack Emanuel's pronouncements. Youths walked about holding hands, always in the same pairs, and cuddled one another openly. I was somewhat surprised that there was nothing particularly suggestive of homosexuality in the initiation rites. Nearly thirty years later, reading Herdt (1981), I wondered about the only part of the male initiation that I did not observe. This was an excursion into the forest, where the boys had to play the flutes and jump over logs. At the time, I had been awake for two consecutive days and nights and, though invited to come along, I was too exhausted and went home to bed. But in 1981 I reflected that the augmentation of semen would be consistent with the Kuma males' ambition to make babies from that substance alone.

I negotiated unsuccessfully with Nadel and my supervisor, Stanner, to extend my period in the field by six months. The negotiations themselves, deliberately protracted, extended my twelve months to fifteen. I might have defied my Canberra mentors and stayed the desired eighteen months if I had been the same person as when I arrived. I had felt independent with my scholarship stipend topped up by a small income derived from stocks I had inherited from my mother. But I had imagined naively that my relations with the field population would be governed by reciprocity of the Malinowskian kind—a friendly, fair return for gifts and services. Instead, the Kuma were apt to insist on a precisely equivalent return for gifts they gave to others while losing no opportunity to gain advantages for themselves. But they had no wish to enter reciprocal relations with white persons.

All Europeans, they reasoned, had unlimited wealth and were therefore morally obliged to give more than they got. Most people professed to believe that they had been mistaken in identifying Europeans as ghosts, but they were convinced that we were all in touch with the spirit world. This was understandable when we all obtained impressive cargo by sending away a *pas* on an aircraft and *kiap*s conversed with unearthly voices by radio. I resisted some of the Kugikas' demands but had to give in to many others. Eventually I sold my stocks, reducing my income to my scholarship stipend of £1,000 per annum tax-free. An unexpected expense was occasioned by an infected finger that urgently required surgery in Lae. In the end I authorized my father to sell my piano so that I would be able to buy a little secondhand car on my return to Australia.

Looking back at the end of my fieldwork, I decided that being beggared by the greedy Kugika was a fair enough return for what I had gained from them. I was elated at what I had accomplished. But, looking back at a field diary now more than thirty years old, I tried to reconcile its record of blunders, disappointments, and ignorance with the remembered exhilaration in work well done among congenial people in enchanting surroundings. There is a simple explanation. Apart from noting, after three months in the field, my delight at being able to understand everything Ka said in the vernacular, I had failed to record my achievements.

My fifteen months with the Kuma changed my life. I had had my weekly day of *kor* (rest), which lasted until the Kugika came home at about 4 P.M. from repairing the Big Road, and once a month or so I paid a duty call upon the ADO at Minj. Otherwise I was constantly at work observing, noting, eliciting explanations, taking down texts and laboriously transcribing them, designing fresh diagrams of group structure, making lists and puzzling over categories that seemed to overlap, in a continually developing relationship with my data and the people who provided them. I was no longer a dilettante anthropologist; I was the real thing, a dedicated researcher struggling to make sense of society and culture. After experiencing the two phases of the great pig festival—*Konggar*, the time and place of building, and the spectacular *Konggol*—I felt that the best way to tackle my Ph.D. thesis would be to focus it on the semantics of Kuma religion. I would relate the sunny complex of birds and flutes to the brutal subjugation of the young men, the treatment of women as "things" (*yap*), the darker divinings of war sorcery, and so on. Much of the relevant data had sprung directly from my focusing on socialization and authority.

This topic, however, was not acceptable to my supervisor, who was himself struggling with the conceptualization of Aboriginal religion and advised me that too little had been written on religion by anthropologists for a student to write a scholarly thesis on it. The argument seemed to me spurious. I knew that he was hoping to use Aboriginal religion to find the key to religion in general and I suspected that he did not want a study with a fresh approach to the topic to appear before his own work was ready. After all, he wanted to have the last word on cargo cults also and had a facility for diverting students who were passionately interested in these to the Aboriginal field or at least to strikingly different topics. With these unworthy thoughts I floundered in search of a more acceptable topic. Stanner himself thought I should write about the women. I had no intention of giving a derogatory picture of Kuma society by focusing on the slave population; I resented the assumption of many male anthropologists that their female counterparts could fill a gap in men's studies simply because they were women (though never typical women); and, although I had ample observational material on what happened to women, I knew the men much better as individuals.

Since I had been working with a hitherto unstudied people, I was required to make an ethnography available to the discipline rather than focusing too sharply on a single aspect. While I was agonizing about having to write a standard ethnography, I wrote a paper on "Aesthetic Expression among the Kuma," delivered in Melbourne in 1955, for ANZAAS (the Australia and New Zealand Association for the Advancement of Science). It was well received and, seeing Nadel waiting for me in the doorway, I hoped for a smile of congratulation. Instead he glowered at me.

"How dare you! How dare you!" he breathed. "Dr. Stanner was to have presented the only theoretical paper in the session."

Meanwhile, a paradox had been emerging. An ethnographic thesis was more desirable than a theoretical one, and students who did not gather enough material for an ethnographic thesis had to make do with theory. And yet a theoretical thesis carried more clout in the long run; ethnography seemed to brand one as a pedestrian fact finder.

There was no day of *kor* for me now, for the demands of my thesis were as unremitting as the sociality of the Kuma had been. I tended to get drowsy in seminars or during the occasional outing through having worked late and having been ready for the world, Kuma-fashion, by seven. I felt that I needed a rest, and when some friends from my life before the Kuma invited me to join them at Shellharbour I accepted gladly. Nadel informed me that I was to give a seminar on a certain date that I knew fell during the University vacation, and I replied that I had arranged to be away then. He bestowed on me the steeliest of his repertoire of steely stares.

"Anthropologists don't need holidays," he sneered.

Shellharbour was a glorious break. Leaving the makings of my thesis back in Canberra, I gave myself entirely to the joys of prawning at night and drifting away the days in swimming and lazing on the beach. I was lazing on the beach when a neighbor of my hostess who had a portable radio told me that "Professor Naydel" had died of a heart attack. I thanked her for the information and went back to sleep. I did not return to Canberra for the funeral.

Canberra anthropology was then much more authoritarian than Sydney had been. Ph.D. students were a lesser species, and I had to tone down my report under instructions from my advisers. Stanner had once walked through the Wahgi Valley, but his companions had been white officials, not their native carriers, personal servants, and police, let alone local people. Both he and Nadel had a preconceived notion of New Guinea society derived from Malinowski's account of the Trobriands. This model was dominated by a genial ethos of reciprocity: giving for gift-cementing friendship. In my account friendship was fragile and tentative across group boundaries; reciprocity was a ruthless insistence on equivalent return and readiness to retaliate. They also had preconceived notions about the universal nature of marriage and the family. They could not readily envisage a nuclear family occupying several different residences (the father sleeping in his own individual men's house, the mother with her pre-pubertal daughters and little sons occupying her own women's house, a grown son sleeping in the group men's house or with a married close agnate, and adolescent offspring sleeping around in individual men's houses where courting ceremonies were held). My advisers thought I was exaggerating the segregation of the sexes. The state of marriage implied for them cohabitation and also the sharing of intimacies, the very thing men of the Kuma wished to guard against. I wanted to argue that the Kuma clan was the "church" in Durkheim's sense and discuss what made it (and not other clans) so, but Stanner insisted on my deleting all reference to this unpopular idea. I was persuaded to understate the degree of domestic violence. My advisers were convinced that marriage had to be reasonably amicable to survive. They did not consider physical violence to be a "social" enough sanction to be a major means of social control. Further, anthropologists were trying to correct the popular prejudice that primitive peoples were brutal savages, and I was drawing attention to savagery and brutality.

I had to deal with religion summarily, so I was deeply hurt when Lawrence and Meggitt did not invite me to contribute to *Gods, Ghosts and Men in Melanesia* (1965), ostensibly because I had already presented an account of Kuma religion. *Pigs, Pearlshells and Women* (Glasse and Meggitt 1969) also passed me by when I had been rethinking Kuma kinship. The male ethnographers of the Highlands appeared to form a club to which I was not admitted.

The Kuma (1959) was my thesis shorn of verbiage. I had thought it was a model of clarity, but anthropologists generalizing about the Highlands managed to misinterpret it. A common error was to confuse clans that were "as brothers" (*angam angam*) in the sense of "as if they were brothers" with "brother" (*angam*) clans with a putative hereditary link through belonging to the same phratry. Mention of a couple of rubbish men

sleeping in houses they had built for their wives in the ceremonial village
became for Meggitt (1964:220) "many men sleep in their wives' houses,"
though the idea of building houses bulging with pig stalls in the cramped
village was bizarre. Not even old men slept in the ordinary "women's
houses"; they all had their own residences. Meggitt (1964:218–222) contrasted Highland societies like Mae Enga, who married their enemies,
with those like Kuma who intermarried with friendly groups. But there
appears to be no equivalent in Mae Enga to the Kumas' "traditional
enemies," with whom the only encounters were attempted killings.
(Witches' confessions that they had given sorcery materials to the enemy
were patently spurious since they would have been slain on sight.) The
groups that were equivalent to the Mae Engas' "perennial enemies" were
clans that were intermittently friendly and hostile. When not at war they
were friendly groups, so I called them "temporary enemies." They married, stopped marrying for the duration of the conflict, and sealed the
peace with an exchange of women. That is, Kuma married people they
had fought. They drew many of their wives from groups that had killed
their clansmen, though the number of clansmen killed by "temporary"
and "traditional" enemies respectively fluctuated over time. Friendship
between clans was neither safe nor permament.

Postpioneering Highlands ethnography was preoccupied for a time
with the proportion of agnates in the local community as an index of the
strength of agnation. The Kuma were consistently reckoned to be low on
the agnatic scale, presumably because I had explored nonconformity and
analyzed mechanisms for transforming the descendants of nonagnates
into true agnates. An "example" I had given (not of nonagnates as such),
explicitly warning against treating it as a "sample," was cited to represent
Kuma as a whole (Kelly 1968). The Mae Enga were reckoned to be
unusually high on the agnatic scale, even after McArthur (1967) corrected
the evidence that led to this conclusion. Meggitt (1965) played down
nonconformity and described only summarily a mode of manufacturing
agnates identical to that of the Kuma. Putative descent groups had been
described from many parts of the world, but the Highlands offered an
unparalleled opportunity to study the processes by which common descent comes to be ascribed or assumed. Some authors, carelessly suppos-
ing that resident nonagnates were immediately assimilated into the clan,
lost sight of the distinction between a putative descent group and a flawed
imitation of an African lineage. "Putative descent group," however, is part
of the vocabulary of the early ethnographies that appears to be now taboo.

The most powerful figures in British social anthropology in the 1950s
were Africanists, and we had to interpret Highlands societies in terms that
made sense to them. But these societies were unstable and, as I argued
(1969) for Kuma, they had developed alternative structures to suit their

changing circumstances. None of us managed to convey the full complexity in a single Ph.D. thesis. Meggitt's analysis of Mae Enga as a lineage system presented one dimension also of Chimbu, Kuma, and Melpa. I do not think our Africanisms prevented us from exposing Highlands society to scrutiny in reasonably illuminating ways before the ethnography of the region was blighted by reliance on secondary sources and bedeviled by the nonanalytic notion of "loose structure." Barnes's model of New Guinea Highlands society (in his influential article of 1962) was evidently drawn from Glasse's Huli, who are unusual in the region, and he set apart Mae Enga (despite striking similarities to the societies from Chimbu westward) as atypical. Many latter-day ethnographers recognize that warfare was endemic to the region but fail to realize that a group in a more "tightly managed" system than that of Abiera (Watson 1971:250) might only be able to survive in that dangerous environment by being efficiently organized for war at all times with rules to live by and its solidarity affirmed and renewed in speech and action. Langness (1964) set an early precedent for the now common confusion of clan and community when he included in-married women as "non-agnates" of "the group."

The changes that have taken place in Highlands society itself have encouraged such sloppiness. Strict protocol in approaching tentatively friendly groups has given way to getting rides on their PMVs (buses or trucks). Judgments that our emphasis on corporate groups was mistaken need to be balanced against the promptness with which tribal warfare broke out with self-government and independence in the face of the success of all colonial authorities in promoting individualism. With coffee smallholding, local government councils, village courts, and national elections, social patterning at the grass roots is less amenable to systematic study. The discrediting of structural-functionalism, however, made it possible for some anthropologists to ignore modern developments and concentrate on particular aspects of culture without indicating the extent to which these were still valid for the people concerned, with working assumptions sometimes reported as deeply held convictions. Some revealed a preoccupation with bodily substances which would have been disabling if the Highlanders had fully shared it.

One might have expected feminist ethnographers to be concerned at the plight of their Highlands sisters. But they have attempted to demonstrate a harmonious integration of women with the rest of society which contrasts strangely with the earlier emphasis on sexual antagonism. Marilyn Strathern's account (1972), still the most systematic of these studies, is also the most convincing, though even this otherwise impeccable scholar occasionally takes at face value a statement by women (e.g., on the ownership of pigs) that reads like their wishful fantasy. It seems that most feminist ethnographers valorize the social condition of Highlands women, partly through political preconceptions and partly because the social condition of women is now different from what it used to be. Missions have had a marked effect on men's treatment of their women-folk, particularly in curbing violence and encouraging some consideration of them as sentient beings. In many places the segregation of the sexes is no longer so extreme and so visible.

When I returned to Kondambi in 1963, people addressed me at last by my personal name. I had sent two copies of my book (Reay 1959) to the ADO with a request for him to give one to Wamdi. This copy was a source of great pleasure to all the Kugika, who peered at the photographs to identify the actors and occasions depicted there. Years later, when some had attained literacy, it was firmly established as a picture book, still unread.

Ruled paper and custom-built hardcover notebooks had given way to floppy looseleaf stenographers' noteboks and a tape recorder. The new notebooks were awkward to use standing up with nothing to rest them on and the paper was too flimsy, so I found myself taking less detailed notes than before. During my earlier visit, listening to the news on my portable battery radio had been firm evidence for the Kugika that I was receiving messages from the spirits. When I could not give them a minutely detailed explanation of radio they were disappointed that I would not trust them with the white people's secret. The bulky Butoba reel-to-reel tape recorder, embarrassingly prominent on public occasions, was yet another device for communicating with the spirits. Councillor Mani, strolling into my field base and finding me playing back a tape, retreated apologizing for interrupting my conversation with the spirits. But people soon recovered from the initial fright at hearing their own voices reproduced, and the younger men nagged me increasingly to record the courting songs. When I taught one how to use the machine and asked him to record a particular event he did so efficiently but managed to squeeze a courting song onto the tape.

Wau was still working for Jim Leahy so he sent his wife, Dire, whom he had trained, to be the first female *manki masta* in the Wahgi Valley. Dire was a classificatory daughter of Wamdi's by actual kin links and so was classified as Penkup. I engaged Tunamp (the Burikup youth who, as a little boy, had carried my notebook) to help her. The men of Koimamkup called upon me to protest that to be fair and just (*kabege*) I must employ someone from their subclan as well as helping the Buri-Penkup. It happened that although Dire and Tunamp hung around my base all day they were so little occupied (even when doubling as my captive informants) that they were privately running a well-attended school for young men who hoped to qualify as household servants, showing them how to sweep floors and, under supervision, iron their clothes with my iron and my kerosene. If Dire had belonged to the wood-chopping sex I would not have needed a second person to help her. I told the Koimamkup that I had no work for yet another employee. But that was beside the point: it was a matter of simple justice (*kabege* again).

Therefore I engaged Nere, a very intelligent youth with (at that time) a fresh and pleasant personality, specifically to help me in my work. He tape-recorded unofficial courts when I had to be elsewhere or wanted to concentrate on noting nonverbal behavior; he helped me greatly with the transcription; and he was an excellent informant. Dire did not consider this to be work and she could not understand why Nere was not required to help her and Tunamp in the kitchen. Nere did not share the common ambition to train for household service, though he would chop the firewood when Tunamp was occasionally absent. He told me that even though he could not read and write he would really like to be a judge. I arranged for him to enter the local vocational school and soon he obtained work as a driver on a plantation. He rapidly adopted the subculture of the drivers of the time. Wearing rolled socks over football boots, they swaggered and bullied, drank to excess, swore mightily, and had a curious habit of aggressively kicking the earth when they were talking. In the early 1970s he lost his last job as a driver and came to me, very drunk, demanding work. My refusal prompted a declaration that working for me was not real work but collecting money for doing nothing.

In 1963, Noibe, a Kugika villager who had been missing eight years earlier, had still not come home. While working on a plantation in New Britain under the Highlands Labour Scheme, he had gone to jail, been released, and disappeared. His close agnates still speculated about his fate. The most popular theory was that Noibe had boarded or been taken on board a cargo ship, often sighted off the coast of New Britain and bound for Australia. Another was that he might have hidden in the bush and found refuge in some New Britain village, married, and settled down. But why had he not returned, bringing his wife and children with him? When I visited Rabaul as a member of a legal committee I made what inquiries I could, but the trail was cold. Noibe's father, who never believed that his son was dead, eventually died and the Burikup people seemed to accept at last that Noibe would never come home.

The early colonial era had suited Wamdi. It had given him power and renown, which Jack Emanuel's attempts to humiliate him did not diminish. But the death of his brother Tai in 1960 changed his fortune. There is no doubt that he would have had a career in the council if he had been able to interrupt his secluded mourning to participate in the first council election.[6] In 1963 he clashed with the visiting fundamentalist missionary, who was fond of pronouncing that Tai was now burning in the eternal fires of hell and that Wamdi himself would suffer the same fate if he continued to oppose the mission.[7] In clashes with the dictatorial missionary, Wamdi's triumphs were now preludes to defeat. His boycott of the mission school left only one Kugika child attending classes, but when this lad went on to boarding school and university the other youths blamed Wamdi for depriving them of schooling. Missionaries and converts who had elsewhere met no organized resistance to their campaign to destroy war-magic had to turn back when Wamdi organized the Penkup men to greet them with a show of traditional weapons. But they came back unexpectedly and Wamdi sent urgently for the Catholic priest to perform the work of destruction instead. Even so, his number-one wife, an eager fundamentalist convert, dashed into the war-magic house to steal a taboo object and publicly destroy it.

From the arrival of the white man Wamdi had been a progressive agent of change, but the missionary's vituperative propaganda branded him a force for evil and a reactionary opponent of modernity and enlightenment. As *luluai* he had proudly upheld and implemented the white man's law, but he greeted both self-government and independence with lawless acts. He mischievously reported to police that fighting had broken out in a certain place and he led them in a futile search around the countryside before they realized that the report was a hoax. In Wamdi's terms it was "hidden talk," though he said he enjoyed the ride. At independence he stole two loaves of bread quite openly from a tradestore. This again was a warning that independence would put an end to law and order. Later he suffered a stroke and limped about, a pitiful and emaciated figure, lonely for his contemporaries who had died. Occasionally he would chatter senselessly, an object of mild amusement to people who accepted that he was eccentric, slightly mad.

The nostalgia of the old people for the old times was evident in a dream of Meian's in 1984. All the Penkup people who were now dead came to see him. Meian and his living companions wore clothes and their skin smelled bad. The dead wore only traditional decorations and their skin smelled good. They all spoke to him and he tried to answer but his mouth was jammed shut.

The past smelled good to Meian, but it is more complex for me. I associate my early fieldwork in the Highlands with three basic experiences: the place, incredibly beautiful and as yet unsullied by tin roofs, steel pylons, and the dust of vehicular traffic; the people, colorful and friendly and eager to share with me their joys and sorrows; and discovery, the recognition of a set or sequence of events clicking shut in my understanding like a poem satisfactorily resolved. The smells are not among my remembered pleasures. The Aborigines I had worked with in eastern Australia were either very clean or very unclean. The yellowish gray smell of long unwashed clothes, the sour odor of stale woodsmoke: these were the smells of fieldwork in the tin humpies. The scent of gum trees in the heat pervades my recollection of fieldwork in the Northern Territory. Of course fieldwork in the Garden of Eden had some pleasant smells, like the appetizing aroma of certain foods being cooked in a steampit or the unexpectedly refreshing smell of clear running water passing through a bamboo tube, but I remember only that they were appetizing and refreshing and not what they smelled like. I remember more clearly the comfort of smoking a cigarette to partially anesthetize my olfactory sense. The stench of pig fat was sometimes overpowering during the Konggol. Then there was the smell of death. The odor of the muddy clay on the mourners' bodies merged with the sickly emanations from a corpse left too long in the sun so that, even now, wet clay smells of decaying flesh and early fieldwork. It does not make me nostalgic for death, but it recalls the joy of discovering things I never dreamed of.

Wamdi was buried and the obligatory pigs killed before Ka Non wrote and told me of the death. If he had sent a telegram promptly I would have attended the funeral and defied the mission's edict that mourning must be silent. Privately in Canberra I wailed, "*Ndab-o! Ndab-o!*" ("Oh, my father!"). His grave is in the hamlet of his old rival Kaa, now the village magistrate. Several years ago the two men decided, without consulting me, on the location of three gravesites—their own and, between them, that of Wamdi's daughter, the anthropologist.

NOTES

1. My fieldwork in the New Guinea Highlands has comprised fifteen months during 1953–55 and, from 1963 onward, numerous periods from two weeks to ten months in duration. It has been financed by the Research School of Pacific Studies, the Australian National University.

2. I had heard of the Wahgi Valley, which the Australian press had dubbed "the Garden of Eden," but it was difficult to get information about Minj and the people living there. The Department of External Territories allowed me to consult a selection of patrol reports but denied me access to all those headed "Native Situation." These dealt with turbulent matters of fighting, disputing, riotous behavior, cargo cults, and antiadministration sentiments. The reports I did see were uniformly bland and only marginally informative. In various more general sources then available it was impossible for someone unacquainted with the Highlands to discover what might be relevant to Minj.

3. White women were prohibited from wearing shorts in Papua New Guinea at that time on the theory that these would "arouse the sexual passions of the natives." But shorts were my most congenial garb and I would be living for an estimated twelve months in the bush, well away from colonial society, so my father's tropical outfitters made several pairs to my own design. They were

extremely modest modified Bombay Bloomers equipped with five generous pockets, the two on the hips scaled to carry my custom-made notebooks. They were marvelously comfortable and, as I intended, they looked terrible and would certainly discourage any sexual passion that happened to be present. Khaki seemed the most practical color. I was only once mistaken for one of the *kiaps*, who also wore khaki shorts. A man who saw my retreating figure from a distance caused my companions some hilarity by sending a message offering me two of his daughters.

4. Mangindam's given name was Non, but he was known more generally as the owner-occupant (*ndam*, "father") of the place Mangi. Ka Non is his son.

5. The overt aim of this treatment was to remove the illness. The medicine man was never summoned, however, until the patient was obviously dying. The treatment identified the cause of death as the work of a distant and anonymous sorcerer. Thus the patient's relatives could not be accused of killing him by witchcraft. A dying big man did not receive this treatment, since people believed that only enemy sorcery, using materials provided by witches in the big man's own community, could kill him.

6. According to people who were present at the election of Mani to the Minj council, no one would nominate. The cadet patrol officer noticed Mani standing erect with his arms folded and, guessing that he was a leader, instructed him to nominate. It was a bizarre choice but no one would shame a clansman by opposing him. Standing with arms folded had been Mani's habitual position since he had missed two months of the Konggol in 1954 through being in jail for badly beating his wife. It expressed his resolve never to beat her again and risk a jail sentence.

7. This was the Swiss Evangelical Brotherhood, a militant fundamentalist sect which changed its name at independence to the Evangelical Church of Papua New Guinea.

SIX

Kainantu: Recollections of a First Encounter

James B. Watson

ARRIVING

It was no magic carpet in the usual sense but a lot of good advice, generous help, and warm hospitality that steered my wife, Virginia Watson, and me to Kainantu and landed me there, as the "advance party," so to speak, late in 1953. Starting in the United States, continuing in Sydney and Canberra, and on into Port Moresby and Lae (with a welcome respite for Christmas in Mumeng), doors were opened, busy schedules put on hold, meals shared, and rich experience plumbed to provide the best possible guidance for a novice going to New Guinea in search of an as-yet-undetermined research site. The Ford Foundation; academic people at Stanford University, the University of Sydney, and the Australian National University; fellow anthropologists in all three places; journalists; administrators; missionaries; former and current patrol officers and medical personnel of the then "Territory"; a pioneer prospector; and ordinary citizens of extraordinary kindness all extended a hand. I am grateful again and truly humbled in recalling all that we were given along the way. Although the prevailing spirit was invariably one of "all in a day's work," what was given was after all a magic carpet in the truest sense.

The tale of the road to Kainantu could easily occupy far more space than the single paragraph foregoing if I were to recall the many favors done us along the way and those who did them. Besides acknowledging debts that wayfarers can seldom repay, such recollections would convey better than mere statement can the fact that we knew our destination only vaguely when we left and could not by any means have found or reached it wholly on our own. Reduced to bare essentials, we sought a situation in which

1. postcontact history was both brief and documentable enough to afford a reasonable "control" of the contact experiences undergone by
2. each of two culturally distinct peoples who nevertheless shared much the same kind and intensity of foreign contact, and
3. a third people, culturally similar to one of the foregoing but whose contact experience was markedly more limited, either by time or distance, and was hence less extensive or less intense than theirs.

The first two peoples, as is likely obvious, were intended to illustrate the significance of *culture*, so far as there were differences of response to the same contact, while the third people was intended to indicate the importance of *degree of contact*.

Roughly this synopsis was what we presented along our way to colleagues and others in a position to give advice as to possible locations. We were initially inclined toward the Central Highlands as an area within which to locate because foreign contact seemed recent and probably documentable enough there to permit one to know with some reliability what the contact experience—at least outwardly—had been. This inclination toward the Highlands was steadily reinforced by most of those who advised us. As the oldest government—even pre-government—station in the Central Highlands, Kainantu progressively emerged as being, on the one hand, new enough to allow the reliability just referred to yet old enough, on the other hand, to permit finding at least some peoples who were, so to speak, contact-seasoned. This meant peoples who, whatever turmoil might still rule their lives, had by now a conventionalized and at least minimally workable set of terms in which they might hope to deal reliably from day to day with outside or foreign agencies, their agents, and their dependents.

A BEGINNING ON THE BIG ROAD

Briefed on village locations, I set out early one morning on a first walk-about "in the Agarabi," as station people called the stretch of country lying to the north. Coursing northward, the "big road" would take me near a number of Agarabi-speaking villages where we might perhaps begin our work. "In the Agarabi," incidentally, may or may not mimic Tok Pisin *long Akarabe.* "Big road" and *bikrot*, in any case, are clearly linked, the latter being Tok Pisin for a road visibly distinct from a local footpath and built at government command. Unmarked but known to its local builders, each separate section of the single-track, unpaved *bikrot* through the Agarabi was built with the corvée labor of villagers living near it. Ideally no group's section would fall within boundaries disputed by another village. But discrepancies could occur, leaving one set of road builders triumphant and smug, a disfranchised set embittered. Although initially such opposition might afford the government an obvious leverage in imposing roadwork assignments, if exacerbated by a particular assignment a boundary dispute could threaten endless wrangling and sometimes bloodshed. Contested or not, sections of the *bikrot* were normally weeded and their washouts filled and bridges repaired by the initial builders. Along with Saturdays for Seventh-Day Adventist adherents and Sundays for Lutherans, the Mondays regularly marked for *bikrot* corvée made the Western week a part of local life.

At least in good weather, with no broken bridges, landslides, or washouts, the *bikrot* afforded slow passage to the occasional jeep. With scarcely a handful of vintage wartime vehicles in working order, however, a passing jeep still drew attention. More often the *bikrot* served people on foot. Yet even foot traffic was still sporadic and normally sparse. Notwithstanding its limited use at the time, the *bikrot* had at least one striking feature beyond its visibility. Using this road, travelers could come and go unhindered. In popular belief if not in actual principle, they were free from direct or magical attack while they kept to the road itself. So specific was this safe-conduct that in the view of some it was void if one left the road for a drink of water or to meet a natural need!

A village's own paths, by contrast, lay within locally claimed and defended territory. They had developed through customary and virtually exclusive local use. Such paths were in essence proprietary, since in this and other fundamental matters each of these numerous village peoples, their small population notwithstanding, had until lately acted as a *nation* in the original sense. Within a given village territory, in 1954 and much later, a stranger remained at risk without convincing business. Once general, fatal attacks on presumed trespassers still would occasionally be carried out, albeit covertly, on certain village paths. Here, in short, the outsider lacked the safe-conduct imputed to the *bikrot*. This safe-conduct covered not only total strangers and persons of unknown purpose but even mortal enemies. Thus Agarabi villages situated directly on a *bikrot* were understandably few: Whatever its advantages to travelers abroad, the blanket guarantee of free access made the *bikrot* unwelcome as a future main street. Between tiny domains interlinked by essentially private paths and an ever-expanding "big road" network, the difference could hardly be much sharper. For all of its present limitations, then, one could hardly doubt the long-term impact of so marked an innovation. One small consequence was my own first experience on the *bikrot*, a meeting with a stranger.

Just around the bend and over the hill from the Seventh Day Adventist mission, where the big road rose to follow a low ridge, I met a fellow traveler. A man of early middle years was coming toward me on his way to the station. With no one else in sight just then, we paused to look each other over and we exchanged simple greetings. "*Yu go we na yu kam?*" (T.P., "Where are you headed?") "*Mi, mi go long stesin. Yu kam long wanem hap?*" (T.P., "Oh, I am going to the station. What place do you come from?") To further break the ice, I asked him where the big road would take me. Where did I want to go? he countered, and I told him of my wish to visit two or three Agarabi villages and talk to people there. He pointed the way to several villages, including Uminufintenu, in fact my immediate destination. As if to justify his curiosity, he volunteered that he was himself Agarabi, wondering aloud about my purpose. "*Mi tingting tasol.*" (T.P., "I am just thinking.")

Was I *misin* (T.P., missionary)? he asked. Then perhaps *kampani* (T.P., trader or storekeeper)? He left out *gavman* (T.P., government or administrative employee), as I recall, leaving me to wonder later if I did not fit the last of that well-known triad of local stereotypes.

His Tok Pisin was good—much better than mine, and in answering him I offered a quick sketch of the response I planned to give at Uminufintenu to this inevitable question. Evidently satisfied, he surprised me with a skeptical synopsis of postcontact local history. I remember it today as almost a set speech, a recital of views that only later would prove to have been familiar at that time, before history would overtake these views.

"Before the *kiap* [T.P., patrol officer or, generically, the Australian administration] came we were always fighting each other. As soon as one fight died down another would spring up. Then the *kiap* came and the *gavman* forbade further fighting. If we thrust aside his words, the *kiap* was very hard on us so we had to give up fighting. By then we were convinced that things had changed for good, so we were content. Now that everyody had stopped doing it, we could get along without fighting.

"Then Japan came. Japan was strong and they chased the *kiap* away. The *gavman* disappeared. With no *kiap* to stop us, we began all over again, just like before. No one forgot a single wrong they held against their enemies. We decided that *kiap* law was finished. We thought at first it was strong but now we decided that we had been mistaken about the *kiap*.

"We returned to our old ways for a while, but after Japan left, the *gavman* came back again. Once more the *kiap* tabooed our fighting. Any people that cast aside his words would be punished really hard—beatings, executions, burning houses, prison for the fighters, killing some. Some Agarabi peoples suffered very badly and some Gadsup people too. Once more we had to quit. But now we are not sure. We wonder.

"The *kiap*'s police are strong, yes, and when they like they can hurt us to make us stop fighting each other. But will it all happen again, just like before? Will we just go back to fighting again as we always have? No one has forgotten anything—who their enemies are, what rotten things they did that have not been repaid. Everyone remembers exactly where to begin again. So we are waiting to see what will happen. That's what we are thinking about."

I could hardly help looking back now, of course, at what was said on the *bikrot* that morning. At the time it seemed an astonishing soliloquy— plainer in terse Tok Pisin to be sure, than when rendered into English. I recall my informant's mention of specific Agarabi and Gadsup villages. Without elaboration, these village names had meant little to me at the time. The villages lay to the east of my present route, closer to the edge of the Markham Valley. There, as I would later learn, Japanese patrols had been active during the Pacific war. The Japanese had briefly established a small base in the vicinity and at least two of the villages would later suffer heavy reprisals. Carried out by Australian forces, quite likely the wartime ANGAU (Australian New Guinea Administrative Unit), this punishment was inflicted for suspected collaboration with the enemy.

My friend of the *bikrot* quite possibly did not distinguish the specific agency or perhaps even the official motive for these reprisals—if indeed he knew it—from the more general restoration of *gavman* following the Japanese withdrawal, and the again-active postwar presence of *kiap*/police power in curbing intervillage hostilities. If not simply invisible to villagers of that day, moreover, the distinction between the interim, wartime ANGAU and the previous and subsequent civil administration (*kiap* government) might well seem academic, one more imponderable of the white man's world. Further complicating matters was the fact that during the war some former *kiap*s (and possibly some later ones) were ANGAU people. At one point a renowned and troublesome sorcerer from Ontabura (a Tairora village) was beheaded by means of a captured samurai sword. This execution was said by fellow villagers to have been carried out by a *kiap*, Masta Tempis, but in fact the executioner was previously if not at the time attached to ANGAU. (Following the beheading, the executioner deliberately mangled the victim's body beneath the wheels of his jeep.) But even if indeed "ANGAU-instigated," the act could be likened to earlier deeds of a *kiap* or his police, whether or not the latter were authorized or supervised. As a particular thorn in the flesh of prewar authority, Tairora-speaking Noraikora people suffered at least one, perhaps two or more, summary executions, carried out within their village where, evidently unaccompanied, the police had apprehended their victim or victims. With his arms pinioned by constables, a prisoner's head was split open with an axe wielded by the sergeant in charge of the patrol. Following this, in at least one case, the victim's body was roasted, in the presence of his fellow villagers, as in a village *mumu* (T.P., earth oven).

Whether carried out by police (authorized, supervised, or neither), by wartime ANGAU personnel, or by prewar or postwar civilian *kiap*s, such distinctions were missed by most villagers if not by all. Or the distinctions were simply irrelevant, as far as villagers could see, in understanding the world in which they must live. I believe my acquaintance of the *bikrot* that morning, in other words, was speaking broadly of "*kiap*," "*gavman*," and "police," without regard to such details as I have sought to sketch. If I am right, it is easy enough to understand his frame of reference.

CHOOSING "CULTURE A"

The choice of Aiamontina as the first phase of a projected comparison of two cultures (three peoples) was acknowledged by the subdistrict office without much comment pro or con. Apparently it was considered an acceptable location for a man and wife and their infant daughter for a several-month stay. They largely left it to us how suitable Aiamontina might be for the research itself. All three of us were by now in Kainantu, temporarily housed and boarding at the station with *kiap* Bruce Burge and his wife in their small bungalow, which was said to be the oldest standing European building in the Central Highlands. No reason was given for second thoughts about choosing Aiamontina, nor did I later find reason for misgivings. Indeed, there were special advantages, both domestic and ethnographic, for starting out at Aiamontina. A single-track, unpaved vehicular road, passable most of the time except for two vulnerable log bridges, ran all the way from Kainantu to the heart of the village. Though we ourselves had no vehicle, there were several wartime jeeps then still in operation in the vicinity. (I think the first government Land Rover reached Kainantu somewhat later.) Hiring a jeep, we could hope in a single trip to move our bulky household and field gear to our eventual house. These impedimenta included our daughter Anne's "meat-safe baby cot" and the heavy petrol generator lent us—for recharging wet-cell tape recorder batteries—by the Department of Anthropology at Sydney. The jeep option obviated the need to recruit a long cargo line for the purpose of moving to the village.

In conversations with the subdistrict office, I recall no reference to the patrol officer Ian Mack, incidentally, much less any mention of his fatal wounding at Aiamontina in 1933 while leading a government reprisal against the village. Certainly there was no suggestion of a special reputation for defiance or rebelliousness, and no hint that the people of Aiamontina were in any singular way marked by prior conflict with the foreigners or their government. Among Agarabi-speaking peoples as well as others within the Kainantu Subdistrict, armed conflict with foreigners would hardly set one people apart from another. If Aiamontina had in some fashion acquired a special name among early or latter-day administrators, no mention was made of it. Like most or all of their neighbors, to be sure, the Aiamontina were sometimes damned by officers as "bigheads" or "*kanakas*" (T.P., derogatory term for native people), this when they failed in some expected compliance, and they were sometimes grudgingly praised when they succeeded. Their comprehension of and adjustment to the new order of local life seemed at least on a par with that of their neighbors. If they had no women who readily spoke Tok Pisin—none, certainly, as outstanding as the famous Anyan (or Onion) of Taiora, "who could keep up with any man"—this was the common situation among their neighbors as well. They managed the requirements of postwar "pidgin culture," so far as I could learn, in a manner neither more nor less adroit or spirited than that of other local peoples. From a contemporary *kiap*'s point of view in 1954, evidently, the Aiamontina were a representative Agarabi people.

To us who lived there in 1954, Aiamontina (the foreigner's rendition of Ayámoentenu) was a large and thriving community, larger than many others in the vicinity. Nearby, to one side of the village, was an Australian coffee planter for whom some of the village's young men worked at times, while on the other side of its substantial territory lay a block of land already earmarked for future alienation to a former Kainantu *kiap*, Tommy Aitchison. There were both Lutheran and Seventh-Day Adventist converts in the community, a "house boy" who walked every day to his work in Kainantu, and numerous present or former day laborers or indentured *kontrak* (T.P., contract or agreement), fluent in Tok Pisin and in the ways of the postcontact order. Neither dead nor dying, under no administrative disgrace, nor even withdrawn into itself in hurt or hostility, Aiamontina openly admitted sharing with many other Agarabi-speaking villages a familiar record of early confrontations with gold miners and government men, of stealing clothes and blankets from settler clotheslines, and of supplying women for sexual purposes in exchange for trade goods or to provide the chance to steal them.

In being no longer the autonomous people they were before contact, making war and concluding peace on their own terms and account, the Aiamontina resembled every other village of their vicinity. The world and everything of theirs within it had shrunk since then. For them as for most others I would meet, the metaphor of present smallness was pervasive—people, pigs, gardens, yields, the local territiory, sometimes the very *kunai* (T.P., sword grass)—a sign as potent as it was poignant. Like others around them, they knew both court and *kalabus* (T.P., jail). They counted corvée labor on the *bikrot* (T.P., vehicular road) Monday's inescapable chore. With the Seventh-Day Adventists (S.D.A.) some of them celebrated Saturday while somewhat more observed the Lutherans' Sunday. Some kept goats at the behest of the S.D.A. mission while more held regular nighttime sessions during which they recited by rote the Kâte language exercises promoted by the Lutherans. Nobody promoted Tok Pisin but it was nevertheless widely used and even more widely understood. The self-conscious use of Tok Pisin words and phrases had already become a fetish for growing boys, while many men spoke the language fluently. Most men and older youths could explain the different course of life after death for each of the two local mission sects: a serial procession of *Telatela* (Lutheran) souls as each in turn left its earthly body, while *Sevende* souls were destined to remain collectively earthbound until the trumpet should sound and all together advance into the Kingdom. As for the goods of this world, like others around them the Aiamontina claimed to have known the local use of money since 1947, when "Mata Sikina" (*kiap* Ian Skinner) introduced it. They thus knew how much they could earn for a day's casual labor and how much a kilo of *kaukau* (T.P., sweet potato) would fetch from a *kiap*, planter, missionary, or trader, as well as what they could buy with a given amount of cash or *kaukau* at any of the trade stores in Kainantu.

Permission had been granted for us to occupy the government rest-house in the village while a house of our own was abuilding. The rest-house could not be ours indefinitely, however, because of the need of patrol officers making their rounds and stopping at Aiamontina from time to time for census taking, medical surveys, or inspecting the village. The Aiamontina resthouse was in any case in doubtful condition, its thatch unlikely to keep out a heavy rain, its walls with large cracks through which the domestic life of the new residents was plainly visible to inquisitive younger villagers. Normally vacant much of the time, it was smilingly said that the empty resthouse served future adults as a house of assignation. It was obviously in our own best interest, as well as a possible boon to the older boys and girls of the village, to vacate as soon as we had a dwelling of our own.

BUILDING THE HOUSE

I would challenge anyone who described the Aiamontina as listless or dispirited, much less as shirkers, but the house-building plan projected by our hosts proved in retrospect to be over-ambitious. Added to their usual tasks and obligations, building our house was quite a strain on the community's labor pool, and the completion of the dwelling with its several rooms seemed at times to drag. Still there were other times, such as when posts were planted and beams lashed between them, or when enough bundles of *kunai* were on hand to keep a thatching crew of several men busy on the walls or roof, that progress was both visible and heartening. During the slower phases, moreover, I kept telling myself that I should not regard the construction of the house as simply a means to an end—as something required in order to do residential fieldwork. It should itself be thought a part of fieldwork in the sense of learning names and getting a sense of individual people and how they dealt with one another, as well as with the materials at their disposal. Thus slack times and delays need not be considered as time wasted or lost. Before we were through, however, many of those who were taking part would be ready, I am sure, to wonder if such a big house were truly necessary.

The sheer amount of *kunai* required for thatching roof and walls was daunting and here, at times, there would be a bottleneck. Proper thatch had to be fetched from a fair distance, and the path to major sources evidently differed from the daily house-to-garden movements of most of the women. That it was women's work to cut and carry the bulky bundles of grass to the construction site, moreover, meant calling upon the busiest members of the community to assume this considerable extra service. Sometimes idled by the lack of ready thatch, the men could protest the women's reluctance to do as they were asked. Eventually some of the girls and boys of the village were induced to help, but they could hardly match the adult women, the true professionals whose heavy bundles each provided many of the hand-sized clutches that thatching helpers made and threw or handed to the thatchers for lashing to roof or wall stringers.

When *kunai* bundles lay gathered in ample heaps on the ground beside the house, and when a sufficient number of thatchers and helpers were on hand—those were the times when the project surged ahead, when the workers' spirits rose, when banter and joking lightened labor to the seeming point of weightlessness, and those tying and tossing the individual clutches of thatch and those placing and lashing these, one beside the next before it, strove to move in precise synchrony, each ready to give or get, toss or catch, just as the other required, actuating one of the simplest and in some ways perhaps one of the sweetest expressions of reciprocity or teamwork humans can know. The mood was then infectious and one could almost think that, rather than disrupting the rhythms of communal life with a house too big, perhaps we were even promoting these rhythms. If that is too much to accept, I think one can nevertheless agree that pride and pleasure were plain on both sides.

ANCIENT ANXIETIES IN A MODERN CONTEXT

Our own house neared completion and everyone knew we would soon be leaving our temporary quarters in the government resthouse. Separated from the village's main settlement by a stretch of garden land, the site chosen for us was some minutes' walk away. Picking a private moment, Moya approached me one day with a warning I did not fully understand.

He began by saying that women and especially small children are weak and vulnerable. They are not strong like men. Those who wish to do others harm therefore seek them out as victims. But children do not know this and a child, unaware that it was poisoned, might innocently accept a banana from the hand of a stranger. It is important to watch over children, he continued, as the people here knew too well. With baby Anne I must be vigilant lest, unsuspected or unseen, someone approach and do her harm.

Moya was speaking of sorcery, plainly, but why to me and why just then? Thanking him for his concern, I wondered aloud how people as new to the vicinity as ourselves could already have such serious enemies. This quite likely convinced him that I missed the point of his advice and might therefore take it lightly. Mildly conceding that newcomers could be unaware of the kind of men he had in mind, he let the subject drop. Anything further was left to me.

Later I would see what was almost certainly on Moya's mind: don't feel safe even if you think you don't have enemies. There are sorcerers who simply like to kill. Wanton killers kill wantonly, in other words, and women and children are their easiest targets. Since no special motive is needed, sheer opportunity is all that matters. What made the advice timely was, of course, our impending move. In the new house, out of sight of the village, we would lack the protection of other people against the lurking sorcerer, and our risk would greatly increase, especially for the baby. Whatever impression I left with Moya, in any case, this recollection obviously shows I did not forget his concern or his timely advice.

The site itself was splendid. The house stood at the brow of a small hill overlooking a grassy ravine and the *bikrot* beyond. Built by government command with village labor, this narrow dirt road was one branch of a growing network radiating outward from Kainantu. To the south one could see where the road crossed a log bridge on its way to the station; in the other direction it led to more distant Agarabi peoples and territories—Punano, Asupuia, Tuta, Namonka, and beyond them to Pomassi and Bidimoia. Somewhere in the distance, on the far side of the road, was Aroyamare, one of several remembered sites where Aiamontina people had previously lived. With alternate syllables accented, the lilt of this lovely place name struck me as Italian. The name was also a reminder of the recurrent movement of local peoples in the recent past.

Our visibility from the *bikrot* and our proximity to it, incidentally, must have played a part in Moya's concern about wandering sorcerers. Who knew what strangers might come unhindered by using this path? Current opinion held that in walking the *bikrot* no one could be challenged—friend or enemy, neighbor or unknown. Persons intent on mischief were as free as those with honest errands. Prowlers and magicians were no longer at risk, and with little thus to stop them they were ranging abroad in search of casual opportunity.

ONE MAN'S TRAGEDY

During the housebuilding we came to know one of our Aiamontina neighbors as an unusually passive onlooker. He followed with interest whatever others were doing but seldom took part himself. A frail and sickly man, his skin hung on thin bones, the kind of skin local people liken to ashes and view as a mark of aging. But he was evidently not an old man. One of his forearms showed a lump as if, in mending, a broken bone had misaligned. He told me about it one day. The lump was not from a break, he said, but from a *katres* (T.P., bullet) that passed through his brother before hitting him.

"That bullet killed my brother and I'm sure it's still in me. You can feel it right here. [He offered me the arm.] I went to the *haus sik* [T.P., hospital or infirmary] in Kainantu one time to ask them to take it out. They told me there couldn't be any bullet there and sent me away. I tried again later with a different *liklik dokta* [T.P., medical assistant]. But he also sent me away. I think that bullet has made me a *bun nating* [T.P., weakling]. I can do very little work. Everyone knows I lack strength. I get tired from nothing, but I wasn't like this before."

Listeners nearby quickly assented, insisting that their kinsman lost his strength only after being hit by the brother's mortal bullet. That a white man or a policeman was involved scarcely needed saying. No villager had ever used a rifle; perhaps no villager ever even held one in his hands. Further questions brought out that this man's wound was but one consequence of a much larger event, an attack on the village by Masta Mek (Ian Mack), a former *kiap*.

This attack took place less than ten years before the Pacific war, when even "controlled" peoples like the Aiamontina would commence fighting again. However imminent, no such future was yet visible during the pioneer phase of *gavman* in Kainantu, and the *kiap*'s law was promoted with vigor and—one must say in retrospect—with some impatience. Impatience reflected the undoubted "wrongness" of whole sets of indigenous behavior, from the viewpoint of those largely oblivious to its long-established roots. Of the measures then used in imposing a ban on intervillage fighting, direct punitive attack on violators was by far the most dramatic. Though in principle a last resort, armed attack by the constabulary was viewed by a number of *kiaps* as the most effective measure they had. Once fighting was banned among a given people, it seemed to some that any subsequent infraction by those very people might well be deliberate, even provocative, and thus might call for "firm" response. All too easily a junior *kiap* could suppose, moreover, that frequent "out-breaks" in his area would be seen by superiors to reflect his own short-comings as a bringer of peace. Nor should one overlook that the superiors were ultimately answerable themselves to an international body spurring Australia to move with dispatch in civilizing New Guinea's Mandated, later Trust, Territory.

Local peoples knew almost nothing of this in 1933 when men of Aiamontina were accused of attacking and killing or helping to kill two Asupuia enemies of theirs. In the view of the *kiap*, evidently, there was no excuse for them since they should have known better. There was furthermore a complicating factor: the victims were erstwhile prisoners of the *kiap*, escaping from Kainantu. These Asupuia men had been imprisoned for their part in earlier intervillage fighting, which had led the *kiap* to move against Asupuia to apprehend them. Now unarmed and in no doubt of their danger, these desperate fugitives were attempting to cross open enemy country on their ill-fated flight from the *kalabus* (T.P., jail). Moving swiftly, once news of the killings reached him, *Kiap* Mack assembled his police and late in the day proceeded to Aiamontina, arriving under cover of darkness. Counting on surprise, the police surrounded the men's house. Shooting through the walls at whoever might be within, they fired point blank at survivors attempting to escape. Nine or ten men were remembered to have been killed besides our neighbor's brother. Based on accounts by their survivors, I have previously written about that nighttime attack and its aftermath (Watson 1960:141–144).

Some Aiamontina may believe that, felled by a villager's arrows, Mack died that very night on the floor of the men's house. (Even the names of the fatal arrows—two types among several score of named types—were said to be remembered.) According to a fellow *kiap*, however, Mack had a well-known medical problem from which he later succumbed, in the hospital at Salamaua, his weakness aggravated by the stress of the Aiamontina experience.

This memoir is not the place for expanding on the event or evaluating different versions of it. The immediate point is that Aiamontina now shared a fate with various other peoples of the vicinity, some Agarabi, many more not. Among these others, of course, were the peoples named by my initial local contact that morning on the *bikrot*. Hardly the first and not the last, the Aiamontina were among those who had directly felt or who would yet feel the *kiap*'s heavy hand. No less than any other people of the area, moreover, they witnessed the deployment of *kiap* power against some of their neighbors, friends and enemies alike. For the *kiap* himself, indeed, delivering an object lesson was explicit in deploying his power. (As guides or bearers for the *gavman*, it might be added, certain Aiamontina men would later themselves assist police expeditions in punishing certain peoples living to the south, hence newer to *kiap* law than themselves.) Like others accused of violating the taboo against intervillage killings—or accused of stealing livestock or tools or of collaborating with the enemy—the Aiamontina were severely punished.

Sometime after learning of his misfortune, I told our neighbor's story to the *liklik dokta* at the infirmary in Kainantu. Fellow villagers, I stressed, fully backed his claim. A conscientious medical assistant, he doubted that a man with such a wound could be helped very much after twenty years. In fact he questioned whether a bullet could still be buried in his body. Telling me nevertheless to urge our neighbor to come in once more, he agreed to remove any bullet that could be found. There was a bullet, and our neighbor returned from his surgery content at last to have the proof and with it, probably, his own vindication in playing so small a role in the affairs of his people. The lead within the bullet's shell evidently had weakened him. Though nearly hollow after so many years inside his body, the casing itself could still be recognized. In dissolving, however, its contents had been a slow poison. If tempted to see this personal tragedy as a metaphor for postcontact history, one must also recognize that the history is not that of Aiamontina alone.

A JOKE THAT BACKFIRED

Shortly after moving into our raw new house, its plaited bamboo floors still green and damp, I lolled in the sun one morning with four or five Aiamontina men, all of them prominent in the building project. Looking across the ravine to the *bikrot*, we talked idly of this and that. A lone figure presently came into view, making his way slowly along the road. He was struggling with what seemed to be a large sack bulging with heavy contents. Despite the distance, my companions soon settled the identity of the traveler: it was Anara'i, *waitpus* or the paramount *luluai* of the Kainantu Subdistrict. An Agarabi speaker from enemy Punano, Anara'i was well known in the vicinity. Bent beneath his heavy burden, he was evidently heading for the station at Kainantu some miles distant. Almost as soon as naming him my companions surmised the contents of the sack and the purpose of the journey. The sack was filled with green coffee, they were certain, and Anara'i was taking this bulky load of beans to Kainantu to present to the government. Lackey that he was, he was stuck with this thankless task in order to demonstrate his loyalty to the *kiap*. Several years earlier the government had issued what was taken to be a standing order to all the peoples of the subdistrict: plant coffee. In presenting Punano's first harvest of beans for government approval, Anara'i could pay his respects to those who made him *waitpus*.

Rolling in the grass where they had been sitting, my companions chortled with delight. What justice that ambitious Anara'i should have to do this stupid thing! Enjoy yourself, *waitpus*! You want to show you are the government's man! Now see what it costs you! You have become the *kiap*'s *kagoboi* (T.P., native carrier)! One jibe led to the next as each man savored what was sure to be the the day's chief event.

Laughter eventually subsiding, they smiled when I asked about their own coffee-growing project. I had only lately been shown a wretched nursery of coffee seedlings. Like all their neighbors, they pointed out, the Aiamontina had been required by the *kiap* to build and keep up this nursery. Grudgingly they did so, but merely as a token of compliance, unconvinced of the alleged purpose of it, and indeed without sufficient care to keep the seedlings healthy. The thatch meant to shield the young plants from the burning sun had mostly fallen down, and as master gardeners they could hardly deny the poor condition of the seedlings. The few scraggly coffee bushes so far actually planted out in rows further confirmed their disinterest. But what did it matter? This was just one more whim of the government, arbitrary and pointless as far as they could see.

A bit of background shows this resistance to be more than merely contrary. With crop after crop, they insisted, villagers of the region had followed the foreigner's urging, in each case assured of the benefits it would bring them to grow it. They had tried oranges, cinchona trees, white potatoes, manioc, pawpaws, pineapples, passionfruit, cabbages, and lately the temperate zone garden crops the foreigner favored for his own table. Some of these failed commodities, they had been told, would be in great demand by foreigners. Almost none of them, however, had produced a worthwhile result. Planted from seed, the oranges were sour, and while having to eat their own white potatoes following a production glut, they wondered how anyone could want such tasteless stuff for food. After a brief flurry, they could no longer sell their passionfruit. Like the potatoes, a few things were at least edible, but unlike maize and tobacco (not to mention sweet potatoes!), which had reached them without foreign urging, even these items had found no significant place in local consumption. As for the cinchona, the government itself had furnished the seedlings for planting. But by the time the trees matured, the government no longer needed quinine and refused the bark they bagged and brought for sale as they had been told to do. The bark was useless to them. Lately it was coffee seeds. Since these were likewise inedible, they would be as worthless as cinchona bark if the white man once more reneged on his promises. In the meanwhile, to keep out of trouble with the *kiap*, they could transplant a few seedlings now and then. The nursery could be spruced up, readied for show on short notice, whenever word reached them that the village was due for inspection. Unlike themselves, on the other hand, the Punano had no choice but to take this coffee nonsense seriously. Since that was thanks to their resident *waitpus*, however, they could blame no one but themselves.

The humor and candor of my companions were reward enough for the morning I spent with them. But the story did not stop there. By evening of that very day word ran like wildfire through the village that Anara'i had returned in triumph to Punano. Only that morning his toilsome journey had been ridiculed as a fool's errand, but lugging the bag of coffee beans to Kainantu had yielded "sixteen pounds" (in Australian currency of the time). Rumor may have exaggerated the sum, but no matter: the effect was the same. No village product or service, it was soon pointed out, had ever commanded so large a payment. Growing coffee seeds might at last provide the reward they felt they had so often been promised. This potent demonstration seemed almost certain to be a turning point in the commitment of local peoples to cash cropping, and so indeed it proved to be. I could only consider my good fortune in witnessing the event.

PERPLEXITY

In the "Conclusion" of *Elementary Forms of the Religious Life*, Durkheim (1915:426) forthrightly observes:

> ... There is no people and no state which is not a part of another society, more or less unlimited, which embraces all the peoples and all the States with which the first comes in contact, either directly or indirectly; there is no national life which is not dominated by a collective life of an international nature.
>   ... there are other groups above these geographically determined ones, whose contours are less clearly marked: they have no fixed frontiers, but include all sorts of more or less neighboring and related tribes. The particular social life thus created tends to spread itself over an area with no definite limits. . . .

One need hardly modernize the phrasing to recognize here an uncompromising assertion of "another [level of] society," of supralocal groups, in short, of an intersocietal or regional social order dominating the life of the local communities it comprises. Such an order, Durkheim adds, is by no means peculiar to Aboriginal Australia, nor are its manifestations peculiar to the religious life. While it is of course those societies and that life that immediately concern him, not only in Australia but everywhere on earth do neighboring peoples irresistibly tend "to confound themselves with each other" (1915:426). This global tendency commonly has its causes in the commerce and intermarriage of neighboring peoples—

the *commercium et connubium* that Marcel Mauss would later also cite as grounding his universal gift.

In essence, surely, Durkheim's assertion is correct. I doubt the statement is excessive, but if it seems so today, one must allow for the blindness of ethnographic localism and the long-standing neglect of a view of regional and global humanity that was once more prominent as well as widely shared. Yet the very "international nature" of Kainantu's collective life points up the irony of choosing such a place as the setting for a comparison of adjacent peoples and cultures: how deeply would these neighbors, competing and cooperating with one another on intimate terms, be confounded by their extramural activity? In one respect, as already mentioned, Kainantu and New Guinea promised to be ideal, offering a situation in which, first of all, contact with civilization was recent and brief enough to permit obtaining a fairly detailed grasp of its history. And I further hoped to find two local peoples for practical purposes sharing the same postcontact history. Yet I was also aiming to find such a pair of peoples with distinctive cultures, this in order to assess how much their pristine differences—as opposed to the degree of contact—mattered in the subsequent outcome. Here was the rub: how distinctive a pair of peoples and cultures was it possible to find in Kainantu, given international conditions?

Durkheim's extramural rule accurately predicts the extensive and frontierless "other society" that we found ourselves facing in the Eastern Highlands. The Kainantu vicinity was itself, or was at least a substantial part of, such a supralocal society. To be sure, New Guinea at large lends rich support to those who stress local practices and meanings and the specific uniqueness of their expression. One might challenge the exclusive emphasis on local diversity and uniqueness, but there is no quarrel with the fact. Diversity is of course a condition repeatedly remarked if not sometimes exaggerated by writers seeking common terms for dealing with New Guinea at large. For our idealized plan, however, the culturescape of Kainantu posed from the start an opposite sort of problem: it was not enough, I felt, to count on minutiae. The ethnographer's measurements are not so fine. We must find among nearby neighbors particularities radical or gross enough to signify in their respective responses to foreign contact. In looking at peoples and cultures whose collective life was "international," the practical question was whether local contrasts could be sufficiently salient and sharp, in spite of much confounding, to permit a workable comparison of two groups ostensibly exposed to the same "outside." If neighboring groups are invariably exposed to, even *dominated* by much the same outside, in other words, how different might they be? And how different might the reactions of such groups therefore be to a newer, postcontact outside?

The commitment to an Agarabi-speaking community implied a faith that among their Gadsup-, Kamano-, or Tairora-speaking neighbors there was an opposable community whose mother culture differed sharply enough to anticipate and perhaps explain differences in post-contact response or development. To justify that faith, in short, I had to find, among the neighbors of the Agarabi, groups differing both in mother culture and in postcontact development. This faith was not blind, of course, if one accepted that communities speaking different languages would have some likelihood of doing other things differently as well. And I tended to look at Tairora speakers as my best bet for a possible contrast because, although related, Tairora was much farther from Agarabi or Gadsup than either from the other. Kamano was more distant still from the rest of the Kainantu group, but we shied away from having to work, within the space of a year and a half, in two languages quite so far apart. The horns of the dilemma! Was good control of a common postcontact history to be had only at the price of finding too little contrast among the peoples experiencing it? Perhaps we wanted to have our cake and eat it too!

As time went on of course I became more familiar with Aiamontina activities, beliefs, and values. On given points of practice or profession I would often ask informants if particular neighbors resembled them. "Just the same as what I have just now told you [about us]" became almost a refrain. Only rarely did the response vary. To illustrate one such exception, however, let me note that several Agarabi men remarked the low-pitched, breathy, guttural, almost grunting sound delivered in unison by Tairora warriors engaging a foe. As best I can recall and represent their report of it, this was something like a continuous "Hunh! Hunh! Hunh!" Unusual for Highland New Guinea languages, evidently, Tairora has a common "h" sound, for local hearers perhaps accentuating the eeriness of the cry. As the Aiamontina saw—or better, *heard*—it, the battle cry was unique to Tairora, whether allies or foes. The sound they made seemed to reinforce a local tendency to compare their southern neighbors to animals, this in such alleged traits as their blind, unswerving purpose, implacable aggression, ferocity, love of violence, and alleged indifference to prudent calculation or human reason. A young male villager asked if I knew about the Kukukuku, as the Anga people were then still called. Only through their fierce reputation, I replied. Never having visited their country, I admitted knowing them only from hearsay. "So it is with everyone," he protested. "Everybody talks about 'the ferocious Kukukuku,' but who has ever seen one?" He had therefore been forced to conclude, he explained, that these infamous yet mysterious people living somewhere to the south were "none other than the very Tairora we have just been talking about. Isn't that just where *they* live? And isn't that just

what *they* are like?" Mistaken identity or not, it was worth noting that no
such comment was made concerning either Gadsup or Kamano peoples.

While this kind of thing belonged on the right page of the ledger, so
to speak, by itself it seemed unlikely to take one very far. Nor was that
page filled with further entries. In respect of housing, crops, garden
practices, kinship, initiation rites, shared myths, magic, and so forth, what
was commonly known or assumed—or commonly said in response to
queries—was that little in everyday life distinguished the Tairora they
knew from Aiamontina people. Similarities like these—the ethnographer's so-called "laundry list"—were evidently seen as comprising for this
vicinity the essential pattern of human life. Those with whom I discussed
the question had no difficulty in portraying Tairora enemies as lesser
mortals, but they cited scarcely any specific customs (such as the guttural
battle cry) as singular markers of this shortcoming, let alone as proving
it. Apparently their criterion was not whether people were fighters using
shields and arrows, wearing battle dress and paint, or retaliating for
similar wrongs and insults. The differences were not so gross or fundamental. Those were things a villager from Aiamontina could take for
granted as basic and true of all his neighbors. If one went to live among
Tairora, apart from the language, the lack of kinsmen, or the suspicion
of outsiders, dealing with daily life would involve little or no practical
handicap. Whatever the differences the Aimontina people perceived in
the Tairora, those differences must be covert or subtle. Recognizing the
very "international" condition he describes, Durkheim might have
smiled. Realizing that vicarious leads were inconclusive, I began to make
plans to visit some of the Tairora villages I could reach and return from
in a single day.

Not all of my informants, however, were villagers. As opportunity
permitted, I had also asked missionaries, *kiap*s, and other expatriates
what, if anything, they considered distinctive of individual local peoples.
Even when not perfunctory, the discussion usually narrowed down to the
four language groups adjacent to Kainantu—Agarabi, Gadsup, Kamano,
and Tairora. Some expatriates could find little to distinguish one local
people from another. Some were unsure of what the different languages
were or even roughly where their boundaries lay. For these, in other
words, "native" or "*kanaka*," at least in this vicinity, had an essentially
uniform meaning. There were, however, a few suggestive leads. The
Reverend Johannes Flierl, a widely known Lutheran missionary from a
family that had pioneered the Lutheran endeavor in the Central Highlands, had more years in the vicinity than anyone else. Mr. Flierl was fairly
terse, but he conceded that, on the whole, Tairora people had been less
responsive to the mission's proselyting efforts than the villagers of other
languages. When asked, he cited certain efforts that had borne little or

no fruit among Tairora, contrasting this outcome to the Lutheran experience among other Kainantu peoples. He demurred, however, when I inquired if he had any possible explanation for the difference.

In recognizing local ethnic differences, an outsider might suppose that *kiaps* would be among the best informed. In fact, they were not. Plainly they were handicapped, among other things, by the system of short-term postings in force in the Department of District Services and Native Affairs. This system put a man in one post for twenty-one months and then, upon his return from a three-month leave "down south," most often sent him next to a different station, not uncommonly a station in a remote or quite different corner of the country. There were exceptions, as when a man requested re-posting to his former station, perhaps to complete some project already in progress there, or for other particular reasons. In any case, in contrast to a missionary like Mr. Flierl, with decades-long experience in the same vicinity, a *kiap*'s knowledge of local peoples, such as it was, was likely to be acquired over a far shorter span of time. It thus was limited to his own immediate contacts with local people and to the written records his office might afford him, such as patrol reports, supplemented by whatever informal comments might have been passed to him by seniors and other predecessors on the station.

The practical work of administering a subdistrict, it seemed clear, could—or at any rate did—proceed without detailed ethnic knowledge of the local people. My impression is that in large part the work concerned internal bureaucratic duties and the intentions and activities of expatriates, so that it would be incorrect to suppose that full time could be devoted to New Guineans or their affairs. Probably no one even nominally in charge of a given vicinity, however, likes being thought anything less than well-informed. One could easily press a *kiap* too hard, in my experience, if the inquiry had the effect of suggesting that he might know more than he knew or more than he chose to impart. The reaction naturally varied with the individual. One man might be brusque and officious in response, dismissing such questions as impractical or of interest only to someone like an anthropologist with the freedom to satisfy mere curiosity. "Our policies are uniform," one might say. "We don't care how different local people may be in their personalities, or even if they really are different." Or, "So long as they obey the law, they're all alike to us. If we have to push some harder than others to make them toe the line, then we just push. There's precious little time to spend looking into how anyone feels about it. Besides, what would be the point? If I decide to make a study of the local people, what good will that do when I'm not back here after my next leave?"

Another officer might stop and ponder the question of differences among local peoples. Even if he himself had little more than odd bits of experience with one village or individual or another, he might offer them for what they were worth, perhaps expressing a wish that he knew more. "The Terrible Tairora" was a phrase once or twice thrown out in certain conversations. But it seemed to be more of a joke or a tease, perhaps prompted by my intractable question, an amusing alliterative label rather than a serious judgment supported by personal experience or a man's knowledge of the cumulative record of contact. It may at most have been a casual summation of station hearsay or echoes from the past. Despite these shortcomings, there was perhaps a certain accuracy to the epithet for, as I would later learn, the prewar and the wartime government had more than once in fact dealt harshly with certain Tairora-speaking individuals or villages felt to be intransigent or guilty of repeated insolence and challenges to authority.

An Australian coffee grower offered one interesting observation, albeit based on narrow experience. Pointing out that he made a policy of hiring workers from various Kainantu villages, Tairora villages among them, he said he considered the latter both straightforward and hardworking. Their one fault, he felt, was that they usually came with an unstated yet nevertheless fixed and limited working goal in mind: earning so much money or trade goods and no more. (They were, in other words, target workers.) Upon reaching that predetermined point, they would abruptly announce their intention to leave the following day and ask for their pay. Since plantation work could not be made to fit nicely into short-run private purposes, however, these precipitate withdrawals often placed the planter in a difficult position. Frequently he needed to keep his full present crew for a while longer in order to complete some piece of work, and he could not afford to pause and seek casual replacements on such short notice. With some of his workers, in such a case, he could explain his plight and appeal to them personally, pointing out that he had always been generous and fair to them. This appeal was often successful, in fact, even in keeping workers beyond their original "finish time." But not with Tairora workers, whom he found to be unyielding. There was nothing hostile or unpleasant about it, he conceded. All was plain and frank. But go they would and go they went, leaving him regretful, not to say resentful.

A FOOTNOTE ON MAPPING, NOMENCLATURE, AND THEIR TACIT ASSUMPTIONS

In 1954, "Taiora" was the label regularly given to the language, the people, and the country lying immediately to the south and southeast of the station. The *kiap*s of the day, for example, spoke of patrolling "the Taiora." "Taiora" appeared on all of the more recent subdistrict maps, a succession perhaps ultimately traceable to the rough sketches of pioneer missionaries and prospectors, or at least to early government patrols. Drawn and redrawn from such previous maps, each succeeding version was subject to revision as omitted groups were found, discrepancies of location noted, or more accurate names emerged. Particularly to the south, discoveries were still being reported, in fact, and map changes were accordingly discussed and sometimes made whenever a patrol would find some compass direction askew, some distance greater or smaller than previousy estimated, or some "little name" initially mistaken for a more inclusive "big name," as when a major locality was erroneously represented by the name of one of its hamlets.

Prior to World War II, without benefit of aerial survey methods, local mapmaking depended almost entirely on compass, eyeball, and footwork, or sometimes, it seemed, just the last two. Place names and ethnic nomenclature resulted from the sometimes casual inquiry of local residents or their neighbors, whose own toponymy, if the truth were known, comprised a bewildering profusion of names, many with astonishingly minute and specific spatial reference. Many of the names of settlements, moreover, were subject to short-term change and replacement as a settlement moved from one specific site to another adjacent to it whose different name nevertheless became the new name of the settlement. From among the answers received what would ultimately become official designations of people and places were chosen and interpreted with something less than full knowledge of local sociopolitical structure, and these were phonetically and orthographically rendered as well as possible by untrained ears. Only thus, one could suppose, might *lamari*, the generic word for water in northern Tairora, become the name of a specific river. Only thus might Ayamoentenu (accent on the second syllable) become "Aiamontina" (accent on first and penultimate). And only thus might "Taiora" become the collective name of some eight or ten thousand people, whose southern and southeastern limits and hence their total number were not yet even known at the time of naming.

By "Taiora" or by whatever other name they might collectively be known, the implied unity of these scores of autonomous local peoples had at least a linguistic base. Beyond that, however, unity was little more than an alien presumption. Nevertheless, the unity ascribed to such linguistic blocs as "Agarabi" and "Taiora" doubtless helped the outsider's sense of disorder or sheer anarchy (thereby strengthening the case for intervention) as one "Taiora" (or one "Agarabi," etc.) group recurrently made (civil?) war on others, this despite supposedly being part of a single people. The unwarranted social and political implications of such collective designations is the larger issue. Beside it, the specific source and original sense of a given name are of course lesser questions. Yet one

naturally wonders about a name like "Taiora"—if and how it was originally used, as distinct from the inclusive sense outsiders gave to it. How
and how much some lesser designation has been stretched in becoming
a much greater one is at least a measure of foreign misconceptions.

Matching the experience of ethnographers elsewhere, Kainantu ethnolinguistic designations often derive from the usage of a neighboring
people, rather than from that of the people designated. "Fore," for
example, seems to have been a name used by more northerly peoples like
the Agarabi and Tairora in referring at large to peoples living to the south
or southwest of them. "Fore" evidently included some or all of the present
Fore but in either case was not necessarily limited to speakers of that
language. The name was not specific to the present Fore, in other words,
and in any case it probably was not their own name for themselves if they
had one. As for the source of "Taiora," I could get no conclusive answer.
Some suggested that "Taiora" might derive from the name of a particular
village named Saiora—or one at least known to the *kiap* and entered on
his maps by that name. "S" and "T" are common allophones of some
Kainantu languages, making Saiora/Taiora a plausible confusion. Some
if not all of the Saiora people do, moreover, speak "Taiora." Still, it is quite
a leap from the name of a single small village at one edge of the country
in question to a designation comprising scores of villages and thousands
of people. If a single village could give its name to so many others,
moreover, why not a village like Arau, with resident Finschhafen cate-
chists going back to the 1920s, or some other such village that had figured
earlier and more prominently in the initial contacts of the foreigners? For
the moment, however, let me pause with this query, returning later to the
source and original sense of "Taiora."

FIRST VISIT TO "TAIORA"

The day eventually came when I set out on foot to visit one of the Taiora
villages closest to Kainantu, close enough to reach and return from before
dark the same day. On government maps my destination was shown as
"Taiora No. 1." A patrol officer with some inkling of the local micro-
history laughingly suggested, however, that my village destination was
more properly "Taiora No. 1½." The first Taiora village reached after
leaving Kainantu, he explained, was not strictly Taiora. Its population was
in fact a mix of Taiora and other people. A *kiap* would doubtless be
reminded of this fact whenever as magistrate he had to hear some Taiora
No. 1 litigant whose testimony the station's Taiora-speaking *tanim tok*
(T.P., interpreter) could not translate. Taiora No. 1, in other words, was
a *hapkas* (T.P., half-caste, or "mixed") village, as several other like communities were known in Tok Pisin. Since I was already unsure whether

even a "pure" Taiora community would suffice for our research, for present purposes, clearly, I must not choose a *hapkas* village.

It was a fine day, clear-skied and warm, the kind of weather that Kainantu area gardeners find ideal for working in their gardens or even just reposing there. On such a day the morning movement from dwellings to garden plots can be virtually unanimous and practically synchronous. It has a distinctly festive aspect, moreover, for this impulse is uppermost for nearly everyone at the same moment, and the day's dedication will have been anticipated, affirmed, and a consensus vocally reached from house to house even before the exodus itself begins. The sound of people stirring from their dwellings and barring the doors with wooden billets is signal enough for that beginning. With chivying and banter, neighbor calls to neighbor as each takes his or her respective path. In a trice, it almost seems, the horticultural surge subsides and the calling grows progressively more distant as the gardeners and their families find their respective plots beyond the village and the place itself is now emptied of all but the very old or infirm. Carried forth to their dooryards by departing neighbors or kin, the latter few may quietly enjoy the warmth of the day. Older children will sometimes drift back from the gardens to taste the freedom of the village entirely on their own, there to pursue their boisterous games, or sometimes mischief, unrestrained by parents or others who might if present complain of the noise and commotion or chase them away. The only monitors, the few remaining elders, would be unable to chase them away but in any case probably would look on amiably despite the commotion. When I eventually reached Taiora No. 1 (or No. 1½) around noon, virtually all the able-bodied people and the littlest children were gone to their gardens, and the village was almost deserted.

The silence of the village and its emptiness made me wonder for a moment if my trip was in vain. But I had in fact been observed. Arrivals and departures are too full of possible meaning and uncertainty, as I could understand, to be allowed to happen unheeded. I need not have worried. Or, to put it differently, if I had wanted to come and go unseen, it is doubtful whether I could have succeeded, or indeed whether any humanly feasible degree of furtiveness could make that possible. Certainly not at midday, or not without the magical invisibility of certain sorcerers.

The stillness was soon broken by long-distance calling, the singing out that is characteristic of the area. This was followed at once by the scampering feet of boys and girls flying to carry the word to people in the gardens or despatched to fly from garden to village and partway back again to report on the unknown visitor. Hurrying along the footpaths to the village, as soon as they could pack their provisions and pick up their babies and baggage, anxious and expectant faces soon began to appear, for the most part in family clusters. The paramount question was obvious if unspoken: who was this white man and what business brought him here?

The initiative was entirely mine, of course. For my part I decided I could not be sure whether word of our presence as far away as Aiamontina would have reached even this borderline northern Taiora village, so I resolved to take nothing for granted in accounting for myself. It never occurred to me that I would be speaking to anyone but men in the first instance, as that was the way it had been in my initial contacts in several Agarabi villages.

Though the day was surely warm enough, a small fire was quickly kindled of grass and twigs. It served if nothing else as a focus for the eyes of my listeners and for lighting their smokes. A group soon gathered around it to sit in a circle. As there were too many people for a single circle, I simply assumed that women would form another circle, probably at a respectful distance behind us. But, lo and behold, the first circle widened and there were women as well as men within it, as also in the second circle accommodating the overflow. I cannot imagine failing to note this intermingling, so sharply did it contrast with all my previous experience. And note it I did, though of course I had no time just then to dwell on it.

I explained who I was and where I was living at the moment and that, knowing nothing about other people around Kainantu, I had decided to make a "walkabout" and so today had come to make their acquaintance. I explained what I did—"my work," as I put it: learning the language, names of people and their connections, what kinfolk were called, how gardens are made, houses built, and so forth, the history of the community, the customs and beliefs. These things were little known or wholly unknown in my America, where there was much interest in such things. That was the work I was now doing at Aiamontina and would still be doing there for a while longer. In the meantime I was thinking about finding a second village in which to live for a while, but for that of course I needed to know if and where my wife, small daughter, and I would be welcome.

I asked for the name of the village and learned that it was Haparira—after the name of the site it currently occupied. (The accent is on the second syllable: hah-PAH-ree-rah.) They said they were an offshoot of nearby Ontabura where most or all of them were still therefore closely connected. They confirmed that what the *kiap* called "Taiora No. 1" was indeed a *hapkas* place, with Agarabi- and Kamano-speaking people in it, but it had at least as many "Tairora." "Tairora"! Who were these Tairora? They were themselves Tairora, I was told, as were also the Ontabura people and the Abiera beyond them (to the south). Tairora went even farther (south) than that, in fact, including what the *kiap* now calls Tonkera, as well as Bonta'a. All of these were Tairora, our big name and a very big line (in fact, a phratry), and the government now calls all of us, including many other people who speak our language, "Taiora." Of course I made a mental note.

I said the Aiamontina had taught me much, but there was still much more I had to learn. I described how this learning took place—asking questions, observing, recording with notebook and pencil, tape recorder, and so forth. One or two people at Haparira were said to speak Agarabi, but no one acknowledged ties to Aiamontina. More of them spoke Kamano or had ties there. Our own conversation was in Tok Pisin, which a number of men spoke well and translated for others, particularly women, who did not. A number of these men had been abroad on *kontrak*.

I remarked that women were sitting down among the men as we talked today, to hear what I, their visitor, had to say. Was there anything unusual about this, I asked, or was it quite the common practice? There was nothing unusual about it, they readily replied, taking no offense that I could see at what might have been too bold a question. Evidently it was just a matter of fact—the way they were—perhaps different from the women of their visitor's people but not for that requiring either amplification or explanation. Like previous exchanges, my question and their reply were translated into the local language for the benefit of the women and other nonspeakers of Tok Pisin. Glancing in my direction, the women seemed to acknowledge my reference to them. But I could detect no hint that either they or their men recognized my own unspoken premise: how different from some Kainantu peoples Haparira women seemed!

Pointing out that I was hoping to get back to Aiamontina by nightfall, I eventually made motions to depart. There was hurried discussion among the group. Eventually a spokesman declared that if I should later decide to come to Haparira, I should let them know. He felt sure that my family and I would be welcome. I mentioned the need for a house, since there was no government resthouse at Haparira to be used even temporarily. There was one old house, someone volunteered, but others quickly rejected this as a practical option, saying that a new house would be a much better idea. Having seen what a project the large, rectangular, multi-roomed house at Aiamontina had proven to be, I emphasized that a round house of the usual size and style would be quite enough, in fact, preferred. I said that of course they should not set to work building a new house until I let them know, and that was the way we left it for the time being. I left exhilarated.

ON CHOOSING TAIRORA AS "CULTURE B"

One day's journey could settle much, or so it seemed that day. "Taiora No. 1" was no longer a curiosity—the village name that was not a village's name. And the choice of "Taiora" as the inclusive name for this large linguistic bloc could also be understood. While obviously posing further questions, the easy mingling of men and women at Haparira at least helped settle where to begin in pursuing answers. No more than a slim thread, this apparent difference of gender-based behavior strongly hinted at further and deeper cultural differences between Agarabi-speaking Aiamontina and Tairora-speaking Haparira. As for the journey itself, the wonderful, wide, yet intimate country always beckoned me. So besides lacking other means of movement, I did not begrudge the time it took to go and come on foot.

It was undeniable, of course, that an entire day had been needed to get what might ultimately seem perfunctory details—mere items. But if there were no other way to do it, and if the significance of given details could not be settled before getting them, then the reward could not be thought as slight as it might later seem, once "everyone" knew with perfect clarity what "no one" could recall as ever having been in doubt. That day would surely come; it always does. So be it, I thought. One could not therefore dismiss the expenditure as misguided or wasteful. Fieldwork had its ups and downs, moments in which one might leap ahead as well as others when the most modest aim took time to fulfill or even went unfulfilled despite honest effort. Between limited objectives and the large amount of time sometimes required for accomplishing them the disparity could be great, but only hindsight could make the expenditure seem avoidable. There was no denying the contrast between grubbing out hard-earned bits in the field, on the one hand, and the soaring summations and agile syntheses of myriad such bits of information, on the other, in books and papers, lectures and seminars, reviews and critiques. There, by contrast, all is ostensibly effortless, smooth, and nimble, nothing sullied unless by defects of logic or the sheer failure of nerve or insight. In such a light the sweaty hands, soggy notebook, smudgy, sometimes cryptic entries, and above all the fumbling attempts at half-framed questions—these could only belong to some other, meaner realm. Yet while in that realm those were the rules by which one labored.

No such second thoughts, however, disturbed my homeward-bound euphoria. I could now meet the *kiap*'s challenge concerning the "Taiora" of his maps. ("Why ask us?" he had countered my inquiry, or words to that effect. "You're the anthropologist.") Whatever the ultimate source of the ambiguity, "Taiora" was surely some foreigner's rendering of *Tairora*. This was clearly the "big name," knowingly or not taken from that of the phratry (or "tribe") so called. That the phratric name was readily available to pioneer mapmakers was as obvious as it was fortuitous: size and location summed it up. Tairora was and is a very large phratry, among the largest of that language group. The name included more of the speakers in question, certainly, than any other single designation immediately accessible to the government's Upper Ramu Post, the eventual Kainantu. Indeed, the phratric Tairora were adjacent to the station, and the Agarabi, on whose former lands the station stands, almost certainly referred to these neighbors and adversaries of their southern border as Tairora—possibly even as "Taiora"! It was these same first villages that any Kainantu patrol would come upon, moreover, in setting forth to the south. That this circumstance in fact affected the case was suggested in the then still current practice of numbering the first two or three Tairora villages in sequence—Tairora No. 1, No. 2 (Ontabura), and so forth—rather than using their proper names. After all, as the people themselves would still say when asked, they were "all Tairora." It would be Tairora still, furthermore, as the patrol called at each of the next several villages on its way south. So the phonetic coincidence of Saiora/Taiora, if it played any part in fixing the designation "Taiora," probably did so after the fact. Still, it would be interesting to know if some pioneer mapmaker, diligent beyond the norm, was actually acquainted with the legend of Saiora emigrants, in the still-remembered past, as indeed the founders of ancestral Tairora, a settlement today known only by its onetime site. To judge from modern accounts, this settlement was destined to become the stem settlement of the future phratry, the main remembered source of the several offshoots today constituting Phratry Tairora. But I knew nothing as yet of any of this, and even if I had known more, one coincidence would still have been enough for the moment.

None of the foregoing argues for choosing the name of a particular phratry, a minority segment, to stand for a language group more than ten times as large. The full size of the language group would not in fact be known for many years when pioneer *kiaps* first began to use the name "Taiora," and by the time those numbers were fully known, the earlier usage was long established. It remained only to recognize the source and original sense of the name and perhaps to correct its rendering on subsequent maps, which have since in fact been corrected.

More immediate to our own concerns, obviously, was what I have called the slim thread: how much importance to give to the hint of divergent gender roles as between two cultures? The evidence of a contrast between Aiamontina and Haparira with respect to male/female relations, to be sure, was ultimately a fact in its own right. Denying that this was extraordinary, Haparira women on a particular occasion had sat down in the same circle with their men to hear a male visitor to their village. On the numerous comparable occasions we had so far observed, in sharp contrast, Aiamontina women did nothing of the kind. In fact the segregation of Agarabi women in such circumstances was not only clear in numerical terms, but even the distance between men's and women's circles accentuated the gender distanciation. The gap frequently placed the women at such a disadvantage that they could scarcely hear what was said in the men's circle. Except when voices were raised, perhaps deliberately for their benefit, one had the impression that women sometimes strained—and probably failed—to hear. Well and good, but granted the accuracy and validity of the observations themselves, what weight could one attach to the possibility that, because gender roles differed between them in this specific way, two cultures might—better still, must—differ significantly in other respects as well?

There is no hiding our will to give weight to such an inference. By now irretrievably committed to Kainantu as the contact setting and to Agarabi as "Culture A," we naturally hoped we had found in Tairora a valid "Culture B." The reader can surely guess what case we made in support of our inference. Among those queried about possible differences among local peoples, it was true, no one had mentioned how Tairora men and women treat each other. Nor could I recall any particular comment at Aiamontina about Tairora women. Adverse or favorable, there was nothing to compare to the views I would later hear from some Tairora men about the women of the neighboring Gadsup. Allegedly immodest, in the view of these critics, Gadsup women made their bark skirts too short and skimpy. And they hung their skirts so low on their waists, according to one detractor, as even sometimes to expose pubic hair. Whether to make Tairora "Culture B," fortunately, seemed to hang on a slightly more substantial lead.

Essentially, we reasoned, if in the presence of male outsiders Tairora men and women can sit comfortably shoulder to shoulder, their family life and socialization practices may well also differ in some fairly basic sense from those of peoples who would themselves find such behavior uncomfortable if not unacceptable. A difference in gender relations such as this, we decided, was no mere checklist item. It could not be compared, for instance, to the variable use of superposed bark cooking drums to increase the content or concentrate the heat of an earth oven. This fairly overt difference, in fact quite familiar to certain neighbor villages of the Kainantu vicinity, hardly suggests profound cultural concomitants. (The skirts of Gadsup women, on the other hand, may signify more.) Had we known at the time what we would learn during a second visit ten years later, we might sooner have settled on Tairora as "Culture B." Ten years later certain Tairora-speaking groups would have female village officials—*luluais* and *tultuls*—exceptional not only among the peoples of the Kainantu vicinity but, so far as I am aware, by no means common elsewhere in New Guinea (see Pataki-Schweizer 1987). Knowing this, of course, made an agonizing long shot in retrospect seem tame. But it also confirmed that, in leading us accurately to "Culture B," the first contact with Haparira people was truly serendipitous.

LOCALE AND PANORAMA

The immediate feasibility of the research design described at the outset of this memoir raised the question whether intuition was a sufficient guide in selecting Tairora as a culture contrasting significantly with Agarabi. Beyond that tactical problem, moreover, there looms a larger issue, namely, the general relation between local and international society and culture. If neighbored peoples preponderantly reflect the imprint of their neighborhood, as Durkheim categorically asserts and a great many others tacitly assume, are these vicinal influences uniformly strong in all aspects of communal and individual life? Or are they more pronounced in some sectors than in others? In what, if any, sectors do distinctive local traits or attributes most typically emerge or endure? Here I can proceed only by exemplification. I cannot, of course, insist that the Agarabi/Tairora comparison is representative of neighboring peoples throughout New Guinea, let alone the world at large. Besides having lived for some time adjacent to each other, these two sets of peoples are also, as noted, linguistic congeners. This obviously means that they have common linguistic ancestors, however long ago that may be and however much or little their subsequent history may have converged or diverged. Although Agarabi differs from Tairora more than from any other language of the Kainantu group, even with a limited background one can readily pick out cognate pairs illustrating some of the "Grimm's Laws" or regular sound shifts: *tangko* = *kaingge* ("fighting shield"), for instance, while *te'i* = *kere*, dialectally varying as *tere* (first person singular). The history of these two sets of peoples will not, of course, be duplicated in any other pairing.

In what ways were Culture A and Culture B most alike, and what were their sharpest differences? For present purposes I shall play the traveler, epitomizing casually from memory while neglecting a wide range of responses. Choosing only a few of the more dramatic contrasts between Culture A and Culture B, in other words, I am reporting them by means of what, without formal specification, I take to be representative if not strictly modal responses. Beyond this acknowledgment, however, I offer no apology for my traveler's role. In one respect, however, I shall remain the ethnographer, namely, in attempting to preserve the anonymity of the two communities I have up till now been calling by name. I believe it will nevertheless serve immediate purposes to focus on some of the ways in which two adjacent New Guinea cultures appear to differ, without calling attention to which is which.

In an interview schedule used in both communities, one of the questions is roughly, "Why do you think the white man came here?" In one community a recurrent response was, "To straighten us out," or words to that effect. Among the shortcomings most often cited as being in need of correction were practices often named in other contexts as well—sorcery, fighting, theft, and adultery. Much the same list of currently indictable practices was also familiar in the other community, to be sure, but correcting local shortcomings was rarely cited as having any bearing on the coming of the foreigners or on their purpose in remaining. Quite simply, the outsiders' attitudes or intentions toward local peoples were not often seen as a possible reason for their presence. Some respondents, in fact, quite logically turned this particular question back to me: "Isn't that something for the white man himself to answer?" they would ask with some puzzlement. "We don't know what brought them here." Or, "They haven't told us why they came." Denying any reliable knowledge of the foreigners' motives, however, some respondents would then suggest conceivable attractions such as "our water," "the gold," or some other widely acclaimed virtue of their own country, conceivably unavailable in the country from which the foreigners came. In the case of gold, of course, the attraction was one the white man himself had identified. Once he became aware of them, ostensibly, it was understandable that these were virtues that might quite well hold a foreigner.

As to the question of fighting, again, a number of respondents in one community spoke of being frankly unable to match the power of the police. They were thus compelled to give up any further resort to open warfare. In several cases this suppression was expressed so graphically as to make clear that no alternative course was even thinkable. "Now our task is to learn what the white man would teach us and to follow his lead," several said, "and that is what we must teach our children." The vision of the future was less clear, incidentally, than the faults of the past, as first the foreigner and now seemingly the people themselves defined those faults.

While recording the responses of members of the other community I was struck by how sharply they differed on the question of fighting. One response in particular stands out from memory: "We X have no need to boast of our reputation. Our name as great fighters is known to all. We had no equals. Before he came we did not know the *kiap*, but once we saw him, we could see he was also a great fighter. So whenever we fought we were very hard on each other. He was hard on us and we were hard on him. Had things gone on as they were going, who knows where it might have led? There might have been no end. Neither one of us could finish off the other, but neither would we stop. The mission finally decided this could not continue, so they summoned each of us in turn to talk about

it. 'People are not marsupials or game,' they said. 'They are not born in
batches but one at a time, and it takes a long while to grow a person. They
should not be born and grown simply to be killed.' After we heard their
words, the mission told us to go home and think over what they had said.
Later the mission spoke to the *kiap*, giving him the same reasons and
telling him to go home and think about what he had heard. Each of us
thought about it. Deciding the mission was right, now we have both
stopped fighting."

One final recollection concerns contrasting responses to the Thematic
Apperception Test. Roughly twenty of these "projective test" cards, some
slightly modified, were used in both villages, as well as in a third. As is
normally done, T.A.T. cards were used in series, one after the other being
shown briefly and privately to a given subject in order to elicit from the
subject stories that to him/her might account for the persons and scenes
depicted in each particular card. For the clinical psychologist such stories
are "projections." No few of the cards (to my view) depict solitary figures
with rather ambiguous facial expressions. In "projecting" themselves
imaginatively into these pictures, so to speak, many subjects in both
communities indeed saw these individuals as isolated, as lonely persons
removed by one means or another from among their kin. But here the
similarity between the two communities largely ended. For the respondents of one community the solitaries were often seen to be dejected over
their isolation. They wonder what their fellow villagers are doing at home.
They brood over whether the latter ever think of the missing person.
They dwell upon the possibility, when he or she dies, that the word may
never reach the faraway kin so that they can mourn. What I (projectively,
no doubt!) take to be the picture of a circus acrobat climbing a rope
proved particularly evocative for some of these respondents. The figure
depicted was the forlorn person him/herself, climbing a forest vine to
reach the treetops in the hope of glimpsing from there the smoke of the
distant village. But (in some accounts) the village is still too far away and
the smoke cannot be seen.

For several subjects in the other community, however, the solitary was
self-willed and undejected. Dejection, in fact, was replaced by something
altogether different, albeit without challenging the solitariness perceived
by most subjects. The isolation is real enough, in other words, but in some
of the stories of this community it is both deliberately sought for and
satisfying. In a representative projection, the solitary has decided to leave
his own people behind in order to search for good land for gardens, pigs,
and a homestead of his own. His initiative has been well rewarded,
moreover, with fine gardens, a thriving herd, two or three good wives,
and numerous lively children. His relatives at home are meanwhile thinking of him, wondering where he went, curious to know how he has fared,

for ever since he left there has been no word of him. Prompted by their curiosity, in fact, one or two of them now think to set out in search of their long-absent kinsman, to discover his whereabouts and learn of his fate. Eventually they come upon him. His prosperity is so plain that the visitors cannot fail to see it, and they congratulate him upon it. At this point one or two of the respondents took the story a step further. So attracted are the visitors by their kinsman's good fortune that they propose joining him, in the express hope of sharing his success. But he rebuffs them. If they would follow his example, he advises them, they must go elsewhere and find good land of their own. One respondent went so far as to see in a particular picture the solitary himself with drawn bow, defiantly on guard lest anyone take his words too lightly and attempt to settle nearby!

International society and culture notwithstanding, there is here ample, albeit anecdotal, indication of local differences. Indeed, once the international comes to be as well theorized by ethnologists as the national has now long been (viz., the "ethnographic isolate"), it may well seem inevitable that local society must strive to develop or retain its differences, this as a part of the endless struggle for continued autonomy in the face of a dominating neighborhood. The question then becomes not whether the dominion of neighbors is absolute—for though great, clearly it is not—but where the greatest freedom for localism is perhaps regularly found.

SEVEN

Meeting the Mendi

D'Arcy Ryan

In 1945, after a totally undistinguished and mindlessly boring hiatus in R.A.A.F. radar, I was discharged in Sydney to resume my interrupted Arts and Law course. Needing a fourth subject, I thought anthropology might be amusing, exotic, and, I'd heard, not too onerous. As taught in A. P. Elkin's department in Sydney at that time, it was all those things; it was also utterly fascinating, opening up horizons of human behavior I'd never dreamed of. Although becoming more and more interested in the subject, I was yet mindful of my predestined "real" career: the law. However, by overloading courses, I managed to take a totally undeserved first in anthropology before moving to the law school. No, this is not mock modesty. Elkin was a kind and humane man, an ex-missionary utterly dedicated to his subject (especially "his own" Aborigines), and he was more impressed by high-minded enthusiasm, of which I had plenty, than disciplined scholarship, of which I had almost none.

Then the law school, and the deadly memorization of cases—cases—and cases! Anthropology had interested me in the theory of law; I worked through Julius Stone's *Province and Function of Law* and looked forward to stimulating classes with its author. But the Sydney Law School, like most others, was for training legal practitioners and did not encourage abstract inquiry about such frivolities as the "Nature of Law." To be sure they had Stone, but it took a long time on the factory floor before one attained him, and most of my fellow students were unaware of his existence.

About the middle of this dreary year, my father died, leaving me an inheritance that I decided to invest in Oxford. Accepted by Lincoln College to read law, I was allotted to Harold Hanbury, who enjoyed a scholarly reputation similar to Stone's. Still, my first year's reading was an exact duplicate of the course I'd already passed in Sydney—and just as soul-destroying. So, after two terms of this, I made the decision and switched to the Institute of Anthropology under Evans-Pritchard, known to all as "E-P." My first interview with that redoubtable scholar was unnerving, to say the least. His opening remark was memorable (I usually remember it about 4 A.M.): "Of course, you must realize that Here, we don't regard any student of Professor Elkin as having even the *makings* of an anthropologist!" The fact that *all* his own works (Nuer, Azande, and the lot) had somehow escaped the notice of the Sydney curriculum did nothing to dispel this curious prejudice.

Enrolled for the B.Litt. (bachelor of letters), I had as my first supervisor Max Gluckman, whose only remark I recall was, "So you're here under your own steam? Exactly how much money have you got?" He left for Manchester shortly afterward. Next came Meyer Fortes, whom I met twice. The first time, we decided I should "clear up this Australian totemism business." The second time, some three months later, was in the tearoom: "Ah,—umm, Ryan, isn't it? Everything going well?" Before I could say "No!" he disappeared in a puff of sulphurous smoke and I never saw him again (I always meant to ask him how he did it). I understand he rematerialized, shortly after, in the Chair at Cambridge. My third, and final, supervisor was Franz Steiner, a small and charmingly understated refugee from Hitler's Europe. He was a civilized person, in the European intellectual tradition. I saw a good deal of him and just occasionally our minds touched. (After a tentative exploration of my knowledge of anthropology, we tacitly agreed not to mention that subject again.) He introduced me to, among other things, the music of Mahler and Bruckner, and he lived in a world of abstract clarity, where people were an irrelevant clutter. He was the only anthropologist I've met who was never in the field, and he died, just as I was finishing my thesis.

After a singularly traumatic viva, conducted by Leach and Kaberry ("For God's sake, Edmund, leave the poor fellow alone!"), I duly curtsied my way through graduation.

In these days, when many postgraduate students are demanding that supervisors be a cross between parent, confessor, and nanny, the casual style of Oxford supervision may seem incredible; indeed, in retrospect, it was. I was rash enough to remark on this at one stage, and received the reply (from E-P): "I'm afraid we don't indulge in spoon-feeding Here!" I came to realize that this meant in practice an almost complete abdication from any sense of duty or responsibility to students, who were singularly blessed to be Here at all. The only universities that could get away with such a system were, of course, those with reputations giving them access to the cream of potential students, who tend to be tough survivors.

Married in London, my Australian wife and I returned to Sydney in

1952. From Oxford, I took with me a degree, an acquaintance with the literature of "totemism," some social experience, and an ignorance of general anthropology (practical and theoretical) that was still virtually intact.

Back in Sydney, Elkin gave me some part-time lecturing while I wondered where the hell I'd go from there. Obviously I needed fieldwork for a Ph.D., and Elkin offered me a study of an aboriginal settlement on the outskirts of a New South Wales country town. Desperately trying to excite myself over this unexotic prospect, I accepted. About a week later, however, he called me in again.

It appeared he had sent a female student to a place called Mendi, in the Southern Highlands of New Guinea. The Highlands, unadministered and virtually unexplored until after the war, were at last being opened up. The Australian National University, under S. F. Nadel, was placing students there, and so obviously Sydney had to do the same, and this young woman, as inexperienced as I, was sent there in 1952. Mendi had been "discovered," en passant, by Karius and Champion in a 1936 patrol; there was another brief contact with a survey expedition in 1938 and then nothing until the first administration post was established there in 1950, with the Methodists setting up a mission a few months later. When Elkin's student arrived, in 1952, the station was officially "open," but anywhere beyond a two-mile radius of the district office was Restricted Territory, where entry required the official permit of the district commissioner, which, in this case, he flatly refused to give: "You don't think I was going to let a young girl go in alone among those people? God, if anything happened to her, I'd be finished!" (I think his decision was a wise one, even if for the wrong reasons. I do not believe that anything would have "happened" to her, but I am sure that a female anthropologist, in that kind of society, would have been at an even greater disadvantage than I subsequently was.)

Anyway, the unfortunate young woman found her movements restricted to within a two-mile radius of the administration office, and set up house on the other side of the airstrip. Within binocular distance of the office verandah, it was an area which neither she nor they had any means of knowing at the time was an interclan no-man's-land—a former battleground between two clans who were long-established enemies. She had the sense to realize quickly that, as far as her work was concerned, her position was totally impossible, so she informed Elkin that she felt she could function better in another area. Elkin, reluctantly, agreed, she reestablished herself in a different district, did a good job, and laid the appropriate foundations for her subsequent professional career. But I don't think Elkin ever quite forgave her. His own thirty years of fieldwork in Australia had led him (and hence, his students) to believe that "fieldwork" meant long, enchanted hours around the campfire, under the blazing desert stars, recording the old men's accounts of the Dreamtime myths that lay behind the intricate rituals that were constantly going on—this interspersed with long discussions of the subtleties of kinship. He was, and I think ever remained, more or less unaware that different cultures involved radically different kinds of fieldwork. Certainly, when he called me in that day to offer me (to) the Mendi, his first protégé's failure clearly rankled. It was obvious that he had no conception of the difficulties the poor girl had had to face. I should, of course, have been warned, but young Mr. Starryeyes, B.A. (Hons I), B. Litt., had no qualms at all (perhaps because I had such a clear image of the bleaker project I was escaping from).

In the next weeks, there followed some desultory discussion of what I would actually do there. The area at that time was virtually unknown. I managed to get hold of one of the rare copies of Kleestadt and Rheinstein's unpublished translation of Vicedom and Tischner's *Die Mbowamb* (1943–48), as well as a short piece by Elkin (1953b) on the *te* (part of the *moka* ceremonial exchange system), the result of a three-week tour—and that was about the total of my homework. Today, when we send students to the field we ensure that they are first familiar with the (usually considerable) literature of the area, and also that they have a fairly clear, if flexible, idea of the aspects of the culture on which they intend to focus. In other words, when they go to the field, their project has at least a tentative title. Not so in my case. I went chortling off to the Great Adventure on a "dragnet" operation, unhampered by any preconceptions or theoretical hypotheses. Even I, however, had some misgivings about quite such an open-minded approach. Apart from making a map of the settlement and taking genealogies, what then? My undergraduate course had included some superficial acquaintance with the Culture and Personality school of Abram Kardiner, Ruth Benedict, Cora DuBois, and so on (in those days we still believed in Freud and Margaret Mead), and I formulated a vague plan along the line of "child-rearing techniques." (In Oxford I had mentioned this interest to Fortes, who said I couldn't contemplate it until I had undergone at least two years of psychoanalysis—and he was probably right.) Nevertheless, that was about the only purposeful idea I took to the field.

Another thing that really bothered me was language. All the anthropologists I knew in Sydney had worked in Pidgin (Australian or Melanesian). But E-P insisted that the only valid ethnography was through the vernacular. I tried to raise this problem in Oxford but discovered that the subject was taboo. E-P had produced his classic study of the Nuer working from scratch in an apparently fiendish tonal language, and none of his students dared confess themselves incapable of the same achievement. I recall confiding in a young lady just back from her first visit to Dinkaland (the Nuer's next-door neighbors) and her response: "Oh yes, language is a terrible problem. I was there nearly three weeks before I could understand a single word! It was *months* before I was really fluent!" This undermined my linguistic ego to the point where I dared not raise the subject again. But the doubts niggled—as well they might!

This account is supposed to be about what I found when I met the Mendi, but it would be neither complete nor accurate without this, however tedious, autobiography of what the Mendi found when they met me. Today, sending a student of my degree of greenness into a totally alien and possibly dangerous environment would doubtless be considered the height of irresponsibility, but then, assorted colonial flags still waved fairly confidently over a large part of the globe and there was the tacit assumption that if the local administration accepted the presence of anthropologists, they would also afford them the protection of government authority from all but the most egregious stupidities. In return for this there was, equally implicit, the agreement that the anthropologist would not foment discontent, undermine government authority, nor rock the boat in any way. In fact, few of us were tempted to do so. Brought up in a colonial heritage that had yet to be seriously challenged, we did not find these restrictions particularly chafing. To be sure, there were unnerving distant rumbles and the world horizon was not as clear as it used to be, but in 1954, despite the fact that important administrative changes were already in progress, I think few of us conceived the possibility that, in only another twenty years, Papua New Guinea, too, would be precipitated into full, indigenous autonomy.

On a professional level, I am not at all sure that going into an unknown culture, as I did, virtually tabula rasa and devoid of all theoretical principles, was necessarily a bad thing. For me, *everything* was new, and an innocent eye can be an acute observer. And, of course, the tabula was not totally rasa; from my desultory "training," such as it was, I had learned that societies had "structure" whose typology, though broad, was limited, and that cultures had definable patterns. This in turn implied concepts of "functionalism" and "cultural relativism": that societies and cultures were (sometimes sloppily) integrated systems developed to serve their members' needs, and that one must suppress any moral responses in trying to understand how they worked. One must endeavor to see things from the local point of view. This approach had not yet emerged as the trendy pretension of "phenomenology," but that was basically what we were all trying to do.

I have indicated that we were given no formal courses in "Fieldwork," and I do not believe, even today, that this can be formally taught. To be sure, students can be instructed in the efficient taking and filing of notes (it took me weeks to realize that if you write on both sides of the paper you can get in a terrible mess). They can be warned about role identification, particularly the dangers of faction alliance, and that even the most trusted informants should always be cross-checked. But these matters are largely beyond the fieldworker's control: by the time you realize there *are* factions, you may be already identified with one of them, which tends to shut off information from the other, and you seldom choose your informants—they tend to choose you. Initially, at least, they are often "rubbish men" who see their association with you as a path to higher status, and who try to compensate with garrulous and misleading chatter for the vital information to which they have no access. And we can tell students something about "leading questions": that informants do not regard you as a tribal brother (even though you in your lost loneliness may so regard them) and they will try to earn their keep by telling you what they think you wish to hear. Above all, students should be warned (and even now, few are) that "primitive" peoples often suffer from boredom, and seek relief in a mischievous, and sometimes malicious, sense of humor, which they take out on this impertinent, insensitive, and unbelievably ignorant outsider who has come prying into their private lives. I tell my students that the best way to cope with this is to remember, constantly, some of the things they themselves have written in questionnaires, or have told the earnest souls who knock on our doors conducting "social surveys." The truth is that a major requirement of a fieldworker is social empathy—that sensitivity which gives one the "feel" of a culture and dictates the appropriate behavior in a particular situation. A few people acquire this art at a very early age; most of us pick up some social skills along the way; and regrettably, some of us (including a disproportionate number of "social scientists") never do. Apropos of this last: it has been maliciously suggested, especially by "sociologists," that anthropologists head for "exotic" cultures because they cannot handle their own. Unfortunately I can think of a number of my colleagues through the years who appear to substantiate this thesis, but not only in anthropology: the "social sciences" in general do appear to attract misfits, especially those of evangelical reformist inclinations. The present point, however, is that I do not believe "social sensitivity" can be formally taught in a classroom. You acquire it gradually and pragmatically—or, sadly, not.

In the fieldwork situation, however, empathy alone is not enough. No matter how deeply one "relates" to "one's people" nor how sensitized one becomes to the nuances of their culture, one is still there on a job and still has to bring back "results," and too much *délicatesse* can mean no information at all. Consequently, it is necessary to learn the parameters of discretion: How far can one push questioning? How long must one wait for information that will probably never be volunteered? How far can one intrude on private situations, knowing one is unwelcome?

A slight mistake here can lead to a frustrating withdrawal of information; serious errors can give rise to a mistrust that impairs the whole project; constant abrasion of local sensibilities can wreck it. We need the respect, or at least the benevolent tolerance, of our subjects; if we lose it, we ourselves are lost. Again, this sort of thing cannot formally be taught because, in this regard, every field situation is unique.

I arrived in Mendi early in 1954. Initial contact, as I have already said, was recent. Brief exploratory patrols had passed through in 1936 and 1938, the war period was a total blank, and serious contact began only with the establishment of a district office in 1950. Very soon after, a Methodist mission was established at Unja, a tract of land about thirty minutes walk north of the station, and it was here that Elkin, through his church connections, had arranged for me to be initially accommodated. I was received by the missionaries with warm-hearted hospitality that I suspect was replaced, after a relatively short time, by a sense of Christian duty. I was lodged in a newly erected hut of woven cane (in the coastal, not local, style), light and airy by day but dankly chilly in the cold Highland nights; the crisp smell of living in a freshly woven basket lingers yet. I took all my meals in the head missionary's house, and the Reverend Gordon Young and his wife Grace could not have been kinder or more helpful. Indeed it was Grace Young who taught me how to make bread, a most useful accomplishment at the time, and a skill I have since maintained. I was soon introduced to the other missionaries and was invited to meals at their separate houses. My first anthropology became a study of the missionaries, and it was soon clear that cultural isolation and small-group loyalty were at least as strong in holding them together as the sense of vocation that they all shared. In other words, the various households didn't seem to like each other much, but there was no one else.

Those first three months were spent in a concentrated onslaught on the language, and all my worst nightmares came true. The three or four local and inadequate Pidgin speakers, trained by the administration, were employed full-time as court interpreters. The mission prided itself on working in the vernacular, of which they had acquired a work-relevant smattering, and Pidgin was actively discouraged. They had, however, phonemicized the language and compiled a short glossary that they generously let me have, saving me months of work, but the structure of the language was almost untapped. With a couple of cheerful young informants, I spent most of every day trying to learn it the hard way: formally, and by pantomime. Heavily inflected (like all the Highland languages), it was, and forever remained, a recalcitrant brute—although I eventually did learn enough of it to do my job. Unfortunately, my contact with a wide range of native speakers was limited by the fact that the locals were firmly discouraged from wandering aimlessly around the mission—a remarkably self-sufficient infrastructure whose major function seemed to be its own self-maintenance. Considering its ostensible purpose, contact with its local flock was amazingly minimal.

As for conversions, I think I can say with some assurance that, in any spiritual sense, there were none. Any Divine Light that reached the Mendi was seen by them as political alliance, with a spin-off of material benefits. The curious rituals in the church each Sunday, with speeches and singing, were a pleasant diversion, especially for the women and children, offering at least novelty and a focus for social meeting. Moreover, here, as in most mission centers, "conversions" gave some status to those who, for one reason or another, lacked it in their traditional system.

This probably had much to do with the personality of the director. A somewhat authoritarian character, a muscular Christian ex-footballer, whose faith in the Bible was uncomplicated by theological subtleties, he was one of Nature's Scoutmasters. Each Sunday morning I accompanied him on his service rounds over a circuit that took us four or five hours on foot. This was a most useful exercise that gave me an idea of the layout of local settlements and introduced me to the arduous task of getting myself around in a mountain terrain along greasy, wet tracks like a switchback railway. The Reverend Mr. Young, of course, not only believed firmly in physical fitness, but he had had years of practice on the local tracks, and my mud slides, barked shins, and stumbles into icy creeks were to him a source of hearty delight, which he shared with me in the most jocular fashion. Interspersed with this cheery ribbing, he regaled me with endlessly repeated accounts of those wonderful days at "College" when he was a prefect supervising initiations and corrective disciplines for "those types who weren't quite measuring up."

It was not only in learning the local topography that these walks were instructive. I had frequently wondered how missionaries went into a completely pagan society and persuaded the people to reconstruct their worldview, abandon the old ways, and "see the light." To the simpler Christian missionary mind, there was no problem: called by God, they obviously had the Light, and sooner or later with His help, the people could not fail to see and accept it. As a good atheist, however, I had mild doubts about this, and our Sunday patrols gave me some clues.

The first time we set out, I was surprised how few people we met. The Mendi did not live in villages, but in scattered farmsteads on defined patriclan territories. In each of these, the focal point was a cleared, grassy danceground surrounded by tall, sighing casuarinas and thick hedges.

Off this wandered narrow paths leading to the various individual houses and gardens. At one end of the danceground were several large, low huts thatched with *kunai* (Tok Pisin, sword grass) and with walls about one meter high, so that the eaves almost touched the ground. These were the lineage houses where the men and youths lived. The front of each house was a sort of ground-level "verandah room," whose open front looked down the danceground. Behind, a crawlthrough aperture led to the sleeping section. These houses were exclusively male preserves; the women, children, and pigs inhabited differently constructed "women's houses" scattered throughout the clan territory, usually conveniently adjacent to the owner's personal gardens. Most of the communal, social life of the clan took place in the danceground area. Although during the day most were busy in their gardens, there were generally a few people around. During our preaching tours, however, the grounds were usually deserted.

One exotic element had special appeal: our progress was always accompanied by shrill calls in a wailing yodel, like a Swiss muezzin (a form of distance communication common among mountain peoples). G. Y. told me, correctly, that it announced the approach of Kundi (himself) with the Good Talk; I don't think he ever realized that it also implied, "So disappear . . . like *quick*!" In any event, he was apparently used to this absenteeism, and on arrival would usually manage to find some local whom he would order, with hearty firmness, to go off and round up a congregation, and within about fifteen minutes odd bodies would straggle in until a dozen or so were assembled. On one occasion I recall, the only person in sight was a man leading a pig by a leg rope, who wished to go about his business and refused to act as messenger. G. Y. solved this problem by seizing the pig rope, tying it to a tree, and telling the man he could have it back after the service: a scriptural exhortation, partly in English by G. Y., and partly in Mendi by a native missionary teacher who accompanied us. (There were several such teachers, coastal men and their families who, because they mixed much more with the locals, had acquired more of the language than had any of the white missionaries.) These curious performances lasted about fifteen minutes and seemed to me, even then, to be received with total incomprehension (as I later found they were).

In these (and most of his other) dealings with the Mendi, G. Y. habitually displayed such a relentlessly jolly insensitivity that I naively wondered why they stood for it and didn't tell us to f—— off (which comes out even ruder in Mendi than in English!). The reason, of course, was obvious. We were white, and although, like everyone else, we lived in separate clans ("Kiap Clan," "Misin Clan," etc.) we did seem to be *amealt* (a politically united "brotherhood"): attack one, you attack them all. At the very beginning of contact, they had had several armed brushes with the early patrols, and the military superiority of the Kiap Clan, at least, was completely established; hence all the other whites in the settlement sheltered, perhaps not fully realizing it, under the same protective umbrella—a fact for which I later had reason to be thankful. Although the Mendi had learned not to retaliate by the time-honored method of assassination, they had, nonetheless, devised other gestures of disapproval. One evening, G. Y. tossed (literally) a trespasser out of his garden enclosure. Next morning, flinging open the front door to greet the dewy dawn, he found on his doorstep an impressive pile of human shit, still fresh enough to be steaming quietly in the crisp morning air.

Relations between mission and administration were formally cordial but socially remote. They met socially at Saturday tennis where the mission contingent arrived en bloc with an elaborate afternoon tea that the ladies had spent the morning preparing. There were also occasional inter-suppers, usually a token mutual ordeal. One example will suffice. The district commissioner and his wife gave an elaborate party, buffet and dancing (it may have been Christmas). The liquor led to a mild relaxation of inhibitions; it was a nice party that would have aroused no comment in Australia. The missionaries, who had already had their evening meal before they arrived, sat in a circle sipping tea and soft drinks, then left, within the narrowest limits of courtesy, dragging a reluctant but discreet anthropologist with them; the party was discussed disapprovingly for days after. A little later, the mission had a return party: supper, singing, and games, starting at 7 P.M. The evening meal at the mission was always at 5:30 P.M. and we had a supper of tea, cake, and biscuits about 10 P.M. before retiring for the night. Now, the administration normally dined about 7:30 or 8:00 and arrived this night suitably stoked for what they suspected might be an "unwhoopee" evening and with voracious appetites, apparently unaware that there would be three sobering hours of soft drink, games, and community singing before they were served an elaborate supper consisting mainly of cakes and tea. The starving young patrol officers (their seniors had all made polite excuses) moved along the luscious spread like a plague of locusts—and took their leave shortly afterward. To this day, I am not sure how far that party was an *intentional* revenge, a defiant assertion of different life-styles, but it was certainly that! At least this experience brought home to me, far later than it should have, the cultural divergencies in my own society—and I knew which life-style was closest to my own.

Shortly after this, when I'd been at the mission about six weeks, I selected my base community and made preparations to move there, once more with the guidance and absolutely invaluable assistance of G. Y. The place was called Māp (pronounced "Mape"), on the main track (there were then no trafficable roads outside the station) about two hours walk north of the mission, or two and a half hours from the station. Māp had one of the most attractive dancegrounds and enjoyed *relatively* easy access to a number of other settlements. It was just above the Mendi River and not far from the fifteen-hundred-foot range dividing the Mendi Valley from the neighboring Wahgi. The place was, in short, ideal for my purposes. The district commissioner had given me permission to occupy a dilapidated patrol hut situated, again ideally, on the corner of the main track and the danceground, and G. Y. had negotiated, in his usual bluff fashion, with the local clan leaders for their consent to my visit. He even sent a mission teacher-cum-bush-carpenter to make the hut habitable: sagging walls were repaired, thatch was patched, and cane matting woven for the floor; a stout, wooden, padlocked door, matting, and built-in furniture (shelves, bed platform, etc.) of slatted bamboos completed the residence. Originally the place had no windows, so these were inserted, paned with old X-ray plates of shadowy spinal columns flanked by the ghosts of tuberculous lungs. It was rugged but not uncomfortable, and in time I got to thinking of it as home.

I am thoroughly ashamed now, when I think of how passive was my own role in all this. I was totally helpless and was inexperienced enough to suppose that this kind of assistance was a normal concomitant of fieldwork. To be sure, I paid, minimally, for these services, but that does not diminish the fact that they were voluntarily and ungrudgingly given. If I seem to be less than kind regarding some aspects of the missionaries, it is because it seems relevant to my account to indicate that our aims, attitudes, and personalities were perhaps not as finely attuned as one could hope. It was also fairly obvious that G. Y. himself was getting his own kicks out of the assistance he organized for me: it was the kind of thing he was good at and enjoyed doing (far more than the actual proselytization work), and my own utter incompetence was a great solace to his educational inferiority complex. This, however, does nothing to diminish my appreciation for his help.

A couple of weeks before my departure for Māp my wife, Pat, arrived and accompanied me on the ceremonial progress to the field base. We arrived midmorning in what must have seemed an impressive procession. Pat and I moved intrepidly ahead and our gear was carried along on poles by a dozen or more cargo-boys, the whole operation totally organized, of course, by the efficient G. Y., who accompanied us with Daniel, the teacher-carpenter who had helped renovate the house. We were also accompanied by Shont, a stocky young man of about twenty-five (?) who had worked on the mission since its foundation, and for whose invaluable services I was once again indebted to G. Y. Shont, honest and reliable, became my majordomo, cook, chief informant and, I like to think, close friend—but I've never been quite sure about the last. Infinitely tactful and patient, even through all the bloodymindedness of my culture shock, honest, frank when necessary, and helpful, there seemed, nevertheless, to be always a barrier between us. He showed little curiosity about my world, and was indulgent, as with a child, in my attempts to penetrate his. But then, all the Mendi were like that. Never in the whole time I was there did anyone actually volunteer any information: if I didn't ask the right questions, I didn't get it. It was probably unreasonable of us to expect more from Shont. For example, it was more than six months before I discovered that his widowed mother was now married to one of my regular visitors who lived about two-hundred meters away. Why hadn't he told me? I'd never asked. Like so many others, his lineage had been dispersed in warfare, his landrights were negligible, and his status handicapped, which was one reason he had reached his present age unmarried. And it was probably also why he had decided to throw in his lot with the mission; indeed, I heard later that, after my final departure, he became a full-time missionary, a traveling symbol of the mission's success.

But back to 1954: as our procession filed up the last of the track, we found a reception committee waiting outside our future house—armed, and one young man with drawn bow and arrow pointed (I couldn't believe it) at *us*! On my earlier renovation visits, the people had seemed, if not enthusiastic, at least accepting—and now this! Oddly enough, in retrospect, I felt no fear at all—it simply never crossed my mind that there could be any real danger. I guess this is what our Colonial Heritage did for us: Mad Dogs and Anthropologists! It turned out I was right: it was indeed no more than a symbolic gesture of anxiety and disapproval, and G. Y., as insensitive as I, immediately defused the situation with his usual hearty authoritativeness: "Ho, ho, put that thing away!"

The explanation, which I pieced together much later, requires a further digression. When the government first established itself in Mendi (as in other new areas), its first step was to negotiate the purchase of a tract of land for the new station, and any missions went through the same procedure. But none of them realized that, under native systems of land tenure, land was alienable only by conquest: it was not a saleable commodity. When the people "sold" land to these powerful, new "clans," they were really buying allies who would strengthen their forces in the endemic clan warfare which was the normal state of life. Although, of course, they were instantly disillusioned about this, their exclusion from what they still regarded as their own territory (as also the failure of the administration to favor their causes in litigation) at that time still rankled. When we started to fix up the old patrol hut, they had assumed it was for only a night or two, as had been customary. When they saw our entourage approaching they realized for the first time that this was no overnight stand. They were apparently about to be lumbered with a permanent white authority in their community—and they felt tricked and indignant: hence our reception.

However, we settled in, disposed our belongings, made G. Y. some tea on our new primus, and then, as the midafternoon storm clouds were piling up from the south, waved him and his helpers off back to the mission.

At last, we and Our People were alone together!

We finally went to sleep that night, listening to the rustling and scrabbling in our woven cane walls. I reassured Pat that it was just rats and not people trying to get in. I was not sure myself, but it turned out that both explanations were correct.

Next morning I emerged, notebook in hand, to begin Field Work. We were, of course, the focus of interest, and not only the local residents but their accessible kin and casual passersby flocked to our house. We became the social center of the area, which was all very gratifying and proper. Our house was like an ongoing tourist exhibition, with constant "oohing" and "aahing" and fingering everything in sight. Not wanting to discourage my contacts, I endured this for several days, although Pat, not sharing my professional dedication, was getting a bit twitchy. And there was the smell. It is, of course, totally taboo these days to suggest that non-European people smell, but the fact is that the Mendi never bathed; moreover, they smothered their bodies with pig fat or, when they could afford it, with a pungent palm oil imported from the south along traditional trade routes. After evenings spent in smoke-filled huts, the aroma was like smoked bacon—not unpleasant, when one got used to it, but distinctive and penetrating nonetheless. And it was both catching and persistent; even today, when I open up old notebooks, that smoky smell takes me back thirty years.

As the first week or two passed, local curiosity abated somewhat, and our flood of visitors gradually dwindled. Shont was instrumental in this: he constantly warned us against keeping open house. His main anxiety, not unfounded, was petty theft. Pat supported him on grounds of privacy, and even I came to realize that organized interviewing and recording were impossible in the present situation. So we instituted times at which I "received" and times at which the house was closed to visitors—which aroused some indignation and resentment. It was during this period that it was explained to me that, as their brother, whom they had welcomed onto their land, I should share everything with them (I could start with those cases of bully-beef they had seen in their inventory of my belongings), but I must also remember that, as I was a foreign outsider, they were under no obligation to share anything whatever with me. I was never able to change this curious doublethink. When they realized that I was not the anticipated cornucopia they lost interest, and their main concern was, what was I doing there? and how long was I going to stay? I gave the anthropologist's standard reply: I wanted to know about their customs to tell my people so we could understand each other better. This met with total incomprehension. What was there to understand? Everybody was born, lived, made their gardens with their kin, fought their enemies, married, had children, and died. That other people might organize their lives differently simply never occurred to them. They were, however, intrigued by our incessant writing, and quickly realized that *shogsho wap* (marks on leaves) was, among white people, a useful way of communicating, but they still had their own method of yodeling, which could convey news of death or a pig feast right through the valley far quicker than any messenger on foot, and their interest was mild. In general, the very concept of "cultural interchange" was outside their orbit.

So, still objects of some curiosity, but ignorant and materially useless, we were left pretty much to ourselves. I did all the things *Notes and Queries* advised: house and garden map, household census, genealogies—battling all the time with that diabolic language. As Ian Hogbin once remarked, it was like living in a goldfish bowl: while you yourself were totally exposed and vulnerable, you looked out on an exotic world going about its fascinating business behind impenetrable and soundproof walls. It was frustrating, but one thought, "Once I crack that language, I'll be right into it!" Ah well, we need our encouraging little fantasies.

After about six weeks the exotic was waning and discouragement waxing. Fortunately we had learned about Culture Shock, and when it began to strike, recognition of the symptoms and their inevitability helped us through. The obvious therapy was to shut up the house, but I was reluctant to do this lest it "alienate my contacts" (regardless of the fact that, living in cultural isolation, we had acquired almost no contacts of any professional value). Pat's solution was to sneak off to secluded cubbyholes in the dense three meter cane grass, where she would curl up for remedial sessions with a good novel, but the local ladies soon latched onto this, and refuges became increasingly hard to find.

During such a period came my first crisis. We awoke one morning early to see a nose pressed against the shadow of rotting lung in the window immediately opposite the bed. The last straw! This had to be stopped! I leapt out of bed, wrapped on a *laplap* (T.P., piece of cloth used as a wraparound garment), dashed out the front door, and tackled the snooper, who had begun to run, and, grabbing him by the wig and bustle, tossed him over the low fence that cut off our back garden. As I was doing so, I thought, "Oh my God! What have I done?" Came the image of G. Y. on that earlier occasion, but I'd be lucky if I got out of this one with just a pile of shit on the doorstep! So I tried to make amends. Watched by a gathering crowd, seemingly more interested than hostile, the Peeping Tom and I sat in the danceground, with me holding his hand trying to explain that one didn't pry into people's houses (which there, too, was true) and how would *he* feel if I tried to watch him sleeping with his wife? He looked at me and sneered, "We Mendi don't sleep with our wives" (which was also true; they slept separately and "cohabited" in secluded corners of the gardens). After about twenty minutes, pursed lips, pointedly looking away from me, the promise of a handful of salt, and much wounded white pride, the episode was smoothed over. I felt overwhelming relief and that I was luckier than I deserved. Ignorant still of the local status system and its pecking order, I had supposed that my snooper, a mature married man, was a respected elder, and I was then unaware that, in local eyes, he had behaved unbecomingly in a way that no respected big man would, and that my reaction, although undignified, had not been entirely inappropriate.

This episode, however potentially fatal it might have been, taught me two lessons. First, specific: that one recognized the truly important men in the community by the authority of their self-control. Second, applying everywhere: one could afford to stage an all-stops-out temper tantrum when one had carefully gauged its potential effects, but one never *lost* one's temper. (I did also wonder what would have happened had I not been white.)

As the weeks went by, it became apparent that my stay on the mission had identified us firmly with that "clan," and that the Kiap Clan was perceived as the dominant one among the white men. I tried at first to indicate that we really belonged to neither; but in the local system, that would put us in the category of "refugee nonagnates"—people who, expelled from their own land by warfare, had taken refuge with kin by whom they were accepted comfortably enough although suffering certain status handicaps. We were thus in danger of being regarded as white "rubbish men." At this point, I decided it was essential to change our clan identification—if that were still possible. This calculated policy, when eventually it became apparent to the mission people, was regarded (quite reasonably) as an offensive mark of ingratitude. (It would also be hypocritical to deny that, for our infrequent rest-and-recuperation visits, the station was rather more fun than the mission.)

Life continued thus for about three months, and our establishment was running smoothly; we had got to know a range of people and, if not accepted, we were at least tolerated. But that was all. I had done all the preliminary mapping, taken what genealogies I could, and written a regrettably inadequate description of the clan structure (which, alas, was subsequently published), and there it stopped. No more information was coming in.

It may be recalled that my original "research plan" was to have been a Mead-type "cultural-personality" study, focusing on child-rearing techniques. The snag was that the Mendi didn't seem to have any child-rearing techniques—or, at least, their concern with this area of life could have been summarized in about half a page. In infancy, kids were given free rein. When they became a nuisance, they were casually swatted so that they quickly learned the difference between "socially approved" and "socially disapproved" behavior. For a boy, this freedom continued up to the age of about seven or eight when he moved to the men's house and began to learn and assume the work of men. A girl stayed with her mother in her woman's house, and began learning her future life of garden work and pig tending as soon as she was old enough to accompany her mother to the garden and trudge back in the evening carrying one sweet potato in a miniature string bag. Doubtless this could have been expanded to a thesis; many have been written on flimsier material.

Obviously, a great deal more was going on in the society than this—but there seemed to be no way I could get at it. Leadership was informal and difficult to identify, for the now well-known system of "big men" had yet to be defined in the literature. I recall a discussion with young informants (all I then had) about "*poshpeya*": A was "*poshpeya*," so was B, C was not quite but might be some day, while D had been but was no longer. It was not until much later, when it dawned on me that "*poshpeya*" was not a Mendi word but the local pronunciation of the Pidgin *bosboi* (T.P., work foreman, leader of a team), that I realized I had been given the basic outlines of the big man system but had been too dumb to see it and follow it up with the right questions.

There was yet another opacity for which I was not perhaps entirely to blame. Among the whites, even in other areas, the Mendi were notorious for their acquisitiveness. The first Mendi word one heard was *ngi!* (give!), or *n'ame ngi!* (give, my brother!). This seemed to form the opening of most conversations. Both administration and mission had warned me about this, and stressed that on no account was I to grant such requests. My personal experiences seemed to bear out this warning: we were constantly asked to "give"—not only our trade valuables like pearlshell, axes, knives, and salt, but even our clothes, or anything we had; all encounters seemed to begin, and end, with this. In language sessions, the first Mendi verb I learned to decline was *ngun* (I give to you) and its other form *kalon* (I give to him)—in all their ramifications. These incessant requests of "gimme, gimme" we interpreted, as did our fellow Europeans, as "begging" of the most self-degrading kind. It was all very well to remind ourselves that they had so little, while we appeared to have access to untold wealth; subjected to this nagging, day after day, our reactions went from amused indulgence, through irritation, to exasperated rage. It became intolerable:

would these people never see us as anything but a local handout agency? As we made it more angrily apparent that we were not going to play their game, the people closest to us began, not actually to withdraw, but rather to lose interest, to the point where virtually my only informants were a few youths, young bachelors, and one or two mature clan nonagnates, men of no importance; and of course, the faithful Shont. I do not know if the latter realized my predicament, but he made no attempt to enlighten me at this time.

What I began to realize only gradually, and mainly in hindsight much later when bits of the jigsaw puzzle had begun to form a pattern, was that this apparent "begging" behavior was the clue to the whole culture. The Mendi were a "gift-exchange" society: the whole of their intricate system of interpersonal and intergroup relations revolved around, and was symbolized and maintained by, the constant formal prestation of valuables (mainly pigs and pearlshell) between individuals and groups. The pattern of prestations not only served to define the significant corporate groups of the society but established the relationships among them. In short, an understanding of the intricate workings of the gift-exchange system revealed the dominant theme of the culture, the major preoccupation of its members, the articulation that made the society a comprehensible organization. But this discovery did not come as divine revelation; it formulated itself, oh so slowly, over a long period of sweat, tears, and tooth-grinding frustration.

At that stage, I had no clue. The literature on gift-exchange was sparse. I knew, of course, about the potlatch and the *kula* and had read the almost metaphysical synthesis of Marcel Mauss's *Le Don*, but they had no apparent relevance to our daily reality of outstretched hands, ingratiatory smiles, and the constant repetition of "Give me, oh my brother!" How could I realize that this was how these other celebrated systems must have looked to any aliens who wandered into them by chance? (All we have from Malinowski is the operating system in all its intricate perfection; even those embarrassing diaries give no indication of the agonies he must have gone through working it out!) What we had interpreted as degraded "begging" was, in fact, an invitation to enter the system, for it was inconceivable to them that anyone of our wealth or significance (the two were synonymous) could possibly be ignorant of its workings or not want to participate in it. After all, what else was life about? If we didn't want to play The Game, why were we there? So, the door was left ajar for us, and we not only didn't enter—we couldn't even see it!

On the other hand, and in the long term, our obtuseness may have been our salvation. One's skill in playing the exchange game was a major factor in personal status and the sole path to becoming a big man enjoying the respect of the community. Had I realized that there *was* a game, and rushed immediately to try and play it, I would probably have been stripped of everything I had and then relegated to the status of an incompetent rubbish man. It would have been rather like an immensely rich dilettante diving in among the sharks of Big Business without the slightest knowledge of how the commercial world operated. As it was, although my "reluctance" puzzled and irked them, and kept them at a distance, my status was, to some extent, protected by my alienness.

The first six months in Mendi were now at an end. It had originally been agreed that, because Mendi was still an anthropological terra incognita (as it was in most other ways), we should make a preliminary reconnaissance of six months, then return to Sydney to collate our data (!) before returning for the grand assault of long-term, intensively focused fieldwork. So we went home. Our farewell was much warmer than our welcome, even though we tried to make it clear that we would be back in six months. We had some doubts whether this fact registered. It did appear that most of them were so relieved to see us go that they tended to suppress the threat of our return.

Back in Sydney, Elkin was kind and encouraging about my poverty of data, although he clearly found my account of our problems incomprehensible. My real encouragement came from seminars in Sydney and Canberra (and the subsequent convivial sessions) in which I exchanged experiences with colleagues also working in the Highlands: Mervyn Meggitt among the not-too-dissimilar Mae Enga, Ralph Bulmer with the Kyaka Enga of the Baiyer Valley, and Bob Glasse with the Huli at Tari. It was Meggitt's verbal account of the Western Highlands *moka* (which Andrew Strathern has since made famous) that gave me the nudge I needed. Meggitt's information was sketchy, as the focus of his research was elsewhere, and it bore little *direct* relevance to the Mendi, but it did ring a number of Mendi bells, and gave me my first coherent ideas about the *kind* of system I had to unravel.

While, in my professional life, things seemed to be running more or less on schedule, domestically, an unforeseen problem arose: my wife announced that she was again pregnant. We already had one daughter, nearly two years old, who had been in her grandparents' care during our first trip. We had planned to take her back with us and establish ourselves as a family unit. But additional pregnancy, childbirth, and infant care in Mendi were just not on! It is unnecessary to describe the ensuing family discussions, which were long, frequent, and occasionally verging on the terse. By certain standards, I should have stayed, at least until the birth— but at what stage thereafter could I have decently left? In this quandary, there was one thing I knew with absolute certainty: if I did not go back at the scheduled time, I never would; any hope of an academic career would be totally annihilated and, at the age of thirty-two, I would have to replan my entire life. Pat, reluctantly, was persuaded to see my point, but I don't think anyone else ever did.

So back I went for the long haul, which turned out to be fourteen months—but this time, completely alone: more alone than I have ever been before or since.

As, once again, my entourage trudged up the road to Māp, I was gratified (and relieved) to find my house much as I had left it: door padlocked, windows in place, walls unpierced. I had been told that various people, administration, mission, and local, had been keeping an eye on it for me, and when I saw it, I felt ashamed that my confidence in these assurances had been less than total. Shont, thank heaven, was still available as my majordomo and had suborned a kinsman, Shabunaik, a squat youth with a wild cast in one eye, whose obliging good nature more than compensated for his sometimes disconcerting appearance. My welcome, which I had been wondering about, was as effusive as the Mendi ever got: "Eh, Eraino, you're back? You told us you would come back. Well, Eraino, there's your house." And then, repeated many times over the next four days, "How long are you going to stay?" As I settled in again, I had the usual influx of curious visitors, including many of the same familiar faces. Then, soon, the fading away as they returned to their daily affairs, and I became, once again, an alien excrescence on the fringe of the community. And for a long time I remained so, only now I had no one to relax with at the end of each frustrating day.

I had my informants, but they were still the same few amicably unhelpful people. In my own little circle, my language began to improve. But I was worried by the fact that, although I could communicate tolerably well with my "regulars," most of whom were young, and could get by with most of the other Māp residents, even occasionally picking up what they said to each other, yet when I met people unfamiliar with me, even some of the more reticent older men of my own community, the Mendi they spoke was almost unintelligible to me—so much so that when I addressed myself to visiting strangers, they often appeared unaware that I was even trying to speak their language. Apart from my own linguistic incompetence, there were two reasons for this. First, it was a "known fact" that, apart from two or three people on the mission station, no white person spoke Mendi, so what was the point of even listening? Second, and much more of a problem, was that my neighbors (i.e., my language teachers) regarded their language, when talking to me, purely as a tool of communication which, discarding all grammatical nuances, had to be stripped down to a sort of baby talk. To the end, I never really broke out of this impasse. Eventually, I built up my language from infant prattle to, say, adolescent chatter, to the stage where I could get across, to a patient listener, anything I wanted to say and could understand anything they wanted me to hear; but mature, formal Mendi always gave me difficulty simply because my regular interlocutors seldom spoke it to me. The even more formal and florid oratorical language, which would have illuminated so many important situations, had always to be para-phrased for me.

Shortly before the end of my first visit, there had occurred an inno-vation. The community had become involved in the arrival of a new ritual complex called Timp. It had been, literally, traded up from the south of the valley, using the mechanisms of gift-exchange. It involved the con-struction of a large and elaborate Timp-house, with many important visitors, long and earnest confabulation on the danceground outside my door, much solemn unwrapping and inspection of pearlshell, and fre-quent episodes of flamboyant oratory. It was as though a galvanic shock had been passed through the whole community. (Analogies? Edinburgh before the Festival, or Perth before the America's Cup.) But alas, it was that "goldfish bowl" again—or, even more, like watching one of those early surrealist "experimental" movies where people performed, with portentous significance, actions that were totally inexplicable. Timp was open only to those mature males able to afford the entrance fee (in other societies, the "initiated," but Mendi had no formal initiation rituals). Women, youths, and outsiders like ourselves were totally excluded. The whole proceedings were shrouded in the most delicious secrecy. I choose that adjective deliberately, because secrecy was an important part of the act: obviously a source of status to those in the know, who revelled in it. There were mysterious comings and goings, men would scurry across the danceground with bundles of building materials, group discussions would stop at my approach, and often I was impatiently waved away. The way the women played their role was interesting. They were supposed to, and did, act as though nothing unusual was going on. I was told that any woman who showed unbecoming interest or curiosity would be punished by gang rape, while male offenders were beaten up and their house gardens wrecked; indeed, one such case did occur at this time. This in-group assertion of differential status is a general feature of human "secret societies." In Mendi, status went to the male entrepreneurs of gift-exchange, and Timp was, in one sense, a ritual reaffirmation of this fact. But the "manifest function" (to use Robert K. Merton's term), the philosophical rationale of what they were doing, was completely closed to me: my questions were met by pursed lips, rolled eyes, and vigorous head shaking. They had told me very little hitherto, but now they had a marvelous excuse for telling me nothing at all.

Came the great day of the opening ceremonies: we were told to stay indoors for the entire two days and, if we *had* to go outside, to do so with a cloth covering our heads and faces. I did toy with the idea of self-assertion, but decided, no doubt wisely, to observe the restrictions. I was rewarded with a small gift of sacrificial pork with the firm injunction that my wife must not see it. It was well known to the donor that Pat and I shared both house and meals and that there was no conceivable way I could have concealed it from her, but the formalities had to be observed, and my reassurance was accepted at its face value. Our exclusion from the "Secrets of Timp" lasted until our departure, and my professional frustration was edging toward an active dislike of My People. In any circles we had frequented, we had never before been socially ostracized.

So, back to my return visit. Timp was still going on, and had spread a little further to neighboring clans. But in Māp, although the later rituals were still in progress, it was noticeable that the first excitement had died. This, I was to discover, is typical of the "sacred life" of that area. New cult cycles arrived intermittently from the south (I never discovered their initial source) and were welcomed enthusiastically as "monotony-breakers"; then boredom set in, they were duly negotiated north to the next recipients, and the community settled down to await the next arrival. My renewed efforts to gain admission were still blankly blocked. After some weeks, I happened to mention this to the assistant district commissioner, Des Clancy, a veteran of many primary patrols, who, without a word of the language, had managed to establish a respected relationship with the Mendi unequalled by any other European. He had the knack, unfortunately rare in the administration, of conveying sympathetic authority with assured ease. Anyway, with a rum bottle between us, Clancy listened to my bitching, and said casually: "Oh, don't worry, I'll get you into Timp, if that's what you want!" With visions of intruding on these so-secret rituals with an armed police escort (not unlike leading a vice squad raid into the Melbourne Club), I tried to discourage him. But no, not to worry, Des would fix it for me. And he did!

Next morning, I dragged my hangover back to Māp, and the following day received a deputation from Eshmalt, our next-door clan, to inform me that *their Timp* was to open the next day, and would I like them to escort me? Gratitude struggled with humiliation. Here, at last, was the almost-despaired-of opportunity. But here also was the failed grass-roots anthropologist, sharing the life of His People, speaking their language (!), whose finger should have been on the very pulse of the culture—and who was confronted with nothing but closed doors; while down there behind his desk in his office, was one who bothered little about personal contact with the local people but who, with a casual wave of the hand, could not only unlock the door, but have a welcome mat placed at the entrance!

Fortunately, professional responsibility prevailed over personal pique, and, next day, I was sponsored into my first Timp. I was given full entree, photographs and all. I hadn't a clue what was going on; it was only much later that my notes slowly evolved into some kind of coherent interpretation. But at least, I was *in*!

And what did I find in there? Well, that very first time, I found Durkheim. As the day-long ceremony wound up to its climax, I became conscious of a mounting euphoria. There was, of course, the thrill of a successful gala opening after months of rehearsal, and there was also the near-ecstasy of participation in repetitious and rhythmic ritual. The group excitement was truly intense, and even I was caught up in its *effervescence*. For one fleeting moment, transformed from Profane to Sacred, I reached out and touched the face of God. So rapturous was this experience that it was a couple of hours before reason returned and *The Elementary Forms of the Religious Life* slid back into perspective as the rhetorical hyperbole that most of it is.

The Māp people seemed a little embarrassed by my debut in someone else's Timp and insisted that I attend all of their own future ceremonies. I then became a regular Timp-goer and my presence was accepted in ceremonies at various places where Timp was at different stages of its evolution. In this way, I was able to synthesize a time-perspective of the full cycle.

But still, no one who really knew would tell me what it was all about. In other areas of investigation, too, the reticence was as complete as before, and once more bleak frustration set in. Nearly eight months in Māp now, and what had I got to show for it? Certainly not a thesis. I already knew that gift-exchange had to be the topic, for every day I was surrounded by that mysterious maze of discussions, planning, negotiation—and from time to time, the actual display and transfer of goods. But for the life of me, I could not figure out how it all worked! In moments of the worst depression I have known, I seriously considered giving up, going home, and finding some new career.

Around this time, came a radiogram: Pat had given birth to twin girls, the double-up being quite unexpected. I had previously explained Pat's absence by the fact that she was pregnant and they had wanted to know, reasonably enough, why she was having the birth with her own clan: had I been beating her, or just defaulted on my marriage exchanges? I thought my proud announcement of twins might resolve this misunderstanding and establish my status as a fecund and respected paterfamilias. The news was at first received with some puzzlement. "Two girls? You mean the one you've already got and another one?" "No, two new ones!" "You mean two in the same belly?" "Yes!" (Pause) "Our pigs do that." Then, doubtfully, "Oh, well, perhaps you'll get a son later?" (The Mendi, in fact, did have twins, but they were not considered a blessing because it was rare for both, and uncommon for either, to survive.) So, back to square one.

Life went on. Sure, I was learning: you can't live alone for a long period in even the most alien culture without learning *something* about it, even if it is only enough to enable you to continue living there. A number of relationships had flowered purely on the level of personal good will. I was a familiar and painlessly tolerated figure over an increasingly wide radius from my home clan. One thing that pleased and encouraged me was that whereas I had formerly been known as "Hunja Erain" (Hunja being the site of the mission from which I had tried to dissociate myself), I was now addressed and introduced as "Māp Erain," indicating, perhaps, a degree of acceptance, but alas with no informative payoff for, despite this minor satisfaction, those doors were still closed. Apart from the ritualistic "secrecy" of Timp, it was not so much reticence about their daily life that I encountered as a complete lack of interest in discussing it with me. If I couldn't see and understand what was going on, what was the point of explaining it to me? My earlier questions must have been of a naiveté that they found literally incredible. I was lucky, perhaps, in one respect: the Mendi, as far as I am aware, seldom lied to me. If they didn't want to tell me something, they just didn't. Any false information I received was due mainly to linguistic misunderstanding, or the occasional leg-pull.

For example, I heard one morning that a near neighbor, whom I knew quite well, was about to perform a ritual with his family ghost-stones. I had never witnessed this, and so, although uninvited, I called into his house compound where I was received affably enough. A pig was tethered for sacrifice, and three or four men were making the usual preparations. Then nothing more happened; we just sat, chatting and smoking, for nearly an hour. I already had some idea of this ceremony, and the owner answered my queries and said he had no objection to my presence. There were sporadic bits of ritual, but no real action for another long period. Finally, one man got up, took two bunches of leaves and, holding them like horns on his head, began a curious, hopping frog-march around the enclosure. After several minutes, he sat down and the long wait continued. Finally, another man arrived, for whom they had apparently been waiting. Immediately, the pig was bashed on the skull with a cudgel and, with appropriate incantations, its snout was bled onto the ghost-stones, which were then returned to their hiding place. Finish. On my return home, I went over the details, as usual, with Shont. Yes, it was all quite orthodox until we got to that hopping dance and its accompanying chant. Never heard of that—he'd check for me. He had the explanation that afternoon. They had seen me sitting there and were afraid I was getting bored. Deciding that somebody should do something, they had improvised that bit of ritual for my benefit.

But I did experience other definable difficulties. One was in my attempts to use hypothetical cases: "What would happen if . . . ?" The language had conditional tenses, but they were only used specifically: "If

X did so and so, I would do this." The query, "Suppose a man did so and so . . . ?" would bring the reply, "Which man? What's his name?" It took me many months to accustom my informants to this alien mode of generalized abstraction although, with the help of Shont, I had some degree of success. Another problem was a blank refusal to speculate about other people's motives. Questions like, "Why did X do that?" were invariably met by the routine phrase, "Can I see into his mind?"

Moreover, in the taking of genealogies and the plotting of kinship networks, names were a special problem. In addition to the clan name, which comes first, each Mendi had a number of personal names (including nicknames) that were used by different people in different circumstances. For instance, when someone died, their name became taboo to their kin, and all people carrying the deceased's name (as many did) had to change it. The many ramifications of this practice made it extremely difficult, for me at least, to know whom we were discussing at any time or to slot them into my kinship charts.

It was after nearly a year of this (eight or nine months into my second visit) that the breakthrough finally occurred. It was, quite literally, an accident, and not at all the mode of entree I would have chosen. But it worked.

One evening at dusk I was lighting up my pressure lamp. I pumped it up and lit it, but there was a blockage somewhere, and the fuel wasn't coming through. Then (never let it be said that my incompetence is limited in its range!) I unscrewed the cap of the compressed tank and peered hopefully inside. All one side of my head was sprayed with hot kerosene which promptly caught fire. Being well-read, literary metaphors of "living torches" ran through my mind and, although temporarily blinded, I could hear someone screaming in the distance; it turned out to be me. Fortunately, I had a full beard at the time which, although providing splendid kindling, did protect me from what could have been serious, permanent damage. It was also lucky that the lamp extinguished itself as I dashed it to the cane-matted floor. Nevertheless, the left side of my head and neck, from nose to ear, suffered third-degree burns.

Shont, Shabunaik, and two or three visitors who were present rallied around, and someone was sent down to the creek to fetch some of the gray clay river silt for a poultice, the local remedy for burns. Naturally, I wouldn't allow them to use this: who knew what kind of infections it would introduce to raw wounds? I had in my first-aid kit a tube of Tanifax for such an emergency, and applied it liberally. (This was, in those days, the traditional household remedy and has since, very rightly, been taken off the market.) It formed a dry, plastic skin over the burns, sealing in, more efficiently than a primitive mud plaster, any infection that might be present. They got me to bed and, in considerable discomfort, I dozed fitfully through the night. During the following day, the pain grew steadily worse, and by the second morning, I was conscious only inter-mittently through bouts of delirium.

It was then decided, with my agreement as far as I can recall, to take me down to the station hospital, which fortunately had recently acquired a full-time doctor. I did not remember much about that journey: the crowd outside the house, murmuring "*Ish!*" (the expletive for regret, sorrow, sympathy); the endless track undulating slowly in a curious, sub-aqueous way that I had never noticed before; the muscular shoulders of the two stocky men who supported my arms as they half-carried me along; the delicate maneuvers as we negotiated the single log that spanned a raging mountain torrent fifteen feet below; and at last, semi-conscious, the hospital. Within forty-eight hours, antibiotics had subdued the infection; scarring, although permanent, was minimal. The hospital had no accommodation for a white patient, so for my ten days of con-valescence, it was the mission again who came to my rescue, and I was lodged in the house of their agricultural officer, David Johnson, and his wife, Beryl, who supervised my recovery with no reproaches at my very obvious change of allegiance. I was helpless and grateful—and embar-rassed.

My comment above that the hospital had no accommodation for a white patient might, these days, cause some raised eyebrows and pursed lips. In the present climate of Third World Studies, it probably sounds like typical colonialist arrogance. But it was a fact that the Mendi, for the first time in their history, had (if they accepted it, and they often didn't) access to a fairly high standard of modern medical expertise which, despite the current trendy nonsense about "folk medicine," was infinitely more efficacious than their own traditional remedies. Whether, in the long run, we have done such people a disservice in lowering infant mortality, prolonging their lives, causing population explosions and thus increasing their struggle for land and survival, which in turn destroyed "the delicate balance between culture and environment," is a matter for purely academic debate. History has happened, and it can't be revoked. In the Mendi hospital, the care and attention in the native wards was the best that local facilities could offer. The patients were housed in condi-tions far more hygienic and comfortable than they would have had at home, and their families supplied the personal needs that would, with us, have been met by the infrastructure of a large hospital staff. Nevertheless, life in those wards was not one to which sick Europeans could easily have accommodated themselves, and I make no apologies for accepting a more comfortable alternative.

After my recovery, which, physically at least, was rapid, I returned to Māp. I walked back alone with no great elation, back to the reluctant "So here you are again!" and the dismal routine of knocking on locked doors. After the usual couple of hours of cheerless trudging, I crossed that nightmare bridge (however had they got me across it!) and found myself on Our Clan land, with some four hundred meters to go. By this time, I had apparently been spotted (where, and by whom, I don't know) for yodels were going out in which I could only discern the words "Māp Erain . . ." As I approached my house, the meeting-group seemed larger than usual. A few of my familiars ran down to meet me and stroked and hugged me with every sign of—I must be mistaken?—affection and enthusiasm! Surely, these could not be the reserved and dismissive people whose casual rebuffs I had endured for nearly a year! Outside my house, a group of older men waited, with smiles that seemed almost timid. There were speeches of welcome and again I was assured, fulsomely, that nothing of mine had been touched. Among this crowd were several of the senior big men who had avoided all my previous attempts to approach them. They also formed part of the deputation which later waited on me. First, they expressed their intense sorrow at my accident and their joy at my miraculous return—they told me that they had planned to give me a big man's funeral (in a hollow tree, no less!) with full mourning ritual. I was deeply moved by all this, and was beginning to revise my whole (rather jaundiced) view of the Mendi. Then, the gracious formalities over, they got down to business: Exactly how much longer was I going to stay there? And what did I want from them anyway?

I droned through the old routine: "I want to explain your people's customs to my people." Whereas previously this had simply not registered, I had now been with them long enough for this incredible concept to dawn: that perhaps we really didn't know how normal people conducted their lives, and I was going to tell my people the proper way to do things. It was a kind of mutual breakthrough: I actually didn't know, so they would tell me. Then I would go away and leave them in peace!

We set up regular informant sessions, with agreed rates of pay. This led to an interesting discovery: although they had no clocks, and couldn't measure "time," they knew that I could, and that one revolution of the big hand of my clock marked a unit of duration to which I apparently attached some importance. So they proposed, when we got down to details, that each informant would have his personal string in which he would tie a knot for each revolution of that big hand. (The function of the small hand, tied as it was to the notion of a twenty-four-hour day, even Shont never quite mastered.) But the new system worked well, and my now willing informants made important decisions about the ultimate payment they wanted (salt, a small knife, an axe, or a pearlshell) and calculated the precise number of hours they would have to work to earn it. This led to a formal distinction between *kalt enggiba* and *kalt pame* ("work talk" and "social chat"), only the former being paid for. And the information just rolled in. Although I hadn't realized it, I had, in those months of frustration, acquired a considerable, though fragmented and incoherent, knowledge of the culture. I really did have a lot of data about marriage rules, mortuary practices, pig feasts, and dances, but what I lacked was the underlying structure that would make it all hang together and weld disparate clumps of ethnographic observation into a comprehensible picture of a functioning social system. But, slowly, gradually, agonizingly, and battling (even then) with that frightful language, it began to emerge. Still, as always, no unsolicited information was volunteered, but I did know what meaningful questions to ask, and these were answered freely to the best of my informants' ability. Thus *a* (I don't dare say *the*) reasonable picture took shape. A pattern formed, and at last, Mendi society began to make sense!

But why this dramatic change: in confidence, attitudes, personal relations—everything? I speculated about this for years after and have come up with two probable explanations.

First, the Mendi had a system of guest responsibility not unlike our law with respect to "invitees." Visitors accepted on one's land, whether welcome or not (i.e., not an acknowledged enemy), were the responsibility of their hosts, who became the legal protectors of their safety. Should they come to any harm, even a self-caused accident, the hosts would be obliged to go through the ceremonies of an injury or death compensation. While the former was simple enough, the latter was enormously complex and could go on, literally, for years. Normally, it was a matter of political status, and hence a source of clan pride, to demonstrate their ability to organize and make such payments. Also, since political alliances implied military strength, the ability to compensate for a friendly visitor's death was a sign of power and, ultimately, a matter of survival. Clans who refused, or were unable, to make such payments established thereby either their hostility or their vulnerability, either of which could lead to interclan warfare and, in the latter case, the extermination or dispersal of the defaulting clan. In the event of my death, the Māp people would have been willing to compensate the Kiap Clan for me, as this would be a matter of great prestige, but it so happened that, at that time, their plans for a forthcoming major pig feast were at a stage where an unexpected commitment of such magnitude would have caused them serious economic embarrassment—indeed, it could have dislocated the whole system. And defaulting on that all-powerful Kiap Clan was a daunting prospect! In other words, although I had, mercifully, survived, they were still expecting me to make heavy claims of compensation which they assumed I had the influence to enforce. My assurance that I would make no such claims was an obvious relief to them.

There was, however, a second factor. White people had been present
in their valley for nearly five years, but they had never heard of one of
us dying, or even seen us seriously sick or injured. I had frequently been
asked, did we get sick and die? Indeed, this was one of the few areas in
which they had shown the slightest curiosity about us. I had now provided
them with visible proof that we were vulnerable and could be physically
injured: We were indeed ordinary human beings just like them! I have
no idea of the relative importance of these two rationales, but I think both
were relevant.

Explanations aside, I reveled in this new freedom. To be sure, there
were still some blank spots. The secrets of the symbolism of Timp ritual
were never fully revealed to me. Perhaps in self-consolation, I began to
formulate the idea that the "secrets" of Timp might not be unlike the
Oscar Wilde story, "The Sphinx without a Secret." It was also Durkheim
who, in one of his moments of intuitive insight, first drew our attention
to the fact that ritual is largely recreation and that the details of its
performance are often spontaneously inventive, like children's games,
and do not necessarily have any coherent, symbolic significance at all. (I
have already given an actual example of this.) My observations of Timp
rituals supported this comforting assumption; as the cycle progressed
from its ecstatic inception through subsequent ceremonies, the onset of
boredom was quite apparent. Ritual became more perfunctory, short cuts
were taken, more attention was focussed on the accompanying pork
exchanges (although fewer pigs were involved), and the Timp leaders
seemed to be devoting more and more time to the parties of visitors to
whom they were passing on the mysteries of the cult. What these "mysteries" really were, I never discovered. Perhaps there really were Secrets
that would have revealed a unique view of Man's Universe? Ah, well! Of
one thing I was and remain quite certain: if mystic speculation about the
Ultimate Questions was an aspect of Mendi culture, no hint of it was ever
revealed to me!

I had thought, in the early stages, and with the Aboriginal Dreamtime
in mind, that "mythology" might give me some cultural insights. But no.
"Who made the land, the hills and rivers?" "Made them? No one made
them, they've always been here!" "What about the sun, the moon, and the
stars?" "What about them? You know the sun, it comes up in the morning
until the rain clouds hide it, and on clear nights, when there is no rain,
the moon is there!" "And the stars?" "Oh, they're holes in the sky where
the Yegi People live." (I never identified these beings and they received
no worship or ritual; they were simply there and of no relevance to human
life.) "When it rains," someone volunteered, "that's the Yegi pissing
through the holes!" There were suppressed giggles, and I realized, accurately, as it turned out, that my leg was being pulled again. (Of how

much such stuff are "mythologies" made?) I then tried to lure them out
with a mélange of Greek and biblical mythology, which was received with
polite but mild interest, and then a dismissive: "We don't have stories like
that!"

On another occasion, much later, I had made a long trip to another
clan's pig feast. The rain came, and we were settled down for the evening
in a section of one of the "long-houses" erected for visitors to such
functions. Crowded together, we sat and smoked and watched the rain
pelting down on the road outside. We chatted desultorily about (need I
say?) pigs, pig feasts, exchanges, and who would be getting what. As the
hours went by even that endlessly fascinating topic became exhausted.
Then someone said, "That rain outside: where do your people say it
comes from?" Now, after more than a year among them, this was the very
first time they had evinced the slightest curiosity about whites or their
beliefs, even though it took an unusual degree of boredom to elicit it. So,
I launched into a simplified, but not too inaccurate, account of rainfall:
"You've seen those puddles after rain when the sun comes out, and the
mist that rises from them as they are warmed by the sun?" Yes, of course
they had. "And you know how the clouds come up the valley each afternoon?" Oh, yes. "Well, the warm mist off those puddles rises and
makes the clouds. Now it's very cold up there, and the clouds turn back
into water which falls down as rain. So the same water keeps going up and
down." After this lucid explanation, about the severest linguistic test my
Mendi had yet undergone, I sat back triumphantly, awaiting the animated
curiosity that would undoubtedly follow. There was a pause, while they
thought it over. I finally broke the silence: "Well, that's what *we* say. What
do your people think about it?" "Oh, we don't know. You may be right."
After this irrelevant interlude, the conversation went back to the things
that really mattered—pigs and pearlshells.

Despite my increasing grasp of the intricacies of the gift-exchange
system, to the stage where I had even begun to participate in a tentative
way, I still could not understand the emotional "obsession" that it generated throughout the whole culture. Then, one day, I had a heated
quarrel with a young man who had been frequenting my house. He
stalked off with the remark, loudly and publicly uttered, "You are going
to the Timbalt pig feast tomorrow. My mother's brother is giving it, and
you will receive nothing!" I dismissed the threat, and duly arrived at the
affair on the next day. As I entered the danceground, all eyes turned to
me, and an audible mutter (snigger?) went around. Shont, who had
accompanied me, said, "Let's go back!" "Why?" "They are saying you will
receive no pork!" However, I stayed, and sure enough, when the time for
distribution came, I was ostentatiously overlooked. Despite the security
of my alien culture, I was surprised to feel utterly and publicly humiliated!

I had, at last, some inkling of what gift-exchange, and the prestige attached to it, meant to a Mendi.

As mortuary rites were important occasions for gift-exchange, I became an assiduous mourner: at the first notes of a distant death yodel, I would be galloping off, notebook and camera at the ready. They had some elaborations of burial style for very important men, but the status of the deceased was usually expressed by the size of the gift-exchanges among the kin. The common mode of burial was in a shallow pit located in the scrub not far from the deceased's residence. After exposure, ceremonial wailing, and, usually, an autopsy, the corpse was interred, undecorated, in a flexed position and with no further ritual. Mendi mortuary rites seemed a classic illustration of the old adage: "Funerals are for the living, not the dead."

On one of these occasions, I found myself watching the final interment of a little, withered old woman. Curled up in a fetal position she looked fragile and pathetic. The rain had arrived early that day, and yellow, muddy water was trickling into the shallow grave, staining the sad little corpse and the green leaves on which she lay. There were only four or five men present, for most mourners did not normally witness the actual burial. As we watched in the mud and rain, one of the men turned to his neighbor and said, "*Ish, n'ame, non ant ngo!*" (Alas, my brother, that's our house, too!). I was amazed. If there was one impression that my life with the Mendi had consistently reinforced, it was that they were utterly practical, pragmatic, down-to-earth materialists: such "spiritual" insight, expressed in poetic metaphor, seemed totally alien to them. I began to wonder, uneasily, how much of their deeper life I had been missing. I worried about this for some time. A week or two later, I found myself at another funeral, in a different clan, but in circumstances quite similar to the previous one. Once again, a small group stood beside the open grave, ready to shovel in the dirt onto the corpse of a middle-aged man. I looked sadly at the deceased, and said quietly to the man beside me, "*Ish, n'ame, non ant ngo!*" He looked at me in surprise: "What did you say?" I repeated it, but somehow felt its sad poetry beginning to drain away. Another man had overheard: "What did he say?" "He said, 'Alas, my brother, that's our house, too' " (quoting me exactly). "Why did he say that?" "I don't know; he's a white man." And that was that. Somehow, I didn't feel like trying the experiment at another funeral. I didn't want to become known as the white man who made silly comments at gravesides. But I can still see the muddy water trickling on to that poor shriveled little corpse—and to this day, I'll *swear* that's what I heard!

Certain of my colleagues have suggested, sternly, that I should include some discussion of the position of women in Mendi. That subject offered no new insights. Like most human societies, the Mendi divided nearly all activity into "male" and "female" domains . . . and never the twain should meet. Since, as in all mammalian species, the males were physically stronger, they could preempt the more exciting and amusing tasks and relegate the monotonous drudgery to the women; by the same means, they could also control the status and political systems to reinforce their own dominance. Any rebellious female who disputed this iniquitous bio-social injustice was bio-socially clobbered, or, if she was sufficiently rebellious and attractive, gang raped.

Rape in Mendi, as in most of the Highlands, was not uncommon. Occasionally, gang rapes were used as formalized "punishment," to keep women "in their place." Sometimes accusations were faked: a married woman, surprised with a lover, would cry "rape" to escape the often nasty punishment for adultery. But there were also rapes for lust, and one of these provided an illuminating episode. A well-developed young girl (twelve? fourteen?) had gone down to the spring for water. There she encountered a mature man, a member of the community, who propositioned, was rejected, and raped her. She rushed home, summoned her kin, and a crowd assembled on the danceground. As there was not much else going on at that time, the "trial" began immediately. The girl described what had happened. She was not traumatized, or distraught with shame, guilt, or anguish, but, by golly, she was indignant and *very* angry: someone had taken liberties with her person to which he was not entitled! The rapist appeared and sheepishly admitted the whole occurrence. The case then revolved on the issue of compensation. Backed by her kin, she demanded a large pig. The rapist argued that, as she was only a little girl, a small pig should suffice. *But* (and this was crucial) the girl was an agnatic member of the clan, with powerful (and husky) kin support, while the rapist was a nonagnatic, distant-kin, guest resident, whose clan had been dispersed in past warfare (in our terms, she was "establishment" and he was a "refugee-migrant"). While the public debate continued, the girl's brothers sneaked off quietly, seized a large pig belonging to the rapist, hid it in the bush, then returned to the "trial" announcing what they had done. The rapist, knowing that he had no power base from which to contest it, accepted this de facto solution, and there the matter ended: kin honor was satisfied, nonagnates were reminded of their position, and there were no apparent repercussions.

This second trip had been planned to last twelve months, but things were now going so well that I extended it another two. Something else was happening, curious and, in a way, alarming. I was beginning to feel "at home." I do not believe that mature people can really switch cultures, and I had never felt a misfit in mine; but if one of those "Armageddon scenarios" had actually occurred just then, and I had found myself stranded forever with the Mendi, I think I could have coped without

disintegrating trauma. But I now had, I thought, most of the information
I needed, and most of what I was likely to get, for I was running out of
questions. In fact, I was becoming blasé. I realized this one day when,
walking through a garden, I saw a neighbor engrossed with a small
structure of twigs. Without pausing, I glanced at him casually and men-
tally noted: "Ah, yes, Molnaik doing rain magic." I had proceeded plac-
idly another ten paces or so, when I suddenly knew it was time to leave.

The announcement of my intention was received with polite regret.
About two weeks later, I had packed, cast a last, rather swimmy-eyed look
around my now-empty house, the ghosts of diseased lungs to which I had
given affectionate names, and my scruffy little vegetable patch. After
hard negotiation, and for an appropriate gratuity, a team of Māp people
had agreed to carry my gear back to the station, and we set off on the last
trek with me doing a "Sanders of the River" out in front, and the millipede
of carriers trailing behind chanting (no, not "Sandy is great, Sandy is
strong" but some lewd variations on the theme of what Māp Erain was
going to do to his wife when he got home). So I arrived at the station in
a gratifyingly triumphant manner. I flew out a couple of days later and
crossed back into my own world. The most acute phase of inverse culture
shock passed in about six months, but I have never been quite the same
since.

In terms of dramatic construction, the story should end there, for the
rest is a slight anticlimax. In my absence, Elkin had retired and been
succeeded by John Barnes, whose views on field data were more updated
and rigorous. Indeed, he was the first of my teachers to suggest that
anthropology might be pursued with some scholarly discipline and not
merely as self-indulgent impressionism. He pointed out that, although
my generalizations were undoubtedly sound, they lacked the quantifi-
cation that would make them conclusive. He suggested that if I could
manage another six months in the field, it would round off the project
neatly.

So I went back. This time, however, it was quite different: I knew
precisely the kind of information I had to get, and how to get it. I knew
by now how the exchange system worked, but I lacked details of how
much had been paid, by whom, and why. My job now was mainly to collect
records of specific payments. (I might add that this exercise not only
solidified my study, but altered its perspective in some important
respects.) Pat joined me for the final three months, and everything proceeded as most fieldworkers plan.

It was not necessary to be based at Māp for this work, so I had built
(this time with generous assistance from the administration) a house on
a bluff overlooking the Mendi River where it rushed through a narrow

gorge just opposite the hospital. I visited Māp frequently, of course, and, although I was received by my old familiars with the same amiable casualness, it was sad to note that my former home had (in just six months) disappeared, and that a few straggling tomato plants, choked with weeds, were the only physical sign that I had ever been there.

I finished what I had to do, and we returned home for writing-up. I have never been back. I am determined to return (possibly next year), and that should make an interesting epilogue. Frankly, the thought terrifies me: most of my informants are now middle-aged or dead—suppose no one remembers me? At least, I have never forgotten them. I still have a trunkful of notebooks, but in writing this, thirty years later, I had no need to refer to them at all.

EIGHT

Encounters with the Huli:
Fieldwork at Tari in the 1950s

Robert M. Glasse

I came to know the Huli and something of their culture during two periods of fieldwork in the 1950s. They were a fascinating people, full of contradictions, and their culture was rich in symbolism, myth, and ritual. Horticulture provided their staple food, the ubiquitous sweet potato. But Huli men sought their identity deep in the forest: there, away from women and their baleful influence, they practiced austerities to foster the growth and maturation of young bachelors. In these forbidden precincts the novices prepared their resplendent, crescent-shaped wigs—the badge of male identity. Led by two bachelor preceptors, they observed the numerous species of birds of paradise and modeled some of their ceremonial dress and dances on these beautiful creatures. Men liked to conceive of themselves as birds: free, sovereign, and flighty, ready to defend their own territories and also to soar skyward to the realm of Ni, the sun deity and progenitor of all the Huli.

If there is a Huli personality, the male version seems to be marked by volatility and volubility. The former was expressed in their readiness to take up arms and their manifest enthusiasm for spectacular rites. The latter, still very much alive today, is their penchant for discussion and argument, for lumping and splitting, fine discriminations, and endless palaver. One day they will make fine lawyers and barristers. Already, some men have become fervid evangelicals, terrorizing their southern neighbors into Christian observances.

This essay tells how I came to study the Huli and the theoretical "climate" of the period; my experience and problems in the field; relations with informants; and the way I chose to formulate my data on descent and corporate group structure the way that I did (1959a, 1959b, 1965, 1968, 1974). My 1979 return to Tari is not discussed here, for the theme of these essays is "pioneer" fieldwork in the 1950s. I will, however, discuss Aidan Southall's recent resolution (1986) of Evans-Pritchard's well-known paradox, which has raised problems of interpreting Highlands data for too many years.

PRELIMINARIES

In 1955 the Southern Highlands of the Territory of Papua and New Guinea remained virtually a terra incognita so far as anthropology was concerned. D'Arcy Ryan had begun fieldwork at Mendi early in 1954 (see chap. 7), but little was known of the several cultures extending to the then-Dutch border. Several patrols had traversed this area as early as 1936 (see below), but little was known of these newly contacted peoples. For me the country west of Mendi represented both an intellectual and geographical frontier. The prospect of undertaking long-term fieldwork among the Huli of Tari Subdistrict, a population believed to number more than fifty thousand souls, was both attractive and challenging. But I should sketch in my background if my approach to fieldwork is to become clear.

I had taken a bachelor's degree in social science at City College of New York in 1951, served two years in the U. S. Army (mainly in Alabama and Japan), and returned to New York only to find that my hope of working at Johns Hopkins University under Owen Lattimore could not be fulfilled. Lattimore had been attacked by the McCarthy Committee, and the Walter Hines Page School of International Relations had been closed down. Disenchanted with the political climate in the United States, I jumped at the chance to pursue graduate studies at the recently established Anthropology Department at the Australian National University in Canberra. Professor S. F. Nadel held the Foundation Chair and the staff included W. E. H. Stanner, Kenneth Read, Peter Lawrence, and linguist Stephen Wurm.

When I arrived in 1954, about a dozen research students were in residence or in the field in Papua New Guinea and Australia. I hoped to pursue my interests in central Asia, but after a few months it became clear that I had little hope of obtaining permission to enter this politically sensitive corner of the world. Nadel encouraged me to change my focus to the Highlands of New Guinea, where Richard Salisbury was studying the Siane and Marie Reay, the Kuma. I quickly agreed to do so and joined Peter Lawrence's stimulating seminar on Melanesian history and ethnography. I devoted the rest of the year to reading the literature on Oceania and New Guinea, especially books by patrol officers and explorers such as Hides (1936), Champion (1932), and Leahy and Crain

(1937). Hides's *Papuan Wonderland* was particularly exciting, and I still remember his evocative description (1936:77–78) of the Tari basin:

> and beyond the gorge, gold and green, reaching as far as the eye could see, lay the rolling timbered slopes and grasslands of a huge valley system. On every slope were cultivated squares, while little columns of smoke rising in the still air revealed to us the homes of the people of this land. I had never seen anything more beautiful. Beyond all stood the heights of some mighty mountain chain that sparkled in places with the colours of the setting sun. As I looked on those green cultivated squares of such mathematical exactness, I thought of wheatfields, or the industrious areas of a colony of Chinamen. Here was a population such as I had sometimes dreamed of finding.

This romantic image whetted my appetite, and events at Tari and Koroba, much reported in the Australian (and, indeed, international) press, drew me further to the Southern Highlands.

Tari was often in the news in 1954. Aerial photographs of the newly discovered Lavani Valley northwest of Tari Station appeared in the *London Illustrated Times* on July 10 and in many Australian newspapers at about the same time. These early reports told of a "lost valley," a landlocked Shangri-La among the mountains—fertile, well cultivated, and with a huge population. (The Shangri-La image, based on James Hilton's well-known novel, *Lost Horizon*, was not new in New Guinea publications; journalists had used it a decade earlier to describe the Grand Valley of the Balim River in then–Dutch New Guinea when an American military plane crashed there in May, 1945, with four survivors [Souter 1963: 195–200].) Press releases about Lavani Valley were garbled and inaccurate but appealed to the romantic imagination. Later it became clear that Lavani contained only a small population, mostly of Duna speakers but with some bilingual Huli, and that the valley soils were poor and the gardens subject to frost damage because of the high elevation. Hardly a new Eden.

While an aerial survey was in progress, John Zehnder, a geologist working with a team from the Australasian Petroleum Company (A.P.C.), briefly visited Lavani. (The A.P.C. patrol had been undertaken with the approval of the administration, although officials in Port Moresby did not know its exact route or timing.) Because much of the country to be surveyed was still uncontrolled and unexplored, the three-man survey team was accompanied by Assistance District Officer Des Clancy, thirteen native police, and a line of carriers. Zehnder's visit to Lavani was only a brief offshoot of the main A.P.C. patrol, which followed a more southerly route toward the Fly River. Later, much to his surprise, when he returned to Port Moresby Zehnder was lionized by the press. The *London Daily*

Telegraph offered to finance a full "expedition" to Lavani. There was talk of filming a major motion picture there, with Peter Finch in the lead role and perhaps Jane Russell playing . . . well, Jane Russell. These pipe dreams never materialized but kept the press in a positive tizzy.

Gradually it became clear that the estimate of a population of one hundred thousand applied not to wind-swept Lavani but rather to the whole Tari-Koroba region. Clearly this was an area that deserved detailed ethnographic study. In October, 1954, the Australian journal *South Pacific* (vol. 7, pp. 909–915) published an official account of the Clancy-A.P.C. patrol and the true story of the journey became available. Meanwhile, the Australian journalist Colin Simpson visited Tari and published a series of colorful articles in various Australian daily and weekly publications. These provided a reasonably accurate picture of some facets of Huli social life. (Later Simpson summarized his reports in chapter 5 of his book, *Islands of Men* [1955]. However, this did not appear until late 1955, when I was already in the field.)

I began to prepare actively for fieldwork in December of 1954: shots, purchasing field gear, official correspondence. My destination in the Highlands was still undecided; the decision was to be mine after talking with Marie Reay in Lae (she had just completed her Kuma fieldwork) and Ralph Bulmer in the Baiyer River Valley, who had preceded me in the field by several months. Ralph and his wife Eileen had settled with the Kyaka Enga, and one possibility for me was to work with the Sau Enga in an adjacent valley. I left Canberra in mid February and visited some of the Sydney anthropologists and linguists while waiting for my ship to depart. I went to see Dr. A. Capell, who would have the best information about what was then known of the Huli language (Wurm had not yet commenced his studies of Highlands languages), and he put me in touch with Murray Rule of the Unevangelized Fields Mission, who had already done some work on the Huli language. Rule was in Melbourne at the time working in the Wycliffe Bible Institute and later, when I had settled at Tari, he generously made available a copy of his preliminary notes on the language.

Sailing on the S.S. *Bulolo* was a salutary, if inebriating, experience. Among the passengers I met Lloyd Yelland, who had formerly been stationed at Tari as medical assistant and thus had firsthand knowledge of the Huli and of conditions at Tari station. He talked at length of his experience with the Huli and during the voyage we became good friends.

The *Bulolo* reached Port Moresby on the twelfth of March. Here we lay over for a few days to discharge and load cargo. I made courtesy calls on administration officials such as Mr. A. Roberts, director of District Services and Native Affairs, and Dr. Gunther, head of the Medical Service. Roberts allowed me to read Southern Highlands patrol reports, and

Gunther generously provided a crate of medical supplies to be used to treat the local population wherever I ended up. Several days later we docked in Lae. Marie Reay was there and made many helpful suggestions on practical matters. As a result I bought most of my supplies (tinned meat, salt, flour, trade goods, etc.) in Madang and had them shipped by DC-3 to Minj. Leaving my stores in the government warehouse, I flew on to the Baiyer River to visit the Bulmers. The flight across the Wahgi Valley was memorable and spectacular; at last I could see the vast expanse of the Highlands laid out before me.

The Wahgi Valley was beautiful, and it was a relief to leave the steamy climate of the coast behind. I made a pilgrimage to Marie Reay's former house, some two miles from the airstrip, and spent the night at the Malaria Control Center. Next day a small plane took me on the twenty-minute flight to the Baiyer airstrip, and there I was lucky to get a lift with the Reverend Mr. Kroenist of the Baptist mission, who took me north by Land Rover to his station. After two hours of hard walking, with two Kyaka youths guiding me and carrying my hand luggage, I reached Yaramanda.

I spent about a week with Ralph and Eileen. This was my real initiation into fieldwork, and I learned much about bushcraft, natural history, and field techniques. Ralph was in the midst of a sociological survey, and we discussed the problem of how to deal with nonagnatic members of the local group, a problem that would bedevil Highlands ethnographers for years to come. Ralph had worked out a series of empirical tests to determine the status of these so-called "sitdown" men. For example: What became of the widows of such men? Who could inherit their widows or whom did the widows remarry? Could a nonagnatic resident inherit a clansman's widow leviratically? Could he marry a daughter of the clan? I made a list of such queries in my diary which would later prove useful in analyzing my own data.

Much as I enjoyed my visit with the Bulmers and the Kyaka, I was eager to begin my own work. A radio message from the district commissioner at Mendi advised that no permit would be needed to enter Tari, provided I remained within the "controlled area," that is, within a radius of two miles from Rumu-rumu (now Tari Station). He mentioned that no accommodation was available on the station, but with my experience of Highlands hospitality so far I was not really worried. So, finally, I decided against going to the Sau, bade farewell to the Bulmers, walked back to the Baptist mission, and took the next available plane to Minj: Tari was my destination.

After a few days wait a Gibbes-Sepik Airways charter flew me, my newly hired cook from Minj, and our gear into Tari. It was Easter Sunday, the tenth of April. Our descent interrupted a cricket match and a picnic for the entire European population of the area, about twenty-five strong, who had assembled for the occasion. Most were from the three recently established missions, plus Bill Crellin, the assistant district officer, and a patrol officer. Crellin offered to put me up for a few days, an offer I accepted most gratefully.

THE FIRST FIELD TRIP: APRIL, 1955 — NOVEMBER, 1956

In a sense my fieldwork began from the moment the Norseman aircraft threaded its way through the treacherous Tari Gap, a graveyard for more than one unlucky pilot. As we descended from ten thousand feet, the Tari Basin lay before us. I could see the pattern of land use, with neatly laid-out sweet potato mounds, old gardens reverting to bush, and new cultivations in the recently cut forest. The settlement pattern was clearly visible, too: dispersed small homesteads scattered among the gardens with no permanent ceremonial grounds as in other parts of the Highlands. From the air I could barely make out the tremendous fighting ditches, for they were often overgrown with dense thickets of sword grass, making them virtually subterranean passageways (see Lloyd Yelland's photograph in the *London Illustrated News*, 2 April 1955).

When we landed I was surprised to see so many Europeans. But as it turned out, this was nearly the entire European population of the subdistrict, and the opportunity to meet these outsiders in one fell swoop was advantageous. But it was of course the Huli I was most eager, indeed anxious, to see. Huli were very much in evidence. Aircraft landings were still a novelty and hundreds of Huli had assembled to watch the cavorting of the cricket players. Despite the photographs of Huli that I had seen, I was still overwhelmed by the majestic appearance of the men. Their wigs glinted in the sunshine with a treasury of bird of paradise plumes. Many men wore face paint: red, white, and yellow colors in elaborate patterns. The men watched our arrival with no hint of shyness. Fortunately, Tongai, my Kuma cook and helper, began to circulate among the Huli, although hardly any could speak Pidgin and no one Kuma. We stayed only a few days on the station, mainly to await the rest of our supplies and to begin walking around the controlled zone, an area two miles in radius from the airstrip, to which we were limited. Outside of this zone, Huli still fought pitched battles. Any European who left the controlled zone faced expulsion from the Territory of New Guinea. Crellin loaned me a Pidgin-speaking Huli interpreter for a few days, and as we walked he explained to the Huli we encountered that I wanted to build a small house, to learn about the living and the dead, about the gardens and the pigs, and to witness the great ritual called the Tege.

We went to Kovari, where Father Michelaud, a Swiss Roman Catholic priest, had erected an imposing bush church and a chalet-style residence using only bush materials. He invited us to stay at Kovari until we located a place to build our own house. I accepted gratefully and the next day we returned with our supplies. It took about a week to find a place to settle. With the help of one of Crellin's interpreters we managed to explain that we were not missionaries, nor patrol officers, nor "doctors," and that we did not intend to build a large "station" or indeed to acquire any land at all. I hoped to find a spot reasonably close to the existing road system (such as it was), not too near Tari Station, and preferably some distance from any of the existing missions. The latter condition turned out to be difficult to meet and I finally decided to settle at Hoievia, not far from the Methodist Overseas Mission, whose Australian and New Zealand staff were very cordial, although preoccupied with establishing their own station and hospital.

To make it easier for the Huli to distinguish me from the other Europeans I began to grow a beard. After a few weeks they began to refer to me as "the bearded one." The name stuck and helped to establish my identity.

Building a house of local materials (woven bamboo, wooden posts, grass thatch, etc.) was time-consuming but necessary. It also gave me the opportunity to hear Huli spoken constantly, to meet people living in the area, and to improve my Pidgin (mostly with Tongai). From time to time the construction would be interrupted by angry moots and public meetings. Even a brief skirmish broke out not far from the house site. By May I was able to move into my semi-finished dwelling: there was the main room with an open fire and a table-cum-desk; a bedroom and storeroom that were relatively separate from the main living area, and—luxury of luxuries—a shower fed by a canvas bucket. Food was prepared in a separate cook-house because of the danger of fire.

My diary notes the seesaw quality of early fieldwork: frenetic activity followed by periods of seemingly endless waiting; the labor supply was unpredictable regardless of the inducements offered. My notebooks were still alarmingly bare. Nevertheless, housebuilding was an important and unavoidable activity. Huli houses are too small, too low, and too dark for the interviewing I planned to do, and I needed storage space not only for our supplies but for the material culture collection I intended to assemble as well.

Establishing rapport with people is of course a precondition of good fieldwork. One of the means I used early on was to provide simple medical care for anyone who needed it. Fortunately, the Methodist Mission Hospital was near at hand for serious problems, but some people came to me, especially early in the morning, to have wounds dressed and minor ailments treated. Soon I learned that some men were leery of my porch dispensary, not because of my limited skills or pharmacopoeia, but because I treated women in the same place. I resolved the problem by making a separate path for women and a separate place for them on one side of the veranda. This was my first real exposure to the apprehension of Huli men (especially bachelors) over contact with women and women's things.

Communication posed a major problem. Huli is a tonal language with a complex verb structure. I feared that I would do little else if I tried to achieve fluency with roughly a year of fieldwork before me (I had no idea at the time that I would be able to return for a second trip in 1959). I decided to hedge my bet. Only a handful of Huli males could speak Pidgin in 1955, yet I would have to find at least one good interpreter. Vocabulary could be easily acquired and my notes are full of word lists, more or less organized into semantic fields. I hoped to learn enough Huli to at least follow simple conversations, and to rely on interpreters during more structured interviews. Eventually, I employed two, sometimes three, interpreters, hoping to ensure that translations did not reflect one interpreter's point of view. It was of course a compromise, but given the lack of knowledge then about the Huli language and my limited linguistic training, it was the best solution at the time.

With the house now livable, I spent more and more time getting to know the area, attending rituals and courting parties, and watching the endless moots, usually concerned with death compensation. At first I had difficulty following the speeches, but at last gradually I became a familiar figure with my ever-present camera and notebook. By then my Pidgin had become fluent and I finally secured the services of a good interpreter. Tongai was making progress, too, with Huli, for he was anxious to purchase plumes of the blue bird of paradise, which were very rare at Minj.

The days, full of activity, passed swiftly. My notebooks began to fill, and I devised a simple system of recording that assigned two numbers to each entry, whether a single paragraph or many pages devoted to the same subject. The first number grouped the entry into one of fifteen topical categories, such as marriage, death compensation, male/female relations, initiation, and so on. The second was simply a serial number that preserved the sequence in which entries were recorded. Two sets of files were thus generated: topical and chronological. I kept them in different rooms close to windows, hoping to save at least one set in event of fire. The fear of losing field notes was perhaps the greatest anxiety I have experienced in the field.

Toward the end of my first three months I began to assemble my impressions for my first report to Canberra. It was still too early to attempt a sociological survey, but I had found some evidence, mainly in vocabulary, that suggested the existence of a segmentary, patrilineal system. I was worried about carrying out a house-to-house census, for no detailed maps were available, and, more importantly, the territories of all the groups in my vicinity extended well into the restricted area. So far I had discovered that Huli possessed genealogies that typically embraced fifteen generations (fifteen was also the base of their counting system). These were usually segmented at three levels, and they had terms to distinguish agnates from people descended from apical ancestors through some kind of female ties. I had witnessed several performances of the Tege, a spectacular multipurpose ritual that included ceremonial exchange, initiation ceremonies, and reciprocal flagellation. Here was ethnography that was complex, rich, and often full of colorful drama.

My appreciation of the Huli as complex individuals sharing an immense cultural heritage grew by leaps and bounds. Every day produced a struggle to comprehend. Every new discovery led to exhilaration, doubt, and usually to a new set of questions, a desire to witness a ceremony another time. No doubt all ethnographers experience the feeling of cultural blindness: the realization that so much of what you see and hear has connections in language, past events, emotions, small but significant details, easily missed, that render the whole enterprise hazardous, difficult, and uncertain. Such is the soft underbelly of fieldwork, the gnawing doubt whether you have got it right, got it all, posed the right question, written it all down. These are the doubts that led me on a trajectory of repetition, asking different informants the same questions, probing for nuance, searching for vocabulary, each discovery subtly undermining yesterday's. Discovery leads to joy; doubt to depression. Ironically, fieldwork seems to make me more like the mercurial Huli, though I feel sure the source of their oscillatory behavior has different roots.

My first report was finished, sent on to Canberra, and later returned with comments. Meanwhile I continued to work on the language and spent more and more time recording the moots, which were nearly a daily occurrence. Huli eagerly explained their grievances to me, for it gave them an opportunity to rehearse their arguments before bringing them to court, where the assistant district officer sat as magistrate. Through these conflict scenarios I began to gain some insight into the social organization. The patrilineal model I had at first embraced began to look like an oversimplification. Instead, a picture began to emerge of rather fluid political groups (i.e., parish-sections), in which both agnates and other cognates seemed to possess significant jural rights. Brothers frequently lived in different parish territories and some men belonged to several parishes at the same time. To complicate matters further, many men moved from one territory to another during the course of their lives.

Wives, too, did not always reside on the same parish territory as their husbands, and co-wives often lived far apart.

Rehearsals for court cases often included the history of interparish wars and the ensuing death compensation payments. These were grist for my mill and I was hard-pressed to keep my notes up to date. In May, a financial crisis erupted. As a veteran enrolled under the G.I. Bill of Rights, I was receiving a monthly stipend of about $100, which paid my everyday expenses. Suddenly the Veterans Administration ruled that because I was *in absentia* from Canberra my benefits would be reduced by 90 percent. No amount of correspondence nor even a visit by Stanner to Washington would budge them. Short of funds, I husbanded my supplies obsessively, determined to persevere. Fortunately the ANU came to my rescue with a grant to cover living expenses.

Between June and September I was exceptionally busy, witnessing several marriages and two performances of the complex multipurpose ritual known as the Tege. Observation took precedence over interviewing. Nevertheless my house had become a gathering place for a number of regular informants, and many evenings were devoted to discussing the events of the day. Whenever newcomers appeared I routinely asked them questions about their genealogies, the segmentation of their parish, and their residential history. These repetitive inquiries often produced unexpected results, stimulating my regulars to comment on similarities and differences in their experience and raising new questions. By now I had become a familiar figure at public gatherings and many of the local people had begun to address me by kinship terms. I began to contribute to payments made by parish sections in my vicinity and to receive a portion when they received prestations.

The pace picked up even more during October and November. I had little chance to keep up a personal diary; instead, recording fieldnotes and genealogies became my primary concern. Whenever there was a chance, I would read through and try to summarize a file; this proved an invaluable exercise, revealing gaps in my data and contradictions that needed to be resolved or at least corroborated. I organized my vocabulary lists into semantic fields, grouping terms about agriculture or hunting or warfare into a single list; this elementary procedure stimulated my informants to produce new words and to add new meanings to those I had already noted down.

During this period I read Murdock's *Social Structure* (1949). I was not particularly concerned with his arguments about kinship terminology, but was struck by his discussion of nonunilineal descent groups, especially those he called "demes." While Huli groups did not conform to Murdock's formulation, his discussion raised the question about alternative models. No longer did I feel it necessary to reconcile my data with the segmentary models in *African Political Systems* (Fortes and Evans-Pritchard 1940). I decided that henceforth I would try equally hard to assemble evidence that Huli possessed a "cognatic" system, or at least that their patriliny was severely compromised. This was an important methodological step, although I continued to be hamstrung by my inability to collect full census data because of restrictions on my movements mentioned earlier. I found it also difficult to obtain clear-cut normative statements about the composition of their descent groups. In some contexts agnates claimed to have superior rights over nonagnates, but in other situations both agreed that agnates and other kinds of cognates had equal rights. To complicate matters further, in certain ritual contexts, parish sections (the effective political units) acted as dual organizations. For example, the patrilineal members of a section would pay for the ritual services of a specialist whose connection to the group must be traced through one or more female ancestors; by the same token, the nonagnatic members would donate a gift of equal value to an agnatic specialist. Thus certain rituals would display the genealogical categories of membership but at the same time indicate their structural equality and reciprocal obligations. In hindsight this formulation is simple enough, but given the lamentable state of knowledge about nonunilineal descent groups in the 1950s and my weak data on residence, I worried a great deal about how best to describe Huli social structure.

At last 1955 drew to a close. Visits to D'Arcy Ryan at Mendi and Mervyn Meggitt at Wabag provided a welcome change and a chance to compare notes. January 14, 1956, was a sad day: the radio announced the sudden death of Professor S. F. Nadel at the height of his brilliant career, leaving the department without a head.

My relationships with the Huli continued to improve as my comprehension increased. Although I relied heavily on a core of about a dozen regular informants, I took advantage of visits by Huli from distant parishes to record basic data on ground names, segmentary divisions of groups, and residential and garden histories. The collection of such routine data could be boring, but it was essential information, often enlivened by the recall of incidents about warfare, marriage, or ritual. My more or less regular informants had grown accustomed to my queries and would pose some of the key questions themselves without prompting. Two men were particularly resourceful and had become my good friends. Dagema, then in his late thirties, was a man of humor and enthusiasm, always eager to explain or to provide some new tidbit of gossip or other information. Handobe was even more useful. A "big man," he possessed an exceptionally acute mind; his knowledge of history and myth was extensive, and his genealogical recall seemingly endless. Now dead, he remains in my mind as one of the most articulate speakers I have ever known. Later he was elected to the House of Assembly as a member from the Southern Highlands (for a photograph of Handobe in Port Moresby, see John Ryan 1969:118).

As my first field trip began to draw to a close, I felt that I had managed to strike a good balance between direct observation and interviewing. I made extensive use of photography, and when small prints were returned to me from Australia I used them to ask questions about the activity depicted, the identity of unknown participants, and the reasons they were there. Unfortunately, tape recorders were not yet on the market and the available wire recorders were expensive and unreliable under field conditions. During the final months of my first trip I began to run out of steam; I grew weary and felt the need to immerse myself from time to time in paperback novels (mostly translations of Zola and the Russian masterpieces). My routine inquiries no longer seemed to yield surprises and became increasingly repetitive. I realized that it was time to leave. In the last few weeks I went over my files, checking to be sure all my rough notes were transcribed. I left Tari in November, 1956, and I can still recall the immense sadness of that parting. I did not know that I would be able to return three years later.

My return to Canberra was delayed for about three months. The American Museum of Natural History had asked me to make a collection of material culture for them, principally in the Highlands but also in New Ireland and Tabar Island. It was an arduous but productive trip, allowing me to gain some firsthand knowledge of numerous cultures and to expand my photographic files.

I reached Canberra late in January, 1957. The Department was in some disarray, for Nadel's chair remained vacant. Derek Freeman had, however, recently been appointed senior fellow and he became my supervisor. It took a few months to get used to living in University House again. Meanwhile I began cross-referencing my fieldnotes and catching up on publications relevant to my work. Ward Goodenough had published a seminal paper, titled "A Problem in Malayo-Polynesian Social Organization" (1955). This gave me the impetus to begin formulating my data without undue reliance on African unilineal models. Still, unraveling the segmentary structure of Huli groups was a problem difficult to resolve with the limited census data I had been able to obtain. Soon it became increasingly clear that I lacked sufficient quantitative data on residence and land tenure to document adequately the social organization. My data were rich on conflict and its resolution, but without the baseline evidence on land and gardens my dissertation was stymied. It was a period of frustration and uncertainty.

Later that year Professor John Barnes was appointed to the ANU chair and I was offered and accepted a temporary lectureship at Sydney University. This was to prove a godsend. It was a pleasure to move to cosmopolitan Sydney after the cloistered atmosphere of small-town Canberra. Preparing lectures on political organization and social control forced me to think through my data and to pinpoint the evidence I would need to present a convincing case. The presence of Ian Hogbin, Mervyn Meggitt, and D'Arcy Ryan on the faculty led to many helpful discussions, not to mention memorable parties. Toward the end of my lectureship I was fortunate to be awarded the Walter Mersh Strong Fellowship by Sydney University. This would allow me to return to Tari in 1959 and to have the following year free to complete my dissertation. I knew I would have to obtain more quantitative data to make a case and prepared printed census cards that would make data collection easier. I designed a form that would allow me to record all of a person's known parish affiliations, residential history, and distribution of present and past gardens: this was the crucial statistical evidence for an understanding of social organization. Meanwhile Davenport's (1959) essay on nonunilinear descent and descent groups gave a new thrust to my work.

THE SECOND FIELD TRIP:
JUNE, 1959–FEBRUARY, 1960

When I returned to Tari in June I found that several important administrative changes had taken place. The success of pacification had led to a great increase in the area controlled by the administration. Now at last it was possible to find parishes whose territories lay entirely within the unrestricted zone, and the construction of new roads and the bridging of streams and fighting ditches made travel much easier. The Huli now accepted the presence of the administration, and the four missions had begun to make converts and establish schools for the children. As my old house was no longer habitable, I decided to move farther away from the Methodist mission to a site about a mile northeast of Hoievia. This time I found a building plot almost immediately and within a few days was living in a new cook-house and actively engaged in the construction of a field house. Getting settled took barely three weeks.

Soon I began to map the gardens and houses of a nearby parish territory. Arduous work, using a pace-and-compass traverse, it took nearly three months. I recorded virtually all parish members, listing their residential, garden, and marital histories, their complex parish affiliations, and actionable grievances. I mean by the latter term all the wrongs or injuries a man could recall that he hoped to avenge if the opportunity arose. Men no longer carried bows and arrows when they were near the station, and more and more boys began to attend the mission and government schools. Sporadic fighting continued in the restricted areas, but with the expansion of the road system and the arrival of the first Land Rover (dismantled and carried over the range from Wabag because it was too big for planes capable of landing at Tari), it now was possible to send a patrol officer and armed constables to quell small clashes before they escalated into wars. The missions began to have an impact, too, although few Huli had been converted at the time. Huli appreciated steel tools, such as axes, knives, and spades, and they were willing to work to obtain them. The value of cowrie shell declined, but pearlshells were still in demand. Huli were especially eager to obtain Australian-bred pigs, which put on more weight than the traditional razorback animals. As warfare declined, the horizons of the Huli began to be extended. The hospital would sometimes fly seriously ill patients to Mendi Hospital for treatment. Young men ranged farther afield in search of work as contract laborers.

At Hoievia I was of course a familiar figure. When visitors from distant parishes came for a visit, the locals were happy to "show me off." But I was glad to play the pet European in exchange for the chance to question visitors from afar. Not only did I meet Huli from distant parishes, but visitors came also from Duna or Enga and even Etoro and Kaluli from the fringe of the Southern Highlands. Whenever possible I took word lists from these visitors and asked, through a Pidgin speaker, about salient features of their social organization. Talking with outsiders in the presence of Huli often shed light on the more tacit aspects of Huli culture. I began to fathom the complex meanings of Huli wigs (Glasse 1974) and male initiation.

Why Huli were so mobile in the precontact and early contact period was not self-evident. I thought the answer might partly lie in the ecology of Tari and paid closer attention to meteorological data, agricultural practices and yields, and the history of famines and other disasters. In turn this led me to a greater understanding of the role of ritual in attempting to exert control over a rather fickle Nature. At the same time the diacritical aspect of rites became clearer: whether a man belonged to a particular parish section depended only partly on principles of recruitment. Performance counted heavily, such as participation in ritual and warfare. Further genealogical inquiries turned up case material that revealed the bases of individual choice. The optative, contingent character of group membership became more visible.

By the end of the year, I realized that my major tasks had been accomplished. I had the quantitative evidence to make a case. During interviews I began to run out of questions. So I began to put my files in order and to make last-minute efforts to close the remaining gaps in my knowledge of Huli culture. Today I consider this a vain hope, but in my innocence I thought it was possible. Finally, a day arrived when I could think of nothing more. It was time to leave again. And so I bought as many pigs as I could afford and a huge quantity of sweet potatoes and other vegetables. I had the pigs slaughtered and with the help of Dagema, Handobe, Minabe, and others prepared a great feast. The event was well attended. I gave all my camping gear and stores to my friends and neighbors. It was a sad parting. I did not know then that nineteen years would elapse before I would see the Huli again. But that is another encounter, well beyond the "pioneer" period.

ASSESSING THE DATA

It took a few months to settle down in Sydney again. I married Shirley Inglis (now Lindenbaum) and we found a flat. In Canberra John Barnes had become my supervisor. This field trip had yielded masses of data that had to be tabulated and quantified. Initially I decided to focus on the three parishes I knew best and then to determine whether the detailed patterns of affiliation found there could be generalized to a broader sample. I expected that the proportions of agnates, nonagnatic cognates, and others fluctuated widely from parish to parish. Instead, a remarkable consistent picture emerged: 27 percent agnates, 58 percent nonagnatic cognates, and 15 percent others (i.e., noncognates). Inter-parish variation rarely exceeded a few percentage points.

At first I wondered whether I had discovered an agnatic system that was breaking down, or a cognatic system in transition to unilineality. The trouble with both of these hypotheses was the remarkable regularity of the above percentages. In a transitional system one would expect much wider variation. More to the point: a person's descent status was clearly relative; a man might be an agnate with respect to parish A, but a nonagnatic cognate with respect to several other groups. Membership in a parish was not guaranteed by genealogical connection. One had to validate it by public acts, such as taking part in parish wars and contributing to death compensation payments, donating pigs for sacrifices, taking part in rituals, and so on. Thus there were degrees of group attachment, and the status of some individuals was ambiguous or disputed. Analysis of land tenure data was instructive. It appeared that in proportion to their numbers, more agnatic members turned out to be title holders than other cognates, and as a category agnates held larger gardens than the rest. Clearly, the system possessed a kind of agnatic bias, even though patrilineal members formed a minority (c. 27 percent) in every parish I examined. Further statistical tests showed that agnatic bias did *not* extend to other jural domains. I will not rehash the details here (see Glasse 1968), but a cognatic model seemed to fit the data better.

As the chapters began to take shape I began to discern that Huli possessed alternative concepts of parish structure which revealed themselves in different contexts. Reading Leach's *Political Systems of Highland Burma* (1954) was helpful, although the cyclical structure that seemed to operate in Burma was not present as far as I could see at Tari. Why the Huli system had assumed this Janus-faced topography remains a question. In 1962 I thought that fluctuating agricultural production might be the key, due in part to the vagaries of high basin (as opposed to high valley) ecology. Tari experienced erratic fluctuations in rainfall, relatively frequent nocturnal frosts, and perhaps occasional showers of tephra emanating from distant volcanoes. Today I am far less certain that this explanation is sound. At best it accounts for only a portion of the data. At any rate, my thesis gradually took shape. While I emphasized the optative, cognatic aspects of the system, I also showed that agnation was also recognized, particularly in exogamy, and that it acted also as a principle of personal identity in an otherwise rather confusing system. My conclusion was that the Huli system was neither fish nor fowl, agnatic or cognatic, but a system *sui generis*.

REFLECTIONS ON THE HULI

In retrospect, it appears that the fundamental error that the early Highlands ethnographers made was the confusion of principles of recruitment with idioms of descent and metaphors of corporate unity. John Barnes (1962) was certainly correct in diagnosing the problem, but it remained for Andrew Strathern to settle the issue in his account of the Melpa, *One Father, One Blood* (1972). I certainly shared this basic mistake when preparing my thesis. Now I believe much of it can be attributed to Evans-Pritchard's influential accounts of the Nuer.

As mentioned above, many features of the Huli social organization resembled those of the Nuer as they appear in the kinship and marriage volume (Evans-Pritchard 1951). But the Nuer of the politics (and ecology) book (1940) seem quite a different kettle of fish. Such was Evans-Pritchard's reputation, however, that no one really questioned his formulations of Nuer social structure, at least not until much later. Recently Aidan Southall addressed this issue (1986) and made a convincing case that Nuer agnation is something of an emic chimera. For example, he pointed out (1986:2):

> It seems that analyzing Nath (Nuer) society as composed of local cognatic lineage segments might have been much closer to the Naths' own emic model of their society and would have made for a much simpler and far more easily intelligible exegesis. But it would have destroyed the stimulating

paradoxical complexity of Evans-Pritchard's account, thereby rendering much subsequent debate redundant. Despite the strongly empirical emphasis of fieldwork in anthropology, the generation of stimulating models attracts more interest than the correct interpretation of empirical data.

Southall's formulation of the Nath lineage (1986:4) aptly fits the Huli case:

> The Nath lineage is not entirely a framework of the living; that is, with living representatives. The lineage is a conceptual structure composed of a genealogical charter of the more remote ancestors, to which tenuous and shadowy framework a motley collection of the living, of very diverse descent, tie themselves by incredibly remote and farfetched links, making the living irrefutably cognatic, however agnatic the dead are thought to be.

Like Nuer, Huli genealogies appear to have an agnatic superstructure until we come down to the level of the effective political unit, the parish section. The section founder, usually but not always a male, is generally situated some four to six generations distant from the present population, although exceptions do occur (Glasse 1968:31). A convenient supernatural dogma effectively eliminates women from genealogies above the level of most parish section founders. This dogma holds that remote female ghosts (collectively referred to as *kepa*) are extremely dangerous to their living descendants, and that one should not invoke their names unless a sacrifice is made at the same time (Glasse 1965). This strongly held belief effectively purges female ancestors from the upper levels of genealogy (with the exception of the wives of parish founders, who have a mythic presence). It also reduces the potential lateral spread of these "pedigrees" and thus keeps them to a reasonable size.

The ghosts of near female ancestors are also dangerous, but much less so; they cause minor illnesses, skin eruptions, or infertility in pigs or women. Unlike the *kepa*, however, the identity of these ancestresses has to be known in order to make appropriate sacrifices to their greedy ghosts. A person who suffers a misfortune would routinely consult a diviner or medium to determine the source of the affliction. Equally important, knowledge of low-level genealogy enables a man to assert rights to land in any parish where he is a cognate. His claim would not automatically provide him with an unchallenged title, but would usually lead to an offer of hospitality in a hitherto alien parish. It would be up to him to convert his status from that of a cognatic guest with possible rights of usufruct to that of a cognatic member with a secure, recognized title to land.

I don't think it is necessary to belabor the point. Huli have a number of concepts of affiliation and corporate group structure which they use strategically when access to resources is in dispute. In my view these concepts cannot be meaningfully assembled into a seamless, consistent theoretical construct. Instead, the Huli employ the notions of attachment and detachment according to their individual assessment of self-interest at any given moment. Of course, self-interest need not exclude notions of generosity, altruism, or competitive prestations; the algorithms of this calculus may be extremely complex. It would be crass to suggest that virtuous behavior is simply tied to material advantage. Yes, it is a factor, but history, precedent, and the struggle to win high regard are also extremely important. The truly "big man" (and they are rare, now and in the past) covets the opportunity to demonstrate his ability to assume a great burden by paying heavy compensation for a death (or by sponsoring a costly ritual) or by avenging a wrong against a formidable enemy. Hence the calculus of a person's self-interest is often subtle, intricate, and idiosyncratic, infused with the memory of past deeds and with a fine appreciation of the audience before whom the drama of choice and decision is to be played out.

To sum up: my first field trip produced much data on the history and character of armed conflict and its resolution. I learned the idioms of descent, but collected insufficient quantitative data on patterns of individual affiliation and group structure. I had witnessed the shadows cast by the social order, but the substance eluded me. My second trip was more successful and resulted in the accumulation of substantial data on land holding, residence, individual mobility, family structure, and so on. Nevertheless, in formulating my data, Evans-Pritchard's oxymoron continued to thwart a full appreciation of the ethnographic and statistical evidence. Today I am rather less enchanted with attempts to perceive a crystalline, totally consistent image of social order. Contradiction, ambiguity, dramaturgy, and poetics are now the order of the day. I find the complexities of Huli culture, history, and ritual to be far more challenging and absorbing. I have written elsewhere of the remarkable paradoxes of pacification, and work in progress deals with indigenous notions of entropy and degeneration. A suitable task for one's middle age?

NINE

Looking Backward and Forward

Andrew Strathern

In his admirable and detailed introductory essay in this volume, Terence Hays has deftly painted a picture of the historical circumstances leading up to and influencing the first incursion of professional ethnographers into the Papua New Guinea Highlands. The fieldworkers of the 1950s in the Highlands provided a rich array of concerns for those who entered the region subsequently, and the vitality of their interests is shown by the fact that many of these themes are still important today. My task in this concluding chapter is to show the legacy of these early fieldworkers to those who immediately followed them, to review something of the political and social climate of those times, and to relate the analytical concerns of the early fieldworkers to themes that are current today. I take first the legacy of ideas as I experienced it in the 1960s and through to the early 1970s.

THE INTELLECTUAL LEGACY

At a personal level, my memory and understanding of this legacy is bound up with my first encounters with the major harvest of books which appeared either just before or just after my first extended period of fieldwork. My interest was equally challenged by discovery of the three volumes of Georg Vicedom's *Die Mbowamb* (Vicedom and Tischner 1943–48) in an obscure corner of the Haddon Library in Cambridge. In bookshops and library shelves I then found Marie Reay's (1959) *The Kuma*, surely an extraordinary pioneering work; Richard Salisbury's (1962) *From Stone to Steel*, one of the few studies which took as its major focus the problem of change seen from an economic perspective; and Ronald Berndt's (1962) ethnographic extravaganza, *Excess and Restraint*.

These books, while obviously sharing a common concern for social organization, were in other respects quite diverse. One theme, however, linked them: the problem of individuality and choice in Highlands societies. It was precisely this question that emerged also from other classic studies of the time; for example, Kenneth Read's (1959) "Leadership and Consensus" article, in which he explored the tension between competition and egalitarianism in Gahuku-Gama society (and followed this with an in-depth case study of the leader Makis in his [1965] book *The High Valley*), and L. L. Langness's (1964) work on the Bena Bena system of kinship and residence. The theme has also continued to be of significance in contemporary writings, for example, with regard to land tenure and access to land (Brown 1978). Finally, Reay's study, alone of those at the time, prefigured the efflorescence of interest in women's roles which occurred in the late 1960s and 1970s (see Gelber 1986 for a summary).

It was surely not by accident, either, that this concern with the individual and with variability and choice in action which emerges from the work of these pioneers coincided in some way with the development in the metropolitan centers of a critique of mainstream structural-functional theory. The first blows in the debate were effectively struck by Fredrik Barth (1966); although his claims for his generative models have not been fully substantiated over time, his emphasis on individual action and the transactional character of much political and economic behavior has certainly left its enduring imprint on theory. It continues to show, for example, in the stream of works by F. G. Bailey (1983) on Indian and European politics and political leaders. The dialectical interplay between individual action and institutional or cultural constraints has been a theme that has consistently influenced my work also (e.g., A. J. Strathern 1971*a*, 1976). Emerging in another context, that of gender relations, it has provided a major leitmotiv in the contrast between *twem* (individual exchange networks, in which women fully participate as actors) and *sem* (corporate group activity, controlled by men) which underpins the work of Rena Lederman (1986) on the Mendi people of the Southern Highlands, first studied by D'Arcy Ryan. What we find is a crosscutting and interweaving of themes to the effect that what is first written about by an ethnographer on tribe A much later provides fertile clues to another ethnographer working on tribe B. In this sense, the precursor of Lederman's work is not so much Ryan as Reay.

Another of the earliest cohort of fieldworkers who was struck by the individuality and variability of social action in the Highlands was James Watson. It is a topic that has continued to guide his work (see Watson 1970, 1983), and one implication of his arguments has come increasingly to the fore in recent years, although it was held less in mind by earlier fieldworkers. This is his view that the explanation for many features of the Highlands societies is to be found in their recent transition from hunting to horticulture. While the Berndts, Glasse, Reay, and Ryan were largely influenced by the British tradition of synchronic ethnography, from which historical questions had been conveniently excised, Watson's team brought to their work an explicit concern, deriving from the traditions of American anthropology, with micro-evolution and saw their task as combining the results of linguistic, biological, archaeological, and cultural anthropological research: the four-field approach written large on the Eastern Highlands countryside. It was not until Jack Golson's startling finds from his Kuk project in Mount Hagen of the Western Highlands Province became available that serious attempts to evaluate the findings and speculation emerging from Watson's work were made. These attempts have most recently culminated in the synoptic work of Feil (1987), based on the idea of divergent pathways of micro-evolution for the Eastern as against the Western Highlands. At an earlier stage Watson's project in the Eastern Highlands was paralleled in the Western Highlands by that of Vayda and Rappaport, who brought an explicit concern with ecological adaptation, and thus implicitly with evolutionary processes, into their work (Rappaport 1968; Vayda 1976).

Watson's own theorizing of the contemporary social structures in the Highlands meshed clearly with the work of those trained in the British perspective precisely since he, too, was concerned with the problem of individual choice and how it is influenced. Looking at this matter from the viewpoint of intergroup relations, he saw the overall processes involved as conducing to the "organized flow" of personnel across group boundaries, stimulated by warfare, the seeking of refuge, intragroup schisms, or personal friendships and affinal ties. His macro-perspective in fact can be integrated with the more locally focused findings of the other studies, which are alluded to by Glasse and Reay in the present volume.

Glasse had to struggle with what is perhaps the most complex system of descent and residence in the Highlands, that of the Huli people (Glasse 1968; see also Modjeska 1977 on the Duna). His very interesting conclusion that the Huli system has to be seen as exhibiting contradictory structural characteristics at lower and higher (more inclusive) levels of group structure was one of the insights which fed into my efforts (A. J. Strathern 1972) to come to grips with the question of descent among the Melpa people. Glasse's work is the beginning of a dialectical viewpoint, or an understanding of contradiction in structures; implicitly, therefore, it is a contribution to theory of ideology in Highlands cultures.

The same is true, but differently, of Reay's work. She asked why, if there is an agnatic ideology of recruitment to the clan among the Kuma people, in practice so many nonagnates are taken in; her answer (Reay

1959) was that in pragmatic terms it was expedient for the Kuma to do this, since such an intake in fact strengthened the clan against its neighbors, whether for warfare or for exchange. This explanation, however, in turn leads to further questions; namely, why in that case is there an agnatic ideology at all, and under what conditions is the practice of taking in nonagnates expedient rather than inexpedient? The second of these questions, but not the first, was addressed by Mervyn Meggitt in his (1965) work on the Mae Enga people, which followed immediately on the heels of the first wave of studies and in turn formed a significant part of the legacy given to fieldworkers in the second half of the 1960s. Meggitt's answer was that membership is restricted by the agnatic rule more firmly as the pressure on available agrarian resources grows. The problem of "nonagnates" was thus decisively brought into a central place in the literature, born from the suggestions of Watson, the observations of Glasse and Reay, and the hypothesis put forward by Meggitt.

Paula Brown was soon to weigh in with her (1962) discussion of "Non-Agnates among the Patrilineal Chimbu," and the whole controversy was fueled by John Barnes's (1962) brief but biting comments on "African models," in which he suggested that descent was something of a mirage in these societies and that they in fact operated by "cumulative patrifiliation." Shortly thereafter, Roy Wagner (1967), basing his views on his ethnographic work among the Daribi, a "fringe Highlands" people, suggested further that the whole debate was misconceived. He called into question the existence of groups, criticized the empiricist procedure of "counting nonagnates," and argued for an analysis of symbolic categories in which conventional meanings were reversed. In the "descent model," descent (as a special case of consanguinity) defines the boundaries of groups, while exchange (exemplified by marriage) relates them. In Wagner's Daribi model, consanguinity relates, while exchange defines, since people are related by consanguineal ties that move across group boundaries, and these boundaries are themselves marked by the transfer of payments to the *pagebidi* (mother's kin), which determine the affiliation of children to their father's group.

All these studies, and others too numerous to mention, revolved essentially around the typological question of how to categorize the basic social structures of Highlands societies. This focus certainly followed in general from the comparative program envisaged by S. F. Nadel in Canberra, in which his students were to supply the ethnographic data and he the cross-cultural synthesis. Each author came to this problem from a distinct angle, however, and it would be simplistic to derive their difficulties simply from the "African model" referred to by Barnes. Barnes's brilliant formulation of the matter perhaps obscured the divergences already existing among the ethnographers at the time, while correctly formulating many vital questions for the next wave of workers such as myself. The Berndts, for example, like the Watsons, were concerned with comparisons between culturally related societies/linguistic groups. While Catherine Berndt carried over her interest in mythology and ritual from their Australian Aboriginal studies, Ronald Berndt seems to have been inspired directly by the obvious surface volatility and turbulence of life in the Eastern Highlands to pose the question of social control: where can order be discerned in a context that is informed by so much variability, choice, and frank expression of interpersonal and intergroup conflict? No matter how chaotic life might appear to be to the outside observer, it must, he reasoned, contain its own customary limits, and these he sought to establish. The fact that some kinds of "restraint" on others were brought to bear by actions that themselves exhibited "excess" gave him his (1962) book title and one answer to his problem. In any case his work provided another platform for subsequent studies of social control and dispute settlement, exemplified partly in A. L. Epstein's (1974) edited volume, *Contention and Dispute*.

Another answer to Berndt's problem, although this has not been explicitly proposed in relation to his work, is to be found in the sphere of the analysis of exchange relations. It is intriguing to consider how this focus emerged out of the earlier one of group structure. The segmentary model of society proposed by the Oxbridge descent theorists consisted of two distinct parts: one, a rule of lineal recruitment and ties with ancestors (stressed by Fortes) and, two, a nesting hierarchy of political groups subject to contextual processes of fission and fusion (stressed by Evans-Pritchard). As the alliance theorists pointed out, this model essentially gave no structural place to marriage and ramifying kinship relationships across group boundaries, which were nevertheless obviously important in the empirical cases of the Tallensi and Nuer. The New Guinea Highlands societies in turn seemed to correspond neither to the pure form of the segmentary descent model nor to the circulating connubia identified for Asia by Lévi-Strauss (1949). It became increasingly clear that not only marriage but the exchanges built up along affinal lines were crucial components of the social process and must be studied as stochastic or emergent phenomena, rule-guided but strategically molded.

Full realization of this point at the comparative level was not expressed in the literature until the appearance of the edited collection *Pigs, Pearlshells and Women* (Glasse and Meggitt, eds., 1969) and my own paper (1969a) on "Descent and Alliance." Many of the early fieldworkers, such as Reay and Ryan, contributed to the Glasse and Meggitt volume, and Reay's (1959) ethnography in particular had provided glimpses of the significance of marriage ties between local groups, both at the individual and the group level. When linked to the study of leadership, this new interest gave birth in turn to the exploration of the big-man complex mooted earlier by Marshall Sahlins (1963) for Melanesia in general. Sahlins's paper served through the 1960s as a benchmark for the Highlands cases, and one could accurately say that my own fieldwork was influenced by the challenge of Fortes's descent model and Sahlins's exchange model. D'Arcy Ryan's (1962) thesis on the Mendi was entirely devoted to this topic of exchange, and it is curious that he did not choose to publish it quickly. Partly as a result, it was left to me to give the first full-length published account of a Highlands system of big-manship and exchange (A. J. Strathern 1971a), following an earlier comparative survey (A. J. Strathern 1969b). It seems ironic, given the clear emphasis in this work on individual action and choice, that some later writers (e.g., Sillitoe 1979) have tended to lump it in with "corporate group theory" or analysis in terms of "patriliny." The point here, however, is that the exchange model was rather slow in developing by contrast with the descent model, and this is what created a mirage of negativity: Highlands systems were defined as *not* like models of African systems. So what were they like? It was only over a decade or more that "New Guinea models" based on properties of exchange relations gave the answer to this question, although indications of the answer had been provided very early on by Read (1959) in his "Leadership and Consensus" paper.

One way or another, it is true that our attempts in the 1960s and 1970s to write new ethnographies on the Highlands were based squarely on the creative efforts of our predecessors, including notably those represented in this volume. I, for example, was able to benefit not only from the pioneering work of Ralph Bulmer, Glasse, Read, Reay, Ryan, and Salisbury, but also from the slightly later work of Paula Brown and Mervyn Meggitt, which injected rigorous quantitative data on societies distinctly similar to the Melpa whom I studied into the available ethnographic corpus. In addition, while I was still in the field James Watson's (ed., 1964) special issue of the *American Anthropologist* came out, providing a provocative set of hypotheses and perspectives which stimulated all subsequent workers. Each of these perspectives has been in turn looked at critically in later years. For example, Langness's (1964) argument that "residence creates kinship" prompted me (1974) to look for mediating concepts that might make sense of this rather stark formulation; Salisbury's (1964) argument on despots led to counterarguments by Paula Brown (1963) and myself (1966); and Meggitt's (1964) "prudes and lechers" hypothesis at least drew attention to the need to look for correlates of sexual antagonism, a task that Gelber (1986) has recently extensively reviewed, while Herdt and Poole (1982) have subjected it to a more radical deconstruction.

Last, one further stream of work had its roots in early analyses of

Eastern Highlands practices by Read and others, namely, male and female intitiation rites, first treated generally by Michael Allen (1967). Allen's specific hypothesis, linking male initiations with patrilineal descent, monocarpellary residential clan structures, and a relative lack of social stratification, has been often reviewed, and not all parts of his original model survive. However, his interest in this theme has been picked up by the ethnographers of Anga-speakers on the fringes of the Eastern Highlands, and from their work has sprung a further concern with ritualized homosexuality and gerontocracy that now spreads beyond the purview of the Highlands to other parts of New Guinea as well (see Herdt, ed., 1982, 1984; Godelier 1986). Godelier has since gone on to open up a large debate regarding the typology of leadership in New Guinea with his (1986) major contrast between "great men" (à la Baruya) and "big men" (à la Hagen), while Herdt, Hays, and Fitz Poole (in Langness and Hays, eds., 1987) have continued to deepen our sensitivity to and understanding of these cults from the point of view of the individuals who experience them.

THE HISTORICAL CONTEXT

The first professional studies by anglophone social and cultural anthropologists in the Highlands were all carried out within the framework of pacification by the Australian colonial administration. The expansion of cash cropping and the elaborate structural changes that led up to and followed political independence for Papua New Guinea in 1975 were all yet to come. Instead, Australian paternalism was in its heyday: district officers ruled like little kings and treated anthropologists with something of the same condescension they displayed toward the "natives"; the local people themselves were still in the stage of cautiously evaluating the characteristics of the rich, strange, and deadly "red people" who had come to stay, for an unspecified period, with them. My own fieldwork began toward the end of this colonial "summer." I sensed its encompassing presence just as much as its imminent demise in the face of turbulent changes unleashed by the very historical period into which it was, for the rest of the world, anachronistically inserted. Keeping in touch with Papua New Guinea, as I did continuously since then, and involving myself in the country's practical affairs as professor of social anthropology at the University of Papua New Guinea (1973–77) and later as director of the Institute of Papua New Guinea Studies (1981–86), it was easy for me progressively to displace those memories of 1964–65 with many subsequent layers of experience, to such an extent that it is hard for me now to search back to my own baseline. These essays by fieldworkers immediately senior to me form, therefore, a means of such time travel for me and for the book's readers. What is equally interesting is to consider how these anthropologists, and others, situated themselves within the framework of colonialism, and how this may have influenced the work they did.

Here my major impression is that the contextual self-conceptualization developed by this wave of fieldworkers took shape from its surroundings as a feeling of being "pioneers," there to make a first harvest of technical results in anthropology and not to write a sociopolitical history. The fieldworkers had to situate themselves, however they could, in the privileged domains of military or civil administration. At their backs were the academic moguls who had sent them out, chiefly A. P. Elkin in Sydney and S. F. Nadel in Canberra, while in front of them were the equally uncompromising figures of the Australian government officials. In between they were able, for short but intensive periods, to sojourn with the actual people whom they had come to study.

There were differences in this respect between the Eastern and the Western Highlands. As Hays points out, the eastern part was much more affected than the western by the Japanese invasion. K. E. Read's earlier work was carried out in the Markham Valley precisely within the framework of military operations. Carriers were recruited, bombs fell, and village life was disrupted. To the west, the reverberations were more muffled. American servicemen were stationed at Mount Hagen; a bomb dropped mysteriously at Ogelbeng, a Lutheran mission station a few miles north of the Hagen patrol post (later township); and flights of planes, like migrating birds, were seen by mystified villagers far south in Pangia and Erave, long before these areas were even under formal administrative control. A secondary effect, it appears to me, of the disruptive events in the east, was a front of cargo cults or cults of adaptation to change which moved across the Highlands in the 1940s, in some places as a response to new economic differentials in access to wealth, in others as indigenous attempts to cope with introduced epidemics such as dysentery and porcine anthrax. Nowhere, therefore, were the effects of the war negligible, but they must certainly have been more obvious in the areas where Read and, to some extent, the Berndts worked than among the Huli and Mendi of the Southern Highlands studied by Robert Glasse and D'Arcy Ryan.

My characterization of these fieldworkers as "co-pioneers" with the patrol officers and missionaries is not meant to be taken too literally. First, Read wrote early papers discussing social change (again, as pointed out by Hays). Second, the anthropologists were given only limited social acceptance either by administrators or missionaries. Insofar as they were accepted, it was because of cultural similarity, at least as assumed by their hosts. It seems likely that all were given security checks and kept under surveillance, discreet or otherwise, as others later experienced also. And, third, none of these anthropologists voluntarily saw themselves as a direct part of the thrusts for change being imposed on the people, while, equally, all had to recognize that they were indirectly a part of this wider process, if only because they were allowed to work only in such places as the administration declared safe to do so. Marie Reay, for example, was not permitted to visit the Kambi (Kambia) area to the south of Minj because it was, at that time, out of bounds. Similarly, Meggitt, who worked with the Central Enga from the early 1950s, at first was allowed to visit only certain groups close to Wabag Station. This context of restricted movement, experienced earlier by the missionaries to a much greater degree, is one which a later generation of fieldworkers in the 1960s onward would find hard to visualize. Ironically, it is also one which we realized only too well in the 1980s as a result of the expansion of tribal fighting in most of the areas that were initially brought under the Australian aegis in the 1930s through 1950s.

How should one describe the attitude of the administrators toward the anthropologists working in their areas of responsibility in the 1950s? First, they appear to have been concerned for their safety as Europeans. Second, they were adamant that the anthropologists should not interfere with administration activities or policies. Third, they gave a slightly grudging acknowledgment to the notion that the anthropologists' findings might be of some use to them, by way of census information, genealogies, accounts of residence patterns, and land tenure. They were interested to know about cargo cults, as also about any unusual pronouncements by the anthropologists, in both cases because of their dislike of anything that would indicate subversion of their own authority. Beyond this, they preferred to keep the anthropologists at arm's length, letting them get on with their work. Essentially the same set of attitudes held in the 1960s, except that now there was more interest in development and change—in numbers of coffee trees grown and in the ways people perceived the newly introduced electoral process, for example. Purely scientific or purely technical debates were of less interest than questions of practical application. Within these limitations, the *kiap*s (Tok Pisin, administrative officers) could be quite helpful, often to the extent of doing more for the anthropologist than the latter desired. When I first began work in Hagen in 1964, the district commissioner, Tom Ellis, had proposed that the local jail inmates build me a field house; in Pangia in 1967, the *kiap* in charge (Frank Leibfried) had already appointed someone to act as my servant ("*Bai yu wok wantaim masta hia*," [T.P., "You're going to work for this white man"] he told the individual concerned). I declined both arrangements, regretting this sometimes when, in Hagen, the people took many weeks to complete a house, and in Pangia I ran through various employees in search of someone congenial. In general, each of the anthropologists who has contributed here experienced the perennial problem of how to establish a separate identity for him/herself while still accepting much-needed assistance from either administrative or mission personnel.

On the side of the people, also, questions of identity had to be carefully negotiated. The reasons why fieldworkers were accepted into Highlands communities readily enough had nothing whatsoever to do with their projects in anthropology and everything to do with their perceived or assumed possession of desirable goods or roads of access to these. Commonly, perhaps more so than has been admitted, anthropologists were also considered to be dead kin returning to their people. Catherine Berndt makes both of these points in chapter 4. Usurufa speakers thought she and her husband, Ronald, could "recover" the indigenous language quite easily and so would not be hard to teach. But also, and contradictorily, they were interpreted as like the other Europeans and so were expected to employ people in building roads and houses and to pay them for this, and also to build a large storehouse for the goods that would arrive and be distributed in due course. Among the Kuma, Marie Reay found a similar set of expectations, including the notion of a storehouse (probably derived from the "government stores" buildings of the administration). In every case, disappointment ineluctably followed. But Highlanders are also realists, and when faced with one disillusionment, they move on to the next level of opportunity and accept a smaller volume of gifts. Every fieldworker has also found, sooner or later, individuals who show a genuine interest in and aptitude for their actual work, and who act as intermediaries in explaining this to their less well-informed community members. The crisis of expectation is followed, therefore, by a period of adjustment.

Missionaries had been stationed in most parts of the Highlands before the anthropologists got there. Some of them also did ethnographic work. Others wanted to know what the anthropologists could find out for them about the indigenous religion and leadership patterns (most popularly, whether there was a word they could use for "God" in the local language). In many instances they, too, offered practical assistance to the incoming ethnographer by way of transport or food supplies. In Ryan's case, his professor, Elkin, himself had church connections and arranged for him to be "initially accommodated" at a Methodist mission station where Ryan spent his time on language learning for the first three months. He notes that the missionaries greeted him "with warm-hearted hospitality" but wonders if this did not reduce shortly to "a sense of Christian duty." Reay obtained good linguistic information from the Catholic missionary Luzbetak but records her later dislike of the Swiss evangelical missionary who denounced all pagan practices in the area as the work of Satan. Glasse, on his arrival, was confused with missionaries by the people and was at first expected to build a large station as they did. Later he was helped by a Swiss Methodist missionary to establish a place of his own at Hoievia, near to but separate from the Methodist mission site. All of these examples indicate the limited, but definite, mutual involvement of anthropologists with missionaries, again in "pioneer" circumstances.

Because of these practical exigencies, in no case do we find the anthropologist directly challenging the activities of either administrators or missionaries. We see that they were tolerated in return and allowed to do their work, always with the underlying assumption that their presence was inevitably temporary and that they had no place in the local power structure. In case they might be tempted to overstep these limits, administrators reminded them from time to time. Reay, for example, was told by Jack Emanuel that she must by no means interfere with the running of his "native" courts. Fortune, of course, was in the Eastern Highlands at an even earlier stage, when the area was only partially pacified, in early 1935, and his observations, which for long lay dormant in his personal papers, are well marshaled by Ann McLean in her chapter. He was ordered to occupy a police post, not a native village, and was constantly restricted in his movement by physical danger. His situation was more closely comparable to that of the 1930s wave of missionary "pioneers" in the region than to that of the 1950s anthropologists in the rest of the Highlands. After six months of fieldwork, he had to withdraw because of an escalation in fighting.

Turning now to James Watson's mature set of reflections on the circumstances of his fieldwork in the Eastern Highlands, we find that these are accompanied by a characteristically thoughtful exploration of theoretical themes relating to the extralocal ties of parish groups and how these build up into ranges of relationships in space, which amount to what he calls "international systems." Of a piece with his (1970) earlier work on "society as organized flow," this new perspective suggests that it was not only pacification and development that induced communication across the Highlands: rather, the basis for this was there much earlier.

Watson also gives us an account of his search for an appropriate pair of field areas. His aims were explicitly comparative, and the societies or cultures he wished to find had to be contrastive in definite aspects. His conception of a micro-evolutionary study embracing a number of local communities was unusual in its day and revealed a vision quite different from that of the "lonely" fieldworker attempting singlehanded to construct a complete account of one people with only marginal reference to their neighbors, as found in the classic "British-style" studies of those days.

One of the most valuable features of this and other chapters in the volume is its thumbnail sketches of the realities of fieldwork, showing us at the same time the facts of the contact situation in the 1950s. While the local people's world had expanded, they correspondingly felt they had shrunk, a self-perception consistent with diminished political status. Watson gives an ironic and tantalizingly brief account of how introduced theologies of the Lutherans and Seventh-Day Adventists were understood in Aiamontina village. Did the people really think that souls, which previously had their own postmortem trajectories, could now be split according to the church one attended? Or did they see these as imaginative projections, guesses? Telling also is the anecdote of the joke that backfired, bringing with it the shocking recognition of how money was to be obtained in future from the sale of coffee, the beginnings of the "big-men and business" era in the Eastern Highlands (see Finney 1973). Finally, the deft contrast the author makes between the grubby and fragmentary circumstances of fieldwork and the "agile syntheses" that we are sometimes able to make out of our experiences after the fact contains a seed of thought for a postmodern time also.

One other topic, also less than adequately written about so far by anthropologists in general (surely it can now be done, when time has passed on) is *kiap* attitudes. I have commented on these as revealed in the chapters by Ryan and Reay also. From Watson's remarks we see the essentially *practical* concerns of the government officers. We see also how they were structurally constrained by the frequent shifts of posting enforced by the administration. But they were equally constrained by their own attitudes, for example the proposition, running flatly counter to the predilections and pursuits of the anthropologist, that local culture did not matter in the context of the uniform establishment of colonial law. If this indeed was a prevalent principle, little wonder that endless local mistakes were perpetrated under the justifying sweep of its mantle.

It is perhaps permissible to add here that the often-praised era of *kiap* control had also its share of brutality, racism, and callousness toward the people, and for this reason alone political development for Papua New Guineans was absolutely to be desired, whatever problems it has brought in its wake. I am convinced that the authors of the autobiographical essays here would all agree with my viewpoint, and that it is helpful to make this statement on their behalf. Especially I write this also on behalf of the many Papua New Guinean academics (including anthropologists) who represent the successor generation both to the original anthropologists and to the local people whom they studied. Again, I am embarrassed to think of how much I also was a part of the colonial power structure and basically did nothing to criticize it at the time. I chose a pathway later of teaching and working in Papua New Guinea as a way of balancing the situation better, at least from my own perspective, by taking part in affairs at a level beyond that of my immediate field area and attempting to make a contribution to the historical process of transition from colonial control to independence. While not all individual anthropologists were in a position to do this, there is a collective responsibility to see that anthropology as such is kept "up to date."

It would be a pity if these essays, representing a "snapshot of the past," also gave the impression that their authors were situating the peoples they studied in some timeless or isolated past unconnected with the present. Ronald Berndt expresses in his chapter his early desire to witness situations of change in the Eastern Highlands, writing that "in the Eastern Highlands context, where many of the people were experiencing substantial alien impact for the first time, it should be possible to influence the course of change through local awareness of the problems and through administrative goodwill." He also writes that the administration "froze" a volatile situation, preventing processes of alteration of territory of groups and leading to "more emphasis on individual acts of aggression," and also "accentuating the occurrence of sorcery." This is an observation matched by many other anthropologists in the Highlands and in itself gives us a clue to the reasons why in many parts of the region violence broke out again after an apparently successful imposition of *Pax Australiana.*

Berndt further tells us about the disruptive effects of Lutheran evangelists and indigenous "police boys," and he records the impact of informal courts that grew up during the period when fighting was banned. And he recounts an incident in which he wrote a letter regarding land claims on behalf of "his" villagers at Kogu. This letter apparently drew the hostility of the Kainantu district officer, who punched the villager responsible for showing him the letter and proceeded to make a decision exactly opposite to that requested by Berndt. The incident shows clearly the hostility, if not resentment, felt by government officers of the day against any intervention by anthropologists in local issues. Patrol officers in fact used distinctly rough-and-ready methods of getting their business done and were not above employing casual violence in pursuit of impressing their power on the local people. The fact that this, on the one hand, won them a grudging acceptance and, on the other, generated a long-term dissatisfaction and resentment against imposed authority is an important component in the history of the Highlands. Berndt's chapter gives us a glimpse of this.

Berndt also tells us explicitly how Catherine Berndt and he intended their investigation to take place and how their respective themes emerged in the course of fieldwork. His explicit focus on early phases of change in political relations and in procedures for redress of wrongs was perhaps unusual. Quite simply, most of the fieldworkers of the 1950s went to the Highlands to do ethnographies of previously undescribed groups. From

Canberra, Nadel devised his scheme of "social structure and religion," though whether from a Durkheimian or a psychological perspective is unclear to me. In Sydney, Elkin's students were sent out also as pioneer ethnographers but perhaps with more of a concern for applied issues. The Berndts were established fieldworkers already specializing in Australian Aboriginal societies, but apart from Catherine Berndt's concentration on mythology they seem to have been able to make few, if any, cross-inferences from Australia to New Guinea in their work. The Watsons were involved in the beginnings of a project of their own devising, which bore the stamp of American anthropology: the Micro-Evolution Project, in which materials from studies of social structure, geography, and prehistory would all be brought together in order to build a supralocal picture of change and movement over time. What actually emerged from it, through an extended number of years, was a series of individual monographs, of which the synthesis has still to be written. Reay, Glasse, and Ryan were all students in the initial, or early, stages of their careers and subject to the demands of their professors. How did they themselves conceive of their studies?

Ryan had completed a bachelor of letters at Oxford but gives no hint that Fortes and Evans-Pritchard, authors of the "African model," ever taught him anything about it. Before going to Mendi, he read a part of the English translation of Vicedom's work on Mount Hagen (Vicedom and Tischner 1943–48) and Elkin's (1953*b*) report on the Enga *te* (or *tee*; ceremonial exchange system), but this was all; he thought of a study on child-rearing techniques, which he did not carry out, noting ruefully that this part of Mendi culture was not highly elaborated. The most irritating side of his fieldwork was the endless requests for gifts which his informants made, but finally he realized that this gave him the clue to the society itself and the focus for his study: the imperative of gift-exchange. By aleatory serendipity, then, he arrived at his topic.

Glasse had more in-depth training in Melanesian anthropology, at the ANU. He visited Ralph and Eileen Bulmer on the way to his own field area in Tari, and there they discussed "the problem of how to deal with nonagnatic members of the local group." That set an orientation for his own work, which came to grips extensively with this problem. It appears that Glasse did initially conceptualize the matter in terms of the African model, but during his fieldwork itself he decided that the Huli system might be cognatic rather than unilineal. At the same time, he recognized that in fact there was a dynamic, even dialectical, dimension of social structure, present in the situational opposition or merging of the categories of agnates and cognates. The Huli case remains one of the most complicated in the roster of accounts of Highlands social structure, although both Laurence Goldman (1983) and Stephen Frankel (1986) consider the system to be agnatic. Glasse turns a neat phrase here, referring to the "Janus-faced topography" of Huli social structure. Consideration of African models comes full circle when Glasse points out that the de facto composition of local groups among the Nuer themselves was widely different from the unilineal model of relations between Nuer political segments as propounded by Evans-Pritchard (1940) in his first book. Barnes (1962) warned us of the same confusion, but he wished to reduce all to the realm of recruitment and "cumulative patrifiliation." Glasse rightly recognized that we have to distinguish between principles of recruitment and idioms of corporate unity. He also notes that there are rhetorical and situational aspects of *both* of these "levels" of discussion, and the whole cannot necessarily be "assembled into a seamless and consistent theoretical construct."

Reay's discussion reveals another factor that I consider to have been of fundamental importance. S. F. Nadel came to the chair in Canberra imbued both with an almost colonialist view of the superiority of British social anthropology and with a Germanic concept of the relationship between professor and student. The combination seems to have been intimidating. Reay reveals that Nadel was domineering and that he intended that his students should "provide him with the data for classifying and explaining the varieties of social structure in the New Guinea Highlands." It seems possible that it was Nadel who attempted to apply the African model in Canberra, although Reay does not exactly say so. She merely complains that as a female she was in any case defined as at the bottom of the hierarchy, and that most of Nadel's theories didn't seem to apply to the facts. She does say that Nadel's own book (1954) on Nupe religion was actually quite useful to her (here is an unconsidered African model, then), and that her reading of *The Nuer* suggested to her that it was "a highly idealized version of the Kuma segmentary system." It is clear that she entered the field largely as Ryan did, without too many preconceptions. Later in her chapter she remarks that "the men of the Kugika organized their lives in terms of group membership," whether as agnates or otherwise. This is also an important point to note, given the suspicions of, for example, Wagner (1974) that groups don't exist, or of Sillitoe (1979) that Wola society has to be analyzed in terms of networks only and not groups. Societies certainly differ throughout the Highlands, but a group emphasis is there in all of them and is emphatically not just a result of the anthropologists' attempts to bolster their theories, as Sillitoe once claimed. Later again in the chapter—as with the others, one has to pick around in these studies to put a whole topic together—Reay comes back to the problem of agnates versus the rest. She is sharp and to the point, arguing correctly that we should always be less concerned with typology and more with process, and she concludes: "The Highlands offered an unparalleled opportunity to study the processes by which common descent comes to be ascribed or assumed."

She goes on to make the interesting observation that with the cessation of warfare many of the rigidities and niceties of behavior vanished. Finally, she notes that pacification on the whole improved the status of Kuma women, and that ethnographers more distant in time from the pre-pacification situation have tended to overvalorize the position of women and underplay the separation of the sexes that held more markedly before. Observations of this kind are potentially extremely valuable guidelines to latter-day commentators. Implicitly, Reay is here looking back across the intervening period, with all the work done in it by later anthropologists, and then suggesting that aspects of their work resulted from the historical period into which it was set. It is a lesson that we need to apply endlessly as time moves on.

It is also interesting to note that whatever the prescriptions of their professors may have been, each one of these fieldworkers came to define his/her own focus of interest. Salisbury, who belonged to this cohort, developed an interest in technological and economic change; Glasse, in cognatic descent; Reay, in "freedom and conformity"; Ryan, in gift-exchange. K. E. Read pursued his own writing bent in his evocative novellike book *The High Valley* (1965); Ronald Berndt found his focus in the problem of violence and disorder; Catherine Berndt, in women. In each case, the interest was shaped as much in the field as before it by the ethnographer's theoretical concerns. Each of our authors here traces that process, and most stick by their original findings, or at least do not radically modify them.

CONTEMPORARY THEMES

It would be an immense task indeed to survey all the work that has been done since the 1950s on Highlands societies. I do not wish even to attempt this here, but it is clear that certain major trends can be observed. Australian anthropologists have continued the themes of social structure and social change, gradually incorporating perspectives from neo-Marxist theory. The work of Rappaport (1968) and Vayda (1976) ushered in a concern with ecology, making Rappaport's work perhaps the most discussed monograph on the Highlands and generating further field projects among the Maring such as those by Healey (1985) and LiPuma (1988). Women ethnographers have continued to concentrate on women, as Catherine Berndt did, but usually with a feminist-Marxist emphasis (e.g., Josephides [1985] and Lederman [1986]). Roy Wagner has inspired others to follow his concern with indigenous conceptions of kinship (e.g., J. F. Weiner [1988] and, notably, also LiPuma [1988], who practically wishes to rewrite Highlands ethnography on the basis of his reading of the Maring, with Wagnerian ideas in mind). The Marxist models of the 1970s found their way into the ethnographic corpus through the work of Maurice Godelier (1986), Chris Gregory (1982), and Nicholas Modjeska (1982), as well as myself (A. Strathern ed. 1982), and in a broad sense they have also inspired the recent synthetic and generalizing work of Daryl Feil (1987), who attempts to build Highlandswide hypotheses on the earlier work of Harold Brookfield, the Watsons, Jack Golson, Bulmer, Modjeska, and myself. In brief, because of the continuing influx of fieldworkers, largely from America, the Highlands has continued to be a battleground, or at least an amphitheater, for new contenders in the theoretical stakes in anthropology as a whole. Unfortunately, indepth studies of material culture, archaeology, sociolinguistics, and biological anthropology are much less in evidence than are studies in sociocultural anthropology, and we need also more monographs attacking directly problems in the analysis of social change, as Meggitt (1977) did for Mae Enga warfare, Finney (1973) for "big men and business" in Goroka, and Sexton (1986) for women's movements in the Eastern Highlands. Fringe Highlands studies have recently come to the fore, pioneered by Roy Wagner (1967) and Ray Kelly (1977) and continued, for example, by E. L. Schieffelin (1976), Bruce Knauft (1985), and James F. Weiner (1988). Weiner's (ed. 1988) recent collection of papers neatly points out what we can learn by looking at the Highlands from a "fringe" perspective and vice versa.

Did the pioneer fieldworkers realize that their studies would usher in such an immense flood of research and so many vigorous debates? They must surely be pleased by the prominence of the Highlands in world ethnography since the 1960s, but if so they do not really betray this feeling in their contributions here. Yet this is in fact their legacy, their ethnographic present to the future that was to become. They succeeded in attracting the attention of anthropologists around the world by their studies. As already noted above, I remember clearly the excitement I felt on first finding and reading Marie Reay's (1959) book on the Kuma, at a time when I was already struggling to read Georg Vicedom's work on the neighboring Hagen area (Vicedom and Tischner 1943–48). I felt that a world of interesting problems was opening out before me—a feeling that was undoubtedly correct. The wry, almost diffident posture that Ryan, Glasse, and Reay adopt in their contributions to this volume is all the more surprising if one recalls their actual achievements.

It would be wrong, however, to sacralize these ethnographers by crediting them with all the foundations of future work. This would be incorrect for two reasons. First, as Hays points out, missionaries had earlier carried out very substantial studies, and some of these had an analytical perspective. Vicedom's work (Vicedom 1938; Vicedom and Tischner

1943–48) is a case in point. Less well known is the fact that Hermann Strauss, Vicedom's colleague at Ogelbeng in Hagen, greatly revised and deepened Vicedom's picture of Mbowamb society in his work *Die Mi-Kultur* (1962). Strauss's work has been undeservedly buried, largely because it was not translated into English until very recently (Stürzenhofecker and Strathern eds. 1990). It supplies, among many other things, the kind of detailed study of a Highlands religion which anthropologists have found difficult, or uncongenial, to produce. Reay, for example, would surely have found Strauss's material more directly relevant to her Kuma ethnography than Nadel's book on Nupe religion.

The second reason why not everything can be attributed to the early ethnographers is one which I have already mentioned: anthropologists of all persuasions and backgrounds have continually been drawn to the Highlands and have brought with them the traditions and ideas of their own departments, countries, selves, and epochs; thus each new wave of ethnographies carries with it the burden of contemporary thought, chiming against the in situ corpus of writings. If the trend continues, we can surely expect to see in due course a spate of Geertzian-and-beyond postmodernist accounts. We shall then certainly be far from the founding figures. As Glasse notes himself, however, "contradiction, ambiguity, dramaturgy and poetics are now the order of the day." Here he seems to be referring to the influence of Victor Turner, who also identified himself at one stage as a postmodernist. It is an appreciative trend insofar as it aims to take into account dimensions of experience which lie outside of the categories of the analysis of structural form, but less so to the extent that it escapes into the hazy world between the twin subjectivities of observer and observed. In any event, the point here is that the Highlands will continue to reflect anthropology in general as well as the influence of the older ethnographers.

The factor of time brings with it an intersection of many vectors of experience. We can identify at least the following: time in the individual life of the ethnographer; time in the life of the people studied, as a historical matter; time in their individual lives; and time in the history of anthropology. These vectors are all recognized by our contributors here. On the whole, they have located themselves sympathetically in their own pasts in order to relive these on paper. It is a worthwhile aim, a kind of "self-emic" representation. Worthwhile also would be a sort of etic stepping outside of oneself to contemplate the emic picture from a new perspective. If I would attempt to do this for myself, I would certainly see a great continuity between my work of the 1960s and my interests today, in particular a strong commitment to ethnography as well as to theory. But I also note how the work I did has at all times been influenced by the vector of history in the life of the people themselves. It is this which has thrown up new problems and made me think about my own received ideas and those of others: for example, the "red box" cult of 1968–72, the switch from shells to money in the *moka* exchanges, and the more recent switch from bows and arrows to guns in warfare, as well as the continuing encroachments of capitalism and politico-bureaucratic organization.

Another significant matter is the alternative, and occasionally opposed, views of ethnographers on the same society at the same or different time periods. The Highlands now has its share of such multiple studies, an inevitable result of the concentration of fieldworkers in the region. There is little doubt that from the point of view of the discipline as a whole, overlapping projects of this kind are potentially valuable, revealing, as they do, aspects of ethnographers and ethnographies which would otherwise remain unclarified. Four examples may be cited briefly to illustrate this point.

First, the debate between Mervyn Meggitt and Daryl Feil regarding the *tee* exchange system among the Enga people. Meggitt, who has worked with the Mae Enga near Wabag in the heavily populated central Enga area, reported (1974) a corporate, male-dominated focus in the *tee* with little independent standing accorded to women. Feil, whose research was carried out among the Tombema Enga of the less densely settled Sau area to the northeast of Wabag, found (1984) more emphasis on individual activities and more independence on the part of the women as transactors in the *tee*. On the basis of this finding, he challenged Meggitt's picture. It is not yet clear whether Meggitt underemphasized women's involvement in the *tee* among the Mae, or whether the Tombema practices, perhaps for ecological reasons, differ from those of the Mae.

A second example comes from the Wahgi area east of Mount Hagen, where Michael O'Hanlon's recent study (1989) has thrown up findings and interpretations that contrast somewhat with those of Marie Reay. There is a dialect difference between the Komblo, with whom O'Hanlon worked, and Marie Reay's Kuma, but they show "fundamental similarities," as Reay herself notes (Reay 1959:2, cited by O'Hanlon 1989:12). Given this, it is clear that O'Hanlon's account of leadership (1989:35–38) diverges from Reay's. Reay's suggestion had been that there was a distinction between "authorized leaders" and "rhetoric thumpers," with the implication that the former held office by succession as elder sons. O'Hanlon, however, found that the term Reay cites for "authorized leader" simply means "eldest," and there is no ideological prescription that the eldest son of a leader succeeds to his position. This is exactly what I found for the Hagen area in the 1960s (A. J. Strathern 1971a). Either, then, the Komblo are more like the Hageners in this respect than they are like the Kuma, or else Reay was misled by the form of the Wahgi term into imputing a kind of succession to leadership which does not in practice occur. O'Hanlon himself (1989:36) points to the possible reason for such a mistake to be made: namely, the existence of an idea of structural replacement, that is, that "within a given group, particular powers and abilities are retained and will find a home in someone in every generation." This is made more significant by the existence of a debate about leadership in Hagen and elsewhere which stemmed from the early German literature on that area, which gives me my third example.

Vicedom, the German missionary ethnographer, clearly believed that prior to European contact a rather clear form of social stratification based on wealth and control of religious cults had developed in Hagen (Vicedom and Tischner 1943–48, vol. 2). Although it was clear from my later fieldwork that aboriginally big men had held a near-monopoly over the use of shells in exchange, it was by no means clear that the society could be described as having social classes or that there was truly succession to leadership within families over time amounting to an institution of chiefship. The big men's monopoly had assuredly been broken by an influx of shells in colonial times, but I was not convinced that the precontact structure was so rigid as Vicedom portrayed it to be. In the event the testimony of Vicedom's colleague Hermann Strauss has tended to confirm my opinion on this issue (Strauss and Tischner 1962; A. J. Strathern 1987; Stürzenhofecker and Strathern eds. 1990).

The rich corpus of studies on the Maring shows a vigorous disagreement at another level between the work done within the framework of cultural ecology by Roy Rappaport (1968) in the 1960s and the much later interpretative-emic work of Edward LiPuma, who writes more from within the worldview of a latter-day Marshall Sahlins or Roy Wagner. LiPuma (1988) refuses the ecological postulate and argues that the Maring make their own universe of meanings, which alone is our proper business to study. Here, while facts are also at issue, the fundamental disagreement is about a theoretical framework. Rappaport is concerned with function, LiPuma with meaning, and this difference mirrors one overall shift within cultural anthropology which has occurred since the 1960s.

Finally, one can conduct yet another exercise. Looking at these accounts of early fieldwork, what ideas seem to spring out as relevant for the future? It may seem a remote or unlikely exercise, given the fact that the most obvious problems today have to do with social change. However, one thing struck me as very "fresh," and it is the same quality that first attracted me to the ethnographies of the 1960s when I encountered them during my apprenticeship: this was the appreciation of variability and choice. R. Berndt repeatedly draws attention to this and links it to innovation; Glasse concludes that crystalline models are unrealistic; Reay's work has always been concerned with the dialectic of freedom and conformity, a dialectic which, as later investigators have shown, is played out contrapuntally with the dialectical relationships of power and control between the sexes.

One reaches back here to the point at which Fredrik Barth first inserted his idea of "generative models" like a wedge into the edifice of theorizing in British social anthropology during the mid 1960s. Since that time many formal models and theories have been pressed into service, only to be demobilized when they proved inadequate. In this way structural-functionalism was finally laid to rest, and its successor ecological functionalism was recognized as a means of identifying constraints but not determinants. Marxist models have similarly been employed less for formal typologizing and more for the analysis of turning points of change in societies. To some, even the concept of "society" is called into question.

The present lacuna in theory provides an excellent opportunity to face again the theme of individual action and the impact of individuals on patterns of change, as well as the enigma of the historical moment when the individual emerges as the collective. Such a theme can provide, in a context of continuing rapid alterations in life, a point of inspiration for ethnographers of the future, as well as a chance for Papua New Guinea people themselves to find their own voices and tell their stories to the world.

BIBLIOGRAPHY

Adams, Philip
    1986   Our Minds Make Morons of Computers. *The Weekend Australian Magazine*, 8–9 February, p. 2.
Allen, Michael
    1967   *Male Cults and Secret Initiations in Melanesia*. Melbourne: Melbourne University Press.
Aufenanger, Heinrich F.
    1955   Die Stellung der ahnen im Glauben und Brauch des Eingeborenen des Territoriums von Neu-Guinea. Ph.D. dissertation, University of Vienna.
Aufenanger, Heinrich, and Georg Höltker
    1940   *Die Gende in Zentral-Neuguinea: vom Leben und Denken eines Papua-Stämmes im Bismarckgebirge*. Ergänzungsbände zur Ethnographie Neuguineas. Wien-Mödling: Missionsdruckerei St. Gabriel.
Australian National University, Research School of Pacific Studies, Department of Anthropology
    1977   Review of Activities from 1952 to 1977, and Some Indications for the Future. Manuscript.
Baal, Jan van, K. W. Galis, and R. M. Koentjaraningrat
    1984   *West Irian: A Bibliography*. Koninklijk Instituut voor Taal-, Land- en Volkenkunde, Bibliographical Series 15. Dordrecht: Foris Publications.
Bailey, Frederick G.
    1983   *The Tactical Uses of Passion*. Ithaca, N.Y.: Cornell University Press.
Barnes, John A.
    1962   African Models in the New Guinea Highlands. *Man* 62:5–9.
Barth, Fredrik
    1966   *Models of Social Organization*. Royal Anthropological Institute Occasional Papers No. 23. London.

Benedict, Ruth
    1935   *Patterns of Culture*. London: Routledge & Kegan Paul.
Bergmann, William
    1971   *The Kamanuku (The Culture of the Chimbu Tribes)*. 4 vols. Harrisville, Qsld.: W. Bergmann.
Berndt, Catherine H.
    1953   Socio-Cultural Change in the Eastern Central Highlands of New Guinea. *Southwestern Journal of Anthropology* 9:112–138
    1954   Translation Problems in Three New Guinea Highland Languages. *Oceania* 24:289–317.
    1955   Mythology in the Eastern Central Highlands of New Guinea. Ph.D. dissertation, University of London (London School of Economics and Political Science).
    1959   Ascription of Meaning in a Ceremonial Context in the Eastern Central Highlands of New Guinea. In *Anthropology in the South Seas*, ed. J. D. Freeman and W. R. Geddes, pp. 161–183. New Plymouth, N.Z.: Thomas Avery & Sons.
    1966   The Ghost Husband: Society and the Individual in New Guinea Myth. In *The Anthropologist Looks at Myth*, ed. John Greenway, pp. 244–277. Austin: University of Texas Press.
    1977   The Language of Myth: An Eastern Highlands Perspective. In *Language, Culture, Society, and the Modern World*, ed. S. A. Wurm, pp. 39–48. Pacific Linguistics, Series C, 40. Canberra: Australian National University.
    1988   Phyllis Mary Kaberry. In *Women Anthropologists: A Biographical Dictionary*, ed. Ute Gacs et al., pp. 167–174. New York: Greenwood Press.
    n. d.   Myth in Action. Manuscript.
Berndt, Catherine H., and Ronald M. Berndt
    1971   *The Barbarians: An Anthropological View*. London: Watts.
Berndt, Ronald M.
    1952–   A Cargo Movement in the Eastern Central Highlands of New Guinea.
    53   *Oceania* 23:40–65, 137–158, 202–234.
    1954   Reaction to Contact in the Eastern Highlands of New Guinea. *Oceania* 24:190–228, 255–274.
    1955*a*   Social Control among Central Highlanders of New Guinea. Ph.D. dissertation, University of London (London School of Economics and Political Science).
    1955*b*   Interdependence and Conflict in the Eastern Central Highlands. *Man* 55:105–107.
    1958   A "Devastating Disease Syndrome": Kuru Sorcery in the Eastern Central Highlands of New Guinea. *Sociologus* 8:4–28.
    1962   *Excess and Restraint: Social Control among a New Guinea Mountain People*. Chicago: University of Chicago Press.

1964   Warfare in the New Guinea Highlands. In *New Guinea: The Central Highlands*, ed. James B. Watson (Special Issue), *American Anthropologist* 66(4,2):183–203.

1965   The Kamano, Usurufa, Jate and Fore of the Eastern Highlands. In *Gods, Ghosts and Men in Melanesia*, ed. Peter Lawrence and Mervyn J. Meggitt, pp. 78–104. Melbourne: Oxford University Press.

1971   Political Structure in the Eastern Central Highlands of New Guinea. In *Politics in New Guinea: Traditional and in the Context of Change*, ed. Ronald M. Berndt and Peter Lawrence, pp. 382–423. Nedlands: University of Western Australia Press.

Berndt, Ronald M., and Peter Lawrence, eds.

1971   *Politics in New Guinea: Traditional and in the Context of Change.* Nedlands: University of Western Australia Press.

Blackwood, Beatrice

1935   *Both Sides of Buka Passage.* Oxford: Clarendon Press.

1939*a*   Folk-Stories of a Stone Age People in New Guinea. *Folk-lore* 50: 209–242.

1939*b*   Life on the Upper Watut, New Guinea. *Geographical Journal* 94: 11–28.

1940   Use of Plants among the Kukukuku of Southeast-Central New Guinea. In *Proceedings of the Sixth Pacific Science Congress of the Pacific Science Association*, vol. 4, pp. 111–126. Berkeley and Los Angeles: University of California Press.

1950   *The Technology of a Modern Stone Age People in New Guinea.* Pitt Rivers Museum, Occasional Papers on Technology, 3. Oxford: Oxford University Press.

Brown, Paula

1962   Non-Agnates among the Patrilineal Chimbu. *Journal of the Polynesian Society* 71:57–69.

1963   From Anarchy to Satrapy. *American Anthropologist* 65:1–15.

1978   *Highland Peoples of New Guinea.* Cambridge: Cambridge University Press.

Brunton, Ron

1971   Cargo Cults and Systems of Exchange in Melanesia. *Mankind* 8:115–128.

Bulmer, Ralph N. H.

1955   First Field Report on the Baiyer-Lanim Kyaka. Manuscript, Department of Anthropology, Research School of Pacific Studies, Australian National University.

1960*a*   Leadership and Social Structure among the Kyaka People of the Western Highlands District of New Guinea. Ph.D. dissertation, Australian National University.

1960*b*   Political Aspects of the Moka Ceremonial Exchange System among the Kyaka People of the Western Highlands of New Guinea. *Oceania* 31:1–13.

1965 The Kyaka of the Western Highlands. In *Gods, Ghosts and Men in Melanesia,* ed. Peter Lawrence and Mervyn J. Meggitt, pp. 132–161. Melbourne: Oxford University Press.

Capell, A.

1948– Distribution of Languages in the Central Highlands, New Guinea.
49 *Oceania* 19:104–129, 234–253, 349–377.

Champion, Ivan F.

1932 *Across New Guinea from the Fly to the Sepik.* Melbourne: Lansdowne Press.

Chinnery, E. W. P.

1934a The Central Ranges of the Mandated Territory of New Guinea from Mount Chapman to Mount Hagen. *Geographical Journal* 84:398–412 + Map.

1934b Mountain Tribes of the Mandated Territory of New Guinea from Mt. Chapman to Mt. Hagen. *Man* 34:113–121.

Clark, Jeffrey

1988 Kaun and Kogono: Cargo Cults and Development in Karavar and Pangia. *Oceania* 59:40–57.

Commonwealth of Australia

1926 *Report to the Council of the League of Nations on the Administration of the Territory of New Guinea for 1924–25.* Melbourne: Government Printer.

1935 *Report to the Council of the League of Nations on the Administration of the Territory of New Guinea for 1933–34.* Canberra: Government Printer.

1936 *Report to the Council of the League of Nations on the Administration of the Territory of New Guinea for 1934–35.* Canberra: Government Printer.

1937 *Report to the Council of the League of Nations on the Administration of the Territory of New Guinea for 1935–36.* Canberra: Government Printer.

Connolly, Bob, and Robin Anderson

1983 *First Contact.* New York: Filmakers Library.

1987 *First Contact.* New York: Viking Press.

Davenport, William

1959 Nonunilinear Descent and Descent Groups. *American Anthropologist* 61:557–572.

Detzner, Hermann

1920 *Vier Jahre unter Kannibalen.* Berlin: August Scherl.

Dexter, David

1961 *The New Guinea Offensives.* Canberra: Australian War Memorial.

Dickie, J., and D. S. Malcolm

1940 Note on a Salt Substitute Used by One of the Inland Tribes of New Guinea. *Journal of the Polynesian Society* 49:144–147.

Downs, Ian F.

1980 *The Australian Trusteeship: Papua New Guinea 1945–75.* Canberra: Australian Government Publishing Service.

1986   *The Last Mountain: A Life in Papua New Guinea.* St. Lucia: University of Queensland Press.

Durkheim, Emile
1915   *The Elementary Forms of the Religious Life.* Trans. J. Swain. London:
(1926) George Allen & Unwin.

Elkin, A. P.
1943   F. E. Williams—Government Anthropologist, Papua (1922–1943). *Oceania* 14:91–103.
1953a   *Social Anthropology in Melanesia: A Review of Research.* London: Oxford University Press.
1953b   Delayed Exchange in Wabag Sub-District, Central Highlands of New Guinea, with Notes on the Social Organization. *Oceania* 23:161–201 + 2 plates.

Epstein, A. L., ed.
1974   *Contention and Dispute.* Canberra: Australian National University Press.

Evans-Pritchard, E. E.
1940   *The Nuer: A Description of the Modes of Livelihood and Political Institutions of a Nilotic People.* Oxford: Clarendon Press.
1951   *Kinship and Marriage among the Nuer.* Oxford: Clarendon Press.

Feil, Daryl K.
1984   *Ways of Exchange: The Enga Tee of Papua New Guinea.* St. Lucia: University of Queensland Press.
1987   *The Evolution of Highland Papua New Guinea Societies.* Cambridge: Cambridge University Press.

Finney, Ben R.
1973   *Big-Men and Business: Entrepreneurship and Economic Growth in the New Guinea Highlands.* Honolulu: University Press of Hawaii.

Fischer, Hans
1965   *Negwa: Eine Papua-gruppe im Wandel.* Munich: Klaus Renner.

Fortes, Meyer, and E. E. Evans-Pritchard, eds.
1940   *African Political Systems.* Oxford: Oxford University Press.

Fortune, Reo F.
1913–   Unpublished papers, Alexander Turnbull Library, National Library,
79   Wellington, New Zealand.
1926   The Stoic. *The Spike* 25(1):37.
1932   *Sorcerers of Dobu: The Social Anthropology of the Dobu Islanders of the Western Pacific.* London: Routledge & Kegan Paul.
1933   A Note on Some Forms of Kinship Structure. *Oceania* 4:1–10.
1939   Arapesh Warfare. *American Anthropologist* 41:22–41.
1942   *Arapesh.* Publications, 19. New York: American Ethnological Society.
1943   Arapesh Maternity. *Nature* 152:164.
1947a   The Rules of Relationship Behaviour in One Variety of Primitive Warfare. *Man* 47:108–110.

1947b   Law and Force in Papuan Societies. *American Anthropologist* 49:244–259.

1954   Studies in Social Anthropology. *Nature* 174:72–73.

1960a   New Guinea Warfare: Correction of a Mistake Previously Published. *Man* 60:108.

1960b   Statistics of Kuru. *Medical Journal of Australia* 1:764–765.

Frankel, Stephen
1986   *The Huli Response to Illness.* Cambridge: Cambridge University Press.

Frazer, James G.
1913   *The Belief in Immortality and the Worship of the Dead.* London: Macmillan.

Freeman, J. D.
1956   Siegfried Frederick Nadel, 1903–1956. *Oceania* 27:1–11.

Geertz, Clifford
1973   *The Interpretation of Cultures.* New York: Basic Books.

Gelber, Marilyn
1986   *Gender and Society in the New Guinea Highlands.* Boulder, Colo.: Westview Press.

Gibbs, Philip J.
1977   The Cult from Lyeimi and the Ipili. *Oceania* 48:1–25.

Gillison, Gillian
1983   Cannibalism among Women in the Eastern Highlands of Papua New Guinea. In *The Ethnography of Cannibalism*, ed. Paula Brown and Donald Tuzin, pp. 33–50. Washington, D.C.: Society for Psychological Anthropology.

Gitlow, Abraham L.
1947a   Economics of the Mount Hagen Tribes, New Guinea. Ph.D. dissertation, Columbia University.

1947b   *Economics of the Mount Hagen Tribes, New Guinea.* Seattle: University of Washington Press.

Glasse, Robert M.
1959a   The Huli Descent System: A Preliminary Account. *Oceania* 29:171–184.

1959b   Revenge and Redress among the Huli: A Preliminary Account. *Mankind* 5:273–289.

1962   The Cognatic Descent System of the Huli of Papua. Ph.D. dissertation, Australian National University.

1965   The Huli of the Southern Highlands. In *Gods, Ghosts and Men in Melanesia*, ed. Peter Lawrence and Mervyn J. Meggitt, pp. 27–49. Melbourne: Oxford University Press.

1968   *Huli of Papua: A Cognatic Descent System.* Paris: Mouton.

1974   Le masque de la volupté: symbolisme et antagonisme sexuels sur les hauts plateaux de Nouvelle-Guinée. *L'Homme* 14:79–86.

Glasse, Robert M., and Shirley Lindenbaum
1971   South Fore Politics. In *Politics in New Guinea: Traditional and in the Context of Change*, ed. Ronald M. Berndt and Peter Lawrence, pp. 362–380. Nedlands: University of Western Australia Press.

Glasse, Robert M., and Mervyn J. Meggitt, eds.
    1969   *Pigs, Pearlshells and Women: Marriage in the New Guinea Highlands.*
                Englewood Cliffs, N.J.: Prentice-Hall.

Godelier, Maurice
    1986   *The Making of Great Men: Male Dominance and Power among the New
                Guinea Baruya.* Trans. Rupert Swyer. Cambridge: Cambridge University Press.

Goldman, Laurence
    1983   *Talk Never Dies: The Language of Huli Disputes.* London: Tavistock.

Goodenough, Ward H.
    1955   A Problem in Malayo-Polynesian Social Organization. *American Anthropologist* 57:71–83.

Gregory, Chris A.
    1982   *Gifts and Commodities.* London: Academic Press.

Griffiths, Deidre J. F.
    1977   The Career of F. E. Williams, Government Anthropologist of Papua,
                1922–1943. M.A. thesis, Australian National University.

Hallpike, C. R., ed.
    1978   *The Kukukuku of the Upper Watut,* by Beatrice Blackwood. Pitt Rivers
                Museum Monograph Series, no. 2. Oxford: Oxford University Press.

Hasluck, Paul
    1976   *A Time for Building: Australian Administration in Papua and New Guinea
                1951–1963.* Carlton: Melbourne University Press.

Hays, Terence E.
    1976   *Anthropology in the New Guinea Highlands: An Annotated Bibliography.*
                New York: Garland.

Healey, Christopher J.
    1985   *Pioneers of the Mountain Forest: Settlement and Land Redistribution among
                the Kundagai Maring of the Papua New Guinea Highlands.* Oceania
                Monographs, no. 29. Sydney: Oceania Publications.

Herdt, Gilbert H.
    1981   *Guardians of the Flutes: Idioms of Masculinity.* New York: McGraw-Hill.

Herdt, Gilbert H., ed.
    1982   *Rituals of Manhood: Male Initiation in Papua New Guinea.* Berkeley, Los
                Angeles, London: University of California Press.
    1984   *Ritualized Homosexuality in Melanesia.* Berkeley, Los Angeles, London:
                University of California Press.

Herdt, Gilbert H., and Fitz J. P. Poole
    1982   "Sexual Antagonism": The Intellectual History of a Concept in New
                Guinea Anthropology. *Social Analysis* 12:3–28.

Hides, Jack G.
    1935   *Through Wildest Papua.* London: Blackie & Son.
    1936   *Papuan Wonderland.* London: Blackie & Son.

Hope, Penelope
    1979   *Long Ago Is Far Away: Accounts of the Early Exploration and Settlement of
                the Papuan Gulf Area.* Canberra: Australian National University Press.

Howard, Jane
 1984   *Margaret Mead: A Life.* New York: Simon & Schuster.
Hughes, Ian
 1978   Good Money and Bad: Inflation and Devaluation in the Colonial Process. *Mankind* 11:308–318.
Josephides, Lisette
 1985   *The Production of Inequality: Gender and Exchange among the Kewa.* London: Tavistock.
Jukes, J. Beetes
 1847   *Narrative of the Surveying Voyage of H.M.S. Fly, Commanded by Captain F. B. Blackwood, R.N. in Torres Strait, New Guinea, and Other Islands of the Eastern Archipelago, During the Years 1842–46.* 2 vols. London: T. & W. Boone.
Kaberry, Phyllis M.
 1941–   Law and Political Organisation of the Abelam Tribe, New Guinea.
 42   *Oceania* 12:79–95, 209–225, 331–363.
Keesing, Felix M.
 1952   Research Opportunities in New Guinea. *Southwestern Journal of Anthropology* 8:109–133.
Kelly, Raymond C.
 1968   Demographic Pressure and Descent Group Structure in the New Guinea Highlands. *Oceania* 39:36–63.
 1977   *Etoro Social Structure: A Study in Structural Contradiction.* Ann Arbor: University of Michigan Press.
Kettle, Ellen
 1979   *That They Might Live.* Sydney: F. P. Leonard.
Knauft, Bruce M.
 1985   *Good Company and Violence: Sorcery and Social Action in a Lowland New Guinea Society.* Berkeley, Los Angeles, London: University of California Press.
Langham, Ian
 1981   *The Building of British Social Anthropology.* Dordrecht: D. Riedel.
Langness, L. L.
 1964   Some Problems in the Conceptualization of Highlands Social Structures. In *New Guinea: The Central Highlands,* ed. James B. Watson (Special Issue), *American Anthropologist* 66(4,2):162–182.
Langness, L. L., and Terence E. Hays, eds.
 1987   *Anthropology in the High Valleys: Essays on the New Guinea Highlands in Honor of Kenneth E. Read.* Novato, Calif.: Chandler & Sharp.
Lawrence, Peter
 1964   *Road Belong Cargo: A Study of the Cargo Movement in the Southern Madang District New Guinea.* Manchester: Manchester University Press.
 1980   Reo Fortune: An Obituary. *Oceania* 51:2–3.
Lawrence, Peter, and Mervyn J. Meggitt
 1965   Introduction. In *Gods, Ghosts and Men in Melanesia,* ed. Peter Lawrence and Mervyn J. Meggitt, pp. 1–26. Melbourne: Oxford University Press.

Lawrence, Peter, and Mervyn J. Meggitt, eds.
 1965 *Gods, Ghosts and Men in Melanesia: Some Religions of Australian New Guinea and the New Hebrides.* Melbourne: Oxford University Press.
Leach, Edmund R.
 1954 *Political Systems of Highland Burma.* Cambridge, Mass.: Harvard University Press.
Leahy, Michael J.
 1935a Stone Age People of the Mount Hagen Area, Mandated Territory of New Guinea. *Man* 35:185–186.
 1935b Tribal Wars in Unexplored New Guinea. *Walkabout* 2(1):10–13.
 1936 The Central Highlands of New Guinea. *Geographical Journal* 87:229–262 + map.
Leahy, Michael J., and M. Crain
 1937 *The Land That Time Forgot: Adventures and Discoveries in New Guinea.* London: Hurst & Blackett.
Lederman, Rena
 1986 *What Gifts Engender: Social Relations and Politics in Mendi, Highland Papua New Guinea.* Cambridge: Cambridge University Press.
Lévi-Strauss, Claude
 1949 *Les structures élémentaires de la parenté.* Paris: Presses Universitaires de France.
LiPuma, Edward
 1988 *The Gift of Kinship: Structure and Practice in Maring Social Organization.* Cambridge: Cambridge University Press.
Luzbetak, Louis J.
 1954 The Socio-Religious Significance of a New Guinea Pig Festival. *Anthropological Quarterly* 27:59–80, 102–128.
 1956a *Middle Wahgi Phonology and Standardization of Orthographies in the New Guinea Highlands.* Oceania Linguistic Monographs, no. 2. Sydney: Oceania Publications.
 1956b Worship of the Dead in the Middle Wahgi (New Guinea). *Anthropos* 51:81–96.
 1958a The Middle Wahgi Culture: A Study of First Contacts and Initial Selectivity. *Anthropos* 53:51–87.
 1958b Treatment of Disease in the New Guinea Highlands. *Anthropological Quarterly* 31:42–55.
McArthur, A. Margaret
 1967 Analysis of the Genealogy of a Mae-Enga Clan. *Oceania* 37:282–285.
Malinowski, Bronislaw
 1922 *Argonauts of the Western Pacific: An Account of Native Enterprise and Adventure in the Archipelagoes of Melanesian New Guinea.* London: Routledge & Kegan Paul.
Mead, Margaret
 1935 *Sex and Temperament in Three Primitive Societies.* New York: William Morrow.
 1972 *Blackberry Winter: My Earlier Years.* New York: William Morrow.

Meggitt, Mervyn J.
  1956   The Valleys of the Upper Wage and Lai Rivers, Western Highlands, New Guinea. *Oceania* 27:90–135.
  1957   The Ipili of the Porgera Valley, Western Highlands District. *Oceania* 28:31–55.
  1959   The Lineage System of the Mae Enga of New Guinea. Ph.D. dissertation, University of Sydney.
  1964   Male-Female Relationships in the Highlands of Australian New Guinea. In *New Guinea: The Central Highlands*, ed. James B. Watson (Special Issue), *American Anthropologist* 66(4,2):204–224.
  1965   *The Lineage System of the Mae-Enga of New Guinea.* Edinburgh: Oliver & Boyd.
  1973   The Sun and the Shakers: A Millenarian Cult and Its Transformations in the New Guinea Highlands. *Oceania* 44:1–37, 109–126.
  1974   "Pigs Are Our Hearts!": The *Te* Exchange Cycle among the Mae Enga of New Guinea. *Oceania* 44:165–203.
  1977   *Blood Is Their Argument: Warfare among the Mae Enga Tribesmen of the New Guinea Highlands.* Palo Alto, Calif.: Mayfield.
  1979   Reflections Occasioned by Continuing Anthropological Field Research among the Enga of Papua New Guinea. In *Long-Term Field Research in Social Anthropology*, ed. George M. Foster et al., pp. 107–125. New York: Academic Press.
Mennis, Mary
  1982   *Hagen Saga: The Story of Father William Ross, First American Missionary to Papua New Guinea.* Boroko: Institute of Papua New Guinea Studies.
Modjeska, Nicholas
  1977   Production among the Duna. Ph.D. dissertation, Australian National University.
  1982   Production and Inequality: Perspectives from Central New Guinea. In *Inequality in New Guinea Highlands Societies*, ed. Andrew J. Strathern, pp. 50–108, 161–170. Cambridge: Cambridge University Press.
Munster, Peter M.
  1979   Makarai: A History of Early Contact in the Goroka Valley, New Guinea Central Highlands, 1930–1933. M.A. thesis, University of Papua New Guinea.
Murdock, George P.
  1949   *Social Structure.* New York: Macmillan.
Nadel, S. F.
  1951   Research Projects in Anthropology. Manuscript, Department of Anthropology, Research School of Pacific Studies, Australian National University.
  1954   *Nupe Religion.* London: Routledge & Kegan Paul.
Nelson, H.
  1971   Contact and Administrative Control. In *An Atlas of Papua and New Guinea*, ed. R. Gerard Ward and D. A. M. Lea, pp. 4–7. Port Moresby: University of Papua New Guinea.
Neuhauss, Richard, ed.
  1911   *Deutsch-Neu-Guinea.* 3 vols. Berlin: Dietrich Reimer.

Nilles, John
    1940   Eine Knaben-Jugendweihe bei den östlichen Waugla im Bismarck-
            gebirge Neuguineas. *Internationales Archiv für Ethnographie* 38(4–6):
            93–98.
    1950   The Kuman of the Chimbu Region, Central Highlands, New Guinea.
            Oceania 21:25–65.
    1953   The Kuman People: A Study of Cultural Change in a Primitive
            Society in the Central Highlands of New Guinea. *Oceania* 24:1–27,
            119–131.
    1987   *They Went Out to Sow: The Beginning of the Work of the Catholic Mission
            in the Highlands of Papua New Guinea 1933–1943.* Analecta SVD-62.
            Rome: Apud Collegium Verbi Divini.
O'Hanlon, Michael
    1989   *Reading the Skin: Adornment, Display and Society among the Wahgi.* Lon-
            don: British Museum Publications.
Osborne, K.
    1970   A Christian Graveyard Cult in the New Guinea Highlands. *Practical
            Anthropology* 17:10–15.
Pataki-Schweizer, K. J.
    1987   Em Strongpela Meri: A Female Leader in the Eastern Highlands of
            Papua New Guinea. In *Anthropology in the High Valleys: Essays on the
            New Guinea Highlands in Honor of Kenneth E. Read*, ed. L. L. Langness
            and Terence E. Hays, pp. 137–162. Novato, Calif.: Chandler &
            Sharp.
Radford, Robin
    1977*a*   Burning the Spears: A "Peace Movement" in the Eastern Highlands
            of New Guinea. *Journal of Pacific History* 12:40–54.
    1977*b*   The Death of Aiamontina and Ian Mack. *Oral History* 5(7):58–72.
    1987   *Highlanders and Foreigners in the Upper Ramu: The Kainantu Area 1919–
            1942.* Carlton: Melbourne University Press.
Rappaport, Roy A.
    1968   *Pigs for the Ancestors: Ritual in the Ecology of a New Guinea People.* New
            Haven, Conn.: Yale University Press.
Read, Kenneth E.
    1946*a*   Social Organization in the Markham Valley, New Guinea. *Oceania*
            17:93–118.
    1946*b*   Native Thought and the War in the Pacific: A Study of the Effects of
            the Pacific War on a Native Community of the Markham Valley,
            Australian Mandated Territory of New Guinea. M.A. thesis, Univer-
            sity of Sydney.
    1947   Effects of the Pacific War in the Markham Valley. *Oceania* 18:95–
            116.
    1948   The Relation between Food Production and Social Structure in Prim-
            itive Societies. Ph.D. dissertation, University of London (London
            School of Economics and Political Science).
    1949–   Notes on Some Problems of Political Confederation. *South Pacific*
    50   3:229–234; 4:5–10.
    1950   The Political System of the Ngarawapum. *Oceania* 20:185–223.

1951*a*   The Gahuku-Gama of the Central Highlands. *South Pacific* 5:154–164.

1951*b*   Developmental Projects in the Central Highlands of New Guinea. *South Pacific* 5:202–207.

1952*a*   Missionary Activities and Social Change in the Central Highlands. *South Pacific* 5:229–238.

1952*b*   Land in the Central Highlands. *South Pacific* 6:440–449, 465.

1952*c*   Nama Cult of the Central Highlands, New Guinea. *Oceania* 23:1–25.

1954*a*   Cultures of the Central Highlands, New Guinea. *Southwestern Journal of Anthropology* 10:1–43.

1954*b*   Marriage among the Gahuku-Gama of the Eastern Central Highlands, New Guinea. *South Pacific* 7:864–871.

1955   Morality and the Concept of Person Among the Gahuku-Gama, Eastern Highlands, New Guinea. *Oceania* 25:233–282.

1959   Leadership and Consensus in a New Guinea Society. *American Anthropologist* 61:425–436.

1965   *The High Valley.* New York: Charles Scribner's Sons.

1986   *Return to the High Valley: Coming Full Circle.* Berkeley, Los Angeles, London: University of California Press.

Reay, Marie

1957   The Kuma: A Study of Tradition, Freedom and Conformity among a New Guinea People. Ph.D. dissertation, Australian National University.

1959   *The Kuma: Freedom and Conformity in the New Guinea Highlands.* Melbourne: Melbourne University Press.

1969   Myth and Tradition as Historical Evidence. In *The History of Melanesia,* ed. K. S. Inglis, pp. 463–475. Canberra: Australian National University, Research School of Pacific Studies; Port Moresby: University of Papua New Guinea.

Robin, Robert W.

1982   Revival Movements in the Southern Highlands Province of Papua New Guinea. *Oceania* 52:320–343.

Ross, William A.

1936   Ethnological Notes on Mt. Hagen Tribes (Mandated Territory of New Guinea) with Special Reference to the Tribe called Mogei. *Anthropos* 31:341–363 + 5 plates.

Royal Anthropological Institute of Great Britain and Ireland

1951   *Notes and Queries on Anthropology.* 6th ed. London: Routledge & Kegan Paul.

Ryan, D'Arcy

1955   Clan Organization in the Mendi Valley, Southern Highlands of Papua-New Guinea. *Oceania* 26:79–90.

1959   Clan Formation in the Mendi Valley. *Oceania* 29:257–289.

1962   Gift Exchange in the Mendi Valley: An Examination of the Socio-Political Implications of the Ceremonial Exchange of Wealth among the People of the Mendi Valley, Southern Highlands District, Papua. Ph.D. dissertation, University of Sydney.

Ryan, John
 1969   *The Hot Land: Focus on New Guinea.* New York: St. Martin's Press.
Sahlins, Marshall
 1963   Poor Man, Rich Man, Big-Man, Chief: Political Types in Melanesia
           and Polynesia. *Comparative Studies in Society and History* 5:285–300.
Salisbury, Richard F.
 1956   Asymmetrical Marriage Systems. *American Anthropologist* 58:639–655.
 1958*a*   Economic Change among the Siane Tribes of New Guinea. Ph.D.
           dissertation, Australian National University.
 1958*b*   An "Indigenous" New Guinea Cult. *Kroeber Anthropological Society
           Papers* 18:67–78.
 1962   *From Stone to Steel: Economic Consequences of a Technological Change in
           New Guinea.* Melbourne: Melbourne University Press.
 1964   Despotism and Australian Administration in the New Guinea High-
           lands. In *New Guinea: The Central Highlands*, ed. James B. Watson
           (Special Issue), *American Anthropologist* 66(4,2):225–239.
 1965   The Siane of the Eastern Highlands. In *Gods, Ghosts and Men in
           Melanesia*, ed. Peter Lawrence and Mervyn J. Meggitt, pp. 50–77.
           Melbourne: Oxford University Press.
Schäfer, Alfons
 1938   Zur Initiation im Wagi-Tal. *Anthropos* 33:401–423.
Schieffelin, Edward L.
 1976   *The Sorrow of the Lonely and the Burning of the Dancers.* New York: St.
           Martin's Press.
Schieffelin, Edward L., and Robert Crittenden
 1991   *Like People You See in a Dream: First Contact in Six Papuan Societies.*
           Stanford: Stanford University Press.
Sexton, Lorraine Dusak
 1986   *Mothers of Money, Daughters of Coffee: The Wok Meri Movement.* Ann
           Arbor, Mich.: UMI Research Press.
Shepherd, Ernie
 1971   Akmana: A New Name in the Continuing Story of New Guinea
           Exploration. *Pacific Islands Monthly* 42(4):40–45, 47, 49; 42(5):37–
           40.
Sillitoe, Paul
 1979   *Give and Take: Exchange in Wola Society.* New York: St. Martin's Press.
Simpson, Colin
 1955   *Islands of Men.* Sydney: Angus & Robertson.
Sinclair, James P.
 1978   *Wings of Gold: How the Aeroplane Developed New Guinea.* Sydney: Pacific
           Publications.
 1981   *Kiap: Australia's Patrol Officers in Papua New Guinea.* Sydney: Pacific
           Publications.
Sinclair, James P., ed.
 1979   *Up from South: A Prospector in New Guinea 1931–1937*, by Jack O'Neill.
           Melbourne: Oxford University Press.

Souter, Gavin
  1963   *New Guinea: The Last Unknown.* Sydney: Angus & Robertson.
Southall, Aidan
  1986   The Illusion of Nath Agnation. *Ethnology* 25:1–20.
Spinks, K. L.
  1934   Mapping the Purari Plateau, New Guinea. *Geographical Journal* 84: 412–416 + plate + map.
Stanley, Evan R.
  1923   Report on the Salient Geological Features and Natural Resources of the New Guinea Territory including Notes on Dialectics and Ethnology. *Territory of New Guinea, Annual Report for 1921–22,* App. B, pp. 1–99 + Figs. 1–80 + 2 maps.
Stanner, W. E. H.
  1962   Foreword. In *From Stone to Steel: Economic Consequences of a Technological Change in New Guinea,* by Richard F. Salisbury, pp. v–xi. Melbourne: Melbourne University Press.
Steinbauer, Friedrich
  1969   *So War's in Tarabo.* Freimund, Germany: Verlag Neuendettelsau.
  1979   *Melanesian Cargo Cults: New Salvation Movements in the South Pacific.* Trans. Max Wohlwill. St. Lucia: University of Queensland Press.
Stocking, George
  1982   Gatekeeper to the Field: E. W. P. Chinnery and the Ethnography of the New Guinea Mandate. *History of Anthropology Newsletter* 9(2):3–12.
Strathern, Andrew J.
  1966   Despots and Directors in the New Guinea Highlands. *Man,* N.S., 1:356–367.
  1969a   Descent and Alliance in the New Guinea Highlands. *Proceedings of the Royal Anthropological Institute for 1968,* pp. 37–52. London.
  1969b   Finance and Production: Two Strategies in New Guinea Highlands Exchange Systems. *Oceania* 40:42–67.
  1971a   *The Rope of Moka: Big-men and Ceremonial Exchange in Mount Hagen New Guinea.* Cambridge: Cambridge University Press.
  1971b   Cargo and Inflation in Mount Hagen. *Oceania* 41:255–265.
  1972   *One Father, One Blood: Descent and Group Structure among the Melpa People.* London: Tavistock.
  1974   Kinship, Descent and Locality: Some New Guinea Examples. In *The Character of Kinship,* ed. Jack Goody, pp. 21–33. Cambridge: Cambridge University Press.
  1976   Transactional Continuity in Mount Hagen. In *Transaction and Meaning,* ed. Bruce Kapferer, pp. 277–288. Philadelphia: ISHI Press.
  1979–   The Red-Box Money Cult in Mount Hagen 1968–71. *Oceania* 50:
  80   88–102, 161–175.
  1987   Social Classes in Mount Hagen? The Early Evidence. *Ethnology* 26: 245–260.
Strathern, Andrew J., ed.
  1982   *Inequality in New Guinea Highlands Societies.* Cambridge: Cambridge University Press.

Strathern, Marilyn
 1972   *Women In Between: Female Roles in a Male World: Mount Hagen, New Guinea*. London: Seminar Press.
Strauss, Hermann, and Herbert Tischner
 1962   *Die Mi-Kultur der Hagenberg Stämme*. Hamburg: Cram de Gruyter and Co.
Stürzenhofecker, Gabriele, and Andrew J. Strathern, eds.
 1990   *The Mi-Culture of the Mount Hagen People, Papua New Guinea*, by Hermann Strauss with Herbert Tischner. Trans. Brian Shields. Ethnology Monographs no. 13. Pittsburgh: Department of Anthropology, University of Pittsburgh.
Taylor, James L.
 1940*a*   Exploration of Unknown New Guinea. *Pacific Islands Monthly* 10(8): 37–42; 10(9):37–41; 10(10):32–37; 10(11):50–54.
 1940*b*   Interim Report on the Hagen-Sepik Patrol 1938–39. *Report to the Council of the League of Nations on the Administration of the Territory of New Guinea for 1938–39*, App. B, pp. 137–149. Canberra: Government Printer.
Trompf, Garry
 1984   Missiology and Anthropology: A Viable Relationship? *Oceania* 55: 148–153.
Ulbrich, Josef
 1960   *Pionier auf Neuguinea: Briefe von P. Alfons Schäfer SVD*. Gesamtherstellung: Missionsdruckerei Steyl.
Vayda, Andrew P.
 1976   *War in Ecological Perspective: Persistence, Change, and Adaptive Processes in Three Oceanian Societies*. New York: Plenum.
Vicedom, Georg F.
 1938   Ein neuentdecktes Volk in Neuguinea. *Archiv für Anthropologie* 24: 11–44 + 3 plates; 190–213 + 2 plates.
Vicedom, Georg F., and Herbert Tischner
 1943–   *Die Mbowamb: Die Kultur der Hagenberg-stämme im östlichen Zentral-*
 48   *Neuguinea*. 3 vols. Hamburgischen Museum für Völkerkunde, Monographien zur Völkerkunde no. 1. Hamburg.
Wagner, Roy
 1967   *The Curse of Souw: Principles of Daribi Clan Definition and Alliance in New Guinea*. Chicago: University of Chicago Press.
 1974   Are There Social Groups in the New Guinea Highlands? In *Frontiers of Anthropology*, ed. Murray J. Leaf, pp. 95–122. New York: D. Van Nostrand.
Watson, James B.
 1960   A New Guinea "Opening Man." In *In the Company of Man: Twenty Portraits by Anthropologists*, ed. Joseph B. Casagrande, pp. 127–173. New York: Harper and Brothers.
 1964   Introduction: Anthropology in the New Guinea Highlands. In *New Guinea: The Central Highlands*, ed. James B. Watson (Special Issue), *American Anthropologist* 66(4,2):1–9.

1970 Society as Organized Flow: The Tairora Case. *Southwestern Journal of Anthropology* 26:107–124.

1971 Tairora: The Politics of Despotism in a Small Society. In *Politics in New Guinea: Traditional and in the Context of Change*, ed. Ronald M. Berndt and Peter Lawrence, pp. 224–275. Nedlands: University of Western Australia Press.

1983 *Tairora Culture: Contingency and Pragmatism*. Seattle: University of Washington Press.

Watson, James B., ed.

1964 *New Guinea: The Central Highlands*. Special Issue, *American Anthropologist*, vol. 66, no. 4, part 2.

Watson, Virginia D.

1965 Agarabi Female Roles and Family Structure: A Study in Socio-Cultural Change. Ph.D. dissertation, University of Chicago.

Wedgwood, C. H.

1930 Some Aspects of Warfare in Melanesia. *Oceania* 1:5–33.

Weiner, James F.

1988 *The Heart of the Pearl Shell*. Berkeley, Los Angeles, London: University of California Press.

Weiner, James F., ed.

1988 *Mountain Papuans: Historical and Comparative Perspectives from New Guinea Fringe Highlands Societies*. Ann Arbor: University of Michigan Press.

Williams, F. E.

1930 *Orokaiva Society*. London: Oxford University Press.

1936 *Papuans of the Trans-Fly*. Oxford: Clarendon Press.

1937 The Natives of Mount Hagen, Papua: Further Notes. *Man* 37:90–96.

1940a *Drama of Orokolo*. Oxford: Clarendon Press.

1940b Report on the Grasslanders, Augu-Wage-Wela. *Territory of Papua, Annual Report for 1938–39*, App., pp. 39–67. Canberra: Government Printer.

1940– Natives of Lake Kutubu, Papua. *Oceania* 11:121–157, 259–294, 374–
41 401; 12:49–74, 134–154.

1941 Group Sentiment and Primitive Justice. *American Anthropologist* 43: 523–539.

Willis, Ian J.

1969 An "Epic" Journey: The 1930 Expedition of Michael Leahy and Michael Dwyer across New Guinea via the Purari River. M.A. (Qual.) thesis, University of Papua New Guinea.

Wirz, Paul

1952a A Description of Musical Instruments from Central North-Eastern New Guinea. Koninklijk Instituut voor de Tropen, Mededeling no. C., Afdeling Culturele en Physische Anthropologie no. 43, pp. 3–22. Amsterdam.

1952b Die Eŋa: Ein Beitrag zur Ethnographie eines Stammes im nordostlichen zentralen Neuguinea. *Zeitschrift für Ethnologie* 77:7–56.

1952c   Die Entlehnung und Assimilation eigenen und fremden Kulturgutes in Neuguinea. *Verhandelingen der Naturforschenden Gesellschaft in Basel* 63:187–214.

1952d   On Some Hitherto Unknown Objects from the Highlands of Central North-Eastern New Guinea. Koninklijk Instituut voor de Tropen, Mededeling no. C, Afdeling Culturele en Physische Anthropologie no. 43, pp. 25–31. Amsterdam.

1952e   Quelques notes sur la cérémonie du "MOKA" chez les tribus du Mt Hagen et du Wabaga sub-district, Nouvelle-Guinée du Nord-Est. Société Royale Belge d'Anthropologie et de Préhistoire, *Bulletin* 63: 65–71.

Wise, Tigger

1985   *The Self-Made Anthropologist: A Life of A. P. Elkin.* Sydney: George Allen & Unwin.

Worsley, Peter

1957   *The Trumpet Shall Sound: A Study of "Cargo" Cults in Melanesia.* London: MacGibbon & Kee.

Wurm, Stephen A.

1960   The Changing Linguistic Picture of New Guinea. *Oceania* 31:121–136.

INDEX

Designer: U. C. Press Staff
Compositor: Braun-Brumfield, Inc.
Text: 10/12 Baskerville
Display: Baskerville
Printer: Braun-Brumfield, Inc.
Binder: Braun-Brumfield, Inc.